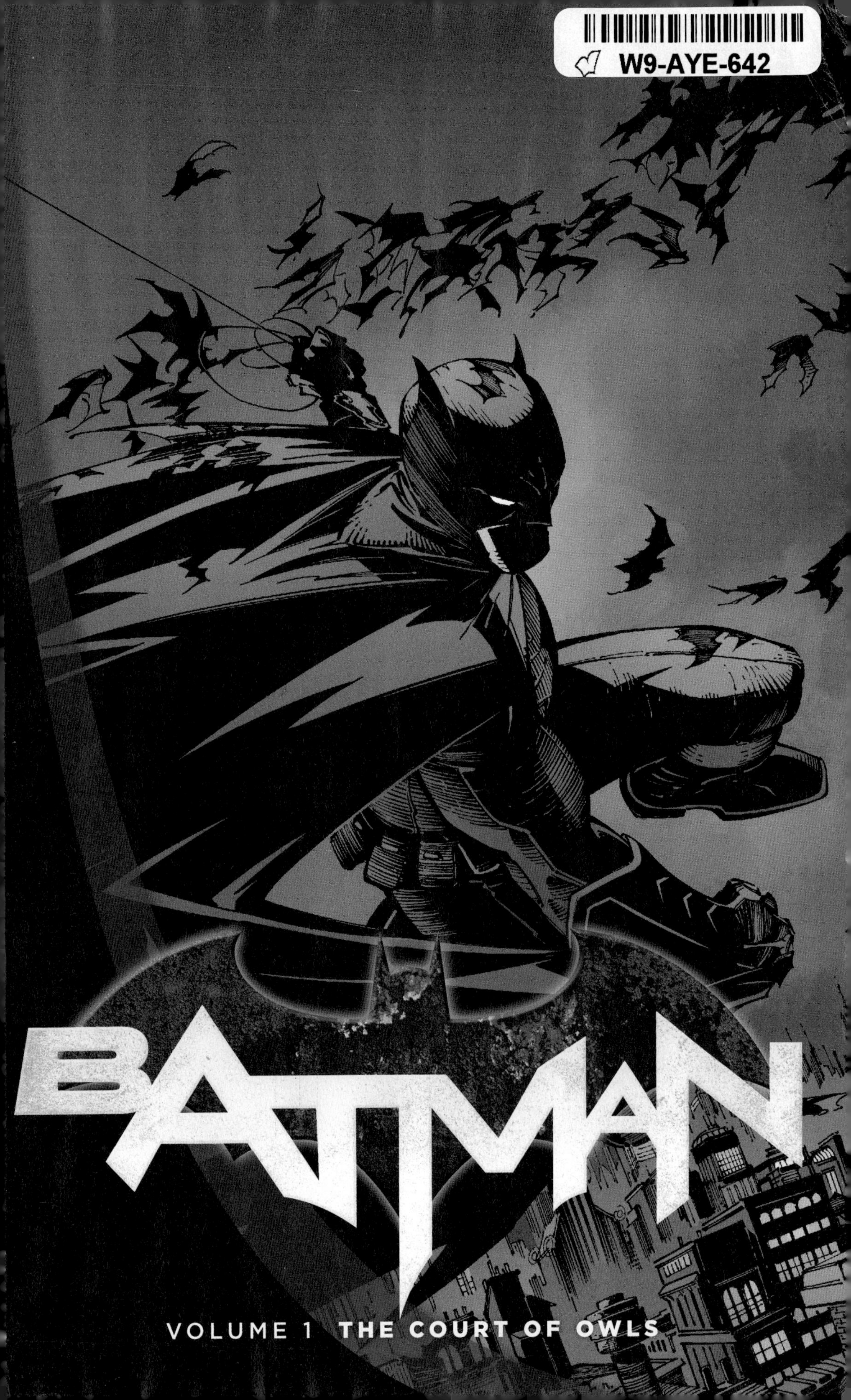
BATMAN
VOLUME 1 THE COURT OF OWLS

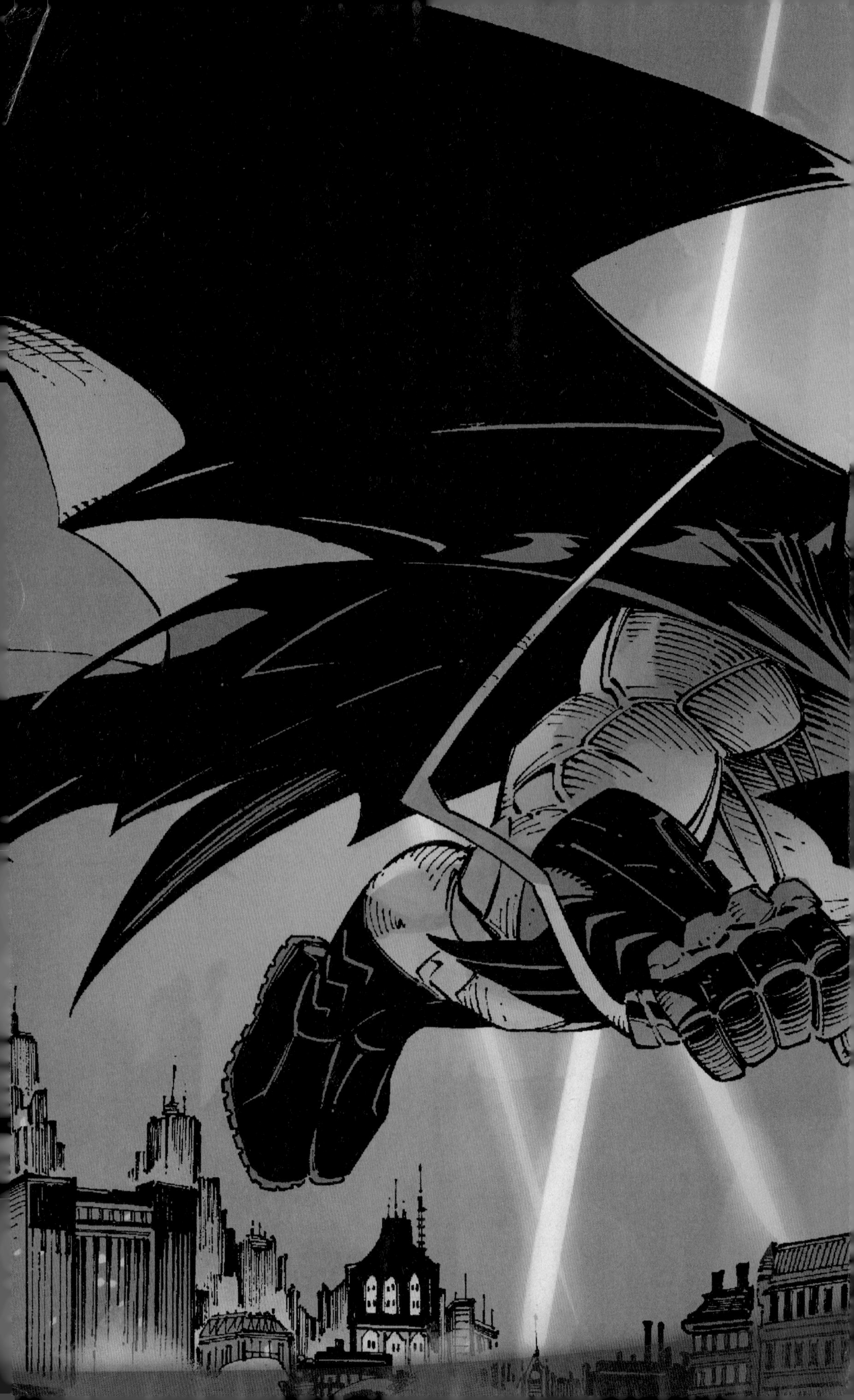

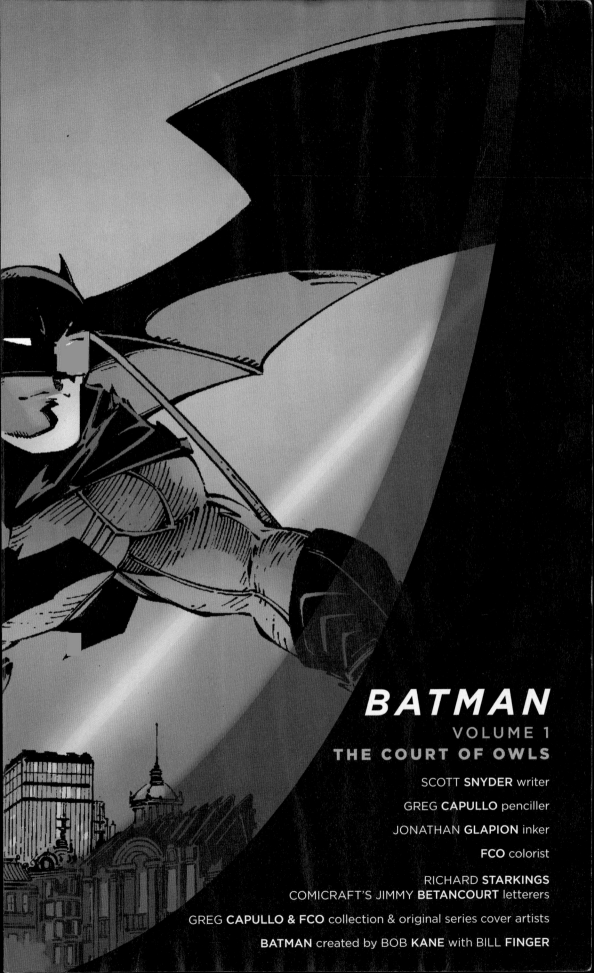

BATMAN

VOLUME 1
THE COURT OF OWLS

SCOTT **SNYDER** writer

GREG **CAPULLO** penciller

JONATHAN **GLAPION** inker

FCO colorist

RICHARD **STARKINGS**
COMICRAFT'S JIMMY **BETANCOURT** letterers

GREG **CAPULLO & FCO** collection & original series cover artists

BATMAN created by BOB **KANE** with BILL **FINGER**

MIKE MARTS Editor – Original Series HARVEY RICHARDS JANELLE ASSELIN Associate Editors – Original Series
KATIE KUBERT Assistant Editor – Original Series JEB WOODARD Group Editor – Collected Editions
PETER HAMBOUSSI Editor – Collected Edition STEVE COOK Design Director – Books ROBBIE BIEDERMAN Publication Design

BOB HARRAS Senior VP – Editor-in-Chief, DC Comics

DIANE NELSON President DAN DIDIO and JIM LEE Co-Publishers
GEOFF JOHNS Chief Creative Officer AMIT DESAI Senior VP – Marketing & Global Franchise Management
NAIRI GARDINER Senior VP – Finance SAM ADES VP – Digital Marketing BOBBIE CHASE VP – Talent Development
MARK CHIARELLO Senior VP – Art, Design & Collected Editions JOHN CUNNINGHAM VP – Content Strategy
ANNE DEPIES VP – Strategy Planning & Reporting DON FALLETTI VP – Manufacturing Operations
LAWRENCE GANEM VP – Editorial Administration & Talent Relations ALISON GILL Senior VP – Manufacturing & Operations
HANK KANALZ Senior VP – Editorial Strategy & Administration JAY KOGAN VP – Legal Affairs
DEREK MADDALENA Senior VP – Sales & Business Development JACK MAHAN VP – Business Affairs
DAN MIRON VP – Sales Planning & Trade Development NICK NAPOLITANO VP – Manufacturing Administration
CAROL ROEDER VP – Marketing EDDIE SCANNELL VP – Mass Account & Digital Sales
COURTNEY SIMMONS Senior VP – Publicity & Communications JIM (SKI) SOKOLOWSKI VP – Comic Book Specialty & Newsstand Sales
SANDY YI Senior VP – Global Franchise Management

BATMAN VOLUME 1: THE COURT OF OWLS

DC Comics, 2900 W. Alameda Avenue, Burbank, CA 91505
Printed by Transcontinental Interglobe Beauceville, Canada. 3/4/16. Ninth Printing.

ISBN: 978-1-4012-3542-0

Library of Congress Cataloging-in-Publication Data
Snyder, Scott.
Batman volume 1 : The Court of Owls / Scott Snyder, Greg Capullo,
Jonathan Glapion.
p. cm.
ISBN 978-1-4012-3542-0
1. Graphic novels. I. Capullo, Greg. II. Glapion, Jonathan. III.
Title.
PN6728.B36S68 2012
741.5'973—dc23
2011051796

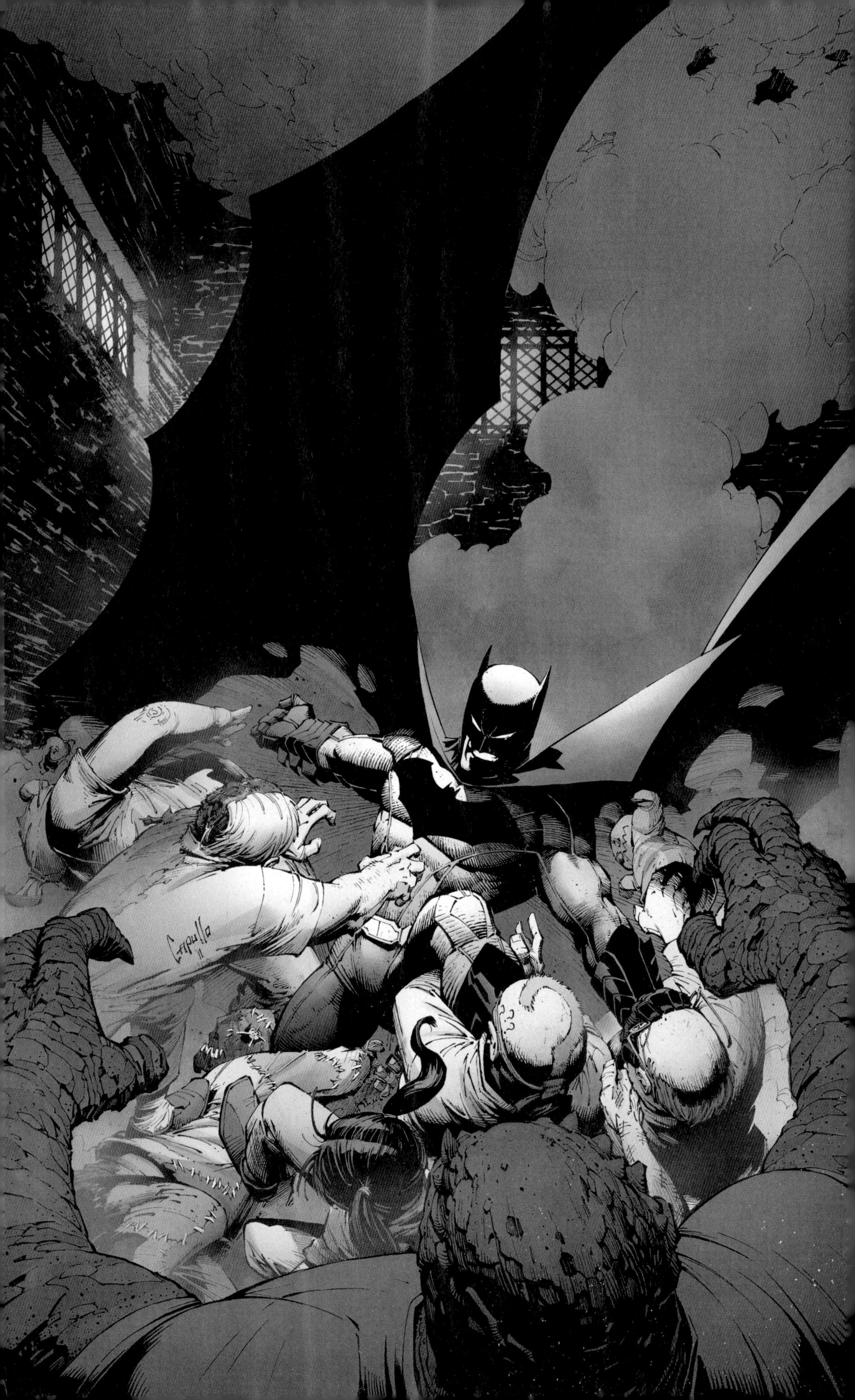

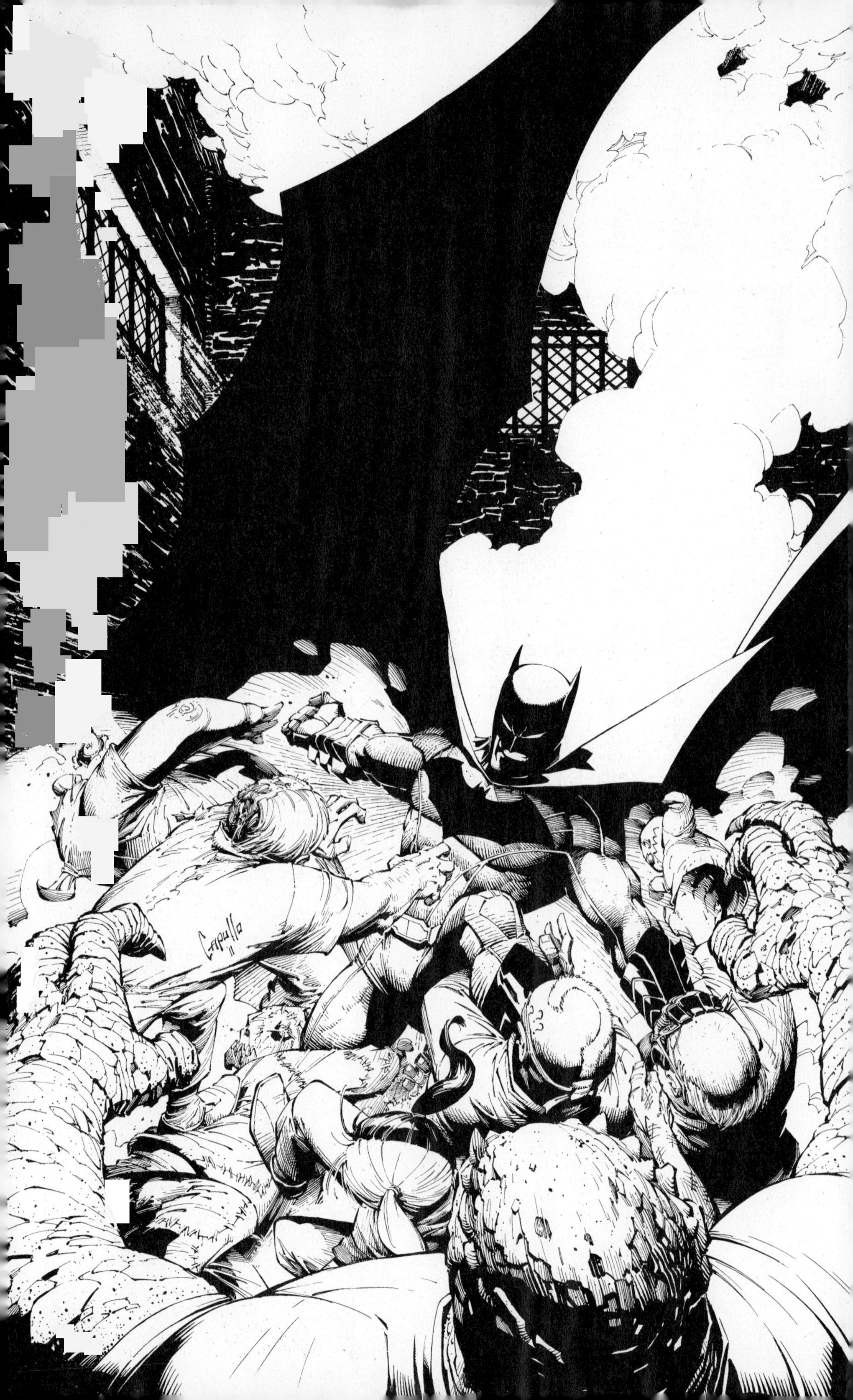

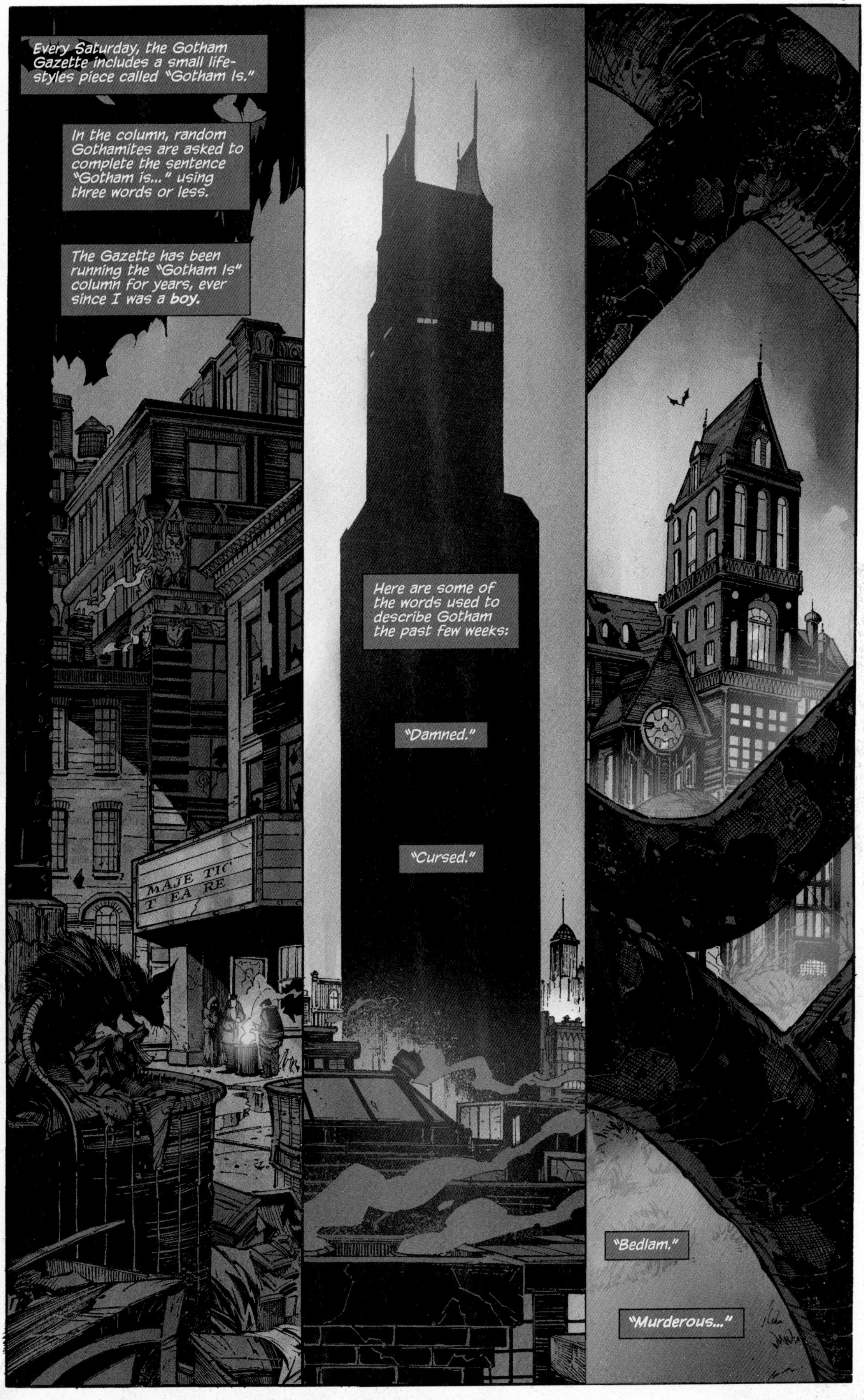
Every Saturday, the Gotham Gazette includes a small life-styles piece called "Gotham Is."
In the column, random Gothamites are asked to complete the sentence "Gotham is..." using three words or less.
The Gazette has been running the "Gotham Is" column for years, ever since I was a boy.
MAJE TIC T EA RE
Here are some of the words used to describe Gotham the past few weeks:
"Damned."
"Cursed."
"Bedlam."
"Murderous..."

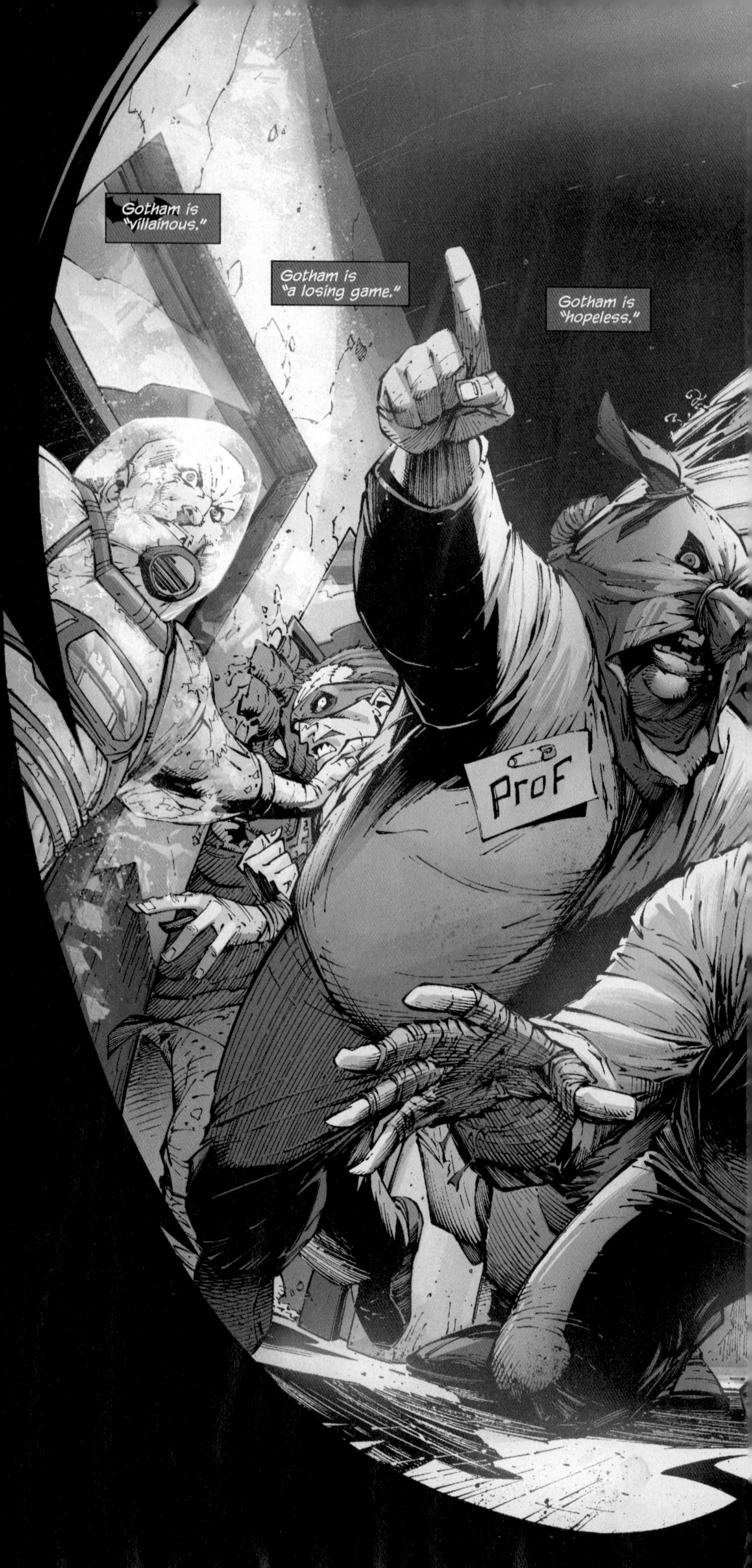
Gotham is "villainous."
Gotham is "a losing game."
Gotham is "hopeless."
ProF

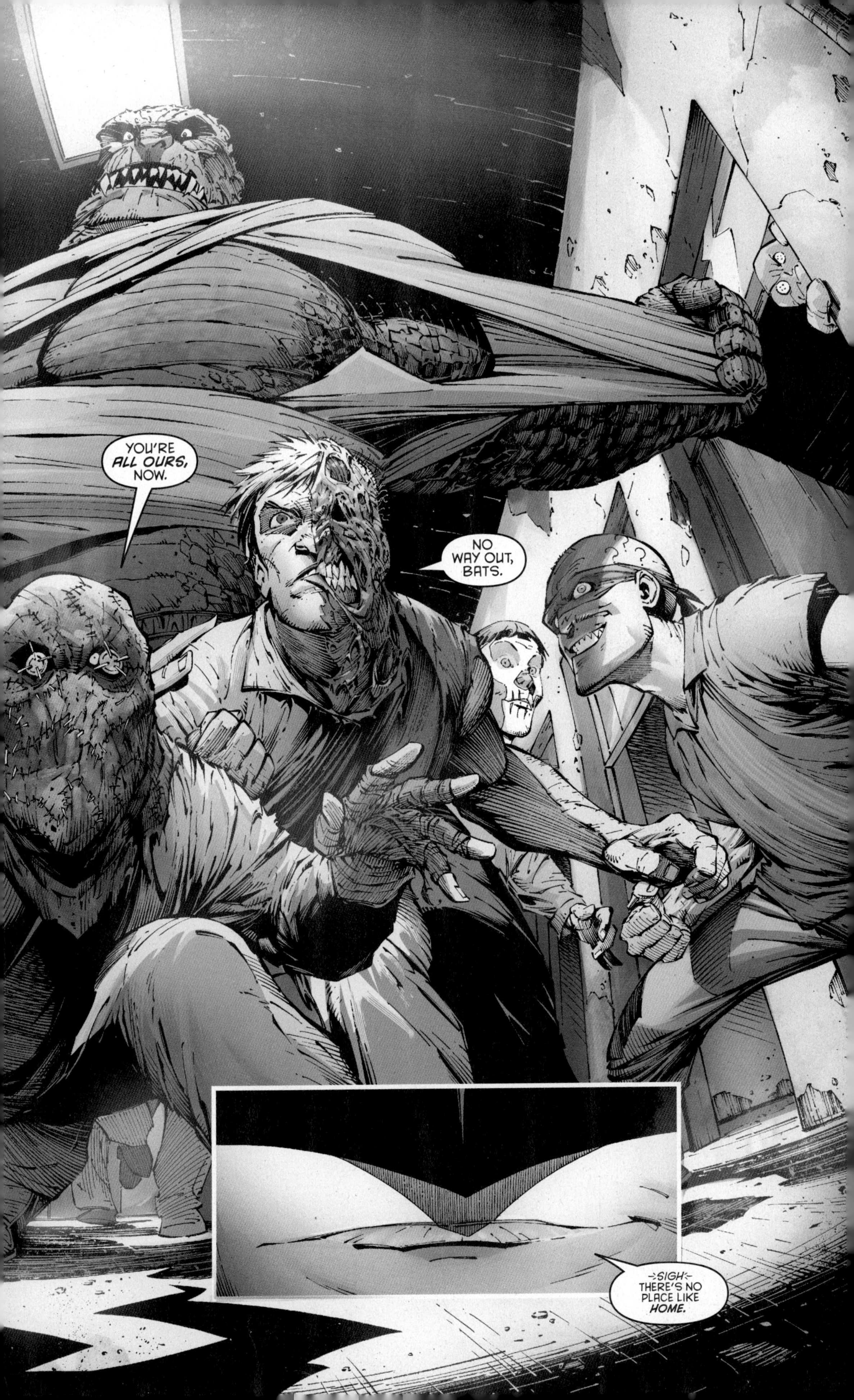
YOU'RE ALL OURS, NOW.
NO WAY OUT, BATS.
-SIGH- THERE'S NO PLACE LIKE HOME.

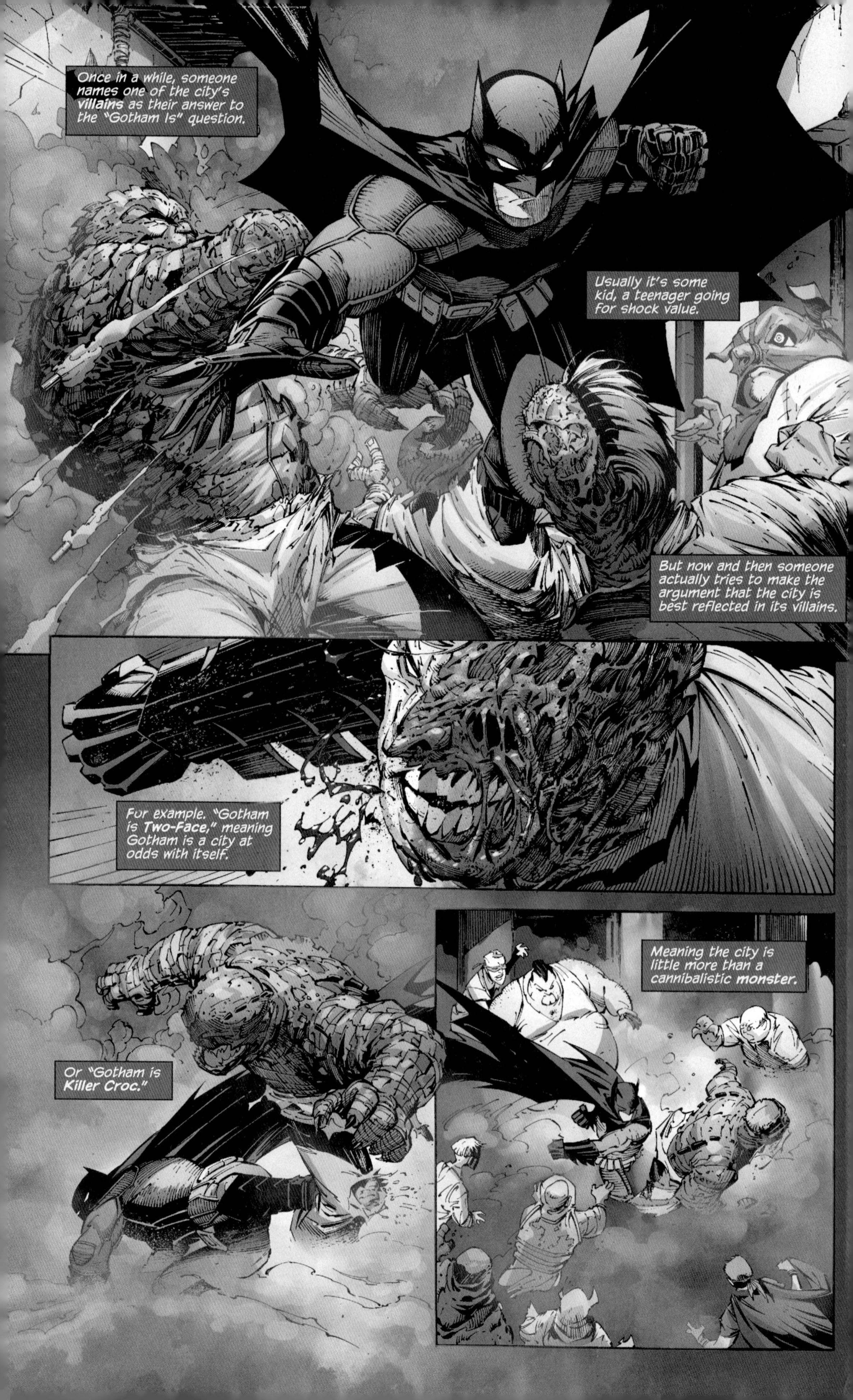
Once in a while, someone names one of the city's **villains** as their answer to the "Gotham Is" question.
Usually it's some kid, a teenager going for shock value.
But now and then someone actually tries to make the argument that the city is best reflected in its villains.
For example. "Gotham is ***Two-Face,***" meaning Gotham is a city at odds with itself.
Or "Gotham is ***Killer Croc.***"
Meaning the city is little more than a cannibalistic ***monster.***

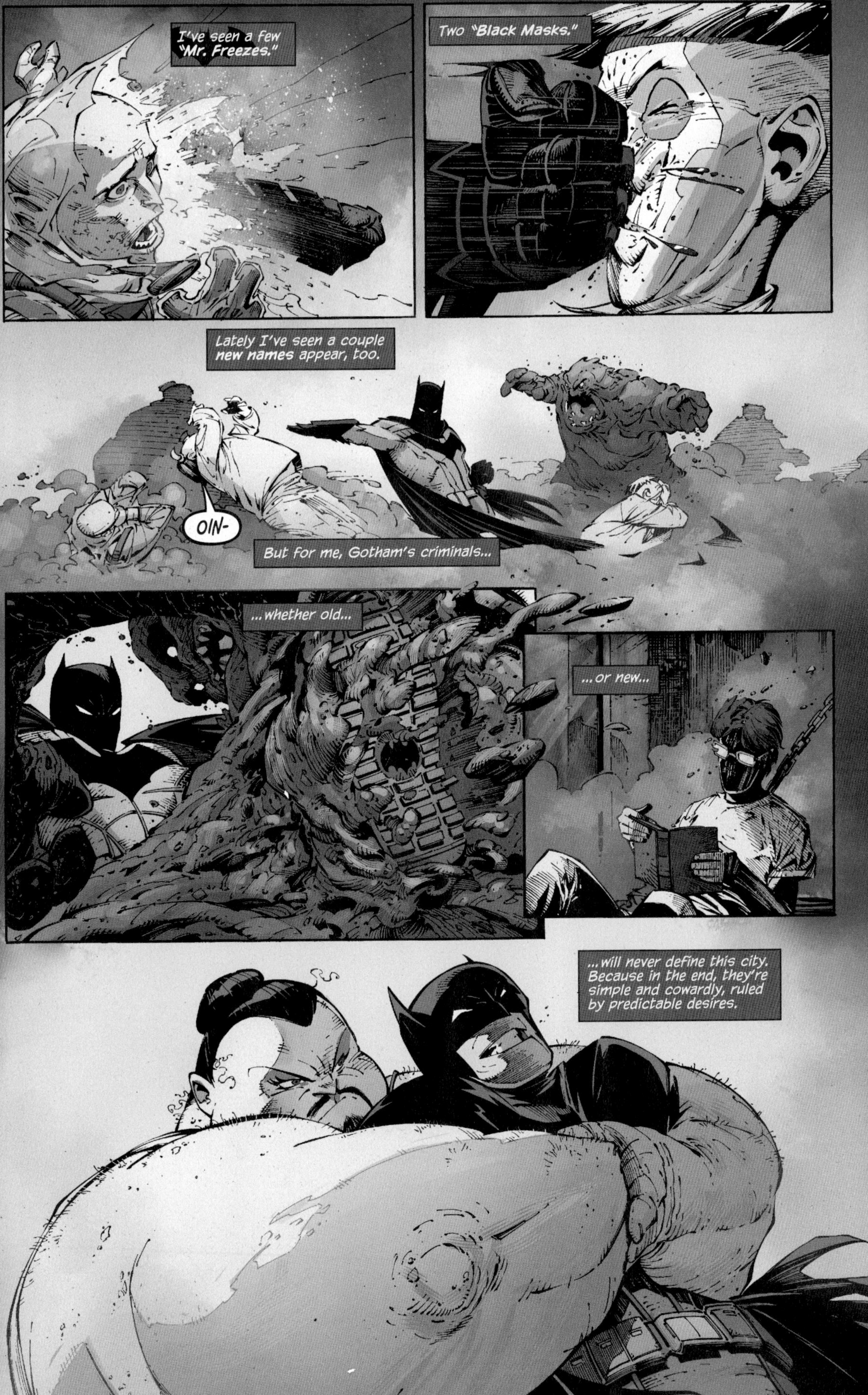
I've seen a few "Mr. Freezes."
Two "Black Masks."
Lately I've seen a couple new names appear, too.
OIN-
But for me, Gotham's criminals...
...whether old...
...or new...
...will never define this city. Because in the end, they're simple and cowardly, ruled by predictable desires.

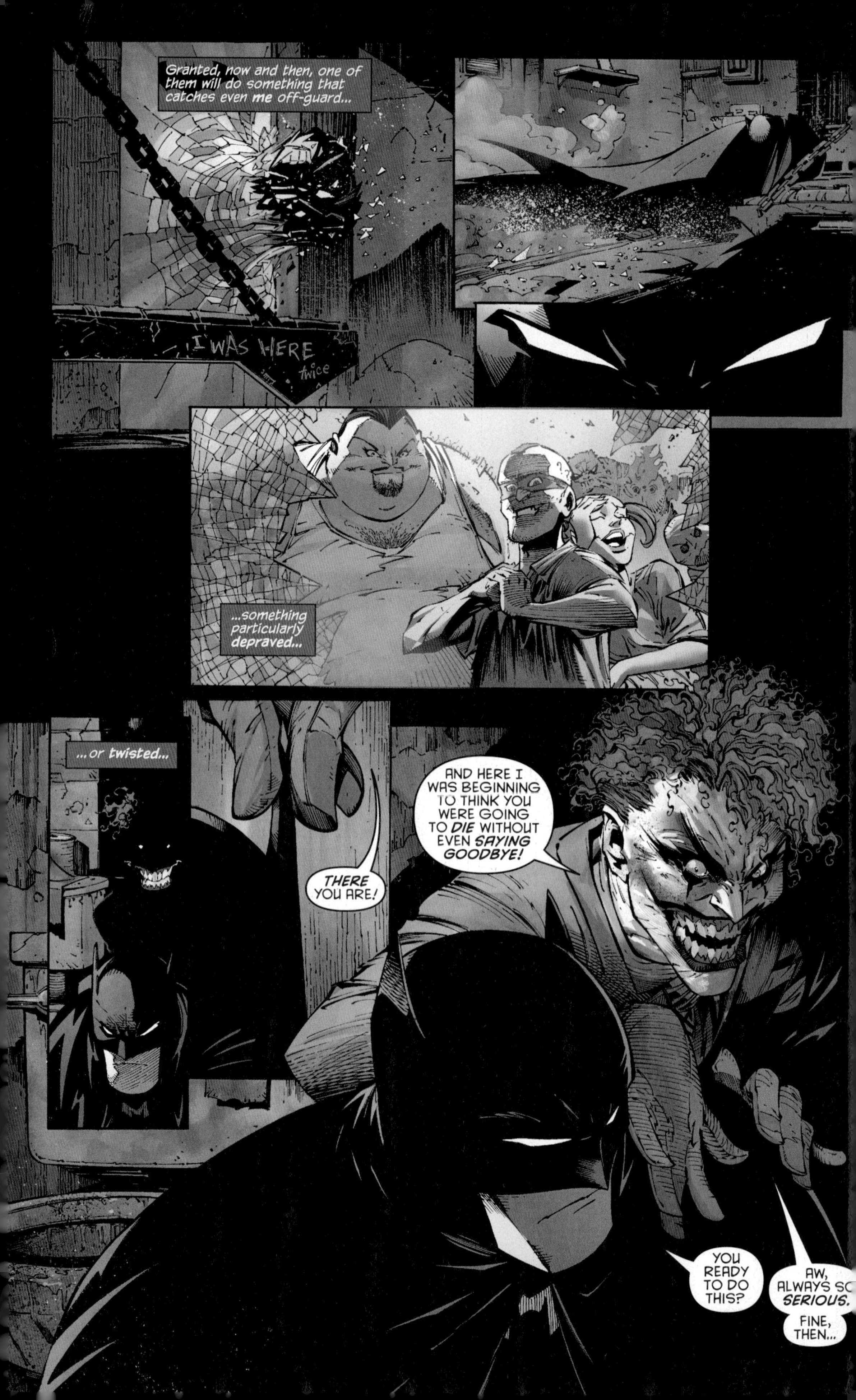

Granted, now and then, one of them will do something that catches even me off-guard...
I WAS HERE twice
...something particularly depraved...
...or twisted...
THERE YOU ARE!
AND HERE I WAS BEGINNING TO THINK YOU WERE GOING TO DIE WITHOUT EVEN SAYING GOODBYE!
YOU READY TO DO THIS?
AW, ALWAYS SO SERIOUS.
FINE, THEN...

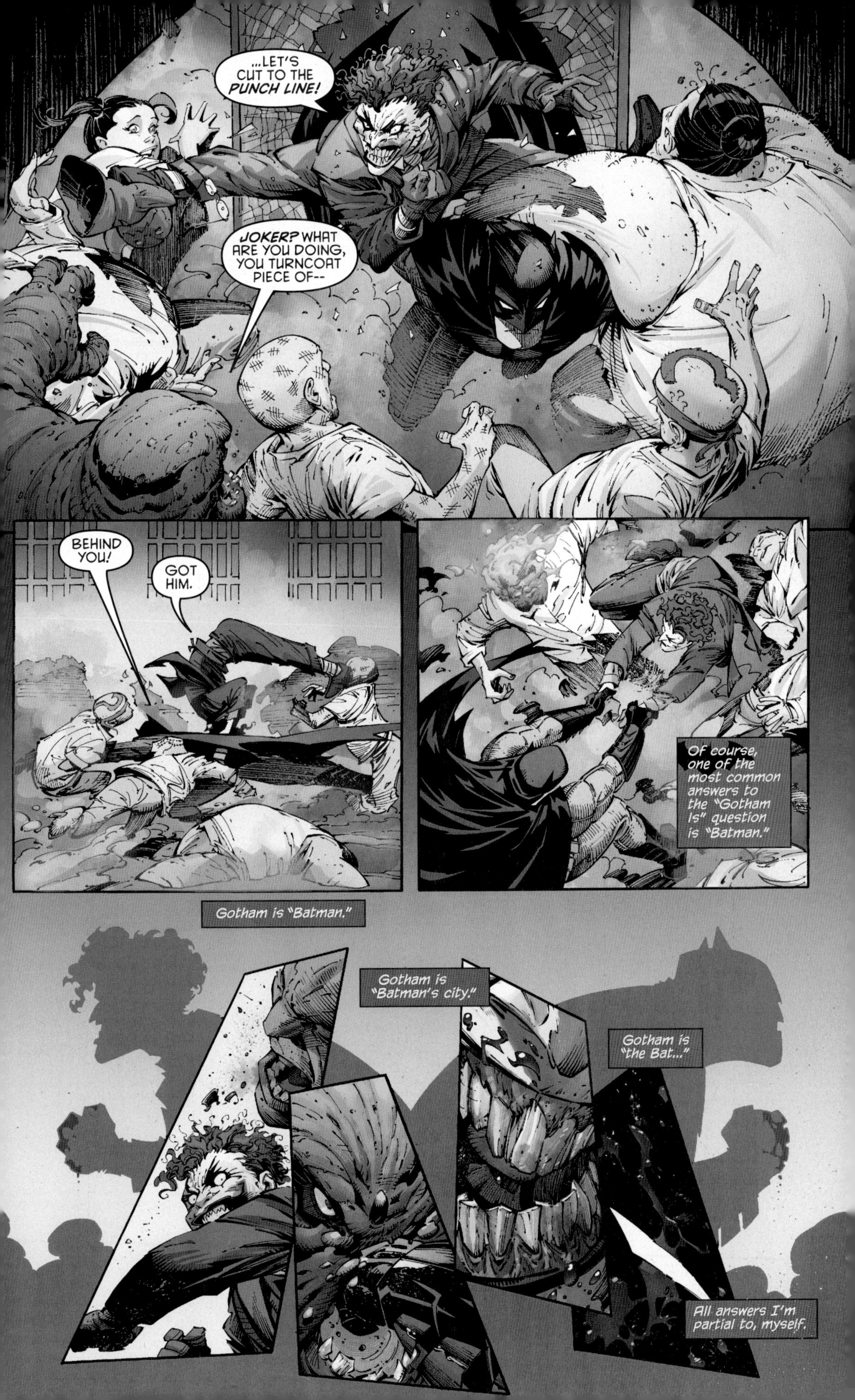
...LET'S CUT TO THE PUNCH LINE!
JOKER? WHAT ARE YOU DOING, YOU TURNCOAT PIECE OF--
BEHIND YOU!
GOT HIM.
Of course, one of the most common answers to the "Gotham Is" question is "Batman."
Gotham is "Batman."
Gotham is "Batman's city."
Gotham is "the Bat..."
All answers I'm partial to, myself.

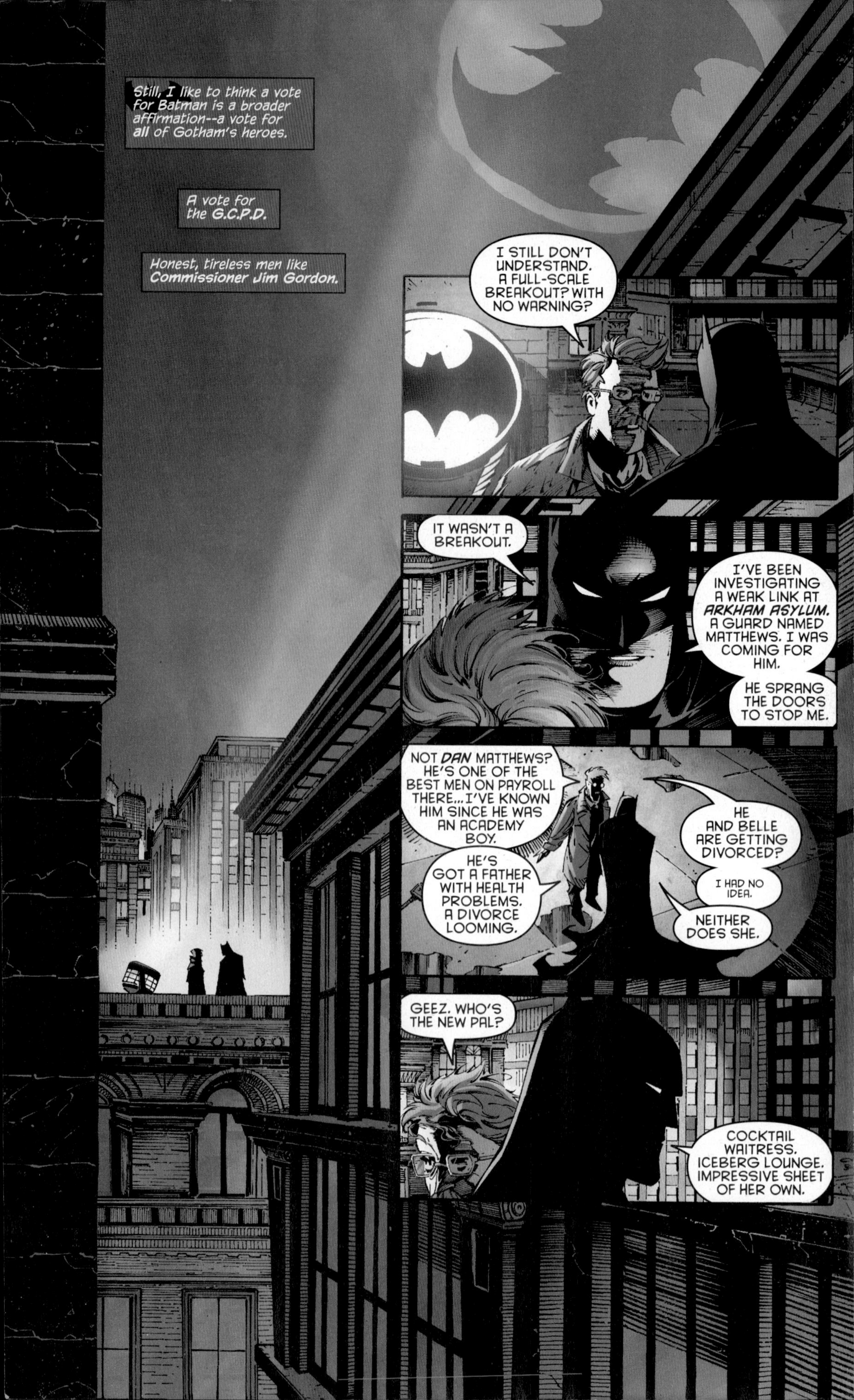
Still, I like to think a vote for Batman is a broader affirmation--a vote for all of Gotham's heroes.
A vote for the G.C.P.D.
Honest, tireless men like Commissioner Jim Gordon.
I STILL DON'T UNDERSTAND. A FULL-SCALE BREAKOUT? WITH NO WARNING?
IT WASN'T A BREAKOUT.
I'VE BEEN INVESTIGATING A WEAK LINK AT ARKHAM ASYLUM. A GUARD NAMED MATTHEWS. I WAS COMING FOR HIM.
HE SPRANG THE DOORS TO STOP ME.
NOT DAN MATTHEWS? HE'S ONE OF THE BEST MEN ON PAYROLL THERE... I'VE KNOWN HIM SINCE HE WAS AN ACADEMY BOY.
HE'S GOT A FATHER WITH HEALTH PROBLEMS. A DIVORCE LOOMING.
HE AND BELLE ARE GETTING DIVORCED?
I HAD NO IDEA.
NEITHER DOES SHE.
GEEZ. WHO'S THE NEW PAL?
COCKTAIL WAITRESS. ICEBERG LOUNGE. IMPRESSIVE SHEET OF HER OWN.

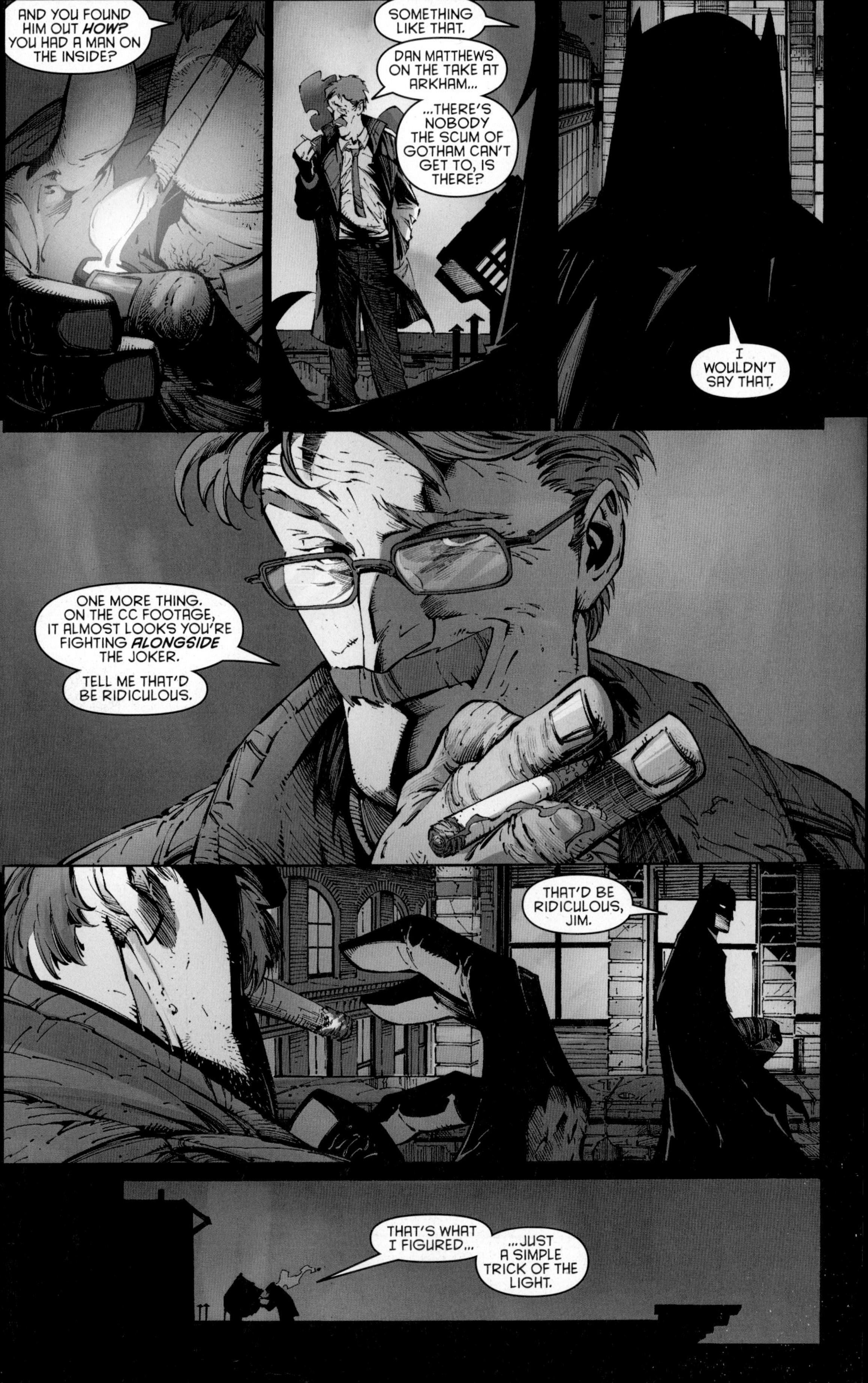
AND YOU FOUND HIM OUT HOW? YOU HAD A MAN ON THE INSIDE?
SOMETHING LIKE THAT.
DAN MATTHEWS ON THE TAKE AT ARKHAM...
...THERE'S NOBODY THE SCUM OF GOTHAM CAN'T GET TO, IS THERE?
I WOULDN'T SAY THAT.
ONE MORE THING. ON THE CC FOOTAGE, IT ALMOST LOOKS YOU'RE FIGHTING ALONGSIDE THE JOKER.
TELL ME THAT'D BE RIDICULOUS.
THAT'D BE RIDICULOUS, JIM.
THAT'S WHAT I FIGURED...
...JUST A SIMPLE TRICK OF THE LIGHT.

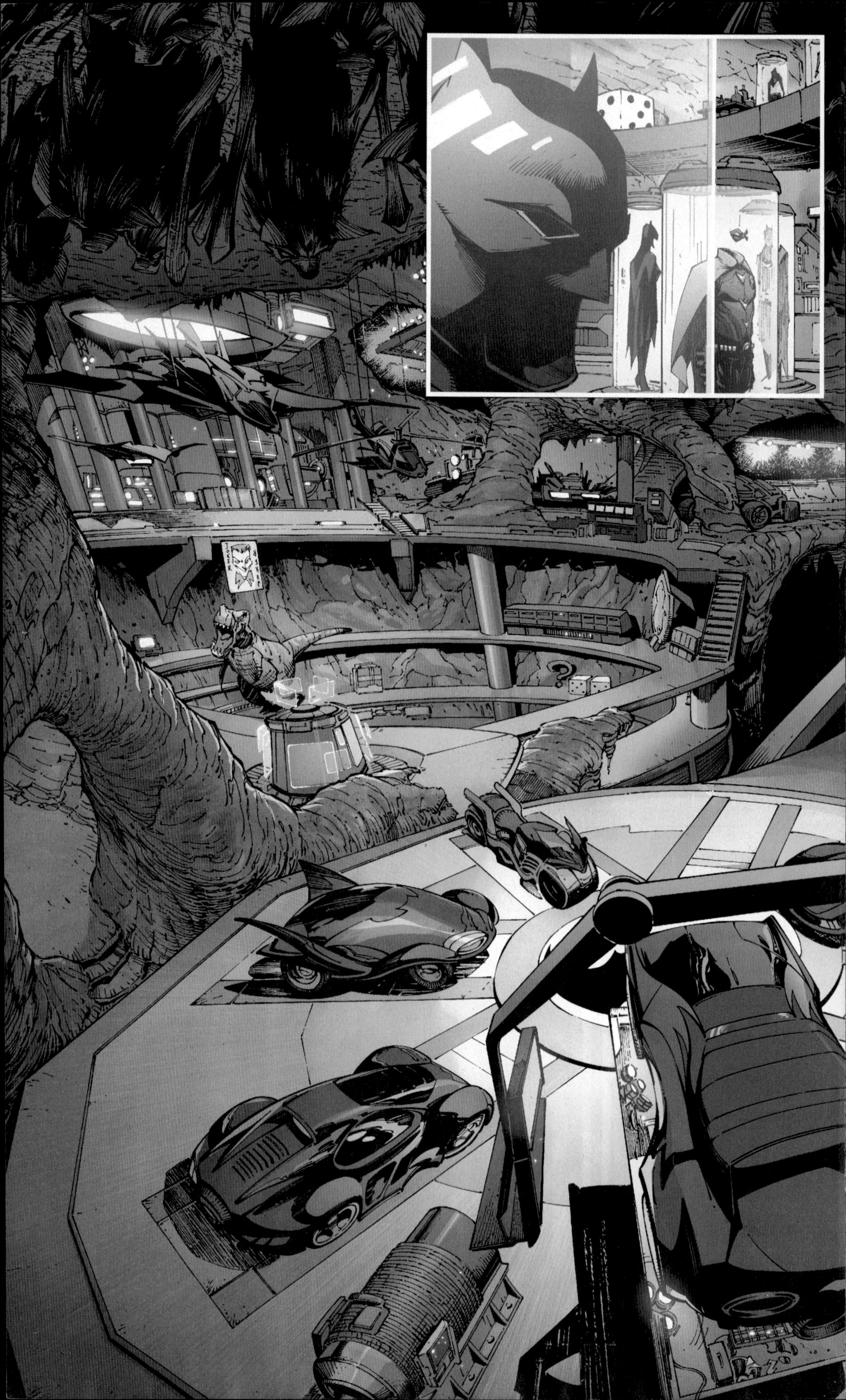
JOKER

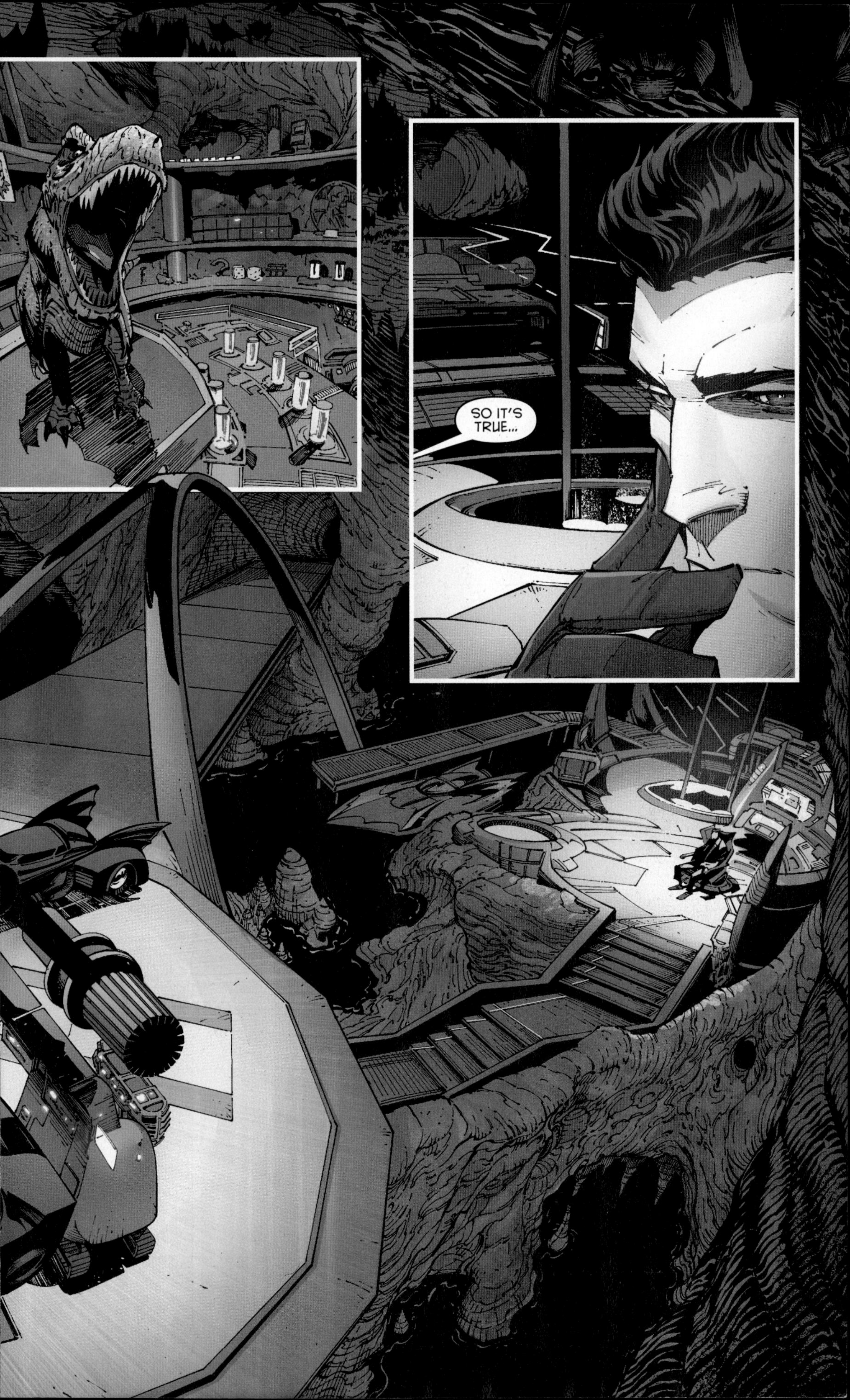
SO IT'S TRUE...

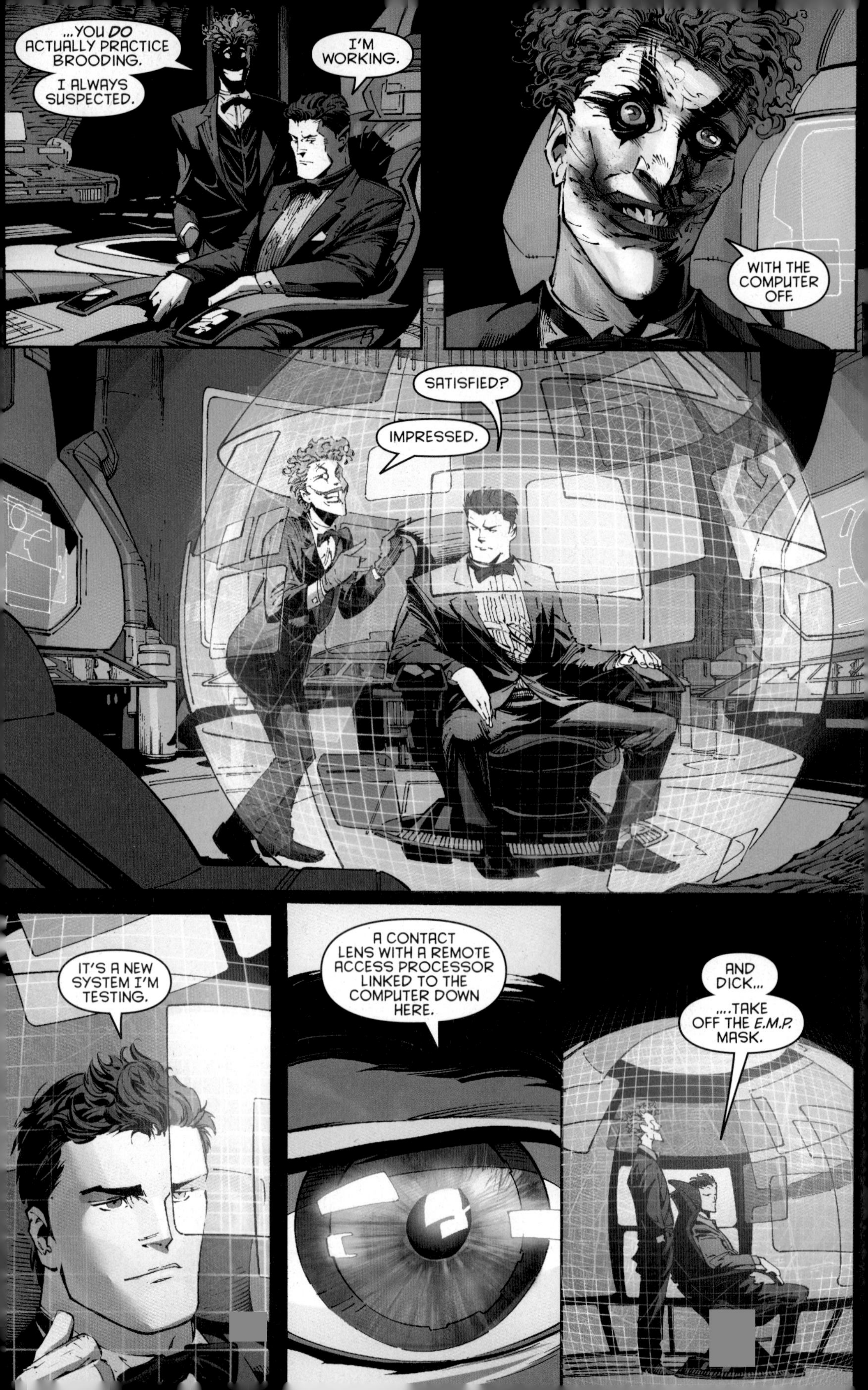
...YOU DO ACTUALLY PRACTICE BROODING.
I ALWAYS SUSPECTED.
I'M WORKING.
WITH THE COMPUTER OFF.
SATISFIED?
IMPRESSED.
IT'S A NEW SYSTEM I'M TESTING.
A CONTACT LENS WITH A REMOTE ACCESS PROCESSOR LINKED TO THE COMPUTER DOWN HERE.
AND DICK...
....TAKE OFF THE E.M.P. MASK.

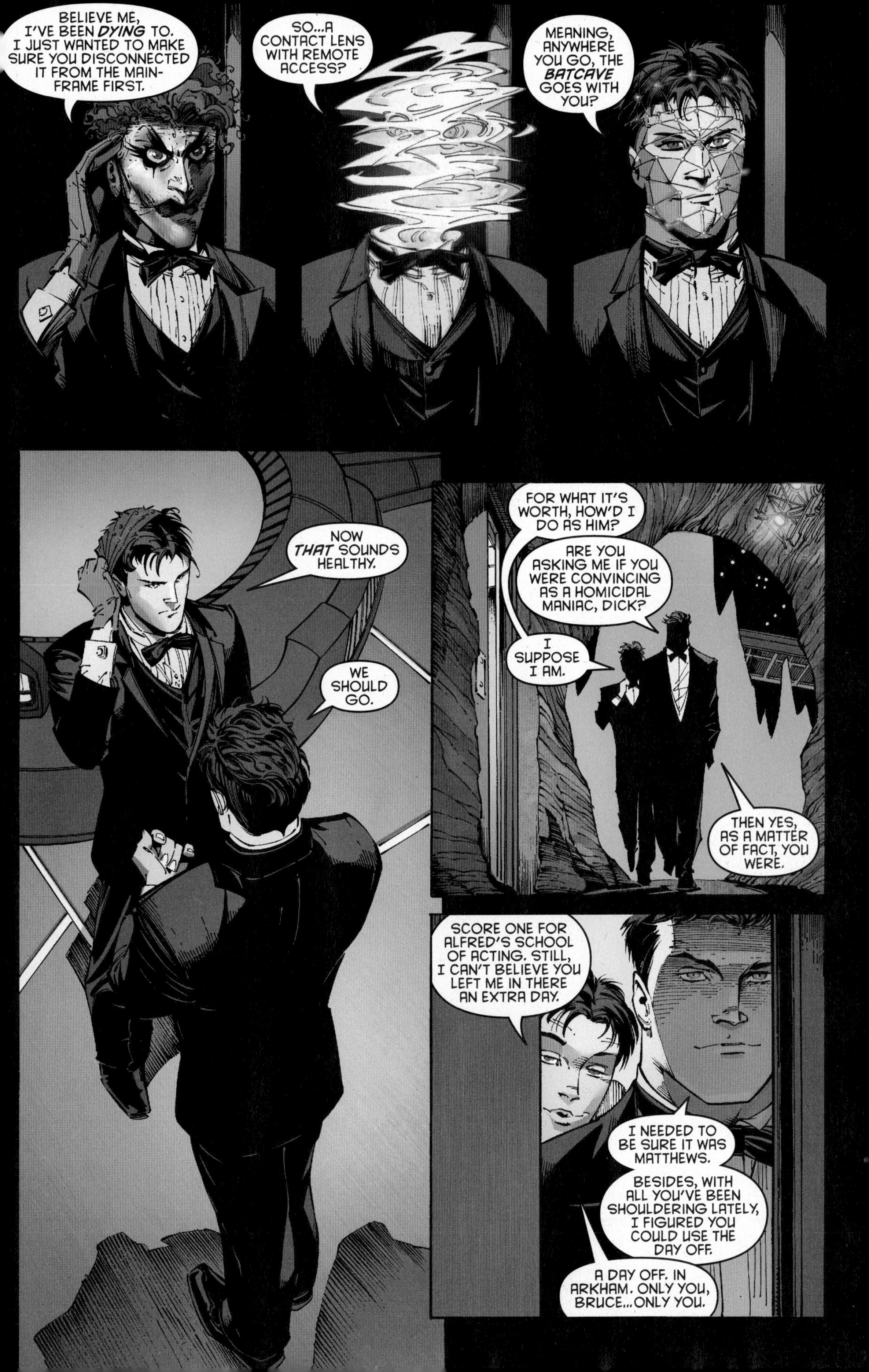
BELIEVE ME, I'VE BEEN DYING TO. I JUST WANTED TO MAKE SURE YOU DISCONNECTED IT FROM THE MAIN-FRAME FIRST.
SO...A CONTACT LENS WITH REMOTE ACCESS?
MEANING, ANYWHERE YOU GO, THE BATCAVE GOES WITH YOU?
NOW THAT SOUNDS HEALTHY.
WE SHOULD GO.
FOR WHAT IT'S WORTH, HOW'D I DO AS HIM?
ARE YOU ASKING ME IF YOU WERE CONVINCING AS A HOMICIDAL MANIAC, DICK?
I SUPPOSE I AM.
THEN YES, AS A MATTER OF FACT, YOU WERE.
SCORE ONE FOR ALFRED'S SCHOOL OF ACTING. STILL, I CAN'T BELIEVE YOU LEFT ME IN THERE AN EXTRA DAY.
I NEEDED TO BE SURE IT WAS MATTHEWS.
BESIDES, WITH ALL YOU'VE BEEN SHOULDERING LATELY, I FIGURED YOU COULD USE THE DAY OFF.
A DAY OFF. IN ARKHAM. ONLY YOU, BRUCE...ONLY YOU.

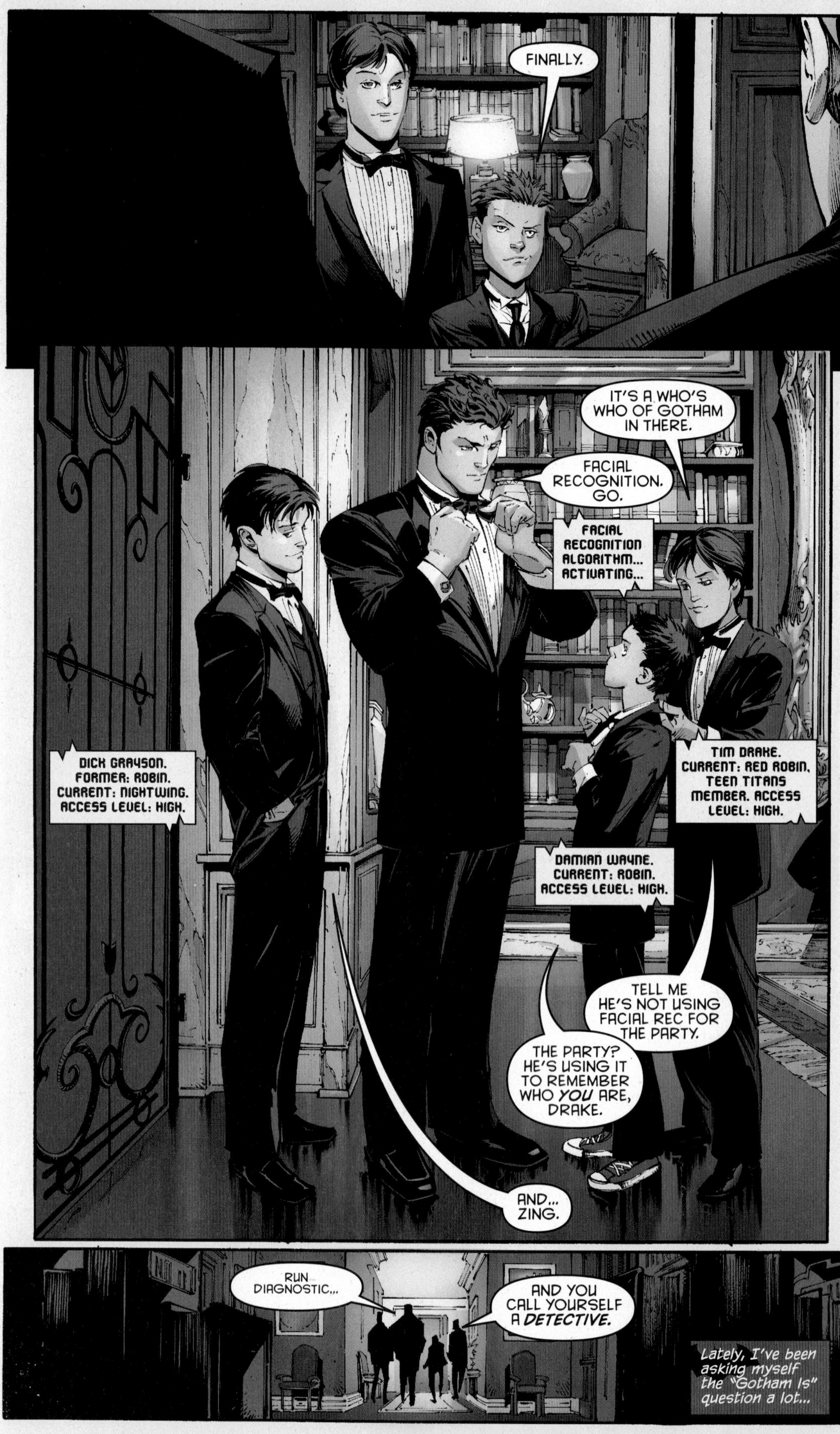
FINALLY.
IT'S A WHO'S WHO OF GOTHAM IN THERE.
FACIAL RECOGNITION. GO.
FACIAL RECOGNITION ALGORITHM... ACTIVATING...
DICK GRAYSON. FORMER: ROBIN. CURRENT: NIGHTWING. ACCESS LEVEL: HIGH.
TIM DRAKE. CURRENT: RED ROBIN, TEEN TITANS MEMBER. ACCESS LEVEL: HIGH.
DAMIAN WAYNE. CURRENT: ROBIN. ACCESS LEVEL: HIGH.
TELL ME HE'S NOT USING FACIAL REC FOR THE PARTY.
THE PARTY? HE'S USING IT TO REMEMBER WHO *YOU* ARE, DRAKE.
AND... ZING.
RUN DIAGNOSTIC...
AND YOU CALL YOURSELF A *DETECTIVE.*
Lately, I've been asking myself the "Gotham Is" question a lot...

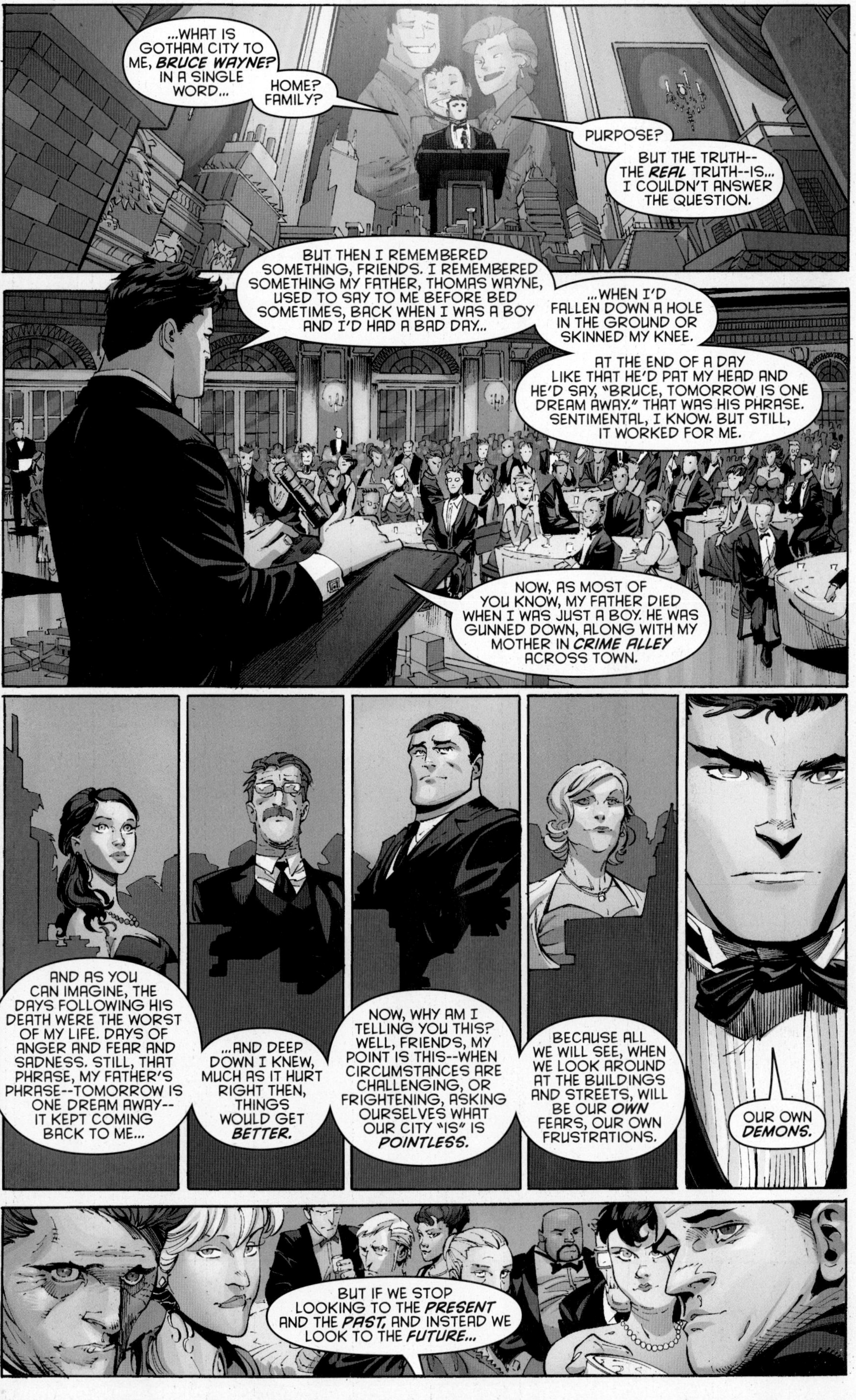
...WHAT IS GOTHAM CITY TO ME, BRUCE WAYNE? IN A SINGLE WORD...
HOME? FAMILY?
PURPOSE?
BUT THE TRUTH-- THE REAL TRUTH--IS... I COULDN'T ANSWER THE QUESTION.
BUT THEN I REMEMBERED SOMETHING, FRIENDS. I REMEMBERED SOMETHING MY FATHER, THOMAS WAYNE, USED TO SAY TO ME BEFORE BED SOMETIMES, BACK WHEN I WAS A BOY AND I'D HAD A BAD DAY...
...WHEN I'D FALLEN DOWN A HOLE IN THE GROUND OR SKINNED MY KNEE.
AT THE END OF A DAY LIKE THAT HE'D PAT MY HEAD AND HE'D SAY, "BRUCE, TOMORROW IS ONE DREAM AWAY." THAT WAS HIS PHRASE. SENTIMENTAL, I KNOW. BUT STILL, IT WORKED FOR ME.
NOW, AS MOST OF YOU KNOW, MY FATHER DIED WHEN I WAS JUST A BOY. HE WAS GUNNED DOWN, ALONG WITH MY MOTHER IN CRIME ALLEY ACROSS TOWN.
AND AS YOU CAN IMAGINE, THE DAYS FOLLOWING HIS DEATH WERE THE WORST OF MY LIFE. DAYS OF ANGER AND FEAR AND SADNESS. STILL, THAT PHRASE, MY FATHER'S PHRASE--TOMORROW IS ONE DREAM AWAY-- IT KEPT COMING BACK TO ME...
...AND DEEP DOWN I KNEW, MUCH AS IT HURT RIGHT THEN, THINGS WOULD GET BETTER.
NOW, WHY AM I TELLING YOU THIS? WELL, FRIENDS, MY POINT IS THIS--WHEN CIRCUMSTANCES ARE CHALLENGING, OR FRIGHTENING, ASKING OURSELVES WHAT OUR CITY "IS" IS POINTLESS.
BECAUSE ALL WE WILL SEE, WHEN WE LOOK AROUND AT THE BUILDINGS AND STREETS, WILL BE OUR OWN FEARS, OUR OWN FRUSTRATIONS.
OUR OWN DEMONS.
BUT IF WE STOP LOOKING TO THE PRESENT AND THE PAST, AND INSTEAD WE LOOK TO THE FUTURE...

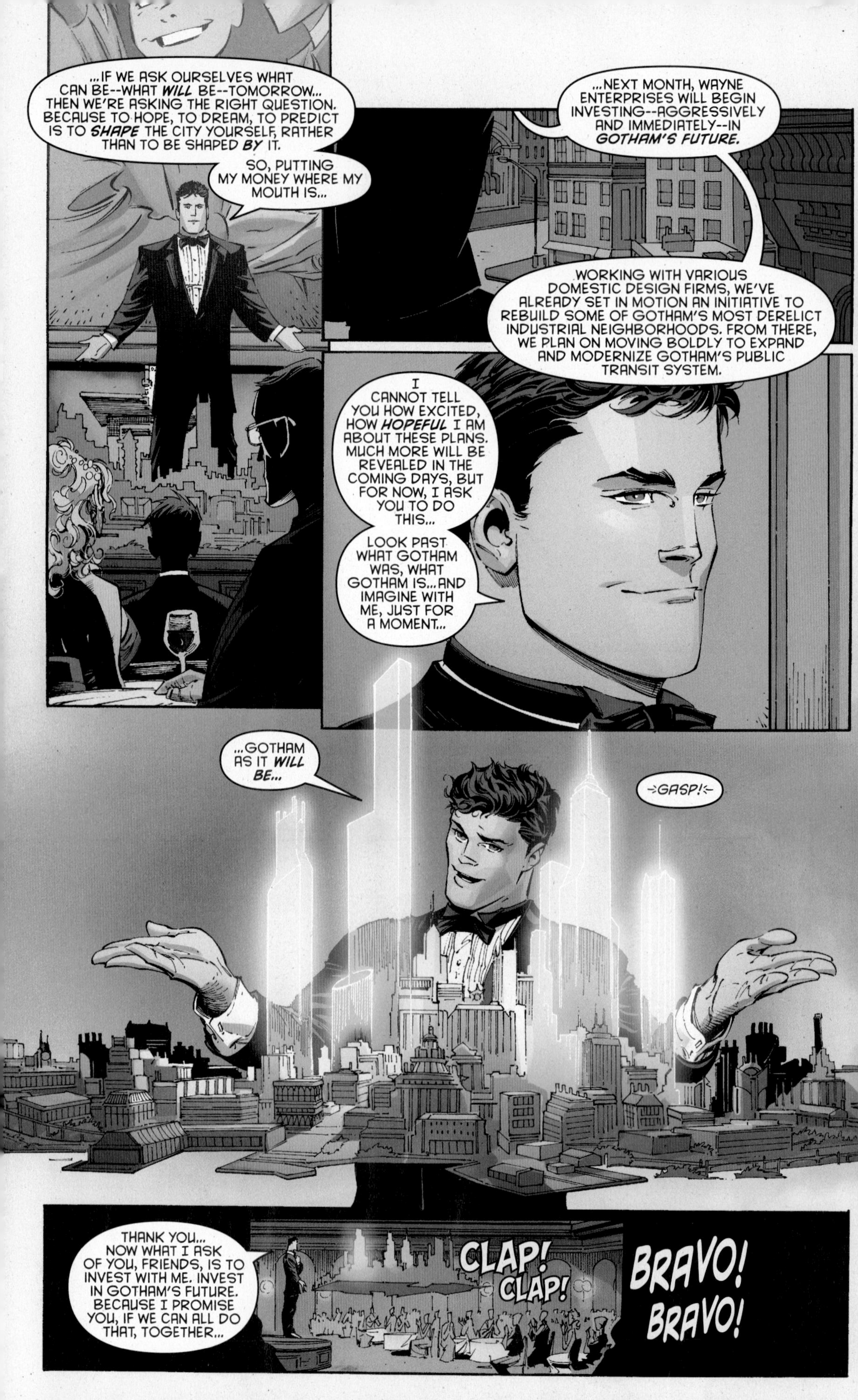
...IF WE ASK OURSELVES WHAT CAN BE--WHAT WILL BE--TOMORROW... THEN WE'RE ASKING THE RIGHT QUESTION. BECAUSE TO HOPE, TO DREAM, TO PREDICT IS TO SHAPE THE CITY YOURSELF, RATHER THAN TO BE SHAPED BY IT.
SO, PUTTING MY MONEY WHERE MY MOUTH IS...
...NEXT MONTH, WAYNE ENTERPRISES WILL BEGIN INVESTING--AGGRESSIVELY AND IMMEDIATELY--IN GOTHAM'S FUTURE.
WORKING WITH VARIOUS DOMESTIC DESIGN FIRMS, WE'VE ALREADY SET IN MOTION AN INITIATIVE TO REBUILD SOME OF GOTHAM'S MOST DERELICT INDUSTRIAL NEIGHBORHOODS. FROM THERE, WE PLAN ON MOVING BOLDLY TO EXPAND AND MODERNIZE GOTHAM'S PUBLIC TRANSIT SYSTEM.
I CANNOT TELL YOU HOW EXCITED, HOW HOPEFUL I AM ABOUT THESE PLANS. MUCH MORE WILL BE REVEALED IN THE COMING DAYS, BUT FOR NOW, I ASK YOU TO DO THIS...
LOOK PAST WHAT GOTHAM WAS, WHAT GOTHAM IS...AND IMAGINE WITH ME, JUST FOR A MOMENT...
...GOTHAM AS IT WILL BE...
GASP!
THANK YOU... NOW WHAT I ASK OF YOU, FRIENDS, IS TO INVEST WITH ME. INVEST IN GOTHAM'S FUTURE. BECAUSE I PROMISE YOU, IF WE CAN ALL DO THAT, TOGETHER...
CLAP! CLAP!
BRAVO! BRAVO!

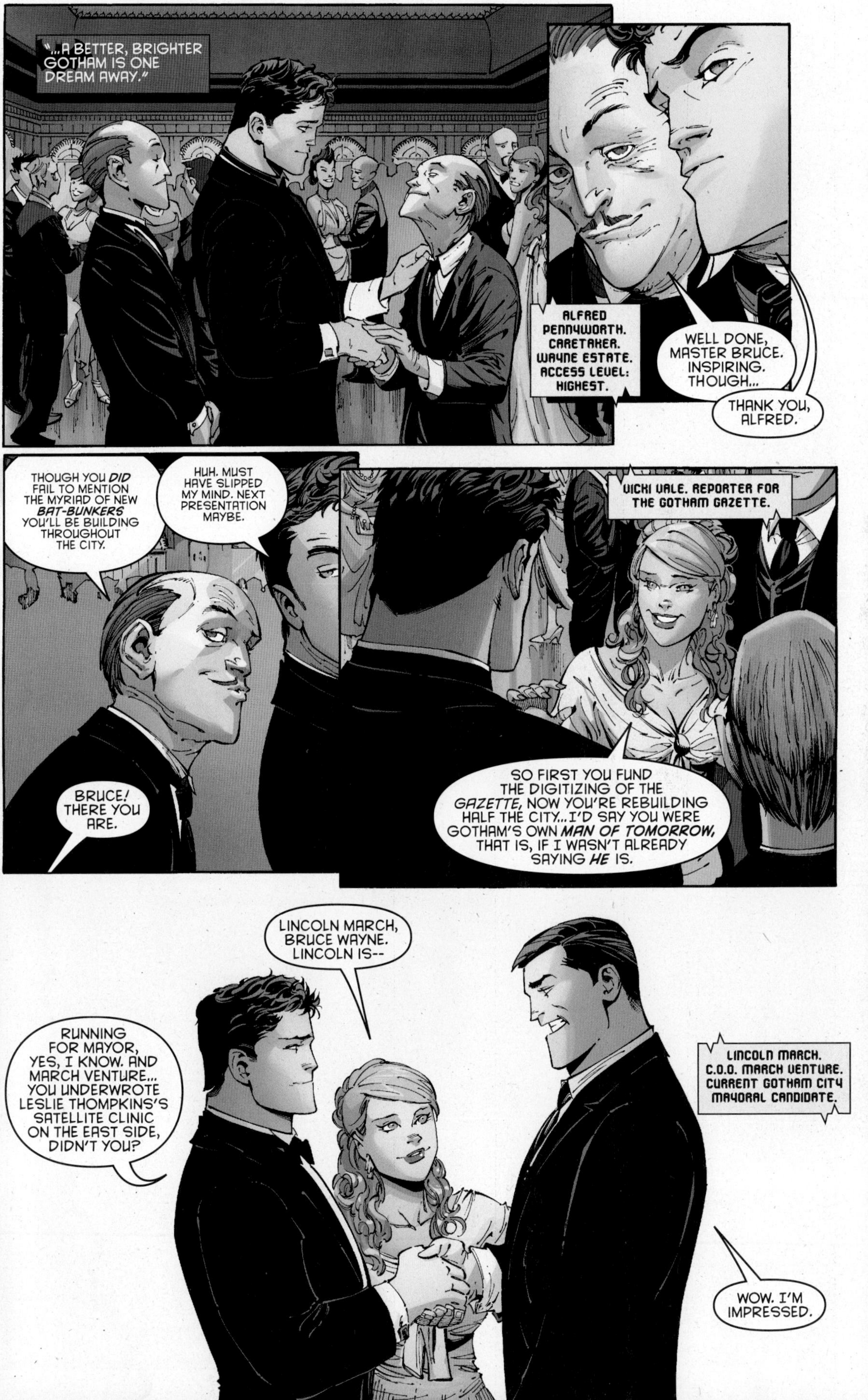
"...A BETTER, BRIGHTER GOTHAM IS ONE DREAM AWAY."
ALFRED PENNYWORTH. CARETAKER. WAYNE ESTATE. ACCESS LEVEL: HIGHEST.
WELL DONE, MASTER BRUCE. INSPIRING. THOUGH...
THANK YOU, ALFRED.
THOUGH YOU DID FAIL TO MENTION THE MYRIAD OF NEW BAT-BUNKERS YOU'LL BE BUILDING THROUGHOUT THE CITY.
HUH. MUST HAVE SLIPPED MY MIND. NEXT PRESENTATION MAYBE.
BRUCE! THERE YOU ARE.
VICKI VALE. REPORTER FOR THE GOTHAM GAZETTE.
SO FIRST YOU FUND THE DIGITIZING OF THE GAZETTE, NOW YOU'RE REBUILDING HALF THE CITY...I'D SAY YOU WERE GOTHAM'S OWN MAN OF TOMORROW, THAT IS, IF I WASN'T ALREADY SAYING HE IS.
LINCOLN MARCH, BRUCE WAYNE. LINCOLN IS--
RUNNING FOR MAYOR, YES, I KNOW. AND MARCH VENTURE... YOU UNDERWROTE LESLIE THOMPKINS'S SATELLITE CLINIC ON THE EAST SIDE, DIDN'T YOU?
LINCOLN MARCH. C.O.O. MARCH VENTURE. CURRENT GOTHAM CITY MAYORAL CANDIDATE.
WOW. I'M IMPRESSED.

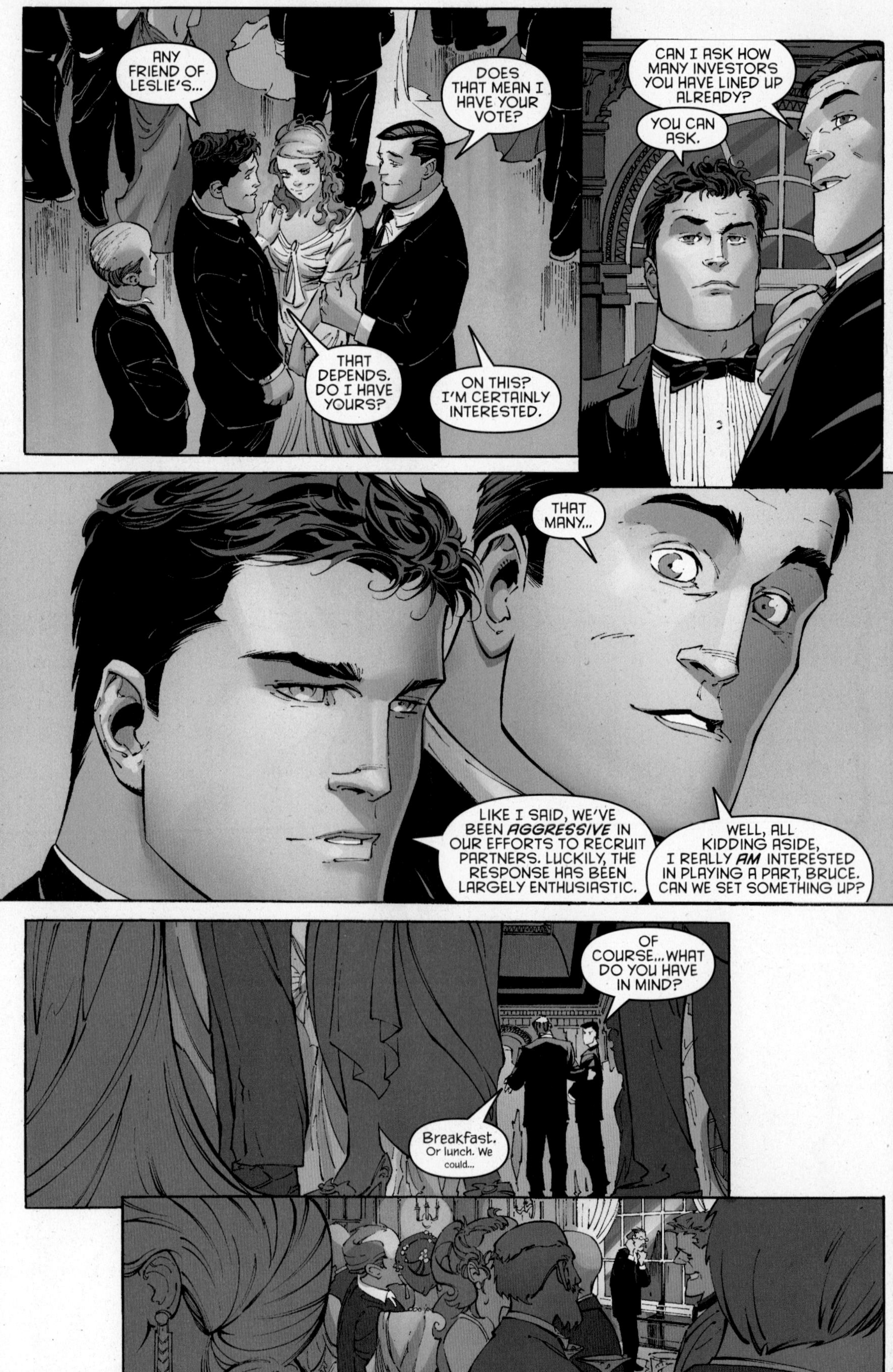
ANY FRIEND OF LESLIE'S...
DOES THAT MEAN I HAVE YOUR VOTE?
THAT DEPENDS. DO I HAVE YOURS?
ON THIS? I'M CERTAINLY INTERESTED.
CAN I ASK HOW MANY INVESTORS YOU HAVE LINED UP ALREADY?
YOU CAN ASK.
THAT MANY...
LIKE I SAID, WE'VE BEEN AGGRESSIVE IN OUR EFFORTS TO RECRUIT PARTNERS. LUCKILY, THE RESPONSE HAS BEEN LARGELY ENTHUSIASTIC.
WELL, ALL KIDDING ASIDE, I REALLY AM INTERESTED IN PLAYING A PART, BRUCE. CAN WE SET SOMETHING UP?
OF COURSE...WHAT DO YOU HAVE IN MIND?
Breakfast. Or lunch. We could...

-:COUGH-COUGH:-
(LIP READ GO).

I'M SORRY. GO ON.

LIP READ ACTIVATING... OCULAR TARGETING TO...

I WAS JUST SAYING I'M ENTHUSIASTIC TO...

HOW MANY STAB WOUNDS? GOD.

ALL RIGHT, I'LL BE RIGHT DOWN. JUST GIVE ME TEN MINUTES TO ESCAPE FROM PLANET OF THE CREPES.

"CREPE." IT'S A PANCAKE. NEVER MIND.

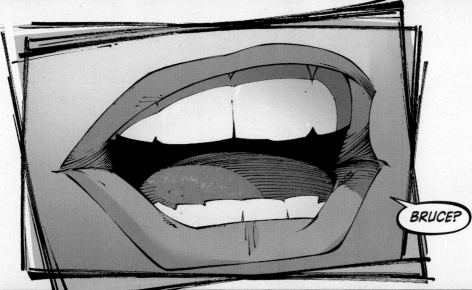

BRUCE?

I'M SORRY, WHAT?

I WAS SAYING I COULD DO AS EARLY AS TOMORROW. LUNCH? TALK ABOUT YOUR PLANS?

OF COURSE. TOMORROW. ALFRED, SET IT UP, WILL YOU? NOW IF YOU'LL EXCUSE ME FOR A MOMENT, LINCOLN...

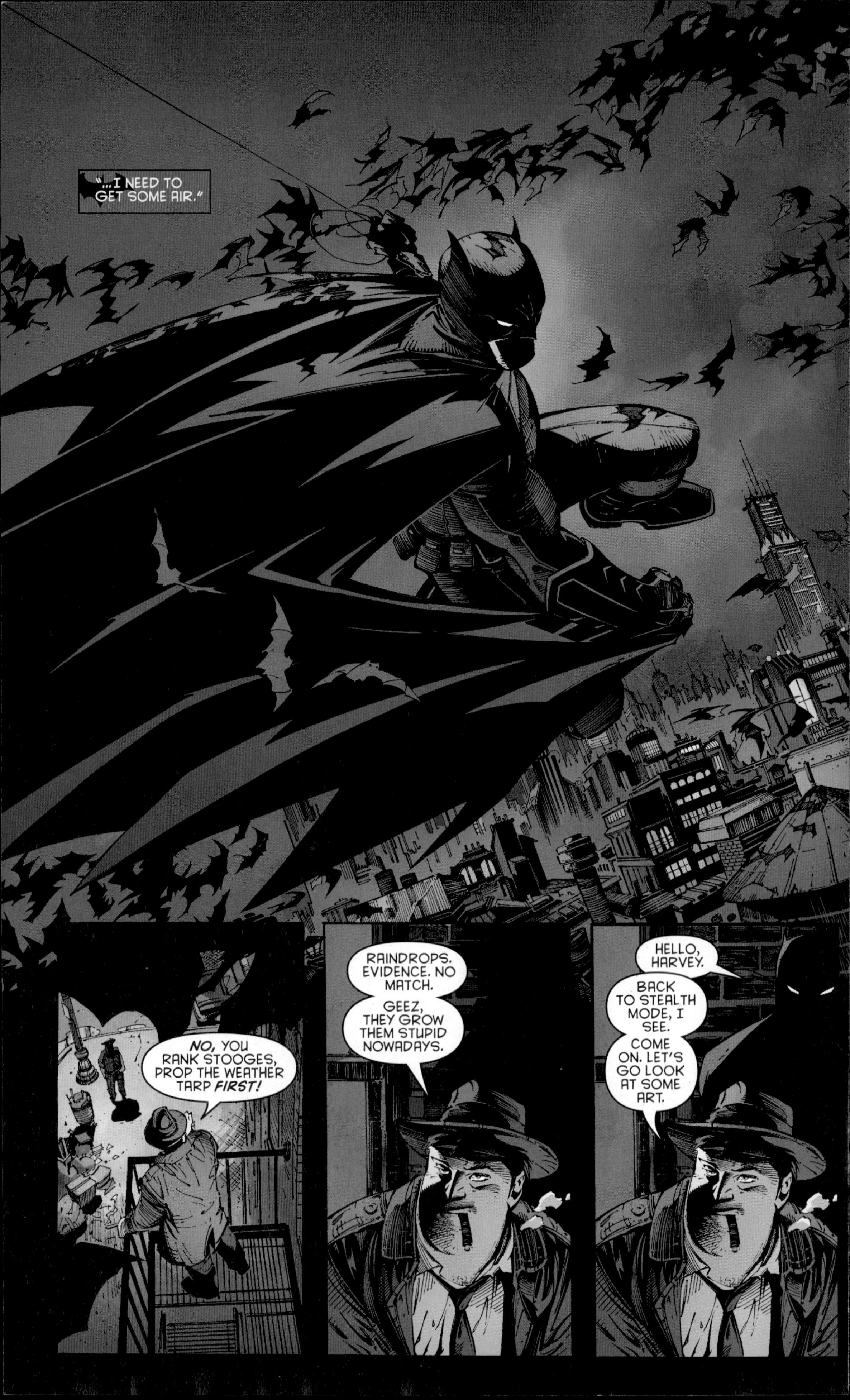

"...I NEED TO GET SOME AIR."
NO, YOU RANK STOOGES, PROP THE WEATHER TARP FIRST!
RAINDROPS. EVIDENCE. NO MATCH.
GEEZ, THEY GROW THEM STUPID NOWADAYS.
HELLO, HARVEY.
BACK TO STEALTH MODE, I SEE.
COME ON. LET'S GO LOOK AT SOME ART.

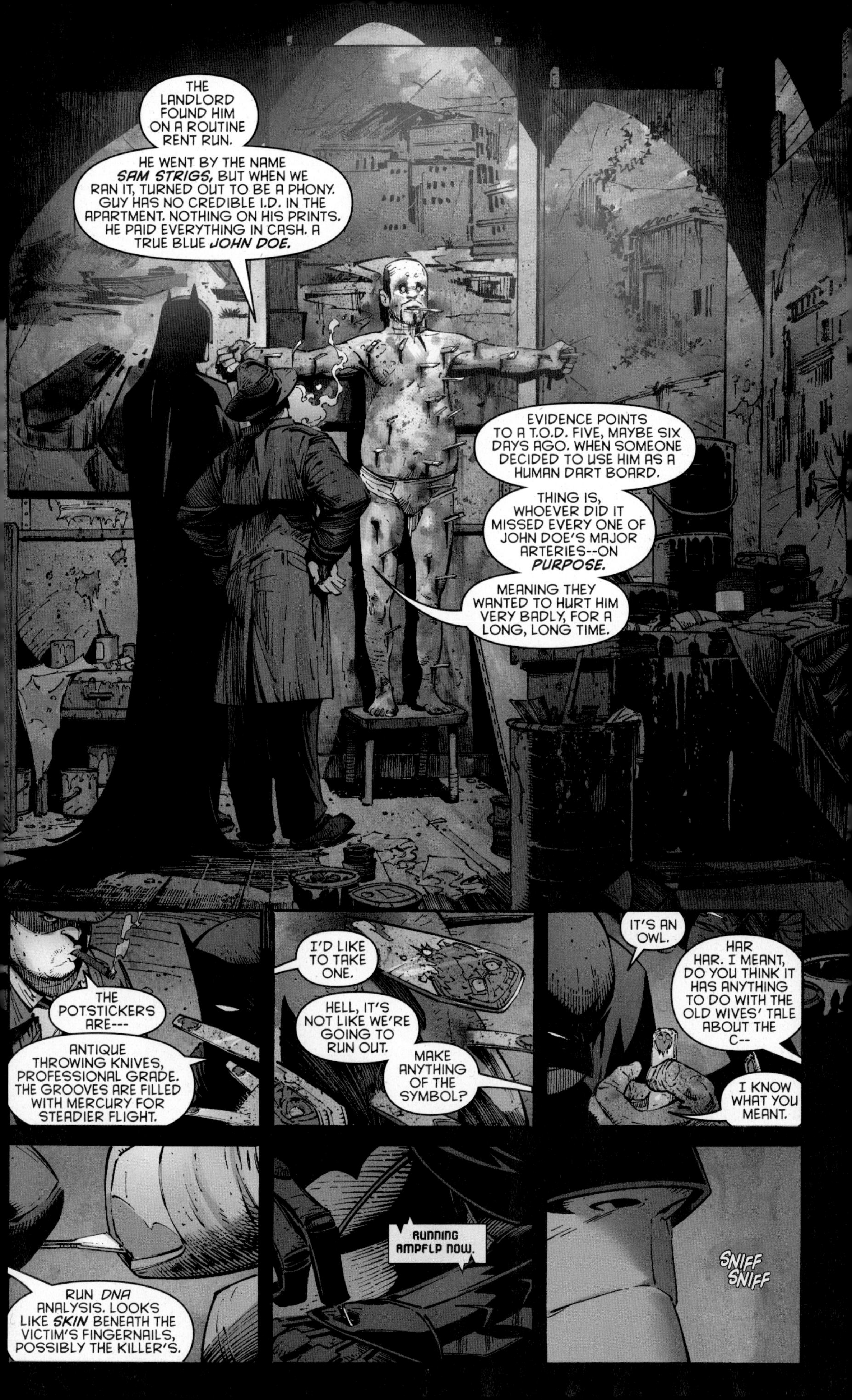
THE LANDLORD FOUND HIM ON A ROUTINE RENT RUN.
HE WENT BY THE NAME *SAM STRIGS,* BUT WHEN WE RAN IT, TURNED OUT TO BE A PHONY. GUY HAS NO CREDIBLE I.D. IN THE APARTMENT. NOTHING ON HIS PRINTS. HE PAID EVERYTHING IN CASH. A TRUE BLUE *JOHN DOE.*
EVIDENCE POINTS TO A T.O.D. FIVE, MAYBE SIX DAYS AGO. WHEN SOMEONE DECIDED TO USE HIM AS A HUMAN DART BOARD.
THING IS, WHOEVER DID IT MISSED EVERY ONE OF JOHN DOE'S MAJOR ARTERIES--ON *PURPOSE.*
MEANING THEY WANTED TO HURT HIM VERY BADLY, FOR A LONG, LONG TIME.
THE POTSTICKERS ARE---
ANTIQUE THROWING KNIVES, PROFESSIONAL GRADE. THE GROOVES ARE FILLED WITH MERCURY FOR STEADIER FLIGHT.
I'D LIKE TO TAKE ONE.
HELL, IT'S NOT LIKE WE'RE GOING TO RUN OUT.
MAKE ANYTHING OF THE SYMBOL?
IT'S AN OWL.
HAR HAR. I MEANT, DO YOU THINK IT HAS ANYTHING TO DO WITH THE OLD WIVES' TALE ABOUT THE C--
I KNOW WHAT YOU MEANT.
RUN *DNA* ANALYSIS. LOOKS LIKE *SKIN* BENEATH THE VICTIM'S FINGERNAILS, POSSIBLY THE KILLER'S.
RUNNING AMPFLP NOW.
SNIFF SNIFF

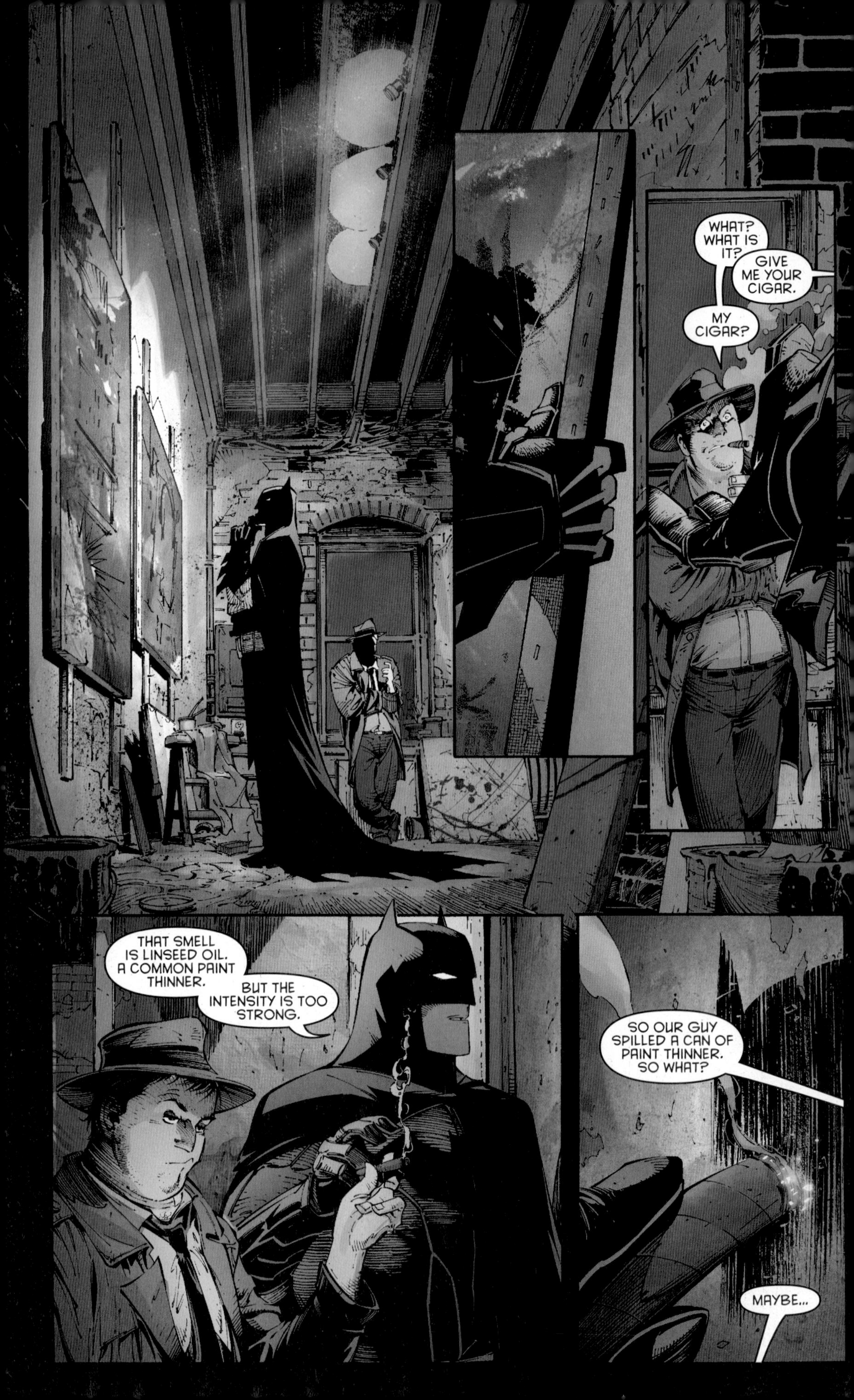
WHAT? WHAT IS IT?
GIVE ME YOUR CIGAR.
MY CIGAR?
THAT SMELL IS LINSEED OIL. A COMMON PAINT THINNER.
BUT THE INTENSITY IS TOO STRONG.
SO OUR GUY SPILLED A CAN OF PAINT THINNER. SO WHAT?
MAYBE...

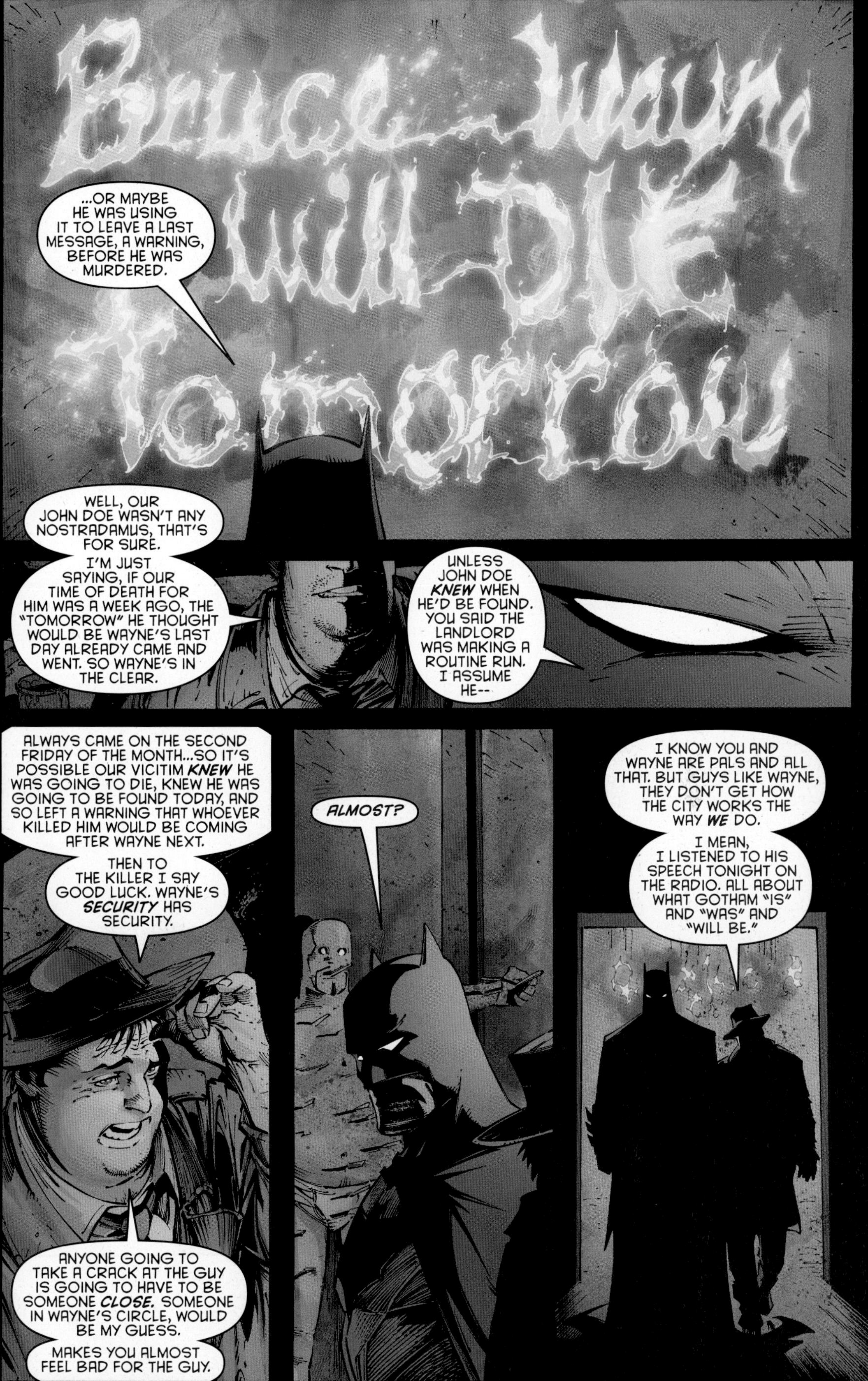
Bruce Wayne will DIE Tomorrow
...OR MAYBE HE WAS USING IT TO LEAVE A LAST MESSAGE, A WARNING, BEFORE HE WAS MURDERED.
WELL, OUR JOHN DOE WASN'T ANY NOSTRADAMUS, THAT'S FOR SURE.
I'M JUST SAYING, IF OUR TIME OF DEATH FOR HIM WAS A WEEK AGO, THE "TOMORROW" HE THOUGHT WOULD BE WAYNE'S LAST DAY ALREADY CAME AND WENT. SO WAYNE'S IN THE CLEAR.
UNLESS JOHN DOE *KNEW* WHEN HE'D BE FOUND. YOU SAID THE LANDLORD WAS MAKING A ROUTINE RUN. I ASSUME HE--
ALWAYS CAME ON THE SECOND FRIDAY OF THE MONTH...SO IT'S POSSIBLE OUR VICITIM *KNEW* HE WAS GOING TO DIE, KNEW HE WAS GOING TO BE FOUND TODAY, AND SO LEFT A WARNING THAT WHOEVER KILLED HIM WOULD BE COMING AFTER WAYNE NEXT.
THEN TO THE KILLER I SAY GOOD LUCK. WAYNE'S *SECURITY* HAS SECURITY.
ANYONE GOING TO TAKE A CRACK AT THE GUY IS GOING TO HAVE TO BE SOMEONE *CLOSE.* SOMEONE IN WAYNE'S CIRCLE, WOULD BE MY GUESS.
MAKES YOU ALMOST FEEL BAD FOR THE GUY.
ALMOST?
I KNOW YOU AND WAYNE ARE PALS AND ALL THAT. BUT GUYS LIKE WAYNE, THEY DON'T GET HOW THE CITY WORKS THE WAY *WE* DO.
I MEAN, I LISTENED TO HIS SPEECH TONIGHT ON THE RADIO. ALL ABOUT WHAT GOTHAM "IS" AND "WAS" AND "WILL BE."

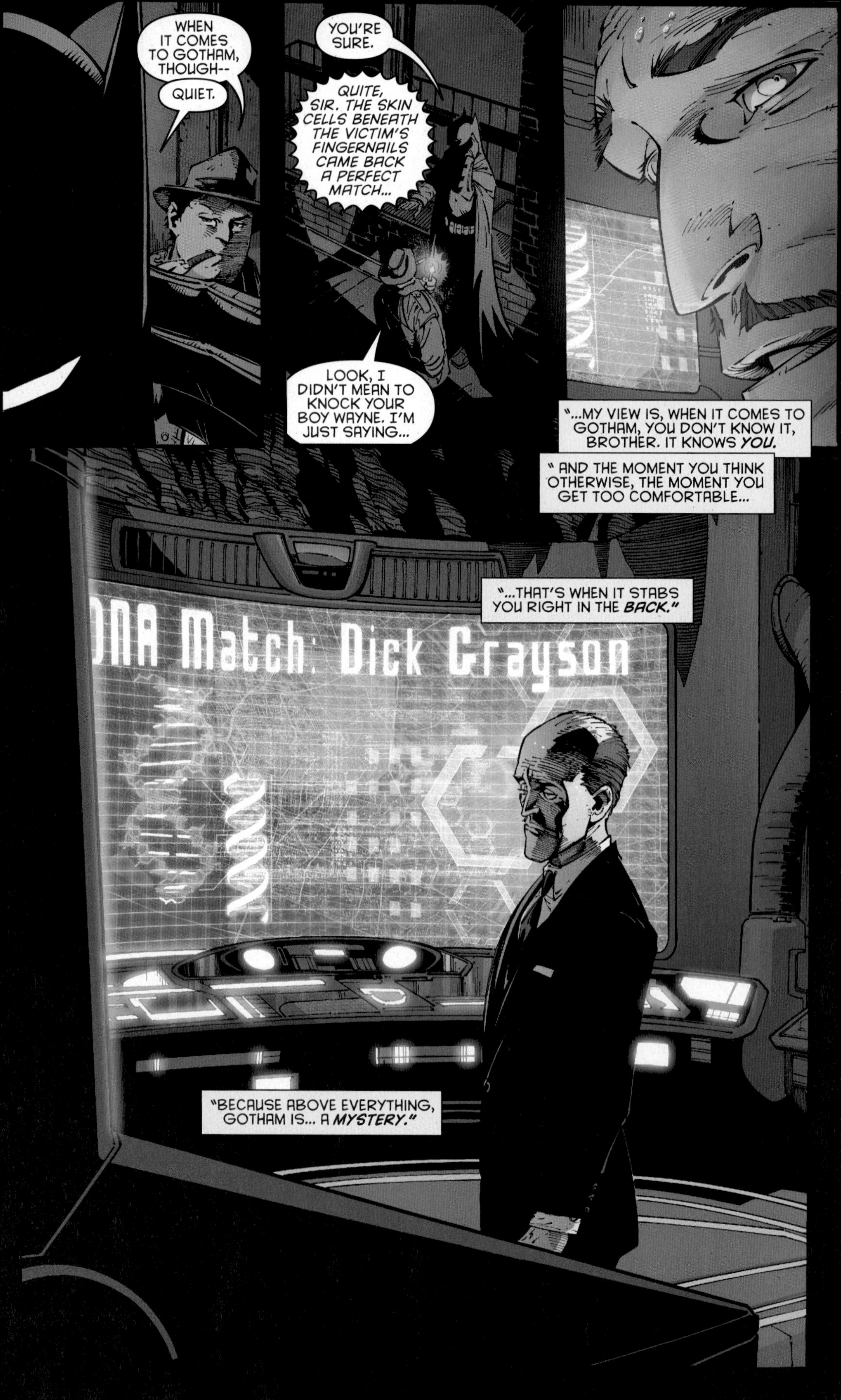

WHEN IT COMES TO GOTHAM, THOUGH--
QUIET.
YOU'RE SURE.
QUITE, SIR. THE SKIN CELLS BENEATH THE VICTIM'S FINGERNAILS CAME BACK A PERFECT MATCH...
LOOK, I DIDN'T MEAN TO KNOCK YOUR BOY WAYNE. I'M JUST SAYING...
"...MY VIEW IS, WHEN IT COMES TO GOTHAM, YOU DON'T KNOW IT, BROTHER. IT KNOWS *YOU*.
" AND THE MOMENT YOU THINK OTHERWISE, THE MOMENT YOU GET TOO COMFORTABLE...
"...THAT'S WHEN IT STABS YOU RIGHT IN THE *BACK*."
DNA Match: Dick Grayson
"BECAUSE ABOVE EVERYTHING, GOTHAM IS... A *MYSTERY*."

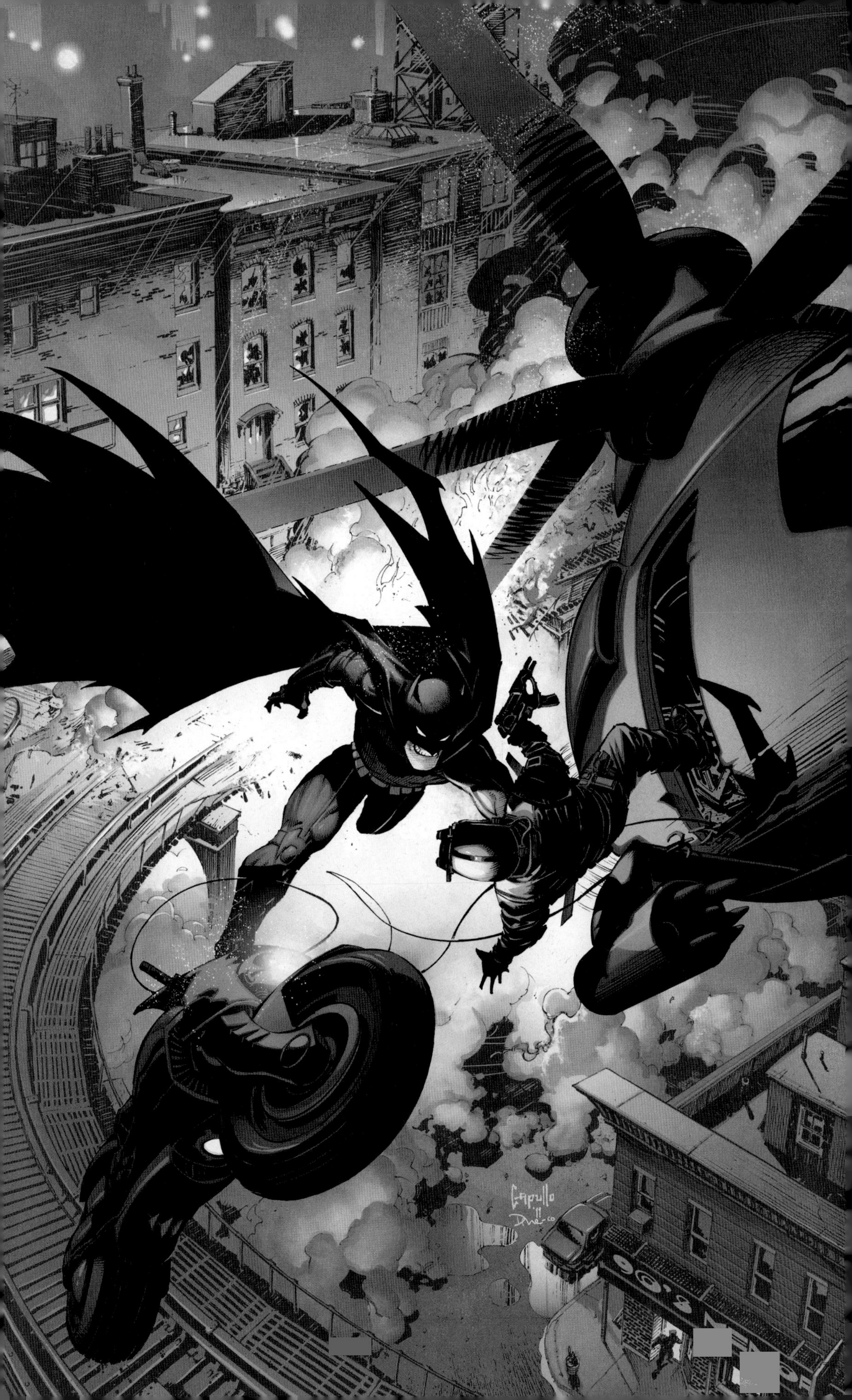

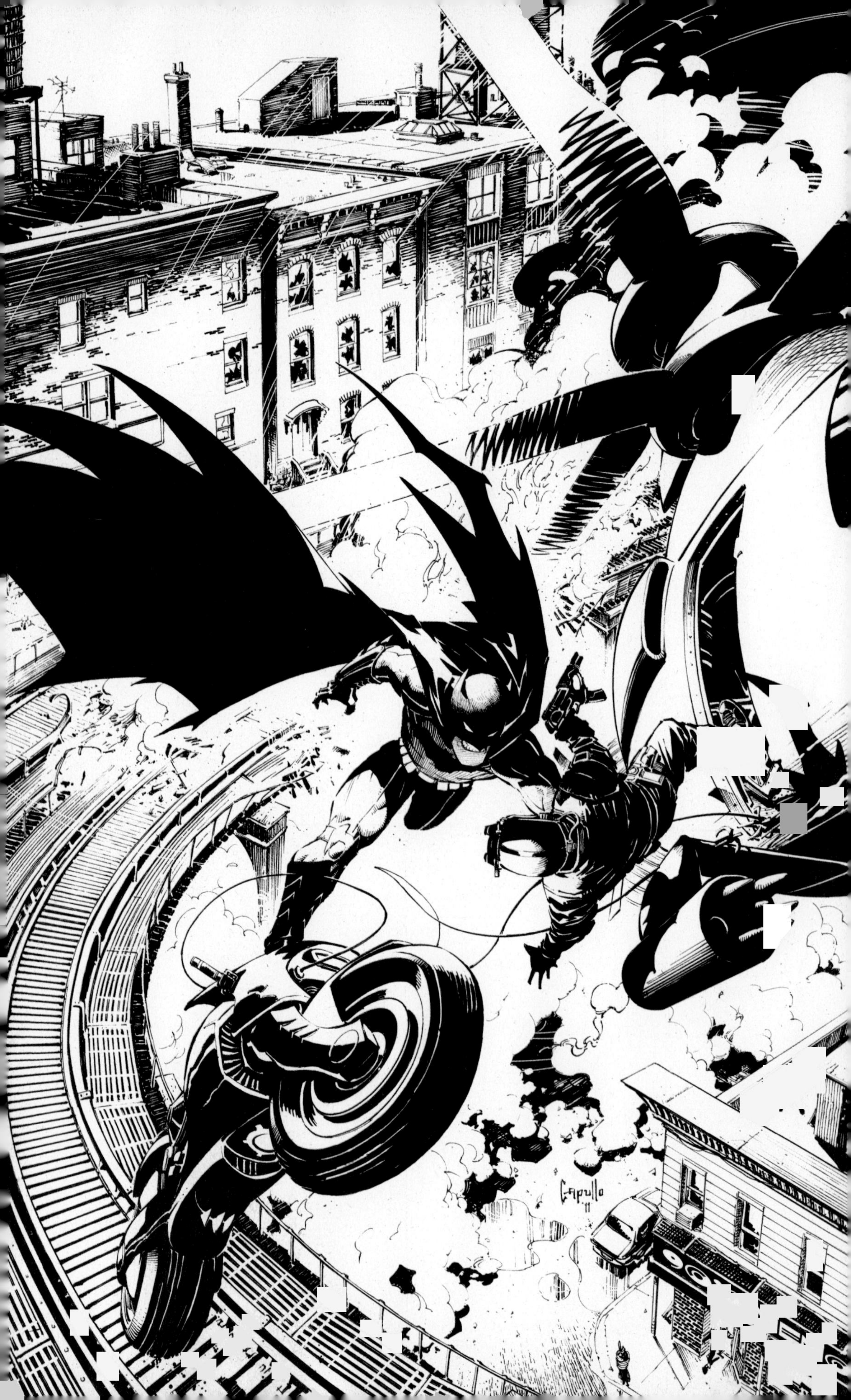
CAPULLO '11

The original Wayne Tower.

If you came to Gotham city today, right now, and took a tour of the building, here are some things your guide would tell you:

The tower was constructed in 1888, under the watch of my great, great grandfather **Alan Wayne**.

He built the tower to serve as a symbol of welcome to people coming to Gotham. And, as your guide will point out, from the ground up, it's designed to give visitors like you the feeling that they're cared for and protected.

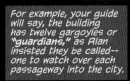

For example, your guide will say, the building has twelve gargoyles or **"guardians,"** as Alan insisted they be called-- one to watch over each passageway into the city.

The five guardians at the first tier were placed there to watch over the five original gateways into Gotham--the three bridges and two tunnels.

Higher up the tower is a ring of seven guardians, one to protect each of the seven train lines that converge at Union Station, below Wayne Tower's base.

And at the top of the tower is the **observation deck**, which Alan insisted remain free and open to the public every weekend, all year round.

For the windows, Alan demanded that only the best glass be used. A kind of double-bonded, laminated float glass, designed to be crystal-quality, weatherproof. And, most important, **unbreakable.**

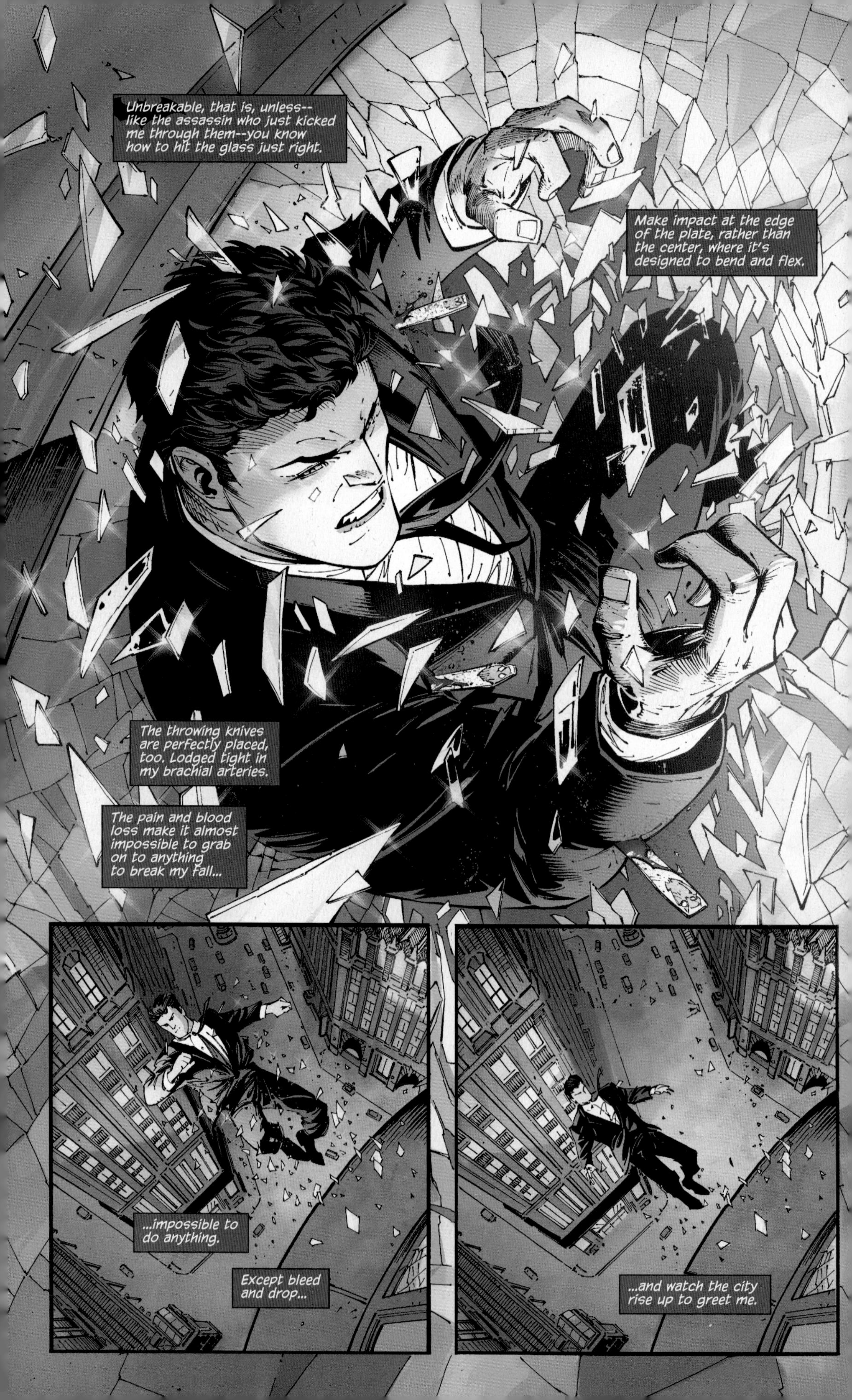
Unbreakable, that is, unless--like the assassin who just kicked me through them--you know how to hit the glass just right.
Make impact at the edge of the plate, rather than the center, where it's designed to bend and flex.
The throwing knives are perfectly placed, too. Lodged tight in my brachial arteries.
The pain and blood loss make it almost impossible to grab on to anything to break my fall...
...impossible to do anything.
Except bleed and drop...
...and watch the city rise up to greet me.

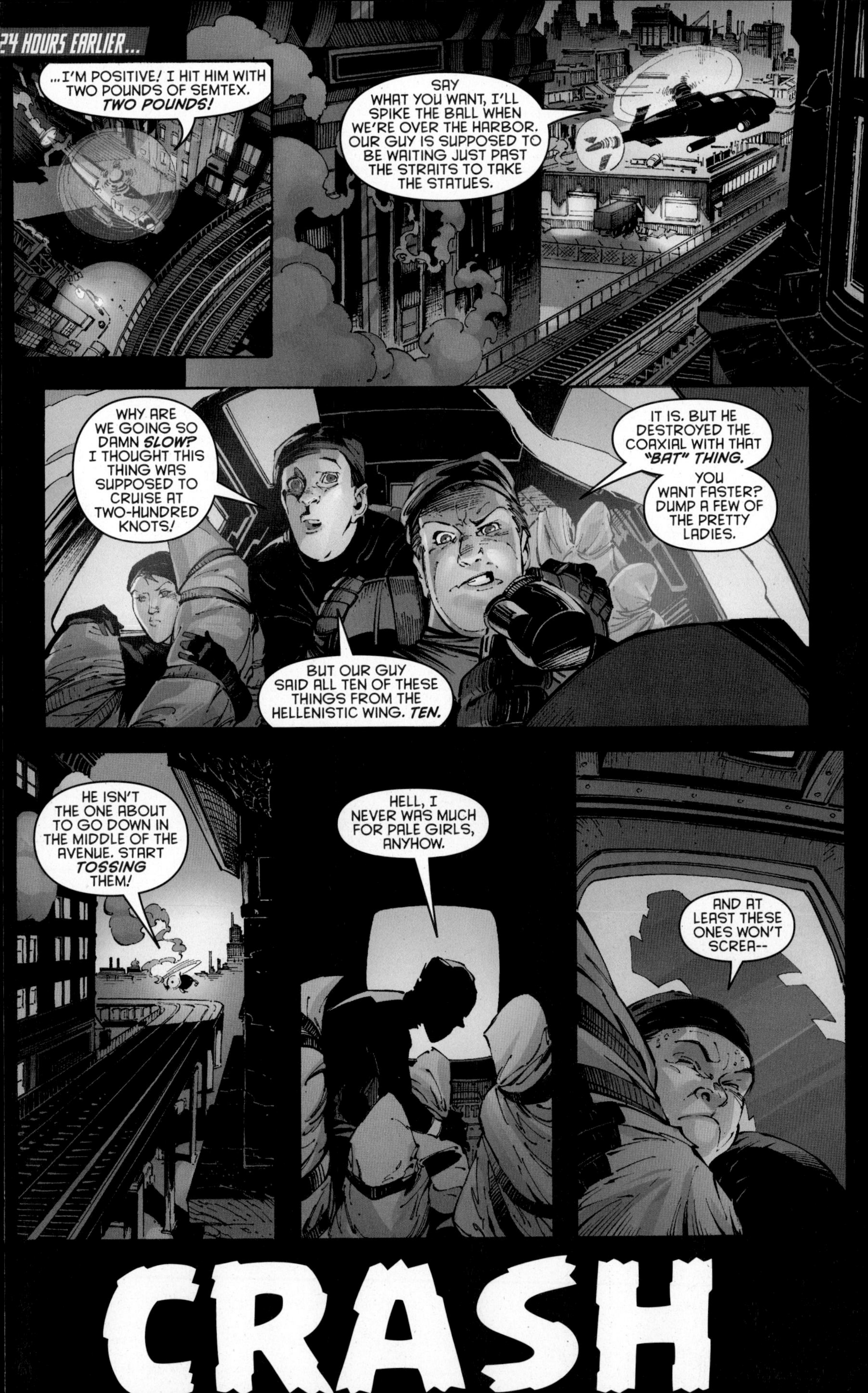
24 HOURS EARLIER...
...I'M POSITIVE! I HIT HIM WITH TWO POUNDS OF SEMTEX. TWO POUNDS!
SAY WHAT YOU WANT, I'LL SPIKE THE BALL WHEN WE'RE OVER THE HARBOR. OUR GUY IS SUPPOSED TO BE WAITING JUST PAST THE STRAITS TO TAKE THE STATUES.
WHY ARE WE GOING SO DAMN SLOW? I THOUGHT THIS THING WAS SUPPOSED TO CRUISE AT TWO-HUNDRED KNOTS!
IT IS. BUT HE DESTROYED THE COAXIAL WITH THAT "BAT" THING.
YOU WANT FASTER? DUMP A FEW OF THE PRETTY LADIES.
BUT OUR GUY SAID ALL TEN OF THESE THINGS FROM THE HELLENISTIC WING. TEN.
HE ISN'T THE ONE ABOUT TO GO DOWN IN THE MIDDLE OF THE AVENUE. START TOSSING THEM!
HELL, I NEVER WAS MUCH FOR PALE GIRLS, ANYHOW.
AND AT LEAST THESE ONES WON'T SCREA--
CRASH

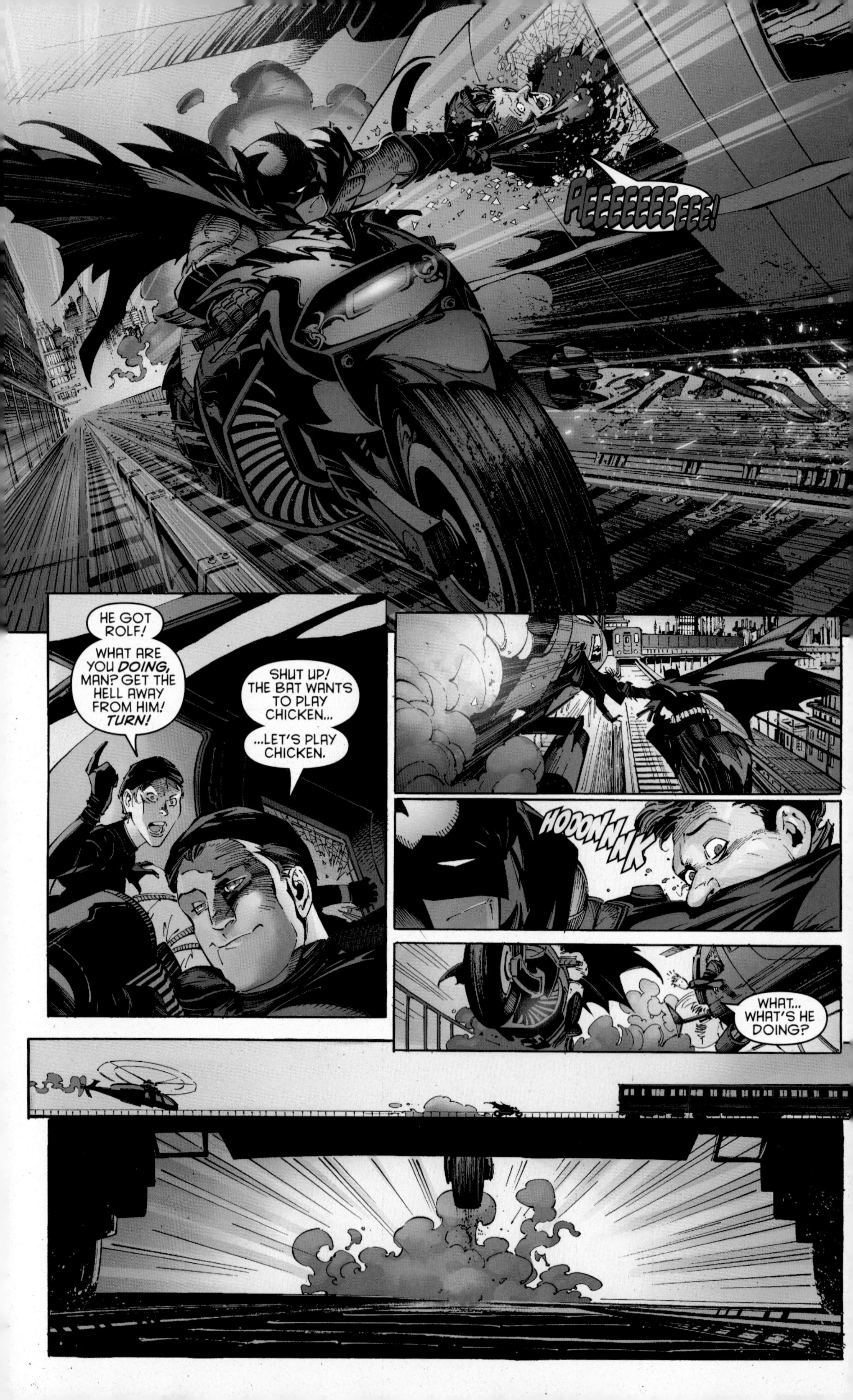
AEEEEEEEEEEE!
HE GOT ROLF!
WHAT ARE YOU DOING, MAN? GET THE HELL AWAY FROM HIM! TURN!
SHUT UP! THE BAT WANTS TO PLAY CHICKEN...
...LET'S PLAY CHICKEN.
HOOONNNK
WHAT... WHAT'S HE DOING?

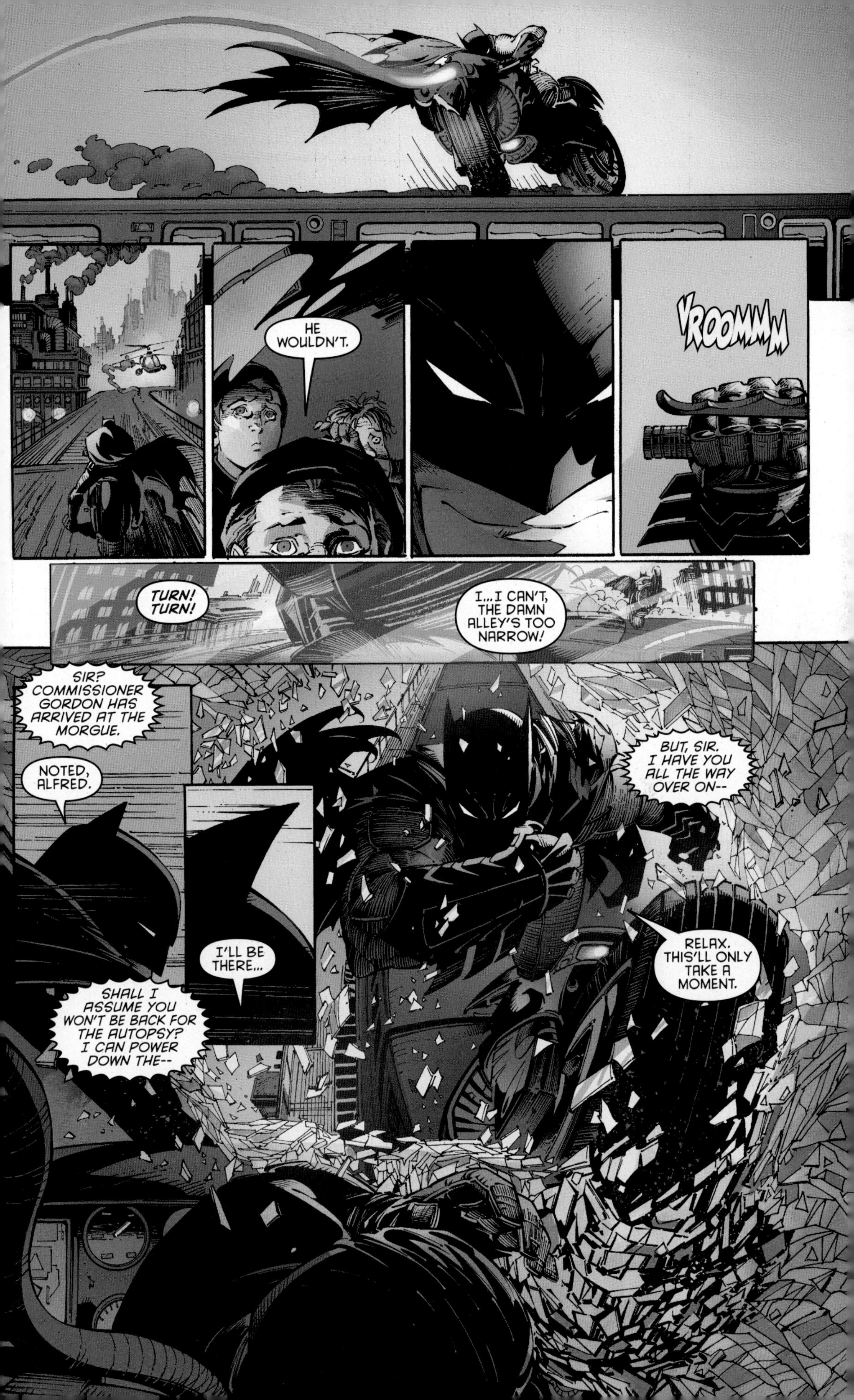
HE WOULDN'T.
VROOMMM
TURN! TURN!
I... I CAN'T, THE DAMN ALLEY'S TOO NARROW!
SIR? COMMISSIONER GORDON HAS ARRIVED AT THE MORGUE.
NOTED, ALFRED.
I'LL BE THERE...
SHALL I ASSUME YOU WON'T BE BACK FOR THE AUTOPSY? I CAN POWER DOWN THE--
BUT, SIR. I HAVE YOU ALL THE WAY OVER ON--
RELAX. THIS'LL ONLY TAKE A MOMENT.

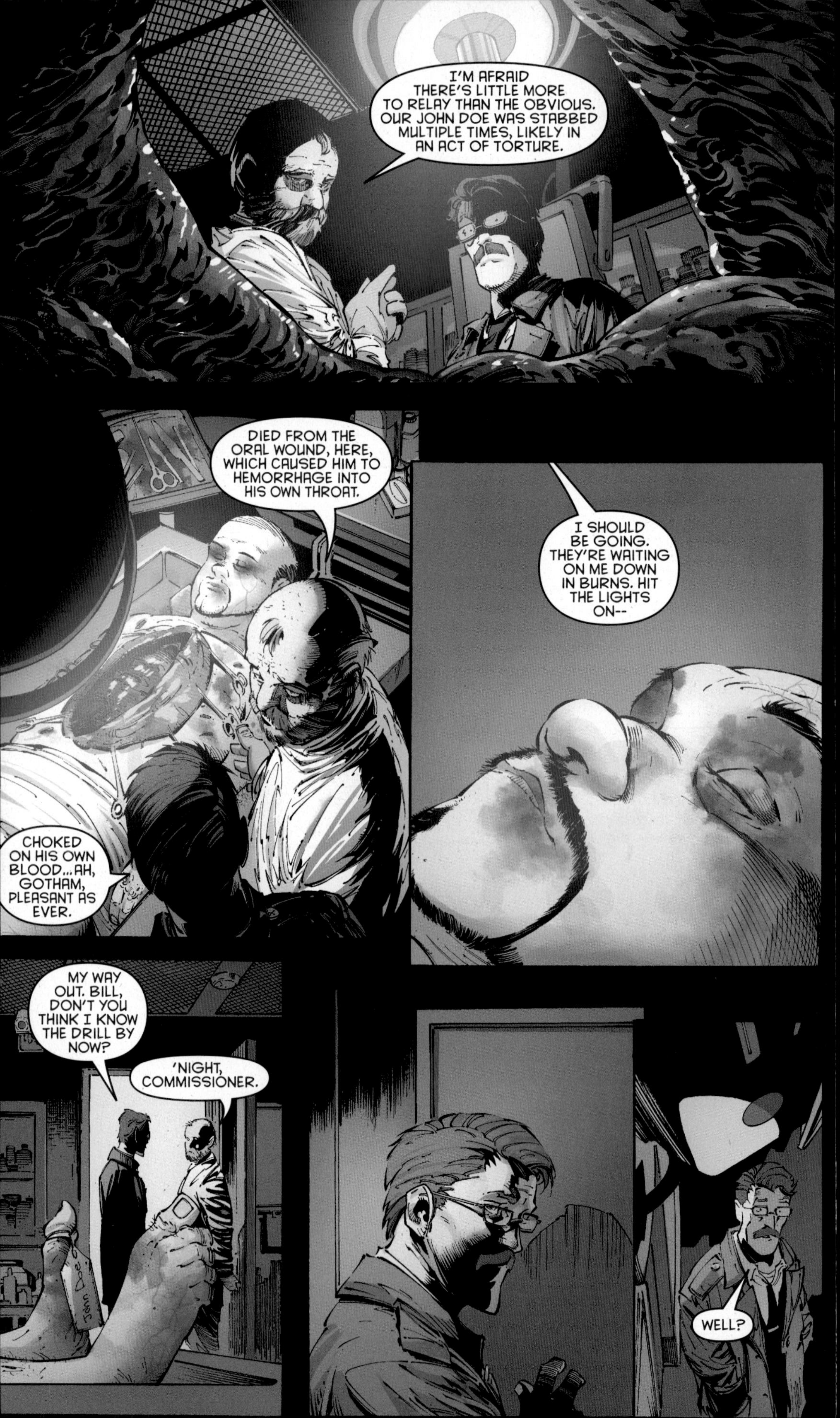
I'M AFRAID THERE'S LITTLE MORE TO RELAY THAN THE OBVIOUS. OUR JOHN DOE WAS STABBED MULTIPLE TIMES, LIKELY IN AN ACT OF TORTURE.
DIED FROM THE ORAL WOUND, HERE, WHICH CAUSED HIM TO HEMORRHAGE INTO HIS OWN THROAT.
CHOKED ON HIS OWN BLOOD...AH, GOTHAM, PLEASANT AS EVER.
I SHOULD BE GOING. THEY'RE WAITING ON ME DOWN IN BURNS. HIT THE LIGHTS ON--
MY WAY OUT. BILL, DON'T YOU THINK I KNOW THE DRILL BY NOW?
'NIGHT, COMMISSIONER.
John Doe
WELL?

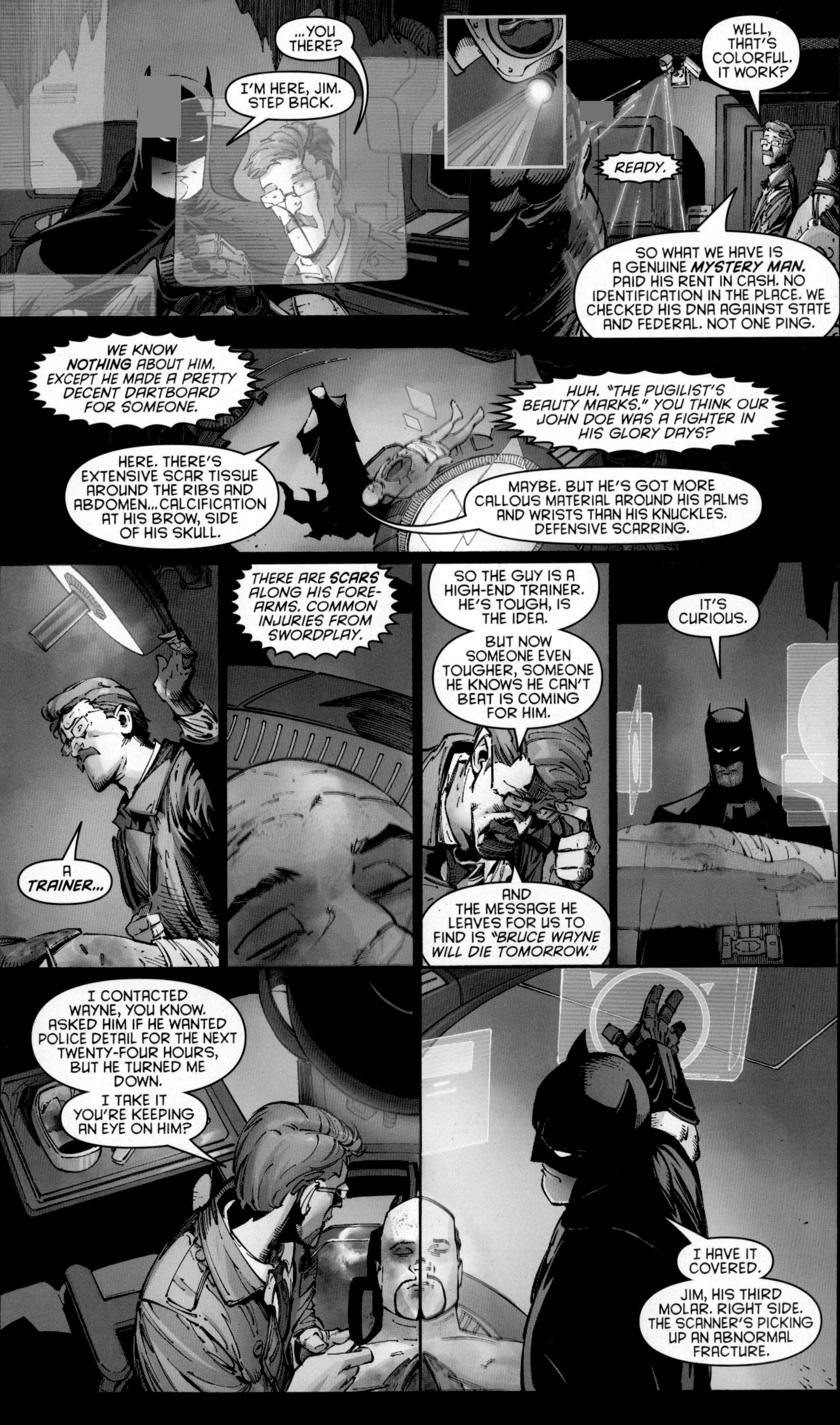
...YOU THERE?
I'M HERE, JIM. STEP BACK.
WELL, THAT'S COLORFUL. IT WORK?
READY.
SO WHAT WE HAVE IS A GENUINE MYSTERY MAN. PAID HIS RENT IN CASH. NO IDENTIFICATION IN THE PLACE. WE CHECKED HIS DNA AGAINST STATE AND FEDERAL. NOT ONE PING.
WE KNOW NOTHING ABOUT HIM. EXCEPT HE MADE A PRETTY DECENT DARTBOARD FOR SOMEONE.
HERE. THERE'S EXTENSIVE SCAR TISSUE AROUND THE RIBS AND ABDOMEN...CALCIFICATION AT HIS BROW, SIDE OF HIS SKULL.
HUH. "THE PUGILIST'S BEAUTY MARKS." YOU THINK OUR JOHN DOE WAS A FIGHTER IN HIS GLORY DAYS?
MAYBE. BUT HE'S GOT MORE CALLOUS MATERIAL AROUND HIS PALMS AND WRISTS THAN HIS KNUCKLES. DEFENSIVE SCARRING.
A TRAINER...
THERE ARE SCARS ALONG HIS FORE-ARMS. COMMON INJURIES FROM SWORDPLAY.
SO THE GUY IS A HIGH-END TRAINER. HE'S TOUGH, IS THE IDEA.
BUT NOW SOMEONE EVEN TOUGHER, SOMEONE HE KNOWS HE CAN'T BEAT IS COMING FOR HIM.
AND THE MESSAGE HE LEAVES FOR US TO FIND IS "BRUCE WAYNE WILL DIE TOMORROW."
IT'S CURIOUS.
I CONTACTED WAYNE, YOU KNOW. ASKED HIM IF HE WANTED POLICE DETAIL FOR THE NEXT TWENTY-FOUR HOURS, BUT HE TURNED ME DOWN.
I TAKE IT YOU'RE KEEPING AN EYE ON HIM?
I HAVE IT COVERED.
JIM, HIS THIRD MOLAR. RIGHT SIDE. THE SCANNER'S PICKING UP AN ABNORMAL FRACTURE.

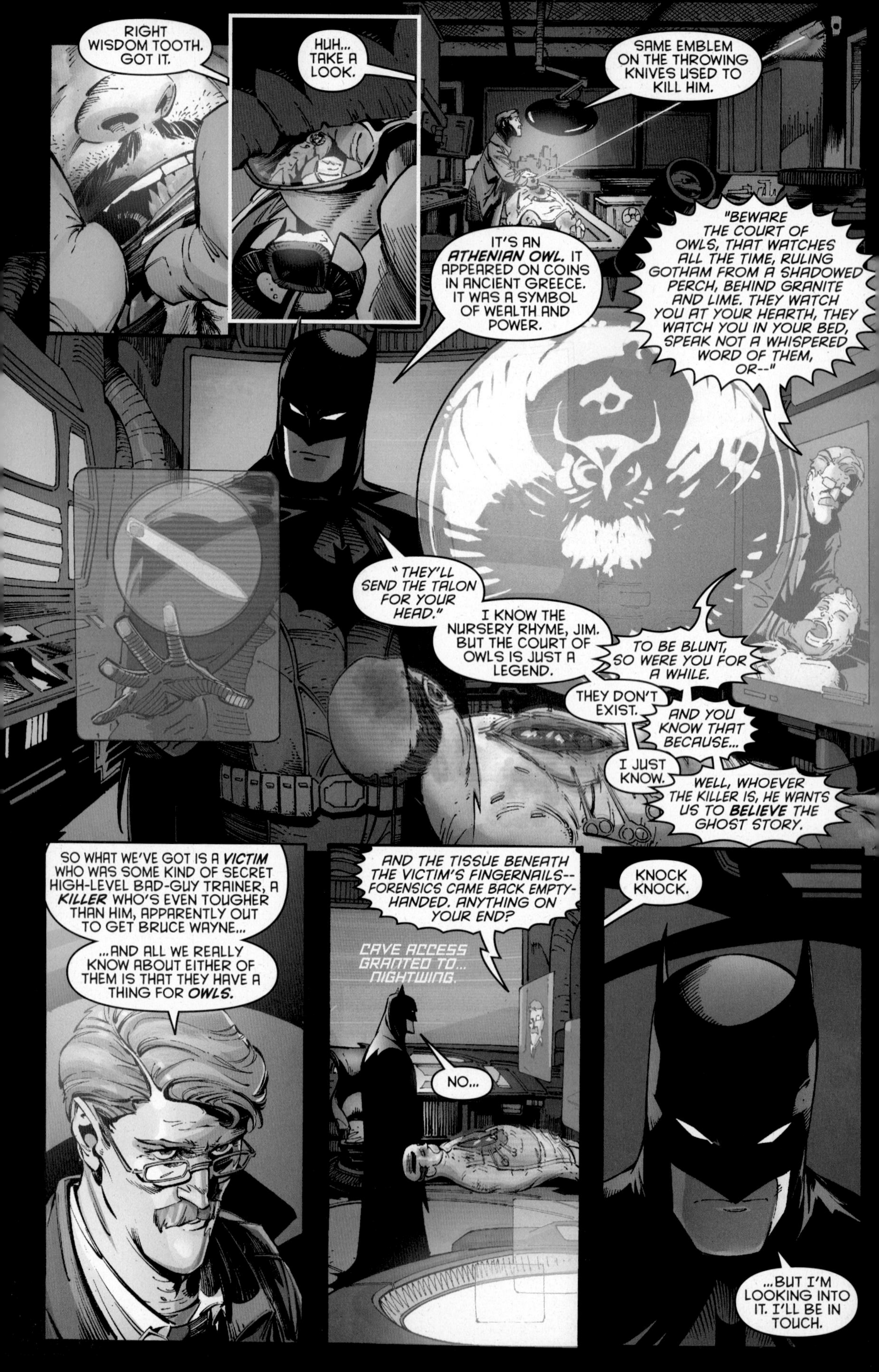
RIGHT WISDOM TOOTH. GOT IT.
HUH... TAKE A LOOK.
SAME EMBLEM ON THE THROWING KNIVES USED TO KILL HIM.
IT'S AN ATHENIAN OWL. IT APPEARED ON COINS IN ANCIENT GREECE. IT WAS A SYMBOL OF WEALTH AND POWER.
"BEWARE THE COURT OF OWLS, THAT WATCHES ALL THE TIME, RULING GOTHAM FROM A SHADOWED PERCH, BEHIND GRANITE AND LIME. THEY WATCH YOU AT YOUR HEARTH, THEY WATCH YOU IN YOUR BED, SPEAK NOT A WHISPERED WORD OF THEM, OR--"
"THEY'LL SEND THE TALON FOR YOUR HEAD."
I KNOW THE NURSERY RHYME, JIM. BUT THE COURT OF OWLS IS JUST A LEGEND.
TO BE BLUNT, SO WERE YOU FOR A WHILE.
THEY DON'T EXIST.
AND YOU KNOW THAT BECAUSE...
I JUST KNOW.
WELL, WHOEVER THE KILLER IS, HE WANTS US TO BELIEVE THE GHOST STORY.
SO WHAT WE'VE GOT IS A VICTIM WHO WAS SOME KIND OF SECRET HIGH-LEVEL BAD-GUY TRAINER, A KILLER WHO'S EVEN TOUGHER THAN HIM, APPARENTLY OUT TO GET BRUCE WAYNE...
...AND ALL WE REALLY KNOW ABOUT EITHER OF THEM IS THAT THEY HAVE A THING FOR OWLS.
AND THE TISSUE BENEATH THE VICTIM'S FINGERNAILS--FORENSICS CAME BACK EMPTY-HANDED. ANYTHING ON YOUR END?
CAVE ACCESS GRANTED TO... NIGHTWING.
NO...
KNOCK KNOCK.
...BUT I'M LOOKING INTO IT. I'LL BE IN TOUCH.

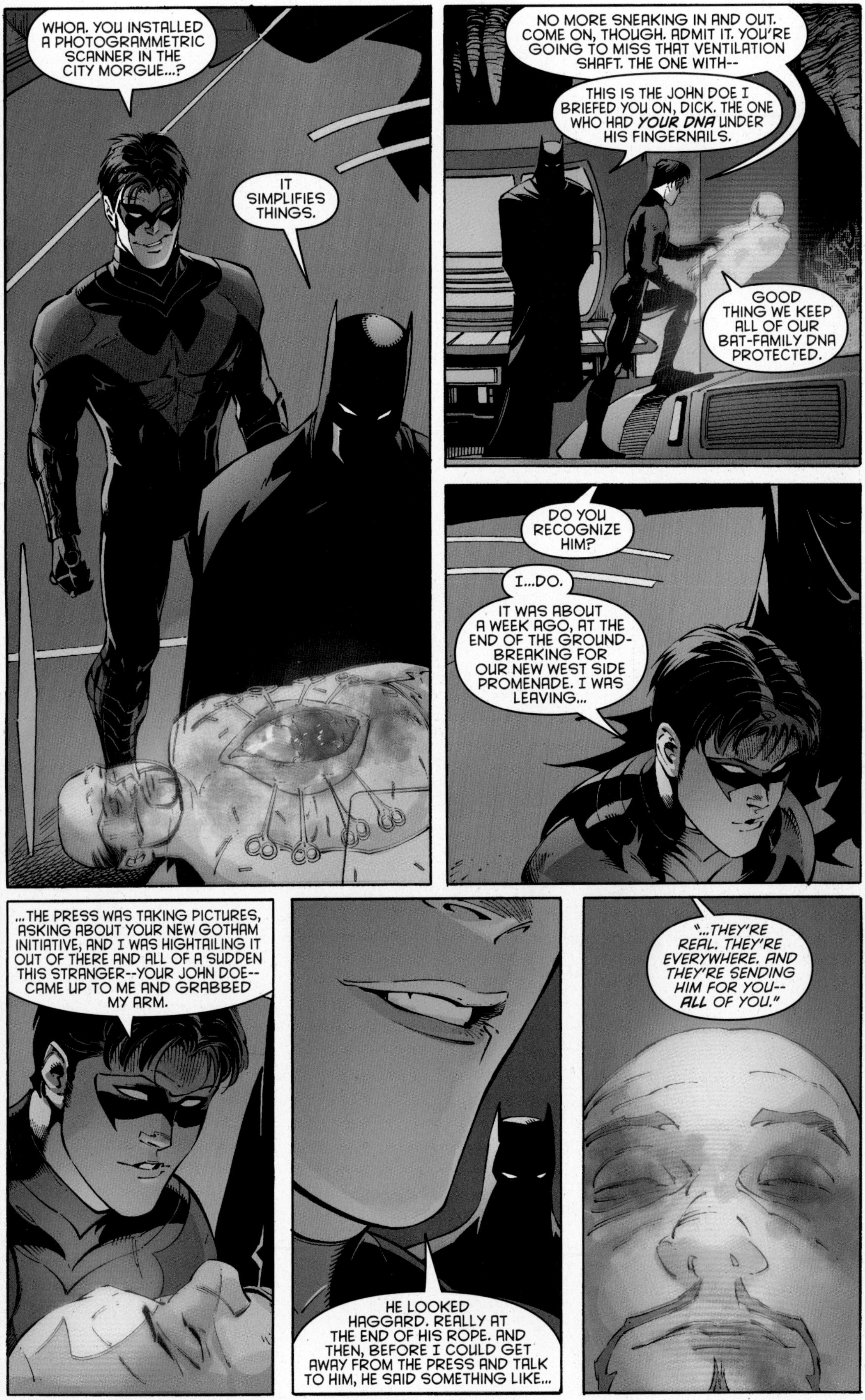

WHOA. YOU INSTALLED A PHOTOGRAMMETRIC SCANNER IN THE CITY MORGUE...?
IT SIMPLIFIES THINGS.
NO MORE SNEAKING IN AND OUT. COME ON, THOUGH. ADMIT IT. YOU'RE GOING TO MISS THAT VENTILATION SHAFT. THE ONE WITH--
THIS IS THE JOHN DOE I BRIEFED YOU ON, DICK. THE ONE WHO HAD *YOUR DNA* UNDER HIS FINGERNAILS.
GOOD THING WE KEEP ALL OF OUR BAT-FAMILY DNA PROTECTED.
DO YOU RECOGNIZE HIM?
I...DO.
IT WAS ABOUT A WEEK AGO, AT THE END OF THE GROUND-BREAKING FOR OUR NEW WEST SIDE PROMENADE. I WAS LEAVING...
...THE PRESS WAS TAKING PICTURES, ASKING ABOUT YOUR NEW GOTHAM INITIATIVE, AND I WAS HIGHTAILING IT OUT OF THERE AND ALL OF A SUDDEN THIS STRANGER--YOUR JOHN DOE--CAME UP TO ME AND GRABBED MY ARM.
HE LOOKED HAGGARD. REALLY AT THE END OF HIS ROPE. AND THEN, BEFORE I COULD GET AWAY FROM THE PRESS AND TALK TO HIM, HE SAID SOMETHING LIKE...
*"...THEY'RE REAL. THEY'RE EVERYWHERE. AND THEY'RE SENDING HIM FOR YOU-- **ALL** OF YOU."*

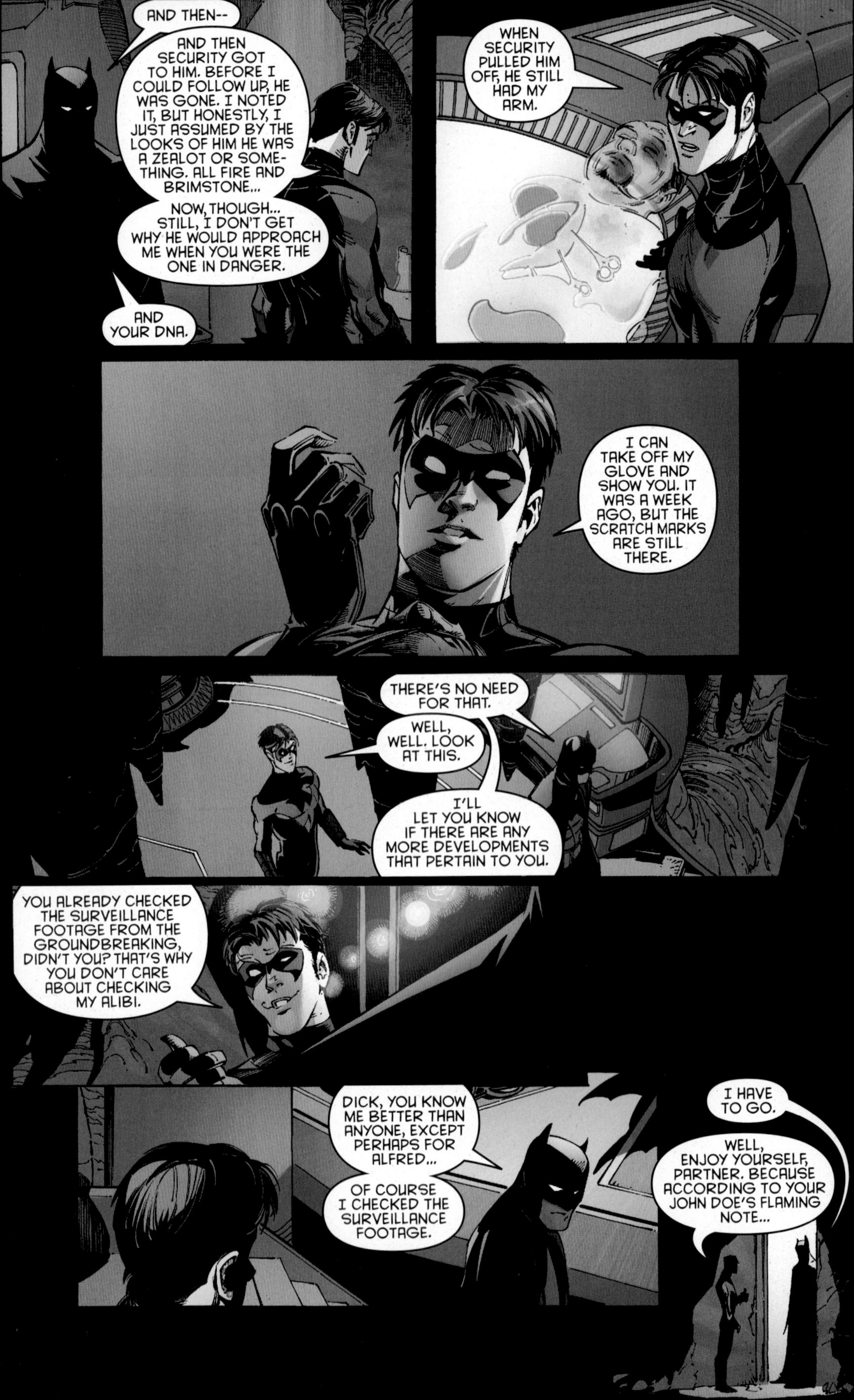
AND THEN--
AND THEN SECURITY GOT TO HIM. BEFORE I COULD FOLLOW UP, HE WAS GONE. I NOTED IT, BUT HONESTLY, I JUST ASSUMED BY THE LOOKS OF HIM HE WAS A ZEALOT OR SOMETHING. ALL FIRE AND BRIMSTONE...
NOW, THOUGH... STILL, I DON'T GET WHY HE WOULD APPROACH ME WHEN YOU WERE THE ONE IN DANGER.
AND YOUR DNA.
WHEN SECURITY PULLED HIM OFF, HE STILL HAD MY ARM.
I CAN TAKE OFF MY GLOVE AND SHOW YOU. IT WAS A WEEK AGO, BUT THE SCRATCH MARKS ARE STILL THERE.
THERE'S NO NEED FOR THAT.
WELL, WELL. LOOK AT THIS.
I'LL LET YOU KNOW IF THERE ARE ANY MORE DEVELOPMENTS THAT PERTAIN TO YOU.
YOU ALREADY CHECKED THE SURVEILLANCE FOOTAGE FROM THE GROUNDBREAKING, DIDN'T YOU? THAT'S WHY YOU DON'T CARE ABOUT CHECKING MY ALIBI.
DICK, YOU KNOW ME BETTER THAN ANYONE, EXCEPT PERHAPS FOR ALFRED...
OF COURSE I CHECKED THE SURVEILLANCE FOOTAGE.
I HAVE TO GO.
WELL, ENJOY YOURSELF, PARTNER. BECAUSE ACCORDING TO YOUR JOHN DOE'S FLAMING NOTE...

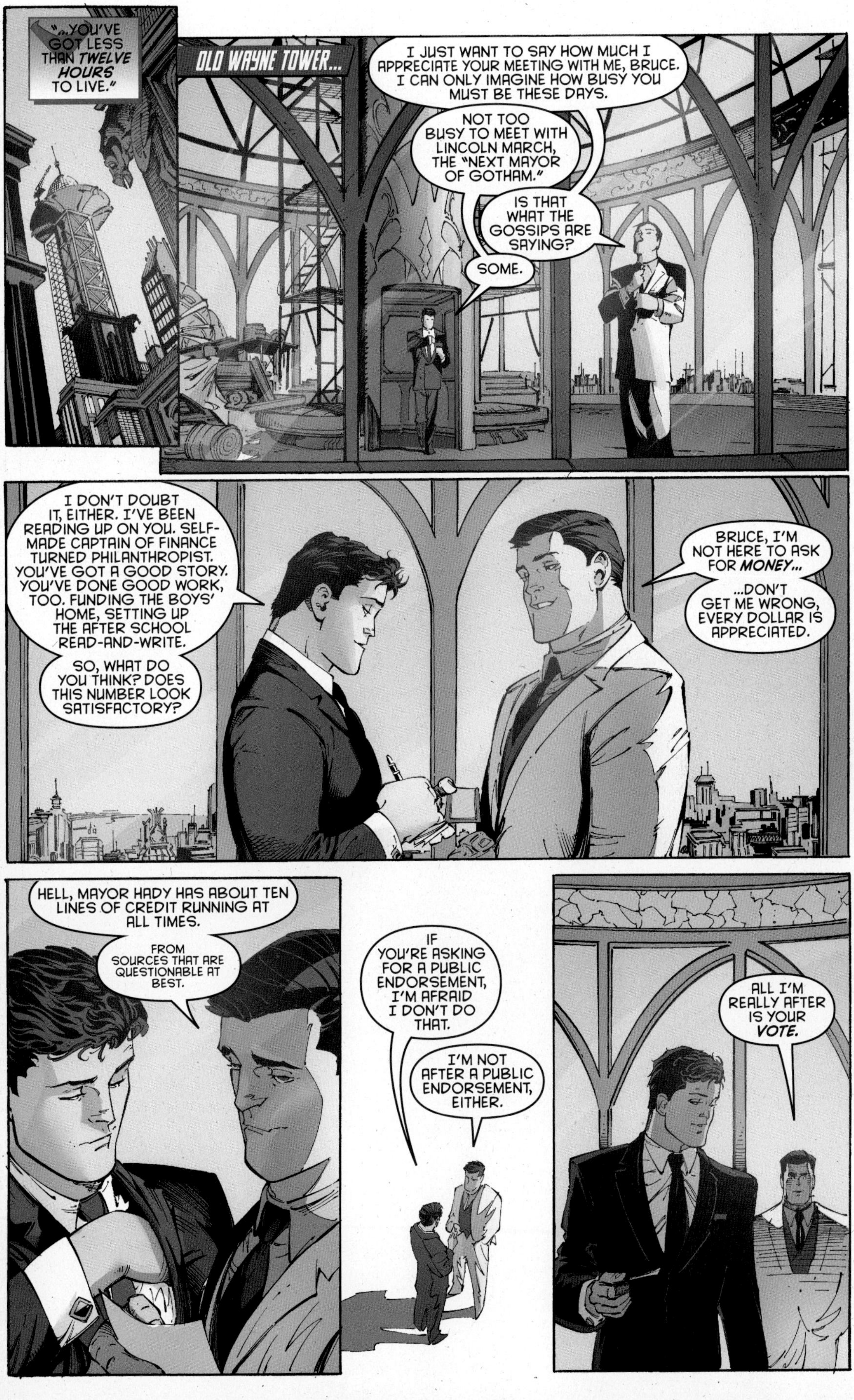
"...YOU'VE GOT LESS THAN TWELVE HOURS TO LIVE."
OLD WAYNE TOWER...
I JUST WANT TO SAY HOW MUCH I APPRECIATE YOUR MEETING WITH ME, BRUCE. I CAN ONLY IMAGINE HOW BUSY YOU MUST BE THESE DAYS.
NOT TOO BUSY TO MEET WITH LINCOLN MARCH, THE "NEXT MAYOR OF GOTHAM."
IS THAT WHAT THE GOSSIPS ARE SAYING?
SOME.
I DON'T DOUBT IT, EITHER. I'VE BEEN READING UP ON YOU. SELF-MADE CAPTAIN OF FINANCE TURNED PHILANTHROPIST. YOU'VE GOT A GOOD STORY. YOU'VE DONE GOOD WORK, TOO. FUNDING THE BOYS' HOME, SETTING UP THE AFTER SCHOOL READ-AND-WRITE.
SO, WHAT DO YOU THINK? DOES THIS NUMBER LOOK SATISFACTORY?
BRUCE, I'M NOT HERE TO ASK FOR MONEY...
...DON'T GET ME WRONG, EVERY DOLLAR IS APPRECIATED.
HELL, MAYOR HADY HAS ABOUT TEN LINES OF CREDIT RUNNING AT ALL TIMES.
FROM SOURCES THAT ARE QUESTIONABLE AT BEST.
IF YOU'RE ASKING FOR A PUBLIC ENDORSEMENT, I'M AFRAID I DON'T DO THAT.
I'M NOT AFTER A PUBLIC ENDORSEMENT, EITHER.
ALL I'M REALLY AFTER IS YOUR VOTE.

MY VOTE... YOU'VE COME A LONG WAY FOR ONE VOTE, LINCOLN.

THAT'S TRUE. BUT I BELIEVE IN WHAT YOU'RE DOING, BRUCE. THIS INITIATIVE TO REBUILD GOTHAM. IT'S A GOOD THING. AND TO BE FRANK, I SEE A FRIEND IN YOU.

A CYNIC WOULD SAY YOU SEE AN OPPORTUNITY.

THAT'S TRUE. AND A CYNIC WOULD SAY YOU'RE SPEARHEADING THIS NEW GOTHAM INITIATIVE FOR THE IMAGE OF YOUR COMPANY. BECAUSE IT'S A PUBLIC HOLDING, AND SO ON. FOR PRIVATE PURPOSES.

IS THAT WHAT THE GOSSIPS SAY?

SOME.

MAYBE THEY'RE RIGHT.

I SHOULD BE GOING. I'LL LEAVE THE CHECK ON THE TABLE.

YOU KNOW, BRUCE, I LOST MY PARENTS WHEN I WAS A BOY, TOO.

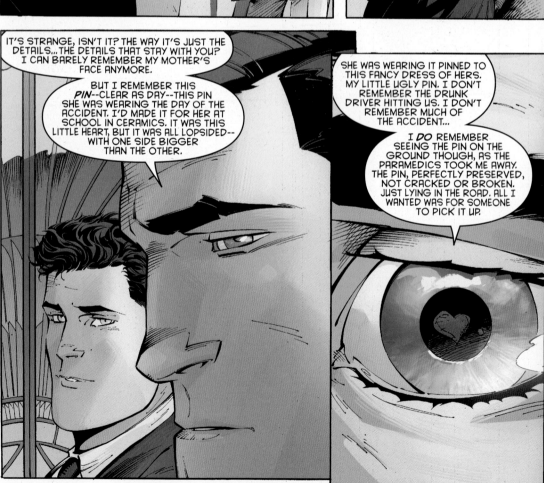

IT'S STRANGE, ISN'T IT? THE WAY IT'S JUST THE DETAILS...THE DETAILS THAT STAY WITH YOU? I CAN BARELY REMEMBER MY MOTHER'S FACE ANYMORE.

BUT I REMEMBER THIS *PIN*--CLEAR AS DAY--THIS PIN SHE WAS WEARING THE DAY OF THE ACCIDENT. I'D MADE IT FOR HER AT SCHOOL IN CERAMICS. IT WAS THIS LITTLE HEART, BUT IT WAS ALL LOPSIDED-- WITH ONE SIDE BIGGER THAN THE OTHER.

SHE WAS WEARING IT PINNED TO THIS FANCY DRESS OF HERS. MY LITTLE UGLY PIN. I DON'T REMEMBER THE DRUNK DRIVER HITTING US. I DON'T REMEMBER MUCH OF THE ACCIDENT...

I *DO* REMEMBER SEEING THE PIN ON THE GROUND THOUGH, AS THE PARAMEDICS TOOK ME AWAY. THE PIN, PERFECTLY PRESERVED, NOT CRACKED OR BROKEN. JUST LYING IN THE ROAD. ALL I WANTED WAS FOR SOMEONE TO PICK IT UP.

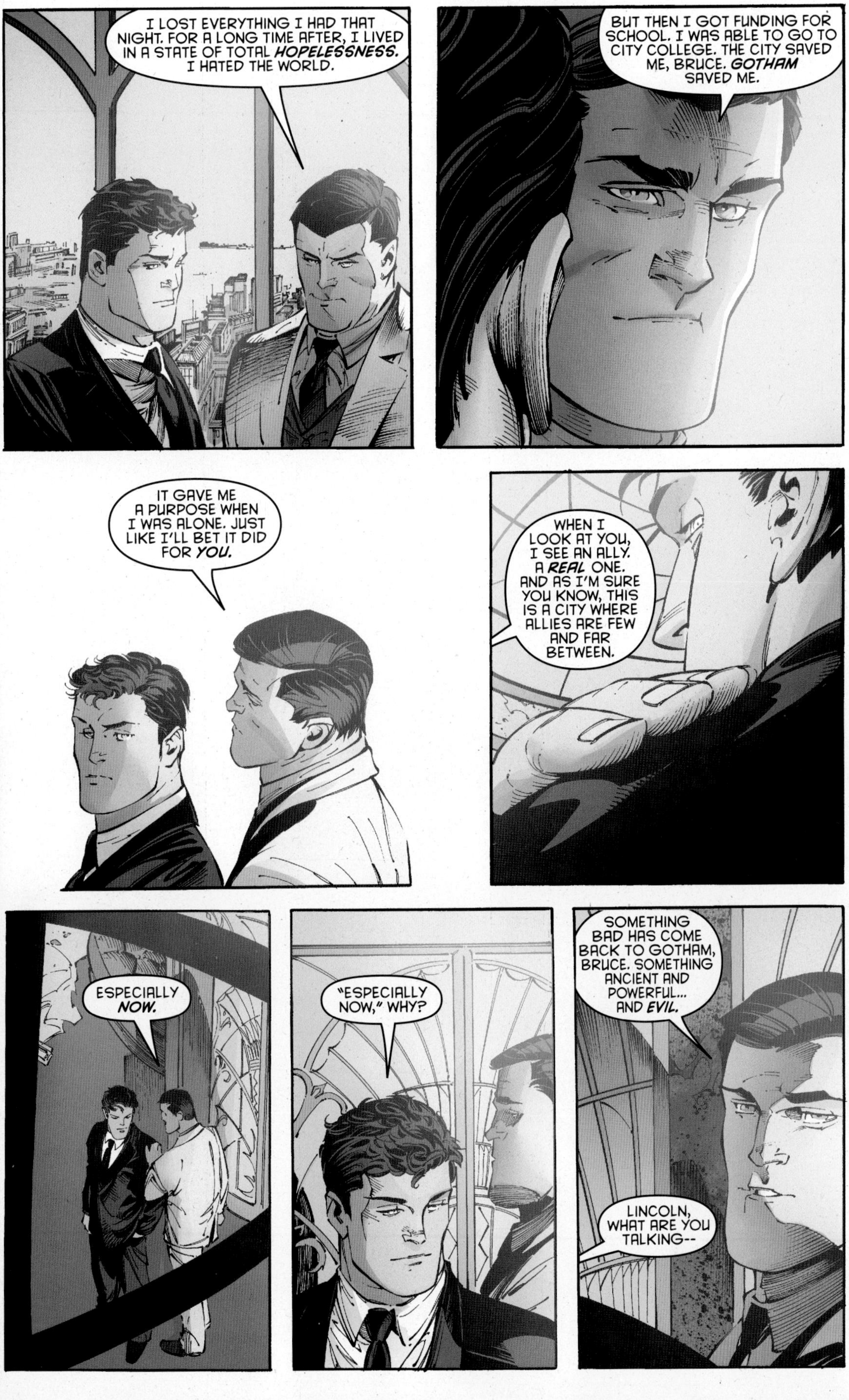
I LOST EVERYTHING I HAD THAT NIGHT. FOR A LONG TIME AFTER, I LIVED IN A STATE OF TOTAL *HOPELESSNESS.* I HATED THE WORLD.
BUT THEN I GOT FUNDING FOR SCHOOL. I WAS ABLE TO GO TO CITY COLLEGE. THE CITY SAVED ME, BRUCE. *GOTHAM* SAVED ME.
IT GAVE ME A PURPOSE WHEN I WAS ALONE. JUST LIKE I'LL BET IT DID FOR *YOU.*
WHEN I LOOK AT YOU, I SEE AN ALLY. A *REAL* ONE. AND AS I'M SURE YOU KNOW, THIS IS A CITY WHERE ALLIES ARE FEW AND FAR BETWEEN.
ESPECIALLY *NOW.*
"ESPECIALLY NOW," WHY?
SOMETHING BAD HAS COME BACK TO GOTHAM, BRUCE. SOMETHING ANCIENT AND POWERFUL... AND *EVIL.*
LINCOLN, WHAT ARE YOU TALKING--

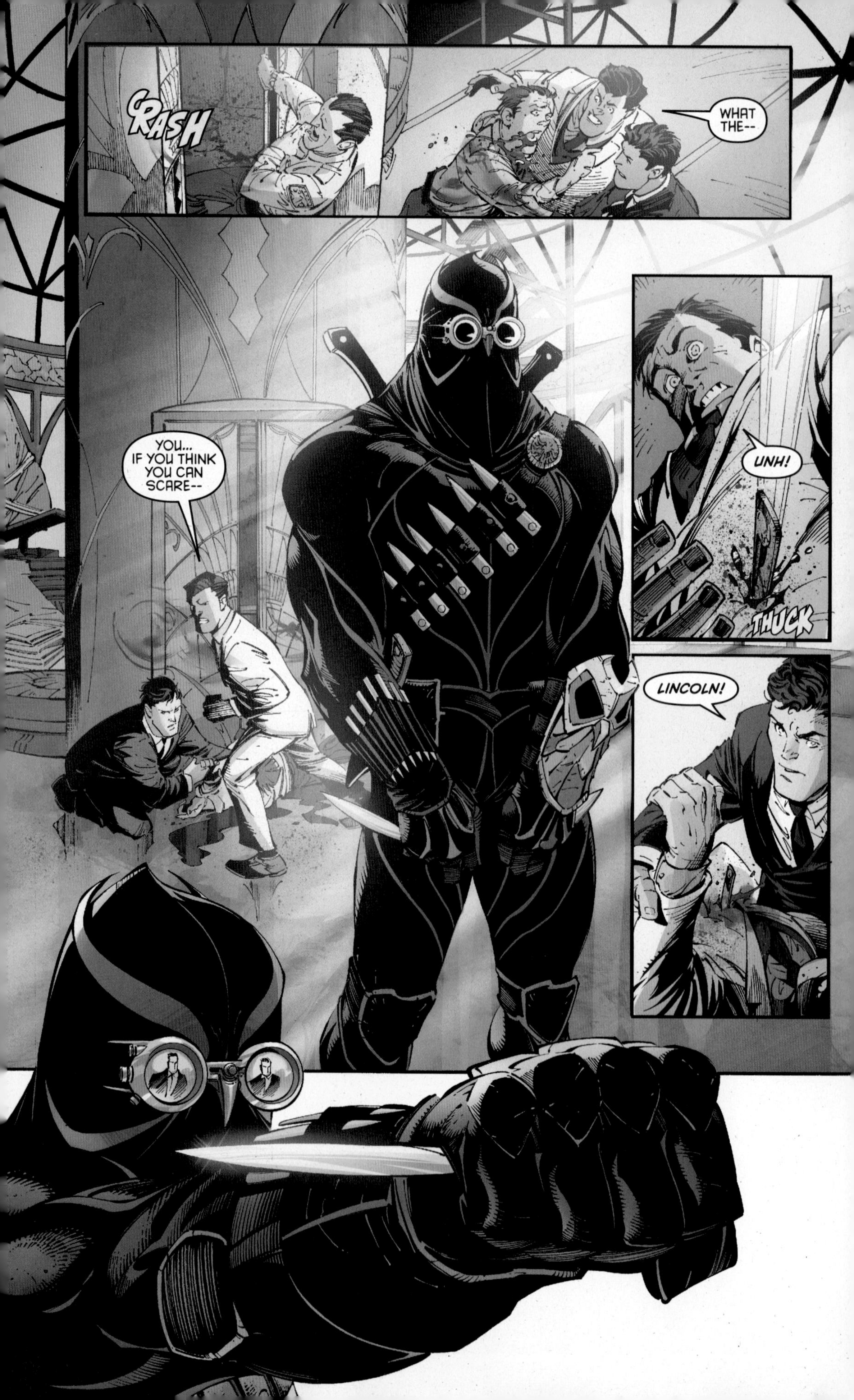
CRASH
WHAT THE--
YOU... IF YOU THINK YOU CAN SCARE--
UNH!
THUCK
LINCOLN!

Don't recognize him.

Someone new.

Someone fast.

Just me and him, but still...have to be careful. Restrain myself. Never know who's watching.

Go for strikes that look like lucky blows.

Solar plexus.

Mandibular nerv--

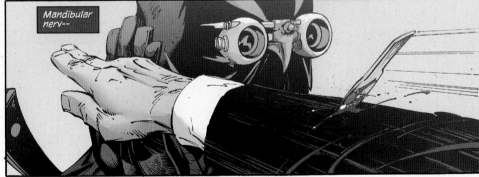

All right. Playtime's over.

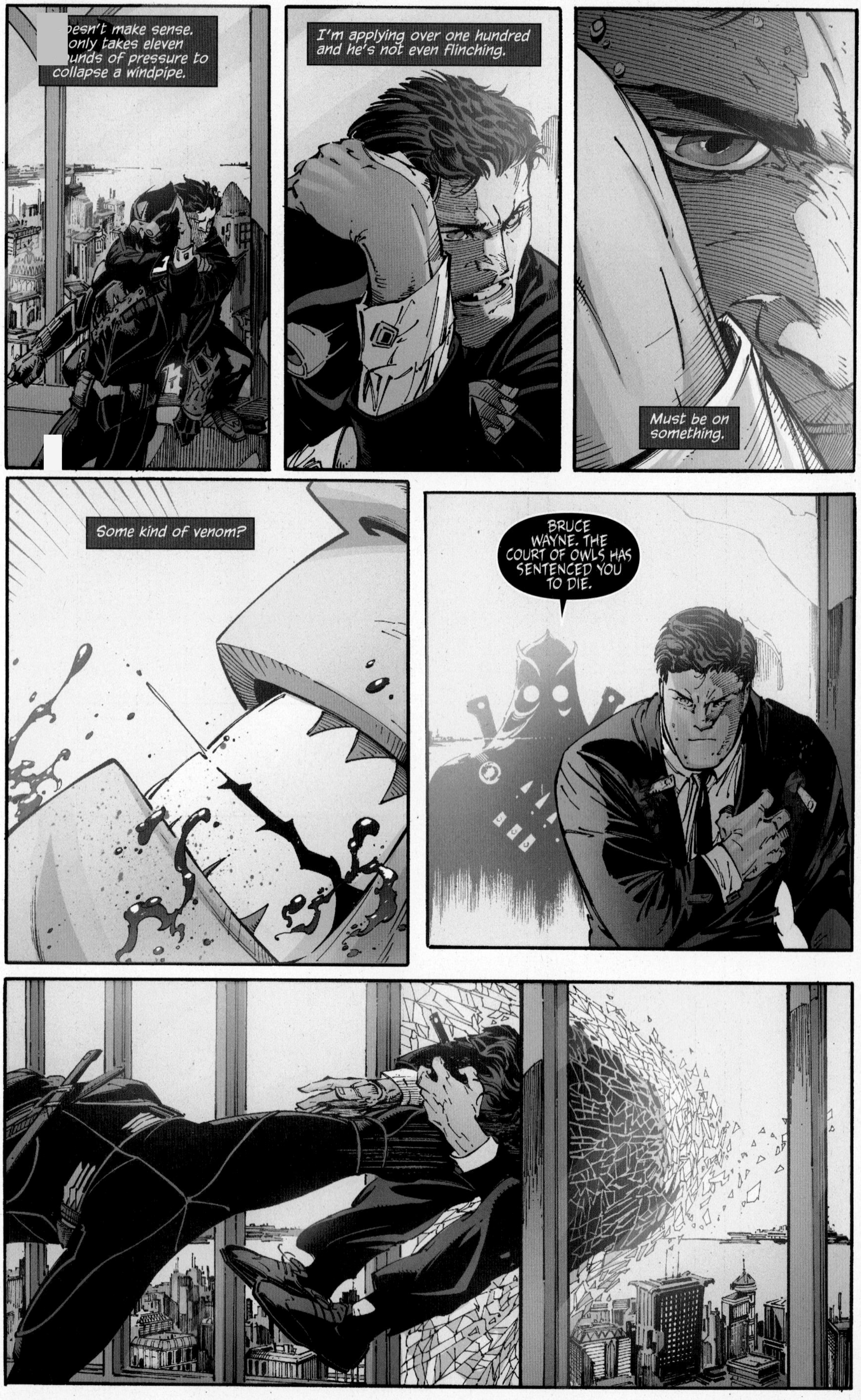
oesn't make sense. only takes eleven unds of pressure to collapse a windpipe.
I'm applying over one hundred and he's not even flinching.
Must be on something.
Some kind of venom?
BRUCE WAYNE. THE COURT OF OWLS HAS SENTENCED YOU TO DIE.

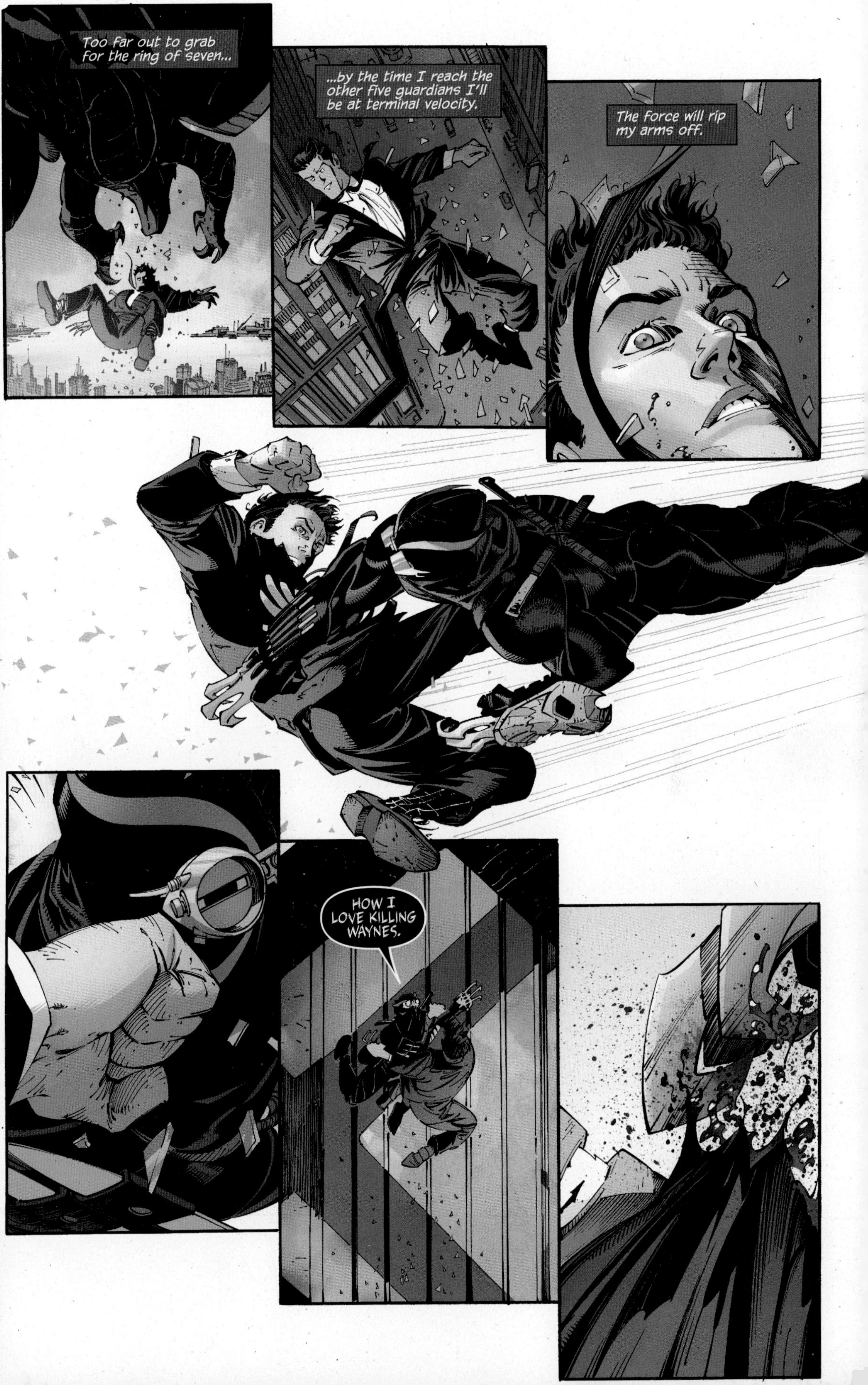
Too far out to grab for the ring of seven...
...by the time I reach the other five guardians I'll be at terminal velocity.
The force will rip my arms off.
HOW I LOVE KILLING WAYNES.

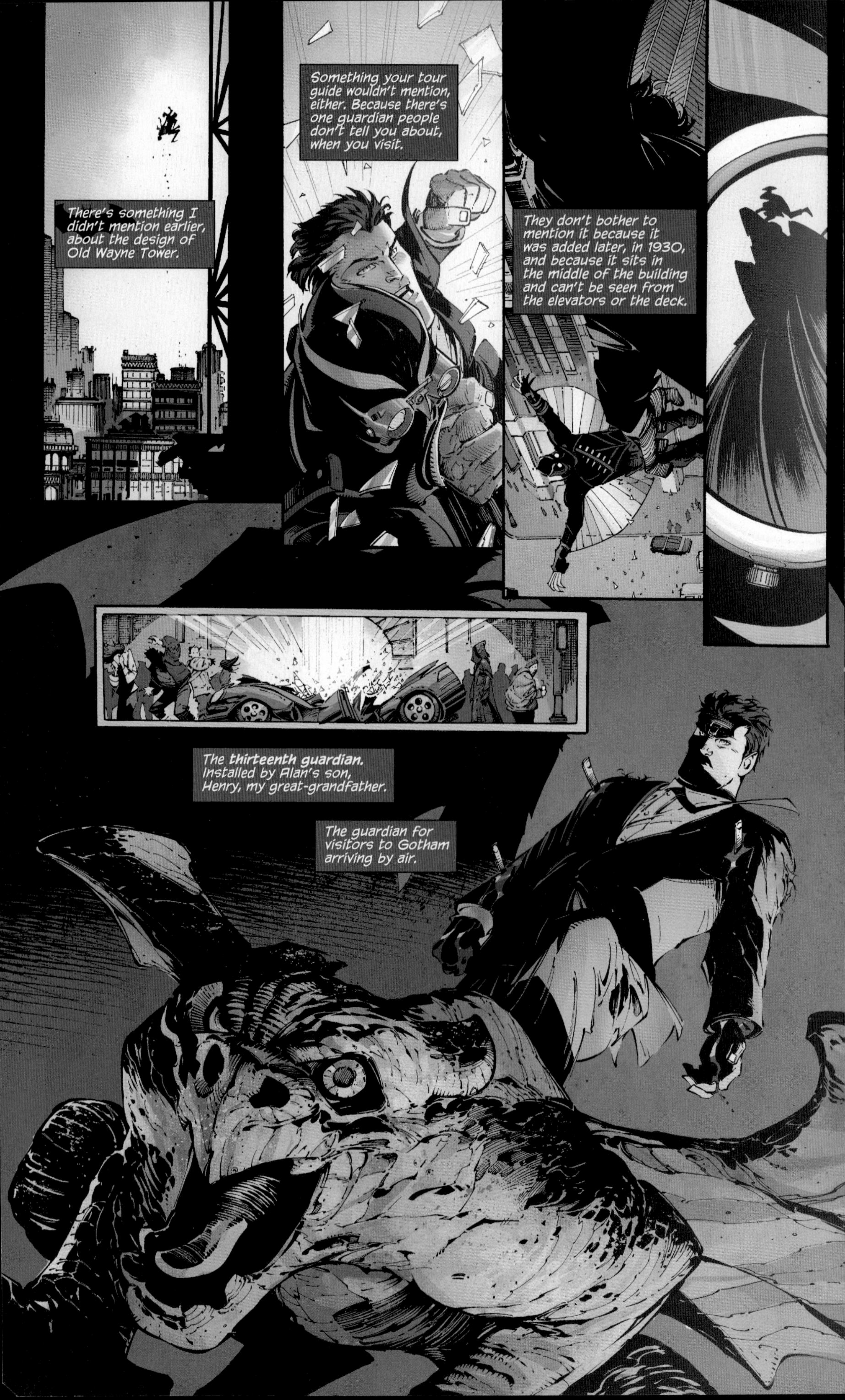
There's something I didn't mention earlier, about the design of Old Wayne Tower.
Something your tour guide wouldn't mention, either. Because there's one guardian people don't tell you about, when you visit.
They don't bother to mention it because it was added later, in 1930, and because it sits in the middle of the building and can't be seen from the elevators or the deck.
The **thirteenth guardian.** Installed by Alan's son, Henry, my great-grandfather.
The guardian for visitors to Gotham arriving by air.

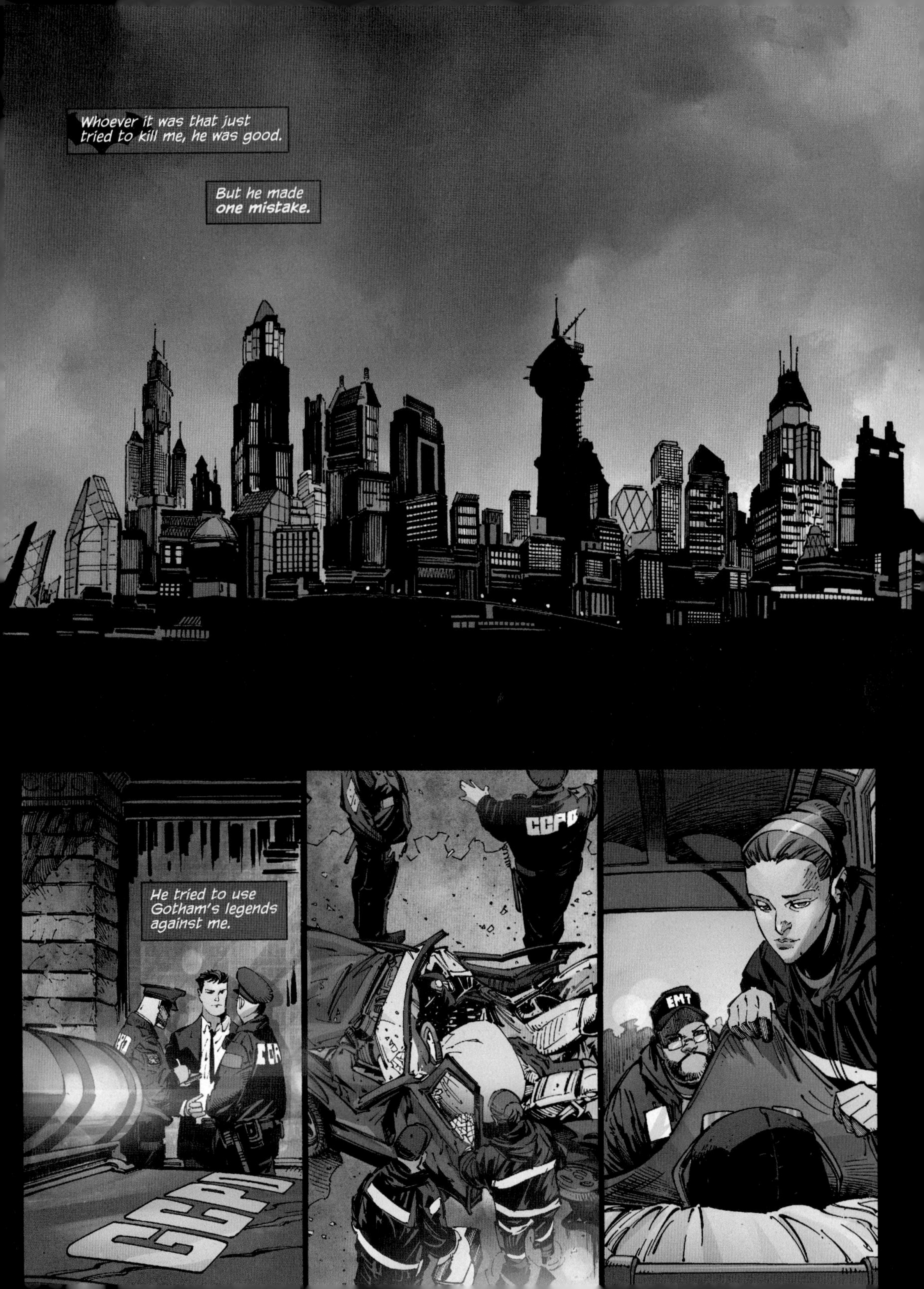

Whoever it was that just tried to kill me, he was good.
But he made one mistake.
He tried to use Gotham's legends against me.
GCPD
GCPD
EMT

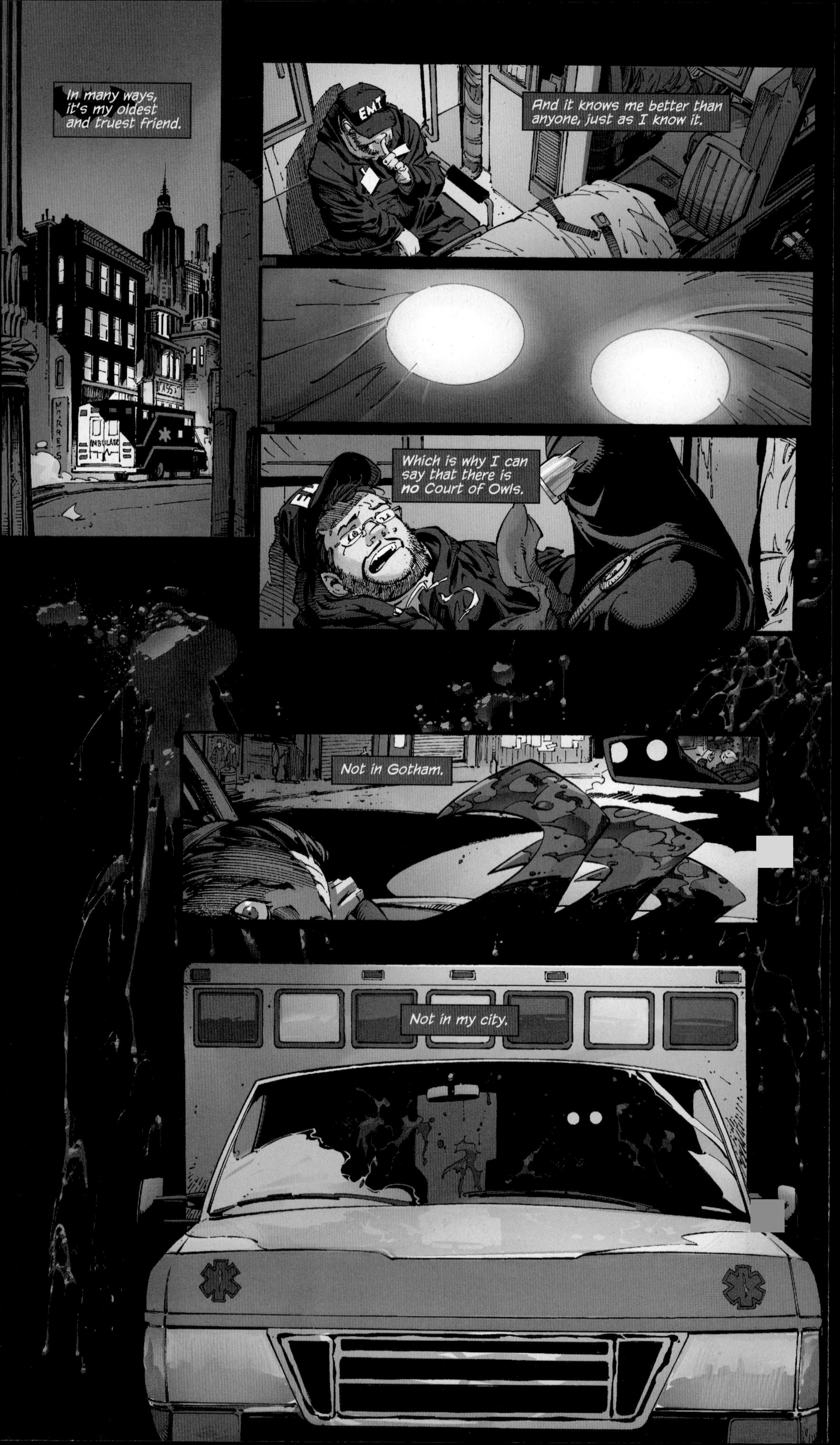
In many ways, it's my oldest and truest friend.
EMT
And it knows me better than anyone, just as I know it.
Which is why I can say that there is no Court of Owls.
Not in Gotham.
Not in my city.

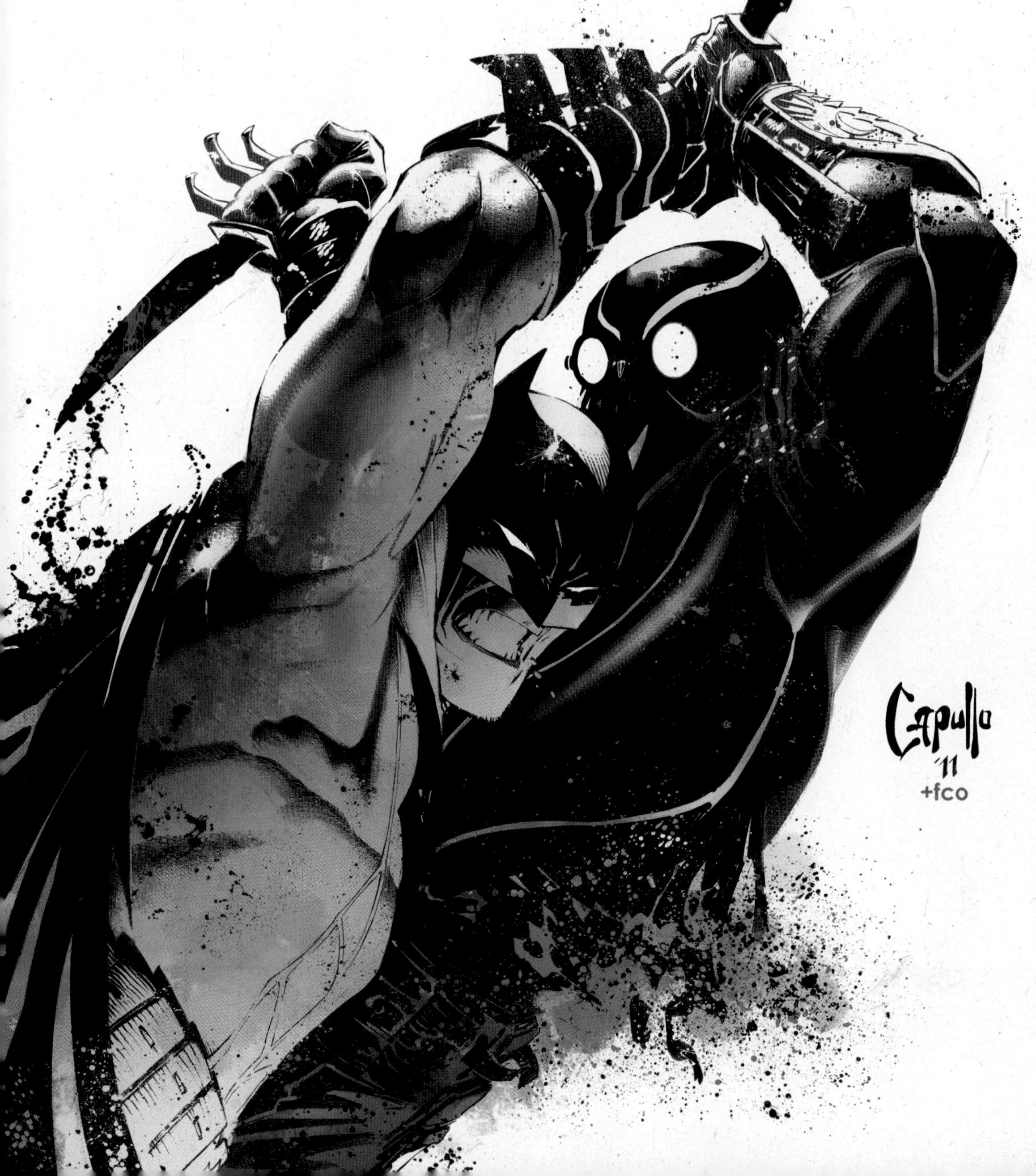
Capullo '11
+fco

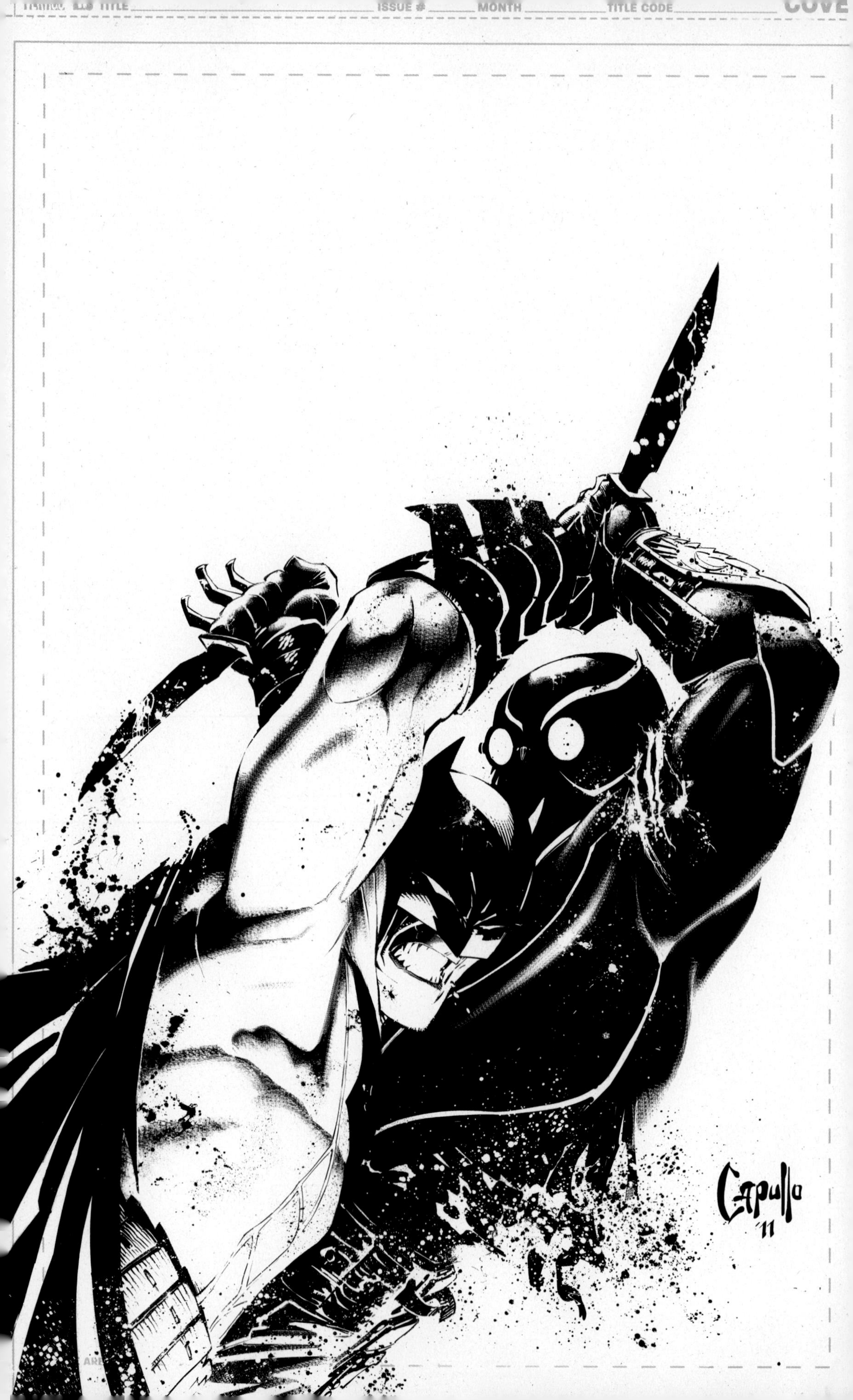
TITLE ISSUE # MONTH TITLE CODE COVE
CAPULLO '11

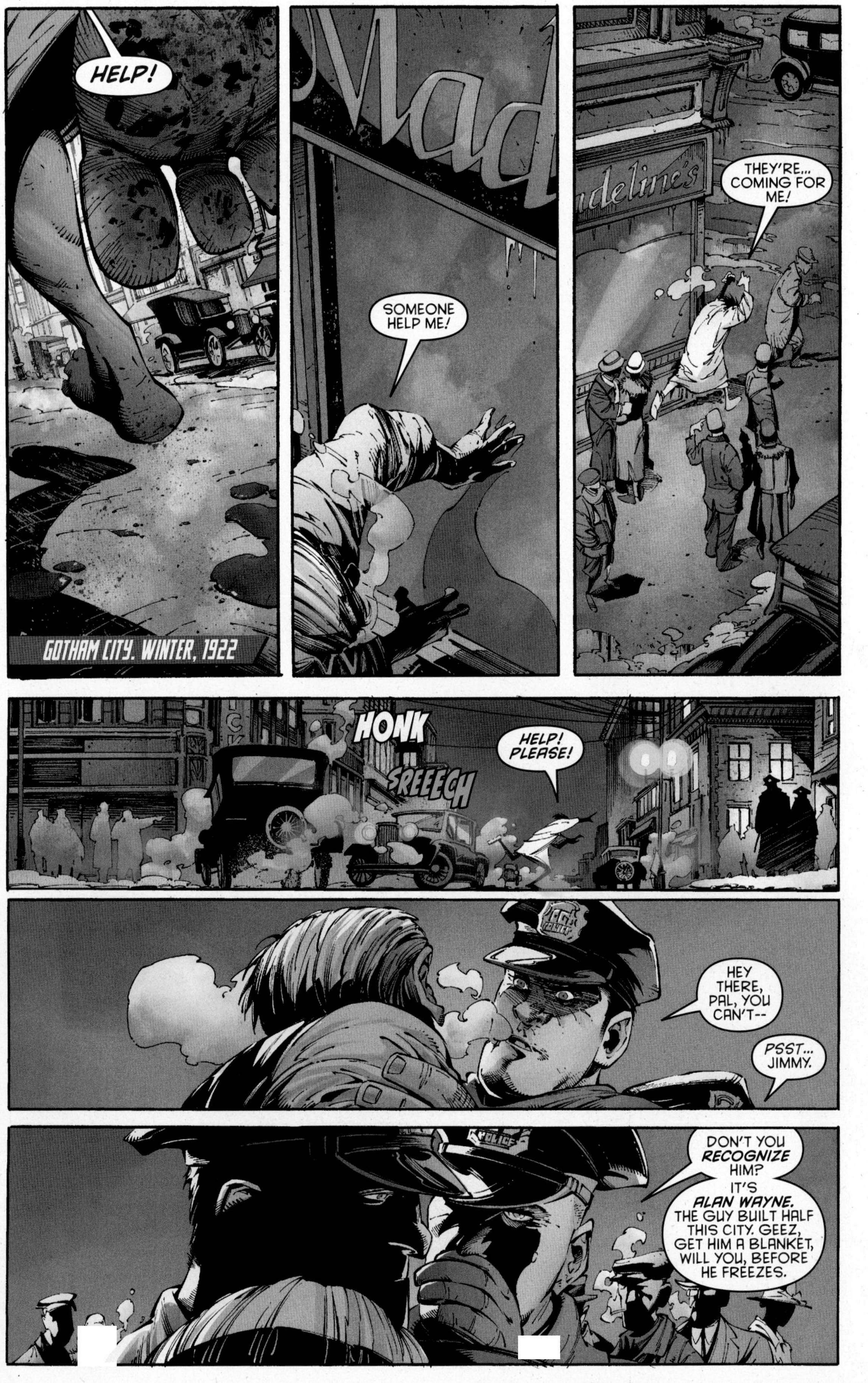
HELP!
GOTHAM CITY. WINTER, 1922
SOMEONE HELP ME!
THEY'RE... COMING FOR ME!
HONK
SREEECH
HELP! PLEASE!
HEY THERE, PAL, YOU CAN'T--
PSST... JIMMY.
DON'T YOU RECOGNIZE HIM? IT'S ALAN WAYNE. THE GUY BUILT HALF THIS CITY. GEEZ, GET HIM A BLANKET, WILL YOU, BEFORE HE FREEZES.

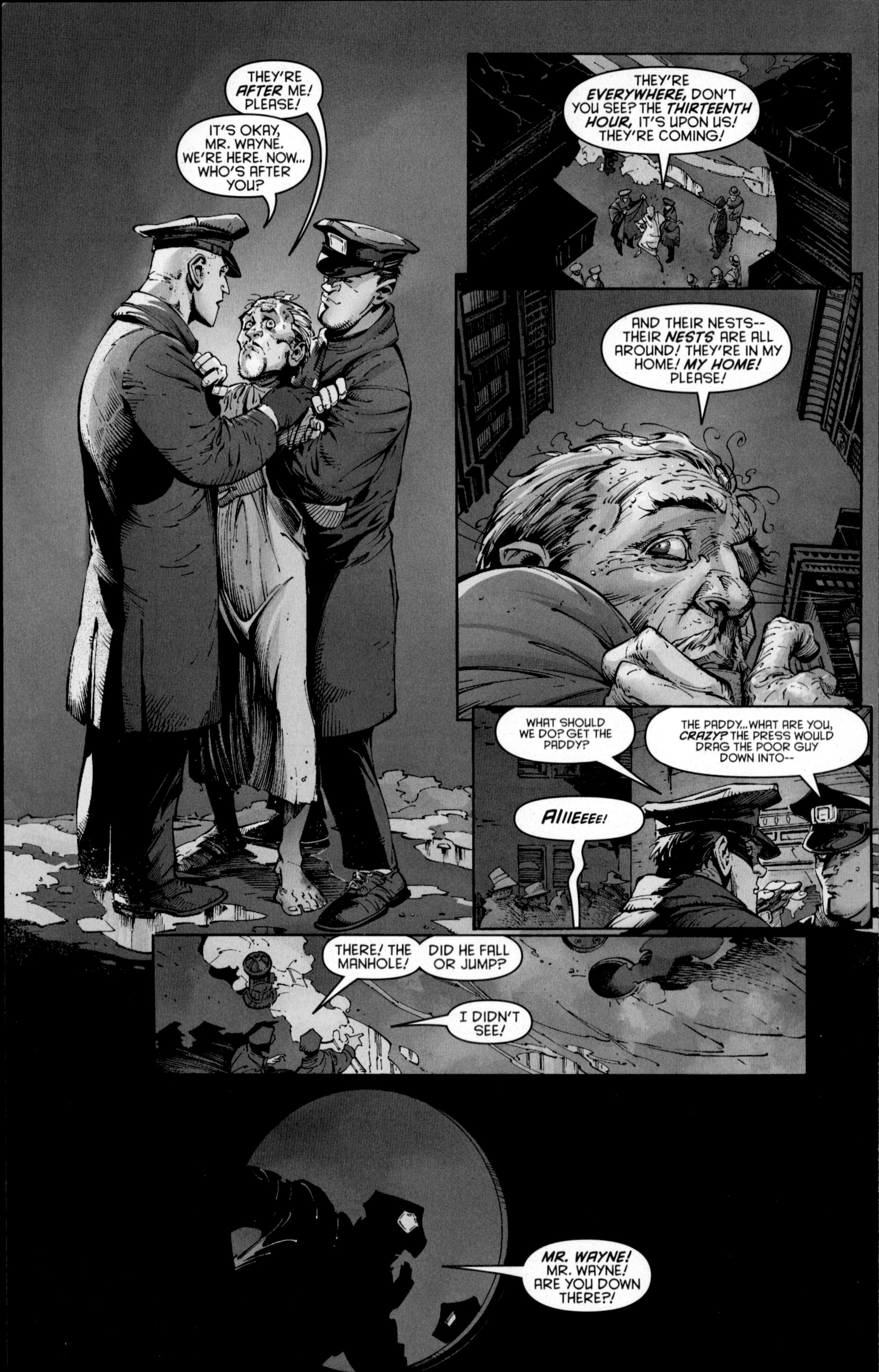
THEY'RE AFTER ME! PLEASE!
IT'S OKAY, MR. WAYNE. WE'RE HERE. NOW... WHO'S AFTER YOU?
THEY'RE EVERYWHERE, DON'T YOU SEE? THE THIRTEENTH HOUR, IT'S UPON US! THEY'RE COMING!
AND THEIR NESTS-- THEIR NESTS ARE ALL AROUND! THEY'RE IN MY HOME! MY HOME! PLEASE!
WHAT SHOULD WE DO? GET THE PADDY?
THE PADDY...WHAT ARE YOU, CRAZY? THE PRESS WOULD DRAG THE POOR GUY DOWN INTO--
AIIIEEEE!
THERE! THE MANHOLE!
DID HE FALL OR JUMP?
I DIDN'T SEE!
MR. WAYNE! MR. WAYNE! ARE YOU DOWN THERE?!

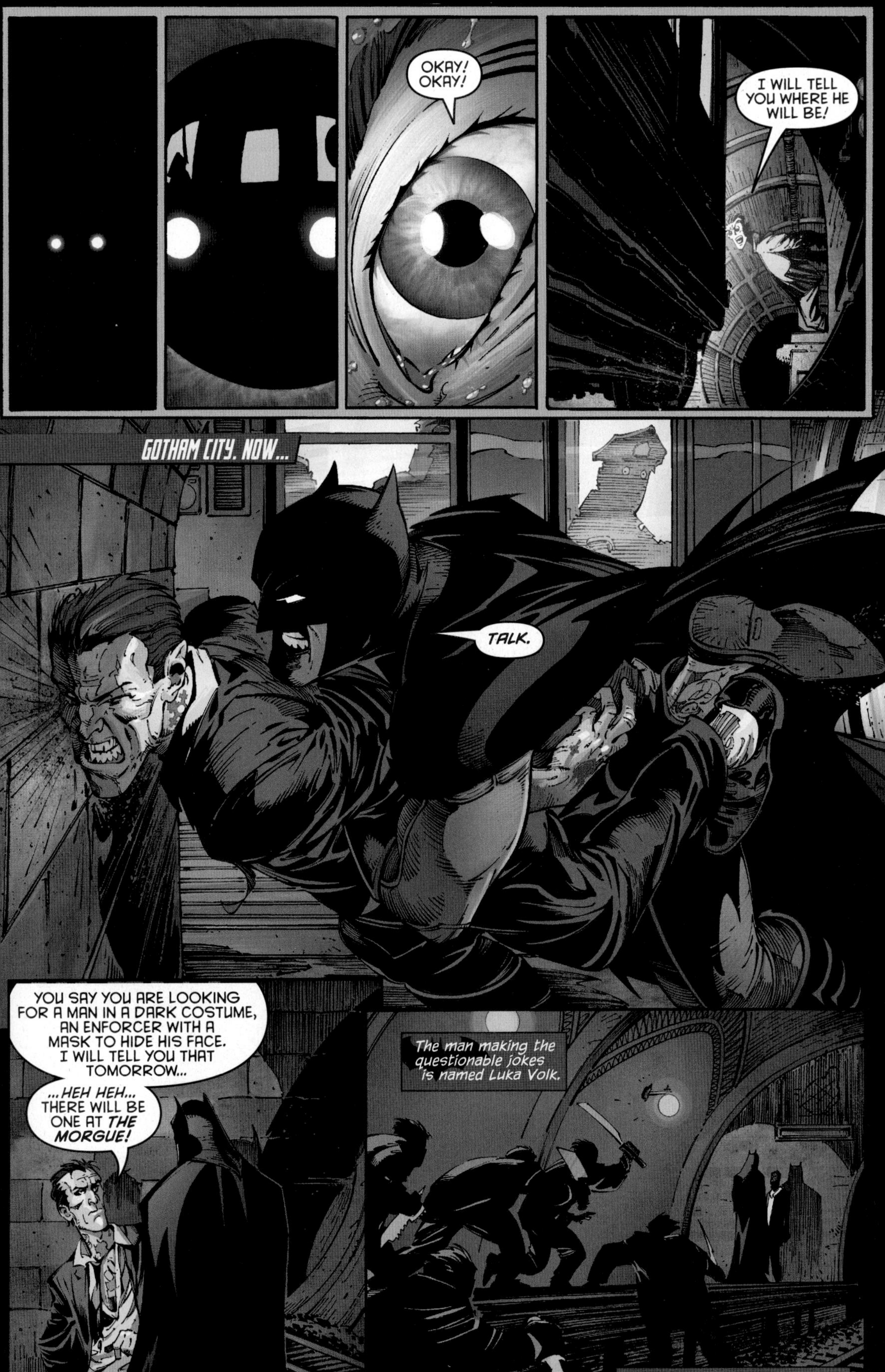
OKAY! OKAY!
I WILL TELL YOU WHERE HE WILL BE!
GOTHAM CITY. NOW...
TALK.
YOU SAY YOU ARE LOOKING FOR A MAN IN A DARK COSTUME, AN ENFORCER WITH A MASK TO HIDE HIS FACE. I WILL TELL YOU THAT TOMORROW...
...HEH HEH... THERE WILL BE ONE AT THE MORGUE!
The man making the questionable jokes is named Luka Volk.
He's the "pakhan" of a Gotham branch of the Ukrainian mob.

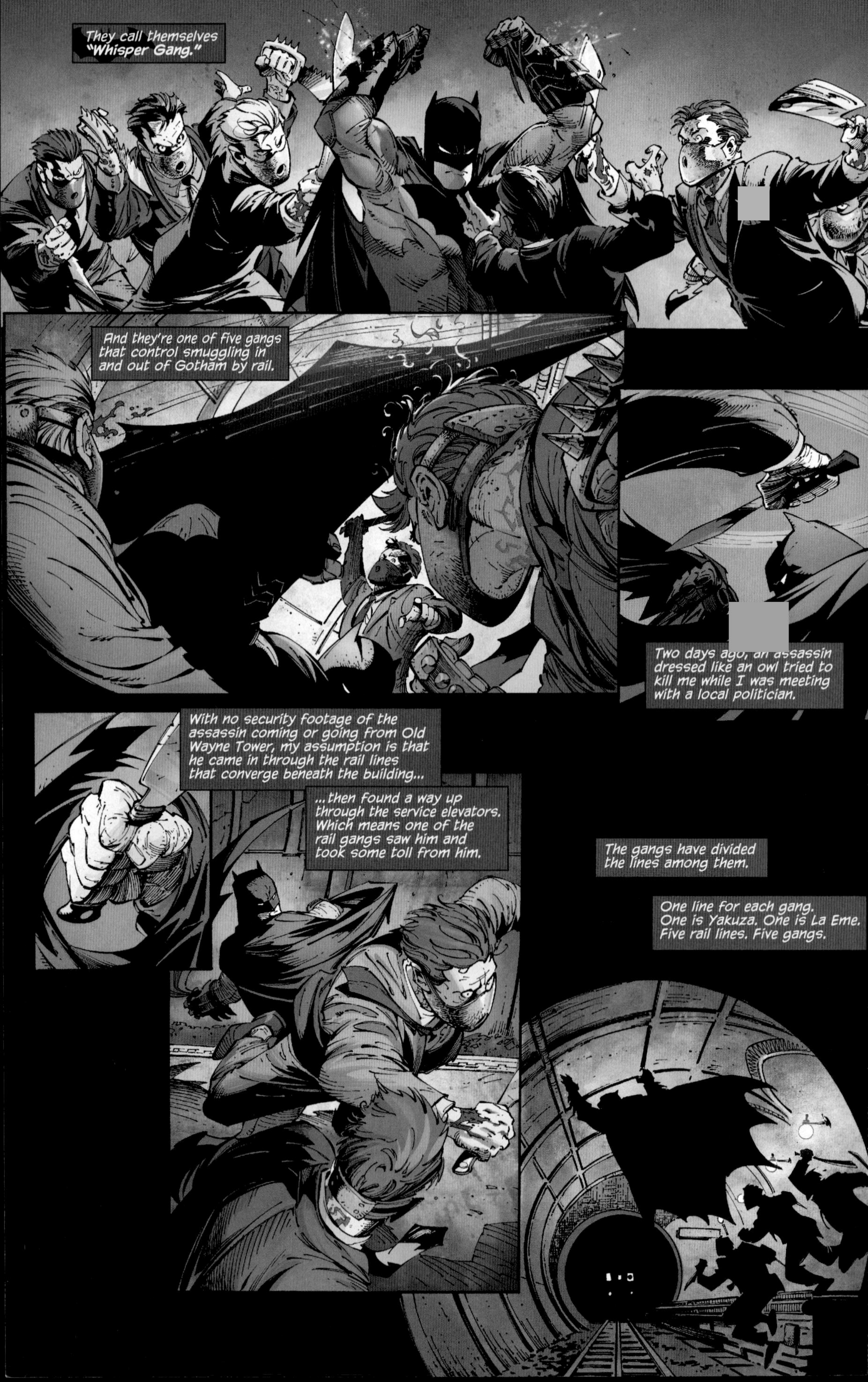
They call themselves "Whisper Gang."
And they're one of five gangs that control smuggling in and out of Gotham by rail.
Two days ago, an assassin dressed like an owl tried to kill me while I was meeting with a local politician.
With no security footage of the assassin coming or going from Old Wayne Tower, my assumption is that he came in through the rail lines that converge beneath the building...
...then found a way up through the service elevators. Which means one of the rail gangs saw him and took some toll from him.
The gangs have divided the lines among them.
One line for each gang. One is Yakuza. One is La Eme. Five rail lines. Five gangs.

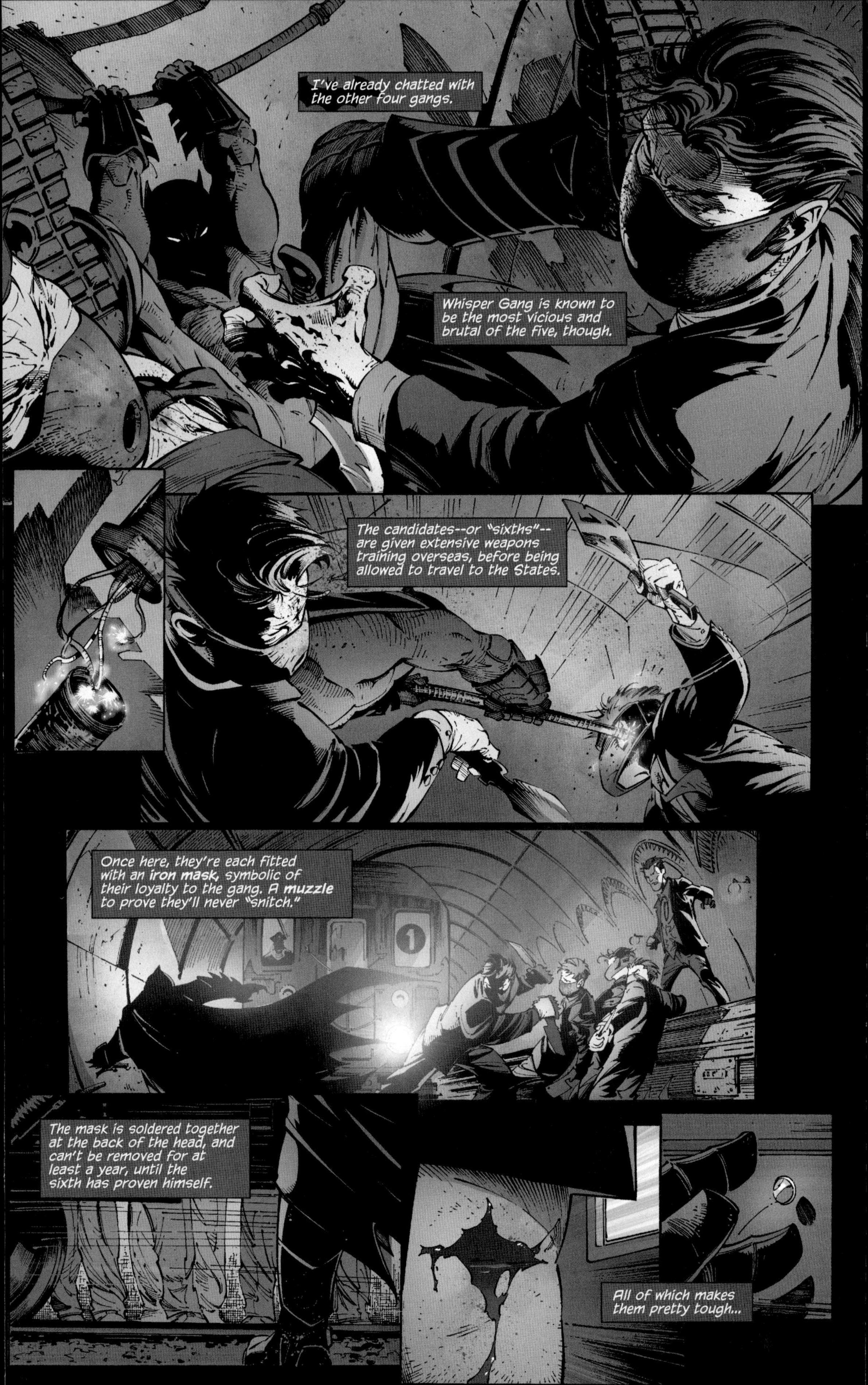
I've already chatted with the other four gangs.
Whisper Gang is known to be the most vicious and brutal of the five, though.
The candidates--or "sixths"--are given extensive weapons training overseas, before being allowed to travel to the States.
Once here, they're each fitted with an **iron mask**, symbolic of their loyalty to the gang. A **muzzle** to prove they'll never "snitch."
1
The mask is soldered together at the back of the head, and can't be removed for at least a year, until the sixth has proven himself.
All of which makes them pretty tough...

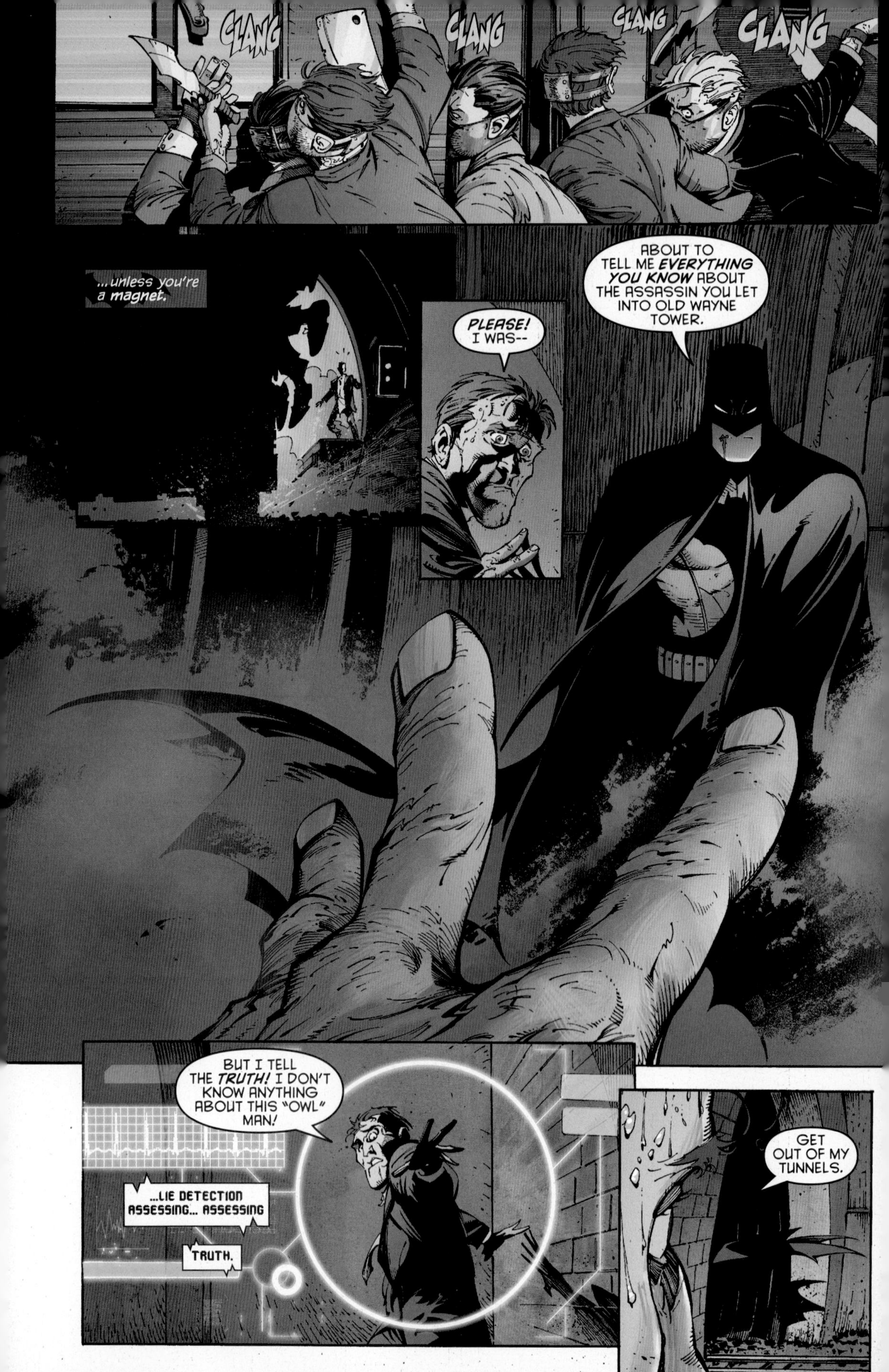
CLANG
CLANG
CLANG
CLANG
...unless you're a magnet.
PLEASE! I WAS--
ABOUT TO TELL ME EVERYTHING YOU KNOW ABOUT THE ASSASSIN YOU LET INTO OLD WAYNE TOWER.
BUT I TELL THE TRUTH! I DON'T KNOW ANYTHING ABOUT THIS "OWL" MAN!
...LIE DETECTION ASSESSING... ASSESSING
TRUTH.
GET OUT OF MY TUNNELS.

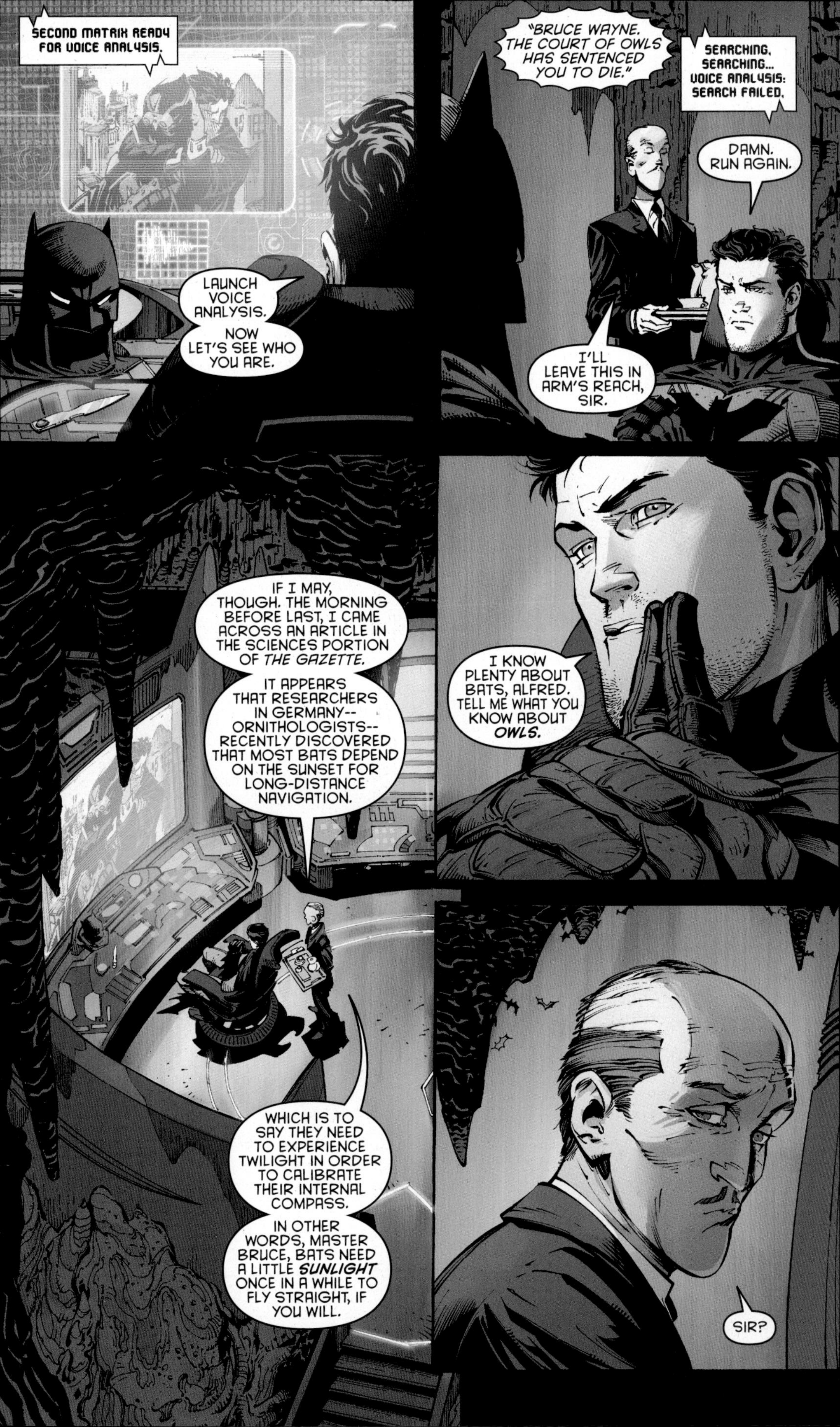
SECOND MATRIX READY FOR VOICE ANALYSIS.
LAUNCH VOICE ANALYSIS.
NOW LET'S SEE WHO YOU ARE.
"BRUCE WAYNE. THE COURT OF OWLS HAS SENTENCED YOU TO DIE."
SEARCHING, SEARCHING... VOICE ANALYSIS: SEARCH FAILED.
DAMN. RUN AGAIN.
I'LL LEAVE THIS IN ARM'S REACH, SIR.
IF I MAY, THOUGH. THE MORNING BEFORE LAST, I CAME ACROSS AN ARTICLE IN THE SCIENCES PORTION OF *THE GAZETTE.*
IT APPEARS THAT RESEARCHERS IN GERMANY-- ORNITHOLOGISTS-- RECENTLY DISCOVERED THAT MOST BATS DEPEND ON THE SUNSET FOR LONG-DISTANCE NAVIGATION.
I KNOW PLENTY ABOUT BATS, ALFRED. TELL ME WHAT YOU KNOW ABOUT ***OWLS.***
WHICH IS TO SAY THEY NEED TO EXPERIENCE TWILIGHT IN ORDER TO CALIBRATE THEIR INTERNAL COMPASS.
IN OTHER WORDS, MASTER BRUCE, BATS NEED A LITTLE ***SUNLIGHT*** ONCE IN A WHILE TO FLY STRAIGHT, IF YOU WILL.
SIR?

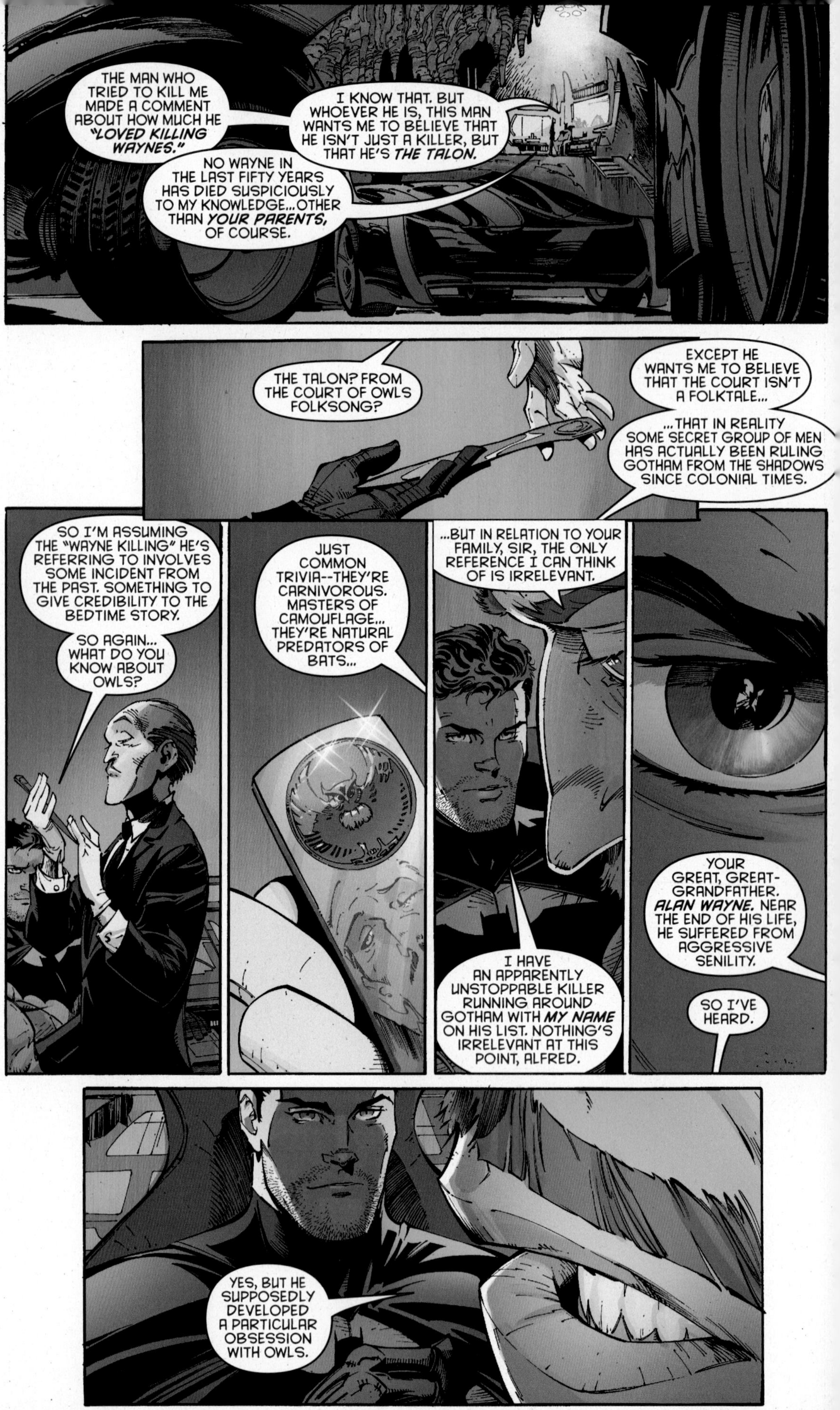
THE MAN WHO TRIED TO KILL ME MADE A COMMENT ABOUT HOW MUCH HE "LOVED KILLING WAYNES."
NO WAYNE IN THE LAST FIFTY YEARS HAS DIED SUSPICIOUSLY TO MY KNOWLEDGE...OTHER THAN YOUR PARENTS, OF COURSE.
I KNOW THAT. BUT WHOEVER HE IS, THIS MAN WANTS ME TO BELIEVE THAT HE ISN'T JUST A KILLER, BUT THAT HE'S THE TALON.
THE TALON? FROM THE COURT OF OWLS FOLKSONG?
EXCEPT HE WANTS ME TO BELIEVE THAT THE COURT ISN'T A FOLKTALE...
...THAT IN REALITY SOME SECRET GROUP OF MEN HAS ACTUALLY BEEN RULING GOTHAM FROM THE SHADOWS SINCE COLONIAL TIMES.
SO I'M ASSUMING THE "WAYNE KILLING" HE'S REFERRING TO INVOLVES SOME INCIDENT FROM THE PAST. SOMETHING TO GIVE CREDIBILITY TO THE BEDTIME STORY.
SO AGAIN... WHAT DO YOU KNOW ABOUT OWLS?
JUST COMMON TRIVIA--THEY'RE CARNIVOROUS. MASTERS OF CAMOUFLAGE... THEY'RE NATURAL PREDATORS OF BATS...
...BUT IN RELATION TO YOUR FAMILY, SIR, THE ONLY REFERENCE I CAN THINK OF IS IRRELEVANT.
I HAVE AN APPARENTLY UNSTOPPABLE KILLER RUNNING AROUND GOTHAM WITH MY NAME ON HIS LIST. NOTHING'S IRRELEVANT AT THIS POINT, ALFRED.
YOUR GREAT, GREAT-GRANDFATHER. ALAN WAYNE. NEAR THE END OF HIS LIFE, HE SUFFERED FROM AGGRESSIVE SENILITY.
SO I'VE HEARD.
YES, BUT HE SUPPOSEDLY DEVELOPED A PARTICULAR OBSESSION WITH OWLS.

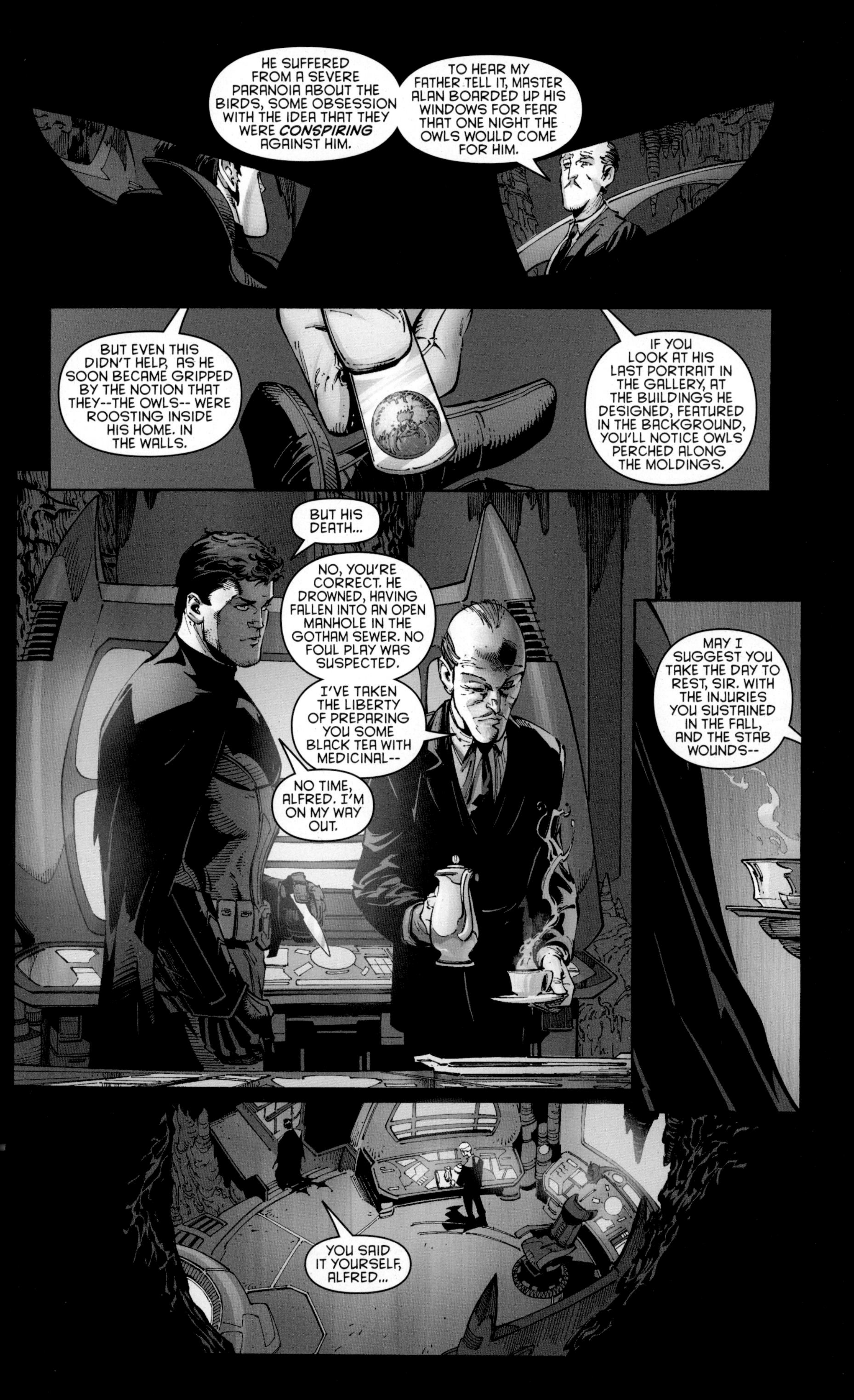
HE SUFFERED FROM A SEVERE PARANOIA ABOUT THE BIRDS, SOME OBSESSION WITH THE IDEA THAT THEY WERE *CONSPIRING* AGAINST HIM.
TO HEAR MY FATHER TELL IT, MASTER ALAN BOARDED UP HIS WINDOWS FOR FEAR THAT ONE NIGHT THE OWLS WOULD COME FOR HIM.
BUT EVEN THIS DIDN'T HELP, AS HE SOON BECAME GRIPPED BY THE NOTION THAT THEY--THE OWLS-- WERE ROOSTING INSIDE HIS HOME. IN THE WALLS.
IF YOU LOOK AT HIS LAST PORTRAIT IN THE GALLERY, AT THE BUILDINGS HE DESIGNED, FEATURED IN THE BACKGROUND, YOU'LL NOTICE OWLS PERCHED ALONG THE MOLDINGS.
BUT HIS DEATH...
NO, YOU'RE CORRECT. HE DROWNED, HAVING FALLEN INTO AN OPEN MANHOLE IN THE GOTHAM SEWER. NO FOUL PLAY WAS SUSPECTED.
I'VE TAKEN THE LIBERTY OF PREPARING YOU SOME BLACK TEA WITH MEDICINAL--
NO TIME, ALFRED. I'M ON MY WAY OUT.
MAY I SUGGEST YOU TAKE THE DAY TO REST, SIR. WITH THE INJURIES YOU SUSTAINED IN THE FALL, AND THE STAB WOUNDS--
YOU SAID IT YOURSELF, ALFRED...

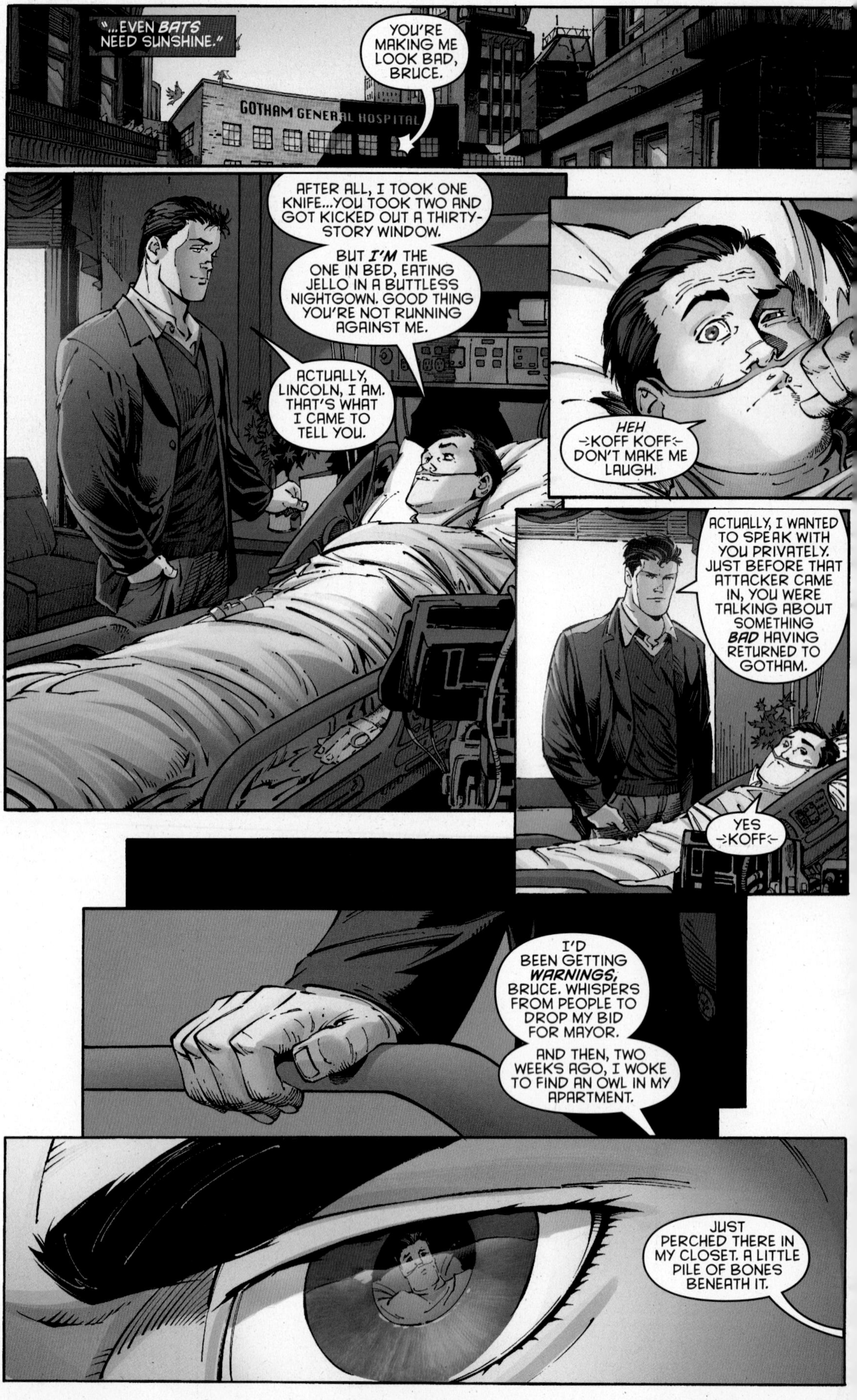
"...EVEN BATS NEED SUNSHINE."
YOU'RE MAKING ME LOOK BAD, BRUCE.
GOTHAM GENERAL HOSPITAL
AFTER ALL, I TOOK ONE KNIFE...YOU TOOK TWO AND GOT KICKED OUT A THIRTY-STORY WINDOW.
BUT I'M THE ONE IN BED, EATING JELLO IN A BUTTLESS NIGHTGOWN. GOOD THING YOU'RE NOT RUNNING AGAINST ME.
ACTUALLY, LINCOLN, I AM. THAT'S WHAT I CAME TO TELL YOU.
HEH -KOFF KOFF- DON'T MAKE ME LAUGH.
ACTUALLY, I WANTED TO SPEAK WITH YOU PRIVATELY. JUST BEFORE THAT ATTACKER CAME IN, YOU WERE TALKING ABOUT SOMETHING BAD HAVING RETURNED TO GOTHAM.
YES -KOFF-
I'D BEEN GETTING WARNINGS, BRUCE. WHISPERS FROM PEOPLE TO DROP MY BID FOR MAYOR.
AND THEN, TWO WEEKS AGO, I WOKE TO FIND AN OWL IN MY APARTMENT.
JUST PERCHED THERE IN MY CLOSET. A LITTLE PILE OF BONES BENEATH IT.

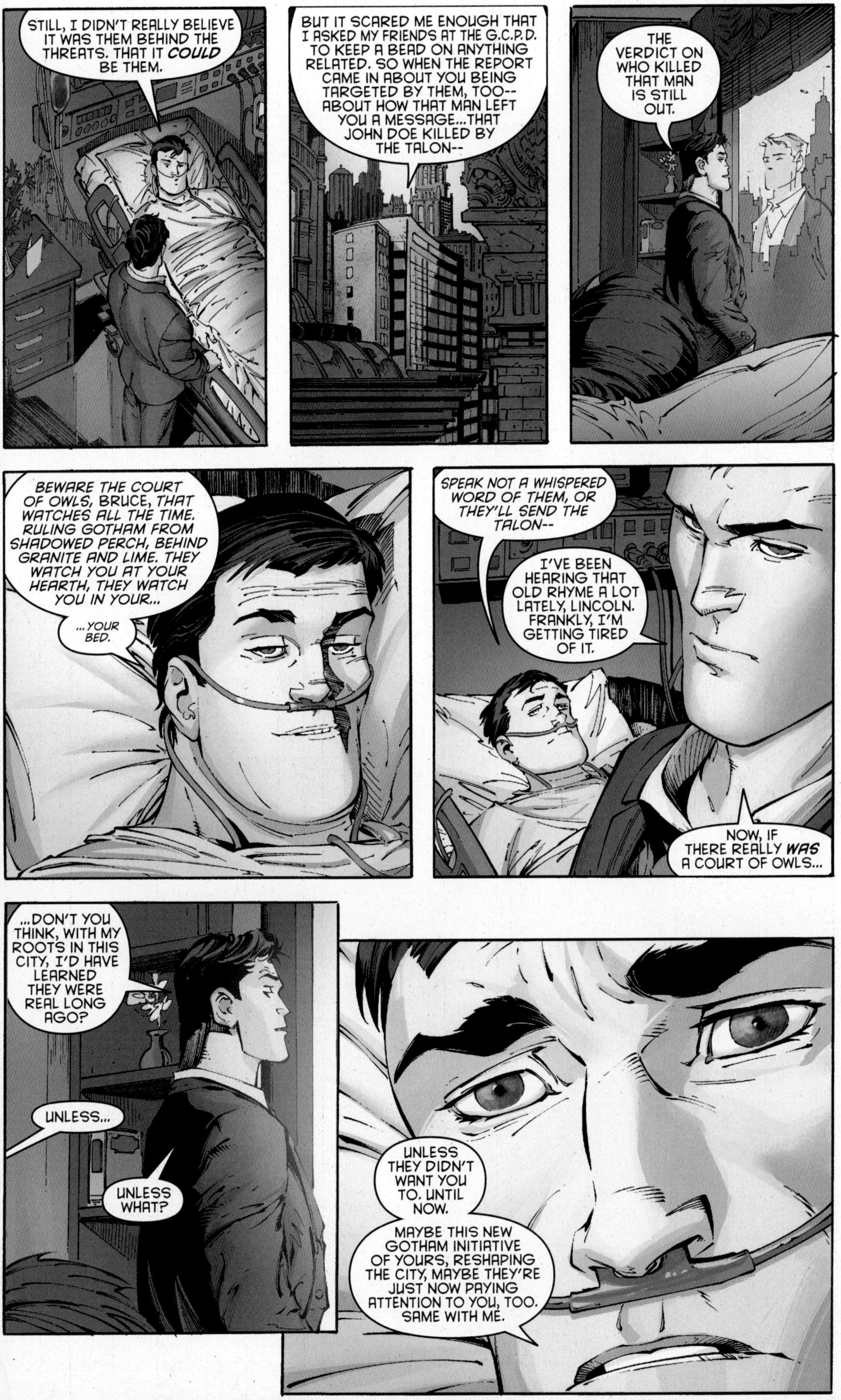
STILL, I DIDN'T REALLY BELIEVE IT WAS THEM BEHIND THE THREATS. THAT IT *COULD* BE THEM.
BUT IT SCARED ME ENOUGH THAT I ASKED MY FRIENDS AT THE G.C.P.D. TO KEEP A BEAD ON ANYTHING RELATED. SO WHEN THE REPORT CAME IN ABOUT YOU BEING TARGETED BY THEM, TOO-- ABOUT HOW THAT MAN LEFT YOU A MESSAGE...THAT JOHN DOE KILLED BY THE TALON--
THE VERDICT ON WHO KILLED THAT MAN IS STILL OUT.
BEWARE THE COURT OF OWLS, BRUCE, THAT WATCHES ALL THE TIME. RULING GOTHAM FROM SHADOWED PERCH, BEHIND GRANITE AND LIME. THEY WATCH YOU AT YOUR HEARTH, THEY WATCH YOU IN YOUR...
...YOUR BED.
SPEAK NOT A WHISPERED WORD OF THEM, OR THEY'LL SEND THE TALON--
I'VE BEEN HEARING THAT OLD RHYME A LOT LATELY, LINCOLN. FRANKLY, I'M GETTING TIRED OF IT.
NOW, IF THERE REALLY *WAS* A COURT OF OWLS...
...DON'T YOU THINK, WITH MY ROOTS IN THIS CITY, I'D HAVE LEARNED THEY WERE REAL LONG AGO?
UNLESS...
UNLESS WHAT?
UNLESS THEY DIDN'T WANT YOU TO. UNTIL NOW.
MAYBE THIS NEW GOTHAM INITIATIVE OF YOURS, RESHAPING THE CITY, MAYBE THEY'RE JUST NOW PAYING ATTENTION TO YOU, TOO. SAME WITH ME.

I'M NOT AFRAID OF GHOST STORIES. AND YOU SHOULDN'T BE, EITHER.

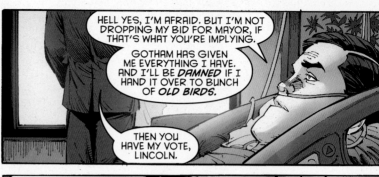

HELL YES, I'M AFRAID. BUT I'M NOT DROPPING MY BID FOR MAYOR, IF THAT'S WHAT YOU'RE IMPLYING.

GOTHAM HAS GIVEN ME EVERYTHING I HAVE. AND I'LL BE *DAMNED* IF I HAND IT OVER TO BUNCH OF *OLD BIRDS.*

THEN YOU HAVE MY VOTE, LINCOLN.

BRUCE, THE HOME FOR BOYS I LIVED IN, AFTER MY PARENTS DIED, IT HAD THIS OLD WOODEN FLOOR. ALWAYS CREAKING. DROVE EVERYONE CRAZY.

NO ONE THE NUNS BROUGHT IN COULD FIGURE IT OUT. THEN ONE DAY SISTER ALISON NOTICED THIS DEPRESSION BY THE CORNER OF THE BUILDING.

TURNS OUT, THE PLACE WAS ON A SINKHOLE. WITHIN A YEAR, THE WHOLE BUILDING WOULD'VE COLLAPSED WITH US INSIDE, IF SHE HADN'T REALIZED IT.

MY POINT IS, SOMETIMES WE BECOME SO CONCERNED WITH LITTLE DANGERS THAT WE DON'T SEE THE BIG ONE, RIGHT BENEATH OUR FEET. THAT'S ALL.

BRUCE?

I'M SORRY, LINCOLN. I HAVE TO GO. I'M GOING TO HAVE MY OWN PEOPLE WATCH YOUR ROOM. THEY'RE THE BEST. GET SOME SLEEP.

BUT, BRUCE, IF THEY'RE WATCHING ME...

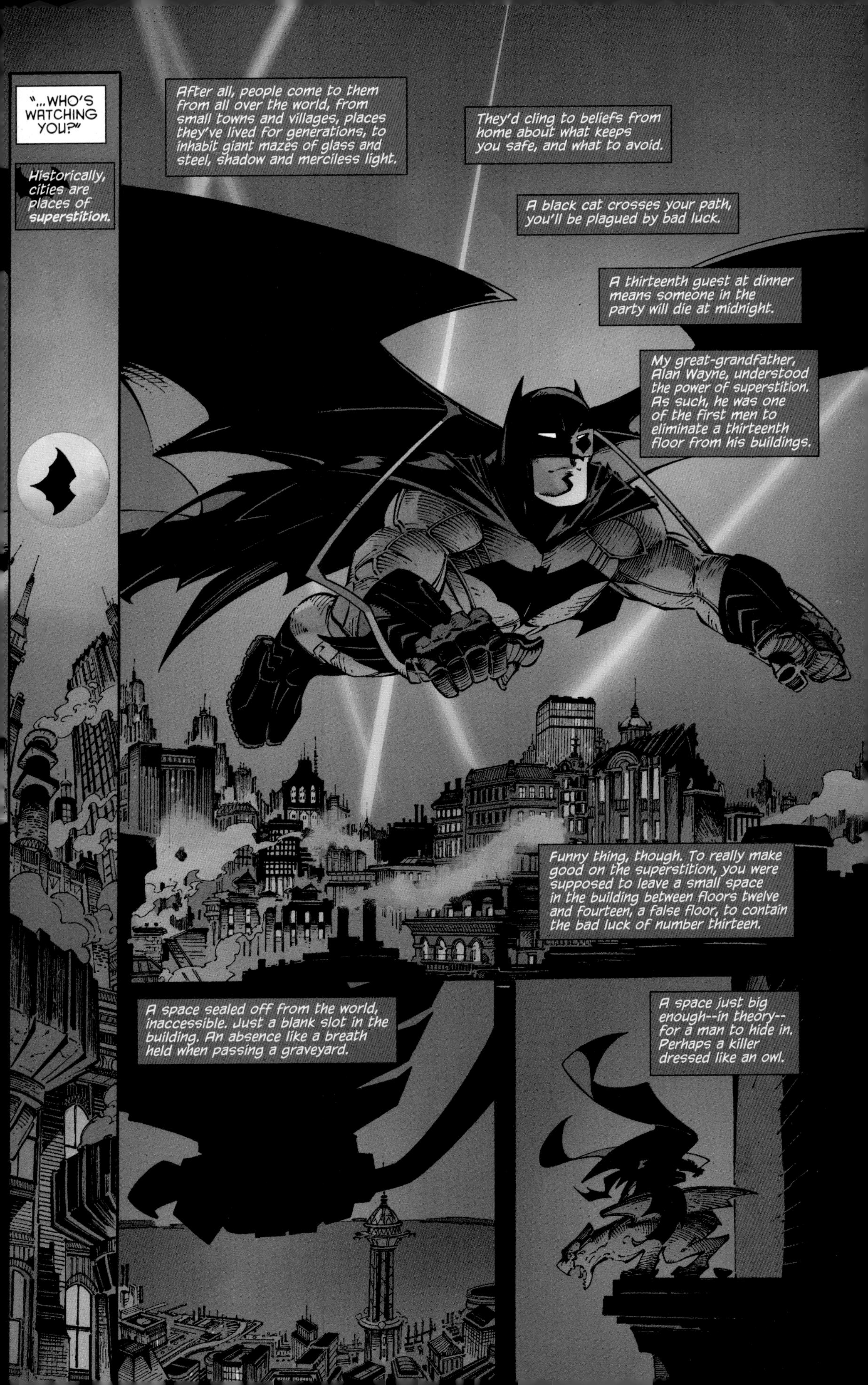
"...WHO'S WATCHING YOU?"
Historically, cities are places of superstition.
After all, people come to them from all over the world, from small towns and villages, places they've lived for generations, to inhabit giant mazes of glass and steel, shadow and merciless light.
They'd cling to beliefs from home about what keeps you safe, and what to avoid.
A black cat crosses your path, you'll be plagued by bad luck.
A thirteenth guest at dinner means someone in the party will die at midnight.
My great-grandfather, Alan Wayne, understood the power of superstition. As such, he was one of the first men to eliminate a thirteenth floor from his buildings.
Funny thing, though. To really make good on the superstition, you were supposed to leave a small space in the building between floors twelve and fourteen, a false floor, to contain the bad luck of number thirteen.
A space sealed off from the world, inaccessible. Just a blank slot in the building. An absence like a breath held when passing a graveyard.
A space just big enough--in theory--for a man to hide in. Perhaps a killer dressed like an owl.

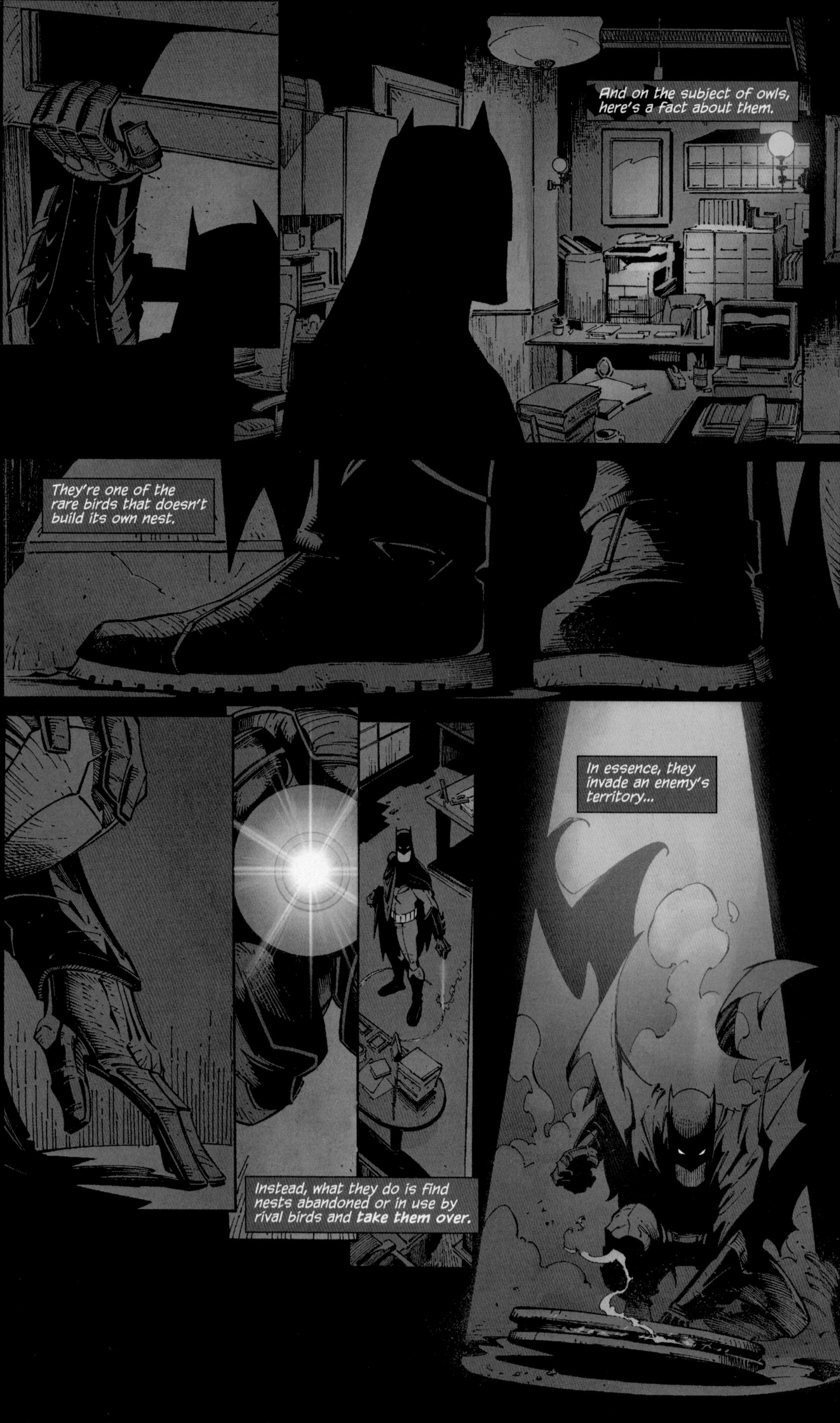
And on the subject of owls, here's a fact about them.
They're one of the rare birds that doesn't build its own nest.
Instead, what they do is find nests abandoned or in use by rival birds and **take them over.**
In essence, they invade an enemy's territory...

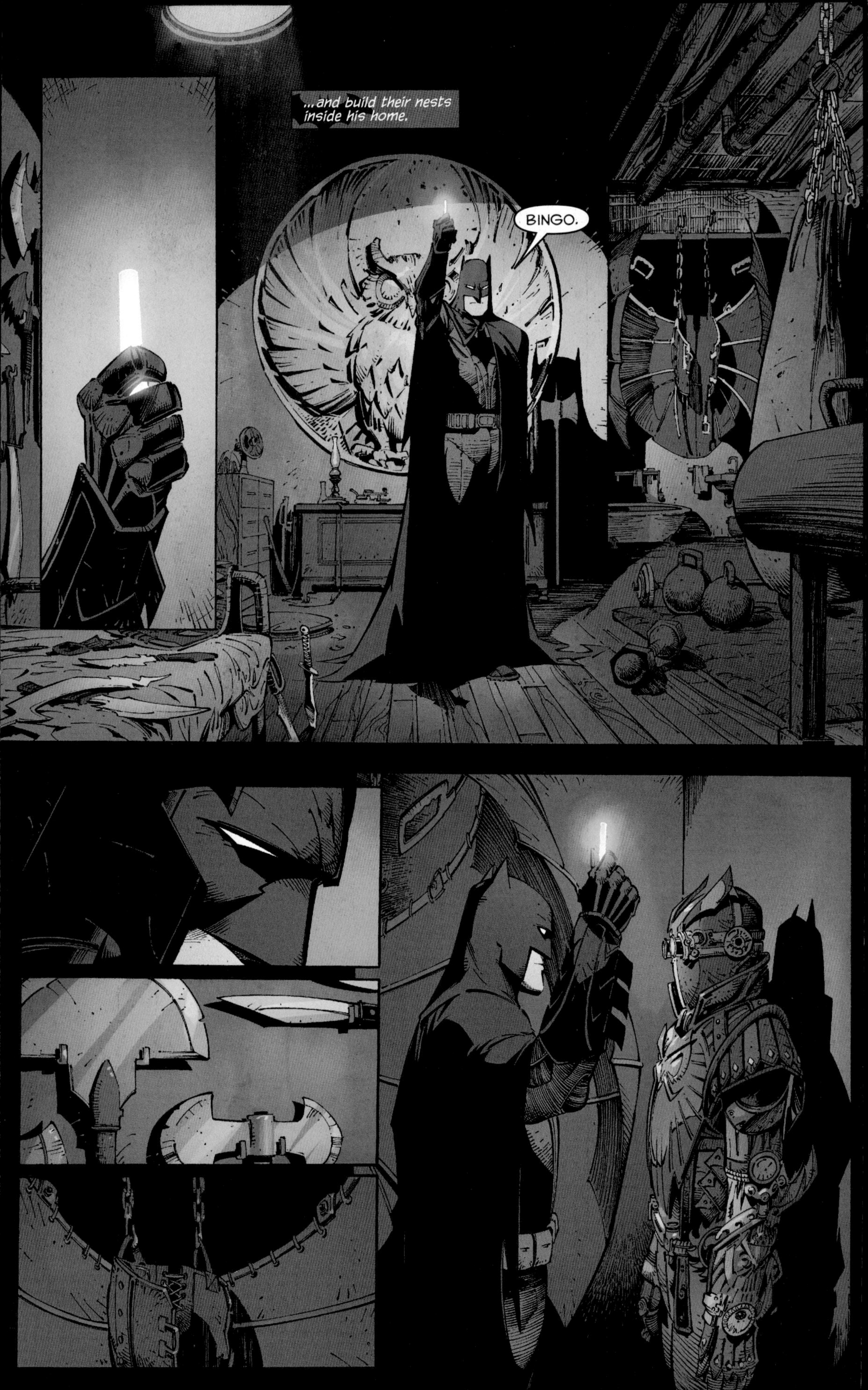
...and build their nests inside his home.
BINGO.

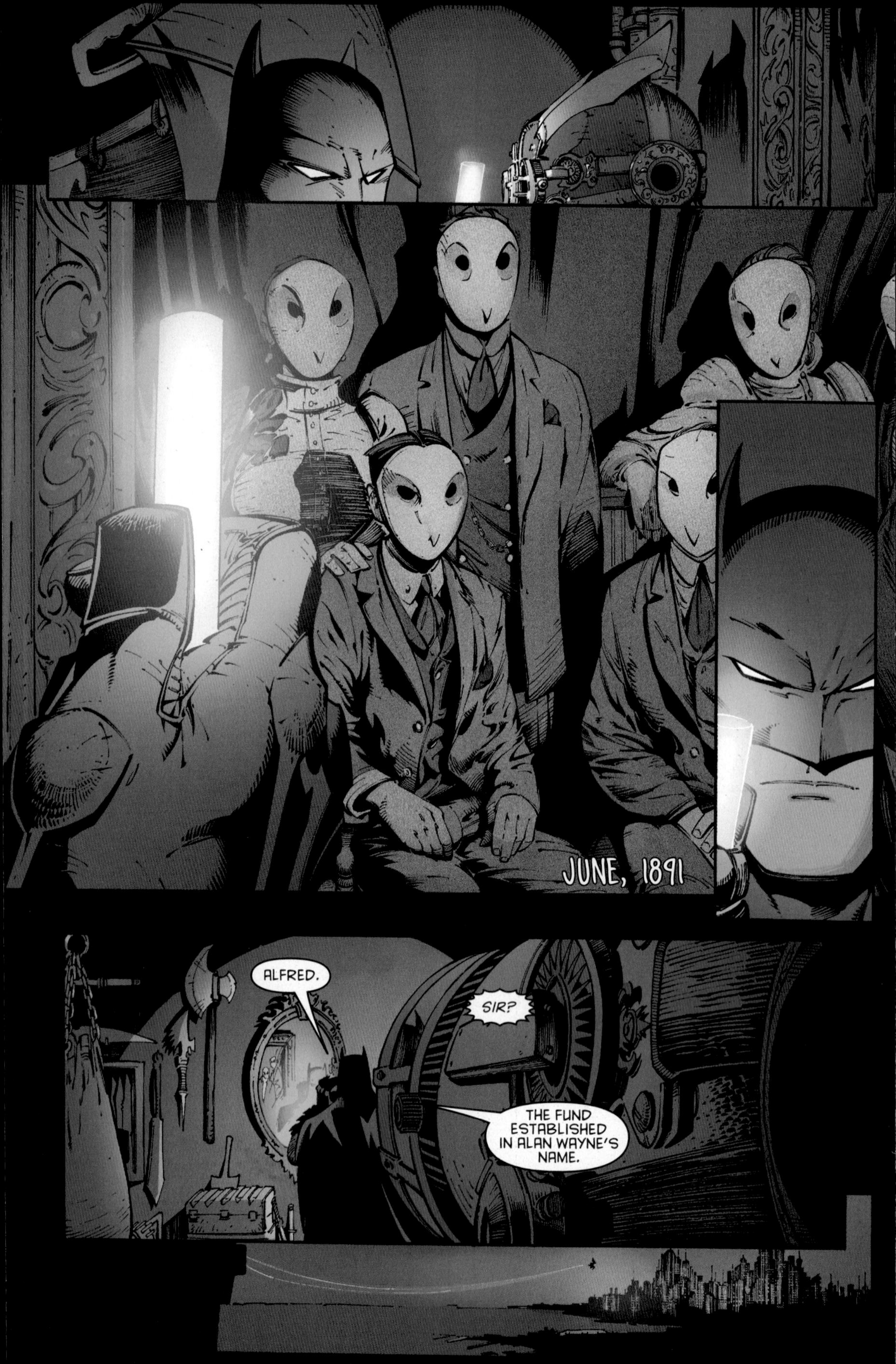
JUNE, 1891
ALFRED.
SIR?
THE FUND ESTABLISHED IN ALAN WAYNE'S NAME.

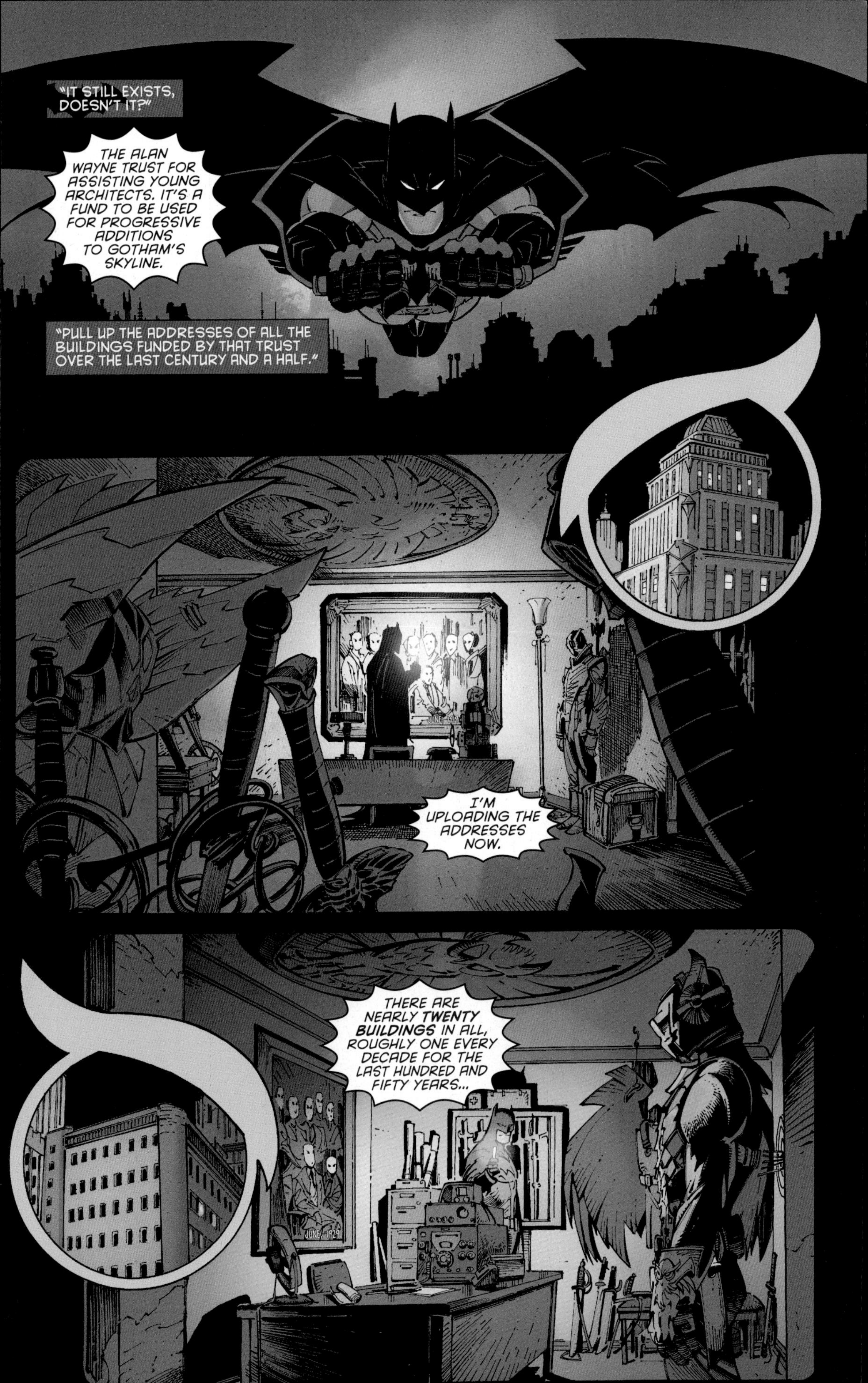
"IT STILL EXISTS, DOESN'T IT?"
THE ALAN WAYNE TRUST FOR ASSISTING YOUNG ARCHITECTS. IT'S A FUND TO BE USED FOR PROGRESSIVE ADDITIONS TO GOTHAM'S SKYLINE.
"PULL UP THE ADDRESSES OF ALL THE BUILDINGS FUNDED BY THAT TRUST OVER THE LAST CENTURY AND A HALF."
I'M UPLOADING THE ADDRESSES NOW.
THERE ARE NEARLY **TWENTY BUILDINGS** IN ALL, ROUGHLY ONE EVERY DECADE FOR THE LAST HUNDRED AND FIFTY YEARS...
JUNE 1929

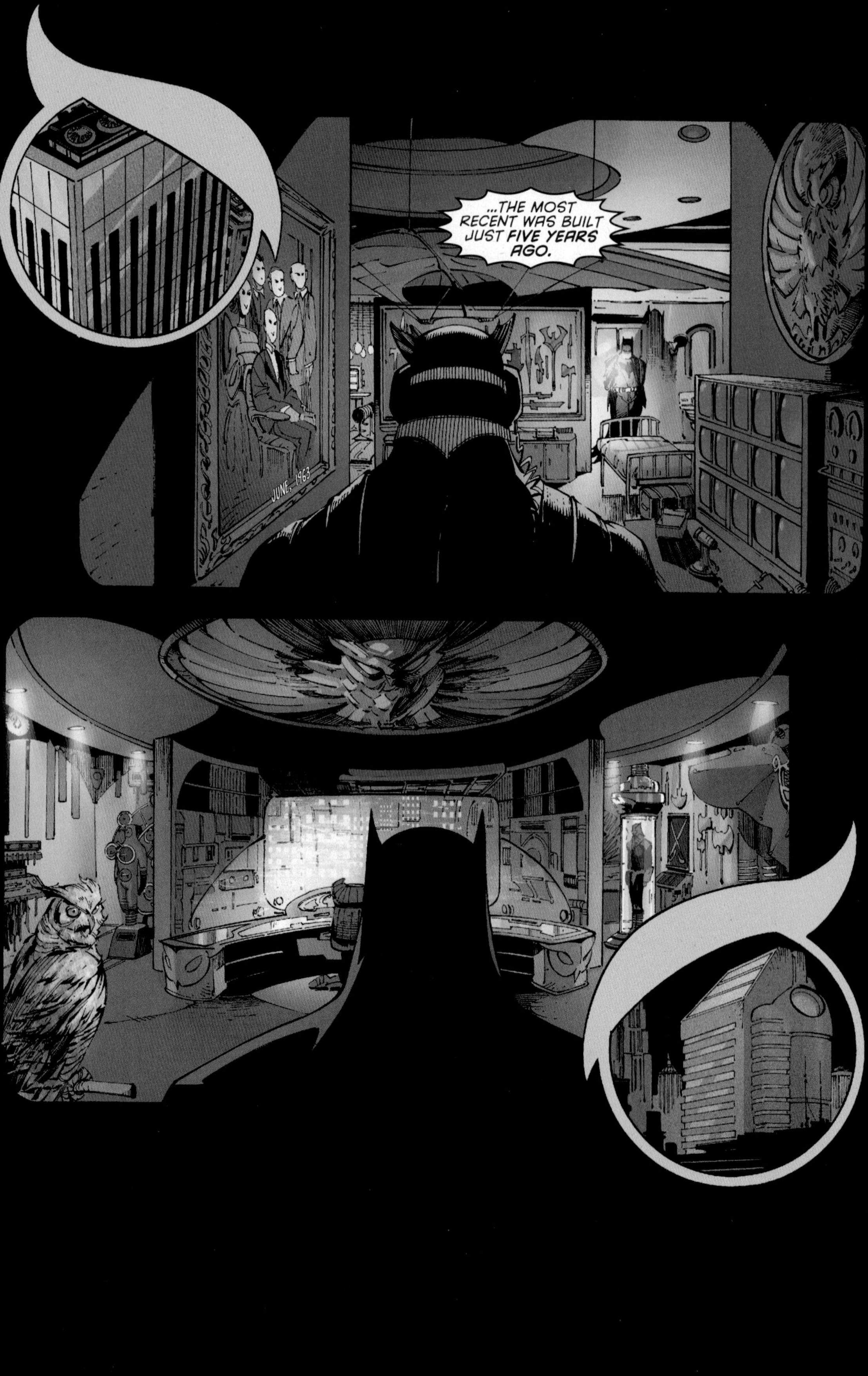
...THE MOST RECENT WAS BUILT JUST FIVE YEARS AGO.
JUNE, 1963

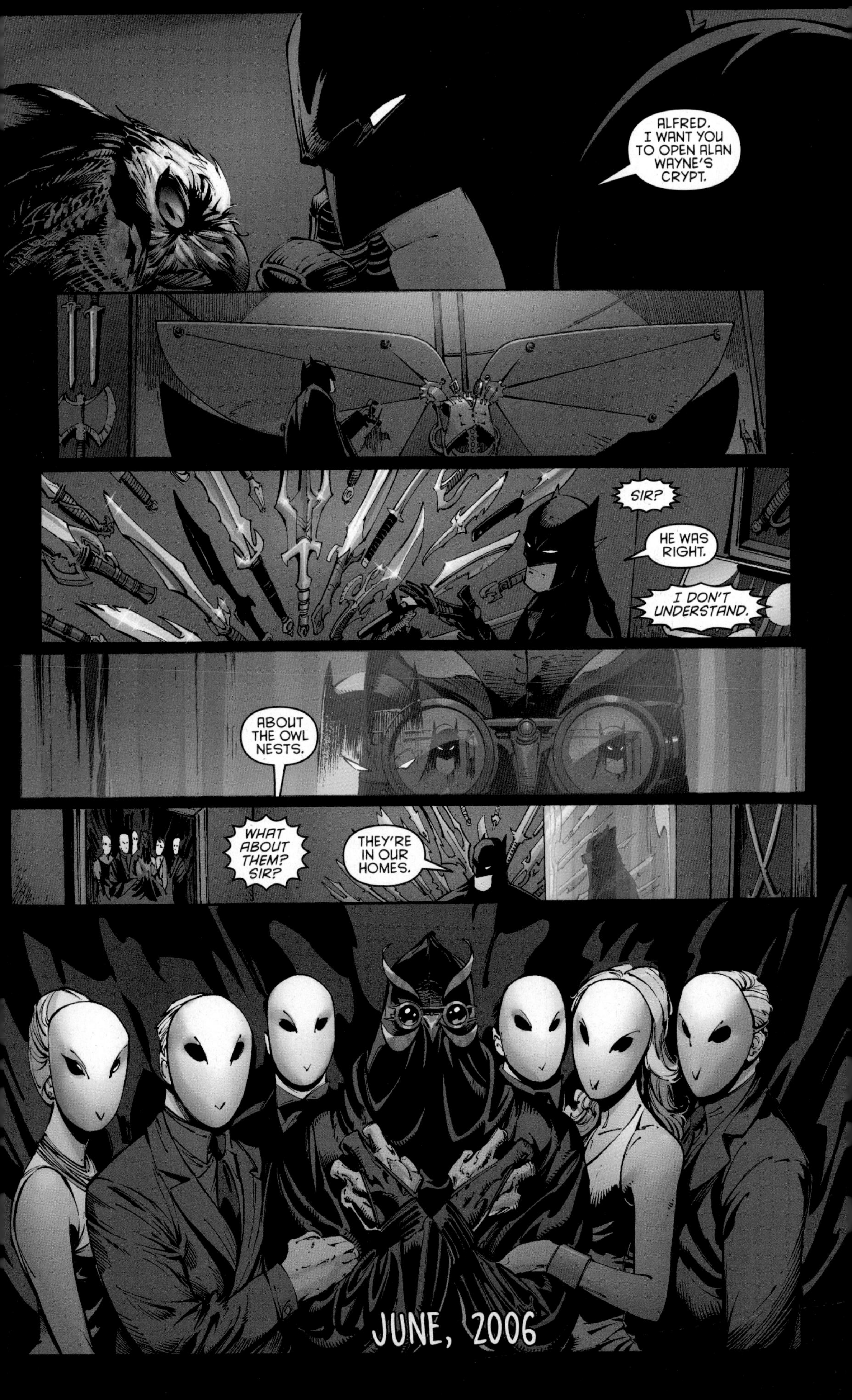
ALFRED. I WANT YOU TO OPEN ALAN WAYNE'S CRYPT.
SIR?
HE WAS RIGHT.
I DON'T UNDERSTAND.
ABOUT THE OWL NESTS.
WHAT ABOUT THEM? SIR?
THEY'RE IN OUR HOMES.
JUNE, 2006

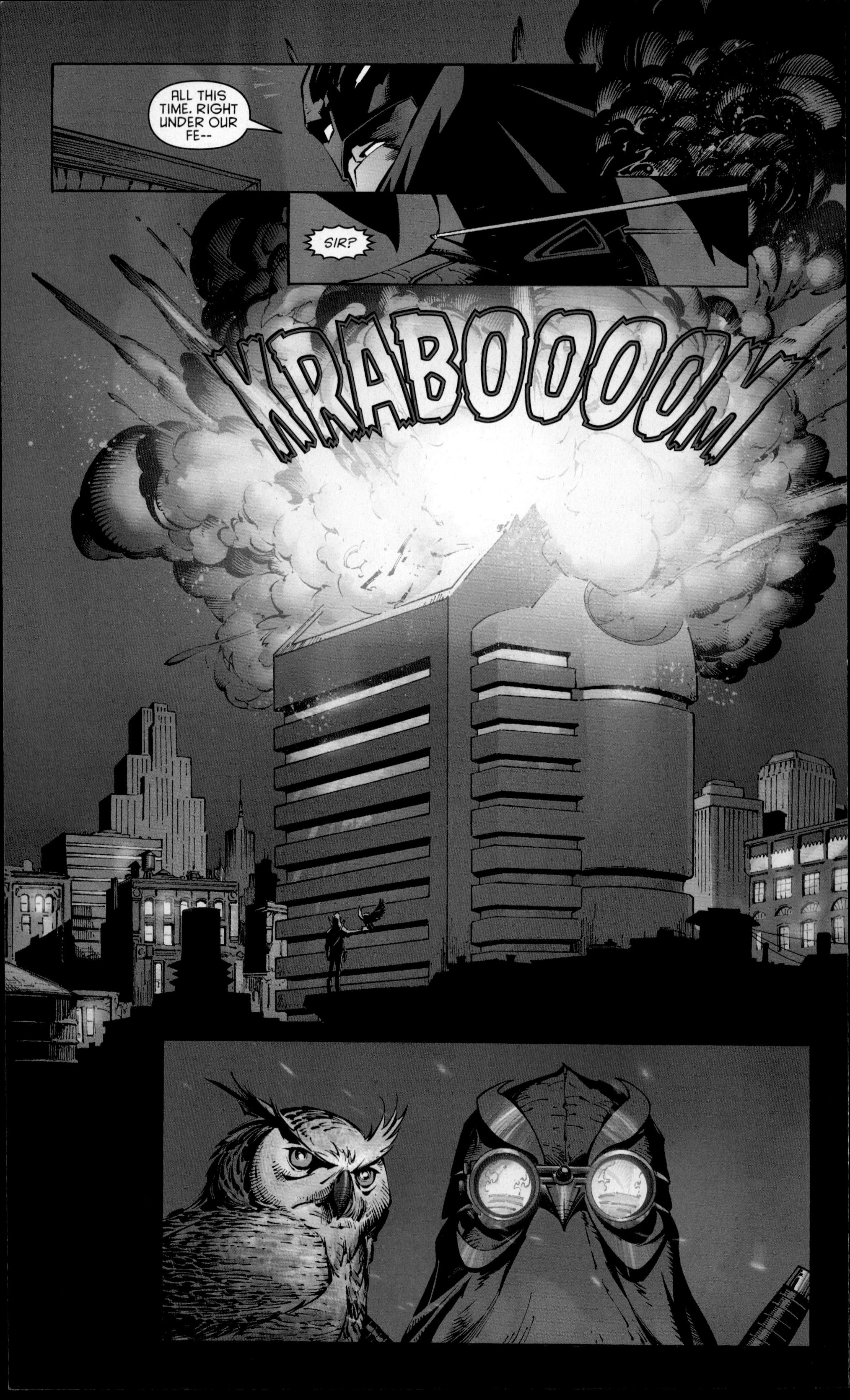
ALL THIS TIME. RIGHT UNDER OUR FE--
SIR?
KRABOOOOM

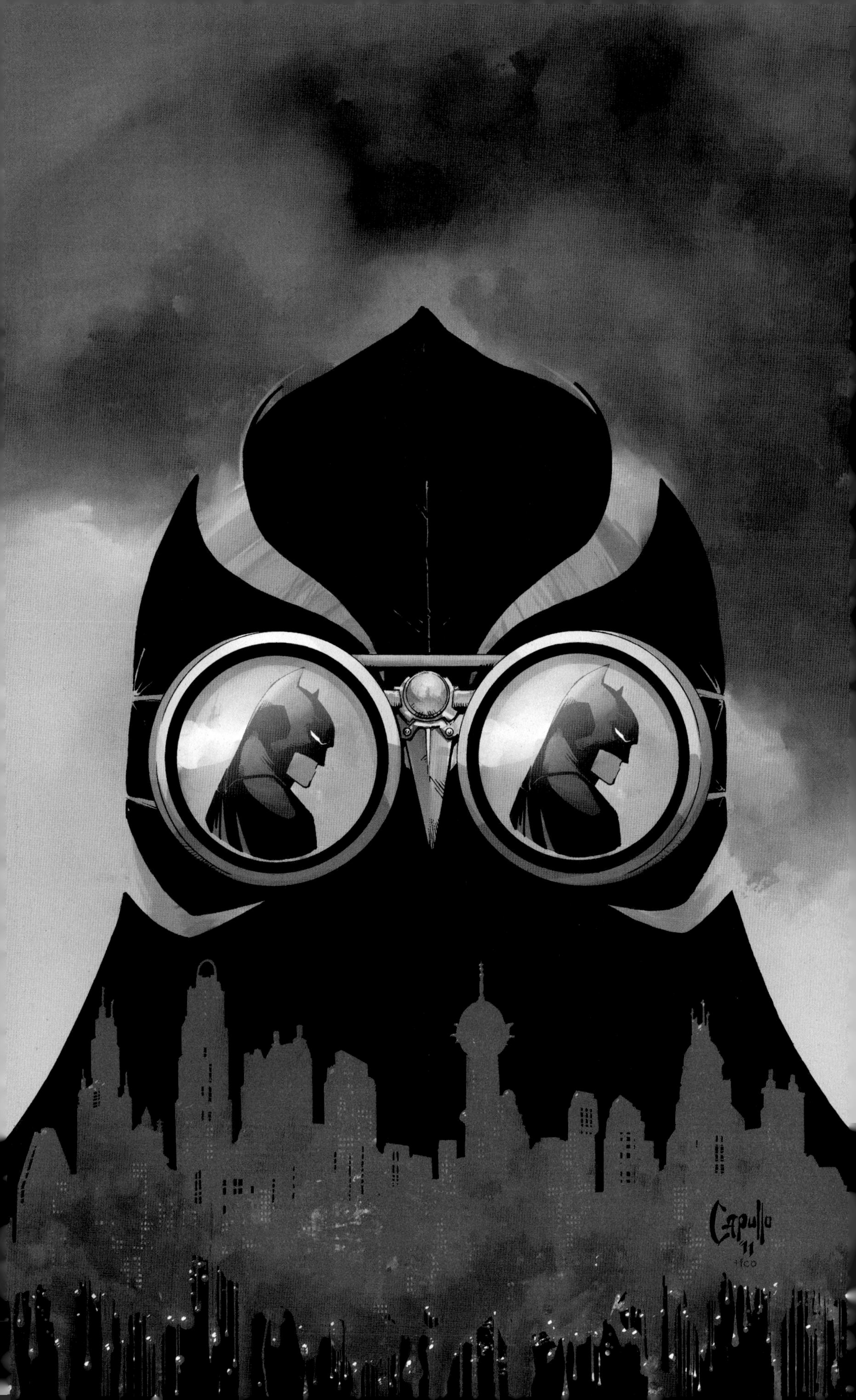

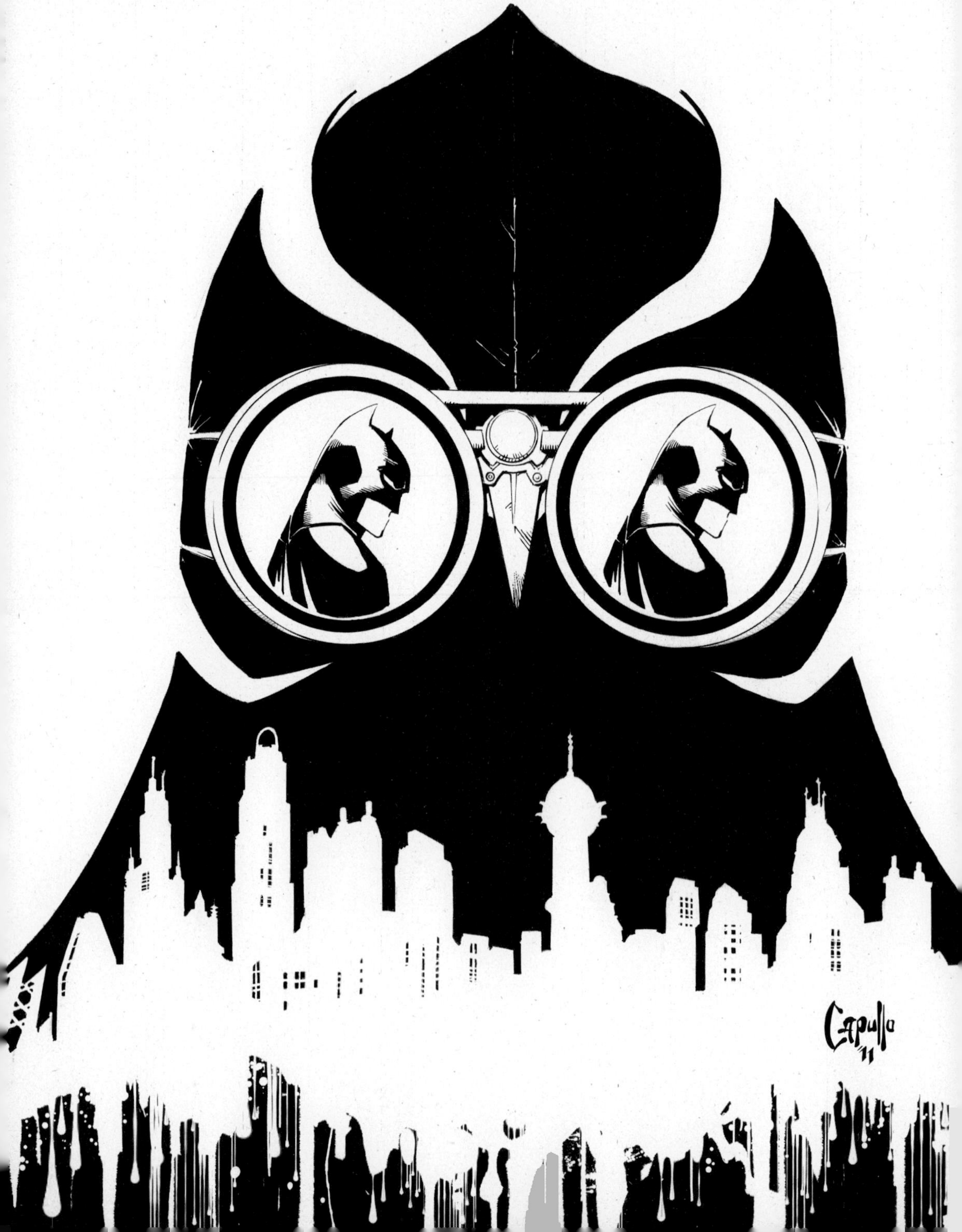
Capullo
'11

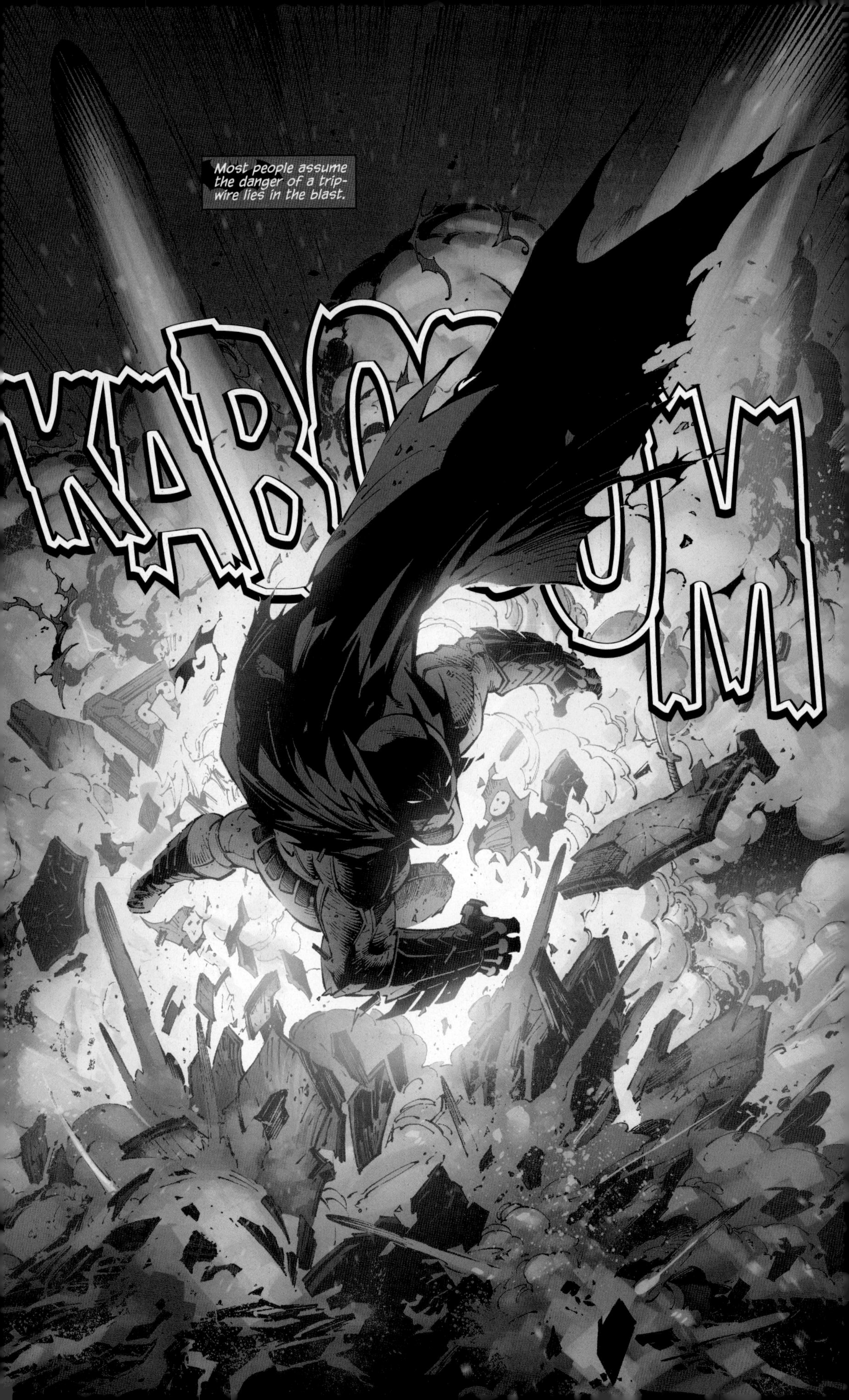
Most people assume the danger of a trip-wire lies in the blast.

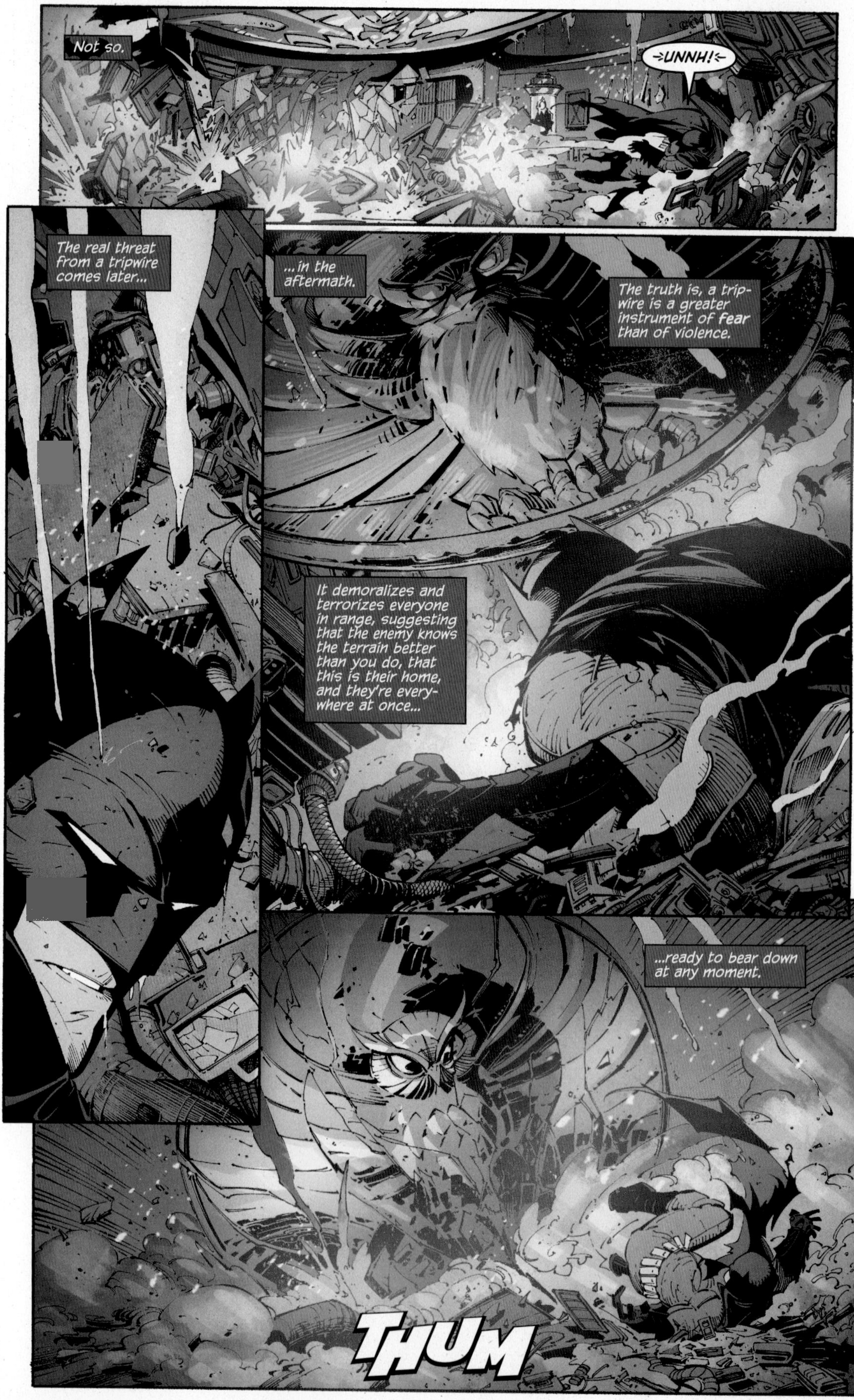
Not so.
UNNH!
The real threat from a tripwire comes later...
...in the aftermath.
The truth is, a trip-wire is a greater instrument of fear than of violence.
It demoralizes and terrorizes everyone in range, suggesting that the enemy knows the terrain better than you do, that this is their home, and they're every-where at once...
...ready to bear down at any moment.
THUM

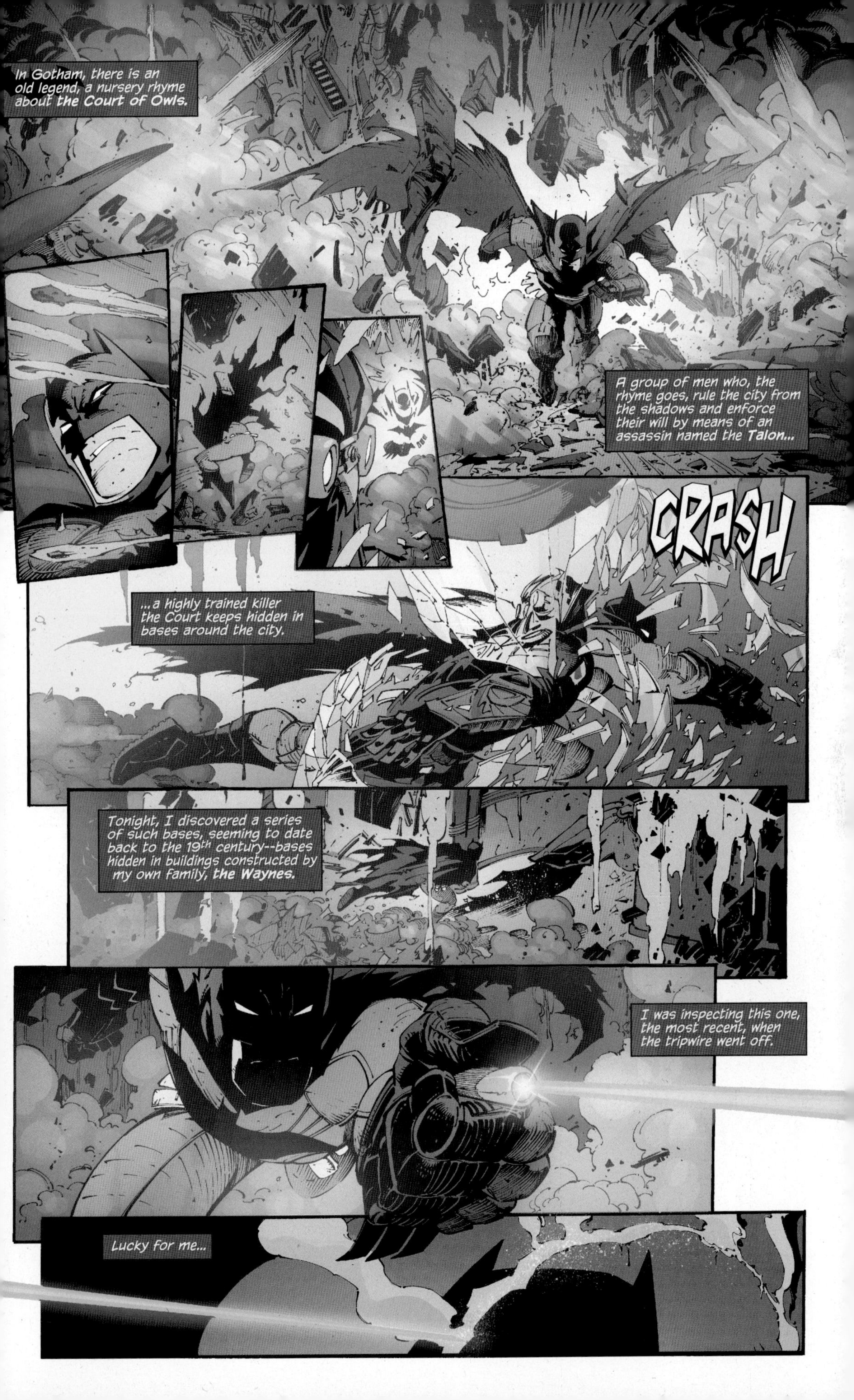
In Gotham, there is an old legend, a nursery rhyme about the Court of Owls.
A group of men who, the rhyme goes, rule the city from the shadows and enforce their will by means of an assassin named the Talon...
CRASH
...a highly trained killer the Court keeps hidden in bases around the city.
Tonight, I discovered a series of such bases, seeming to date back to the 19th century--bases hidden in buildings constructed by my own family, the Waynes.
I was inspecting this one, the most recent, when the tripwire went off.
Lucky for me...

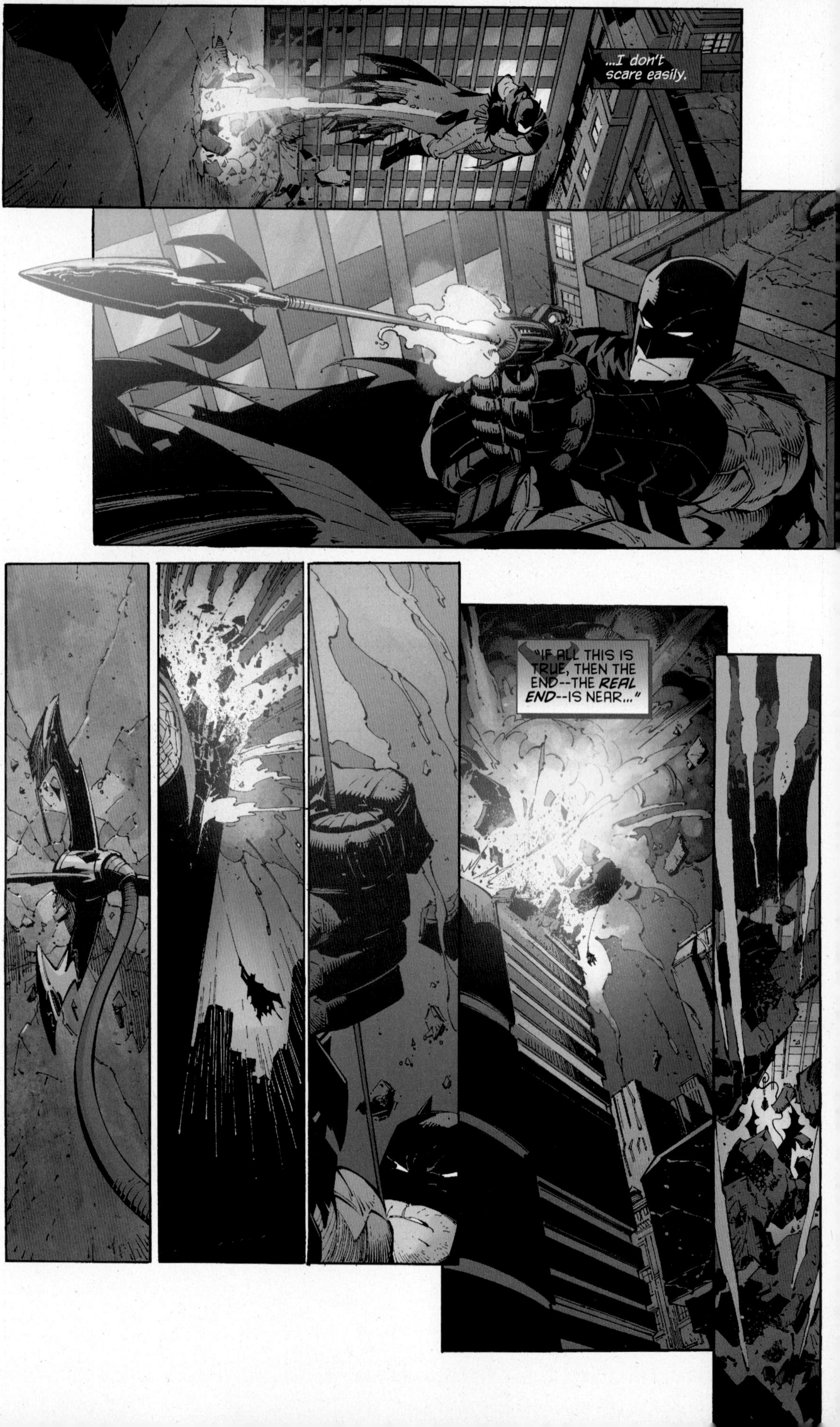
...I don't
scare easily.
"IF ALL THIS IS
TRUE, THEN THE
END--THE REAL
END--IS NEAR..."

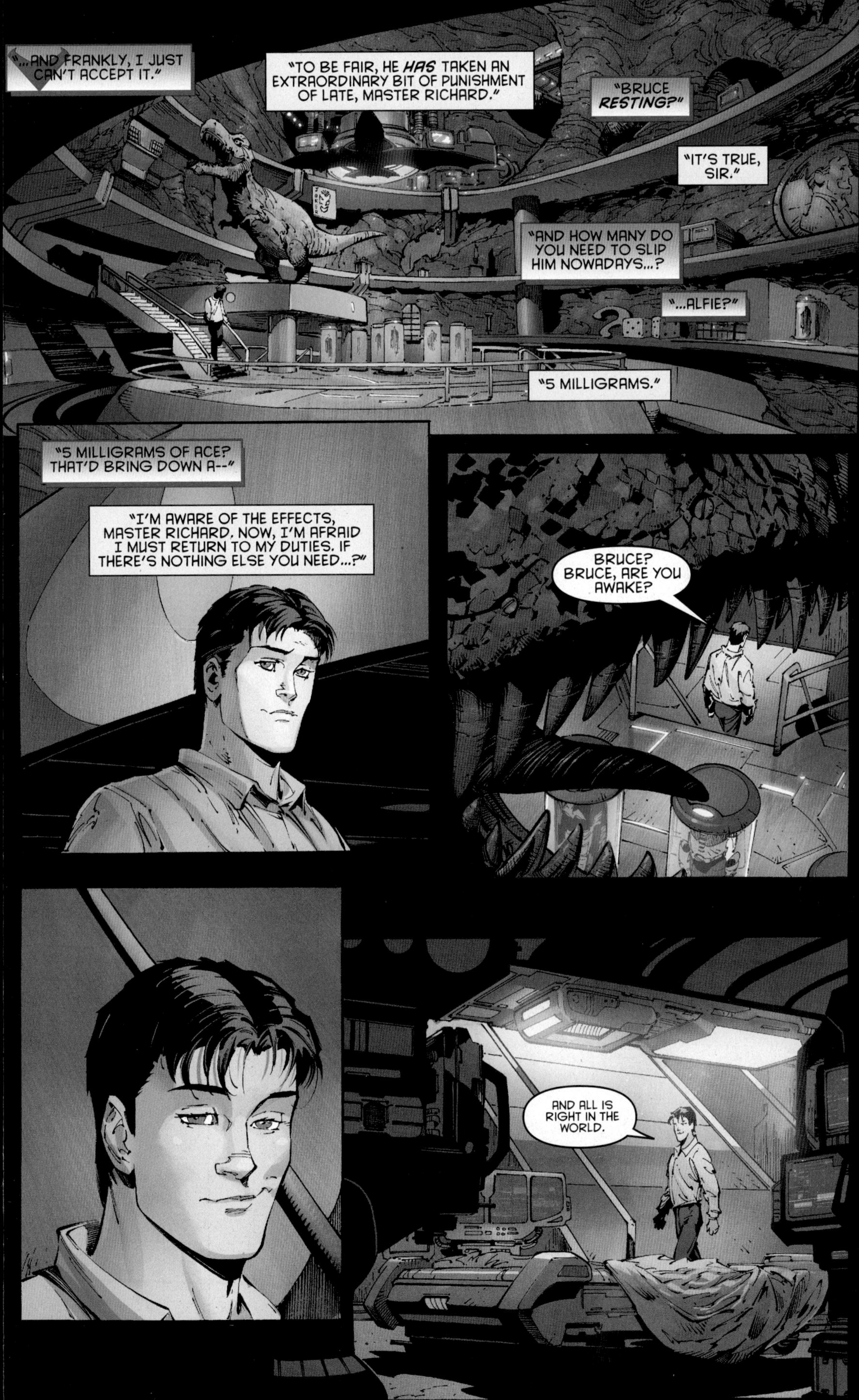
"...AND FRANKLY, I JUST CAN'T ACCEPT IT."
"TO BE FAIR, HE HAS TAKEN AN EXTRAORDINARY BIT OF PUNISHMENT OF LATE, MASTER RICHARD."
"BRUCE RESTING?"
"IT'S TRUE, SIR."
"AND HOW MANY DO YOU NEED TO SLIP HIM NOWADAYS...?
"...ALFIE?"
"5 MILLIGRAMS."
"5 MILLIGRAMS OF ACE? THAT'D BRING DOWN A--"
"I'M AWARE OF THE EFFECTS, MASTER RICHARD. NOW, I'M AFRAID I MUST RETURN TO MY DUTIES. IF THERE'S NOTHING ELSE YOU NEED...?"
BRUCE? BRUCE, ARE YOU AWAKE?
AND ALL IS RIGHT IN THE WORLD.

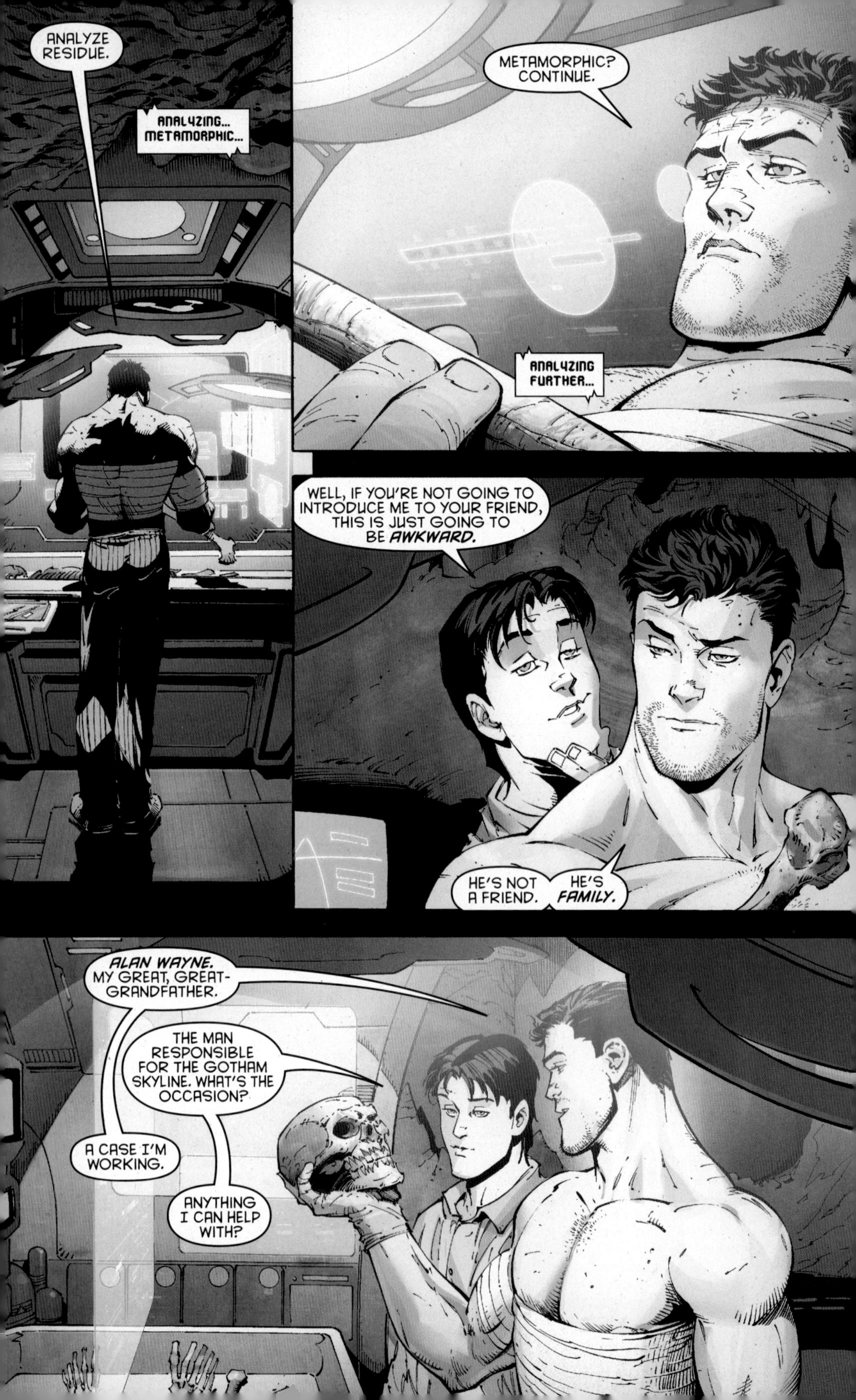
ANALYZE RESIDUE.
ANALYZING... METAMORPHIC...
METAMORPHIC? CONTINUE.
ANALYZING FURTHER...
WELL, IF YOU'RE NOT GOING TO INTRODUCE ME TO YOUR FRIEND, THIS IS JUST GOING TO BE AWKWARD.
HE'S NOT A FRIEND.
HE'S FAMILY.
ALAN WAYNE. MY GREAT, GREAT-GRANDFATHER.
THE MAN RESPONSIBLE FOR THE GOTHAM SKYLINE. WHAT'S THE OCCASION?
A CASE I'M WORKING.
ANYTHING I CAN HELP WITH?

I'M FINE. COMPUTER. ANALYZE.

ANALYZING FURTHER...

I MET WITH COMMISSIONER GORDON EARLIER, JUST TO TOUCH BASE...HE MENTIONED WHAT'S GOING ON.

THE DISCOVERY OF THE COURT OF OWLS BASES. HE SAYS HE THINKS THE DATES ARE LEGITIMATE.

I'M STILL RUNNING TESTS, BUT YES, RIGHT NOW THEY APPEAR TO BE AUTHENTIC. STILL, I'M NOT ENTIRELY CONVINCED.

HE MENTIONED THAT, TOO. YOU KNOW, HE THINKS YOU MIGHT BE OVERLY SKEPTICAL ON THIS ONE FOR SOME REASON.

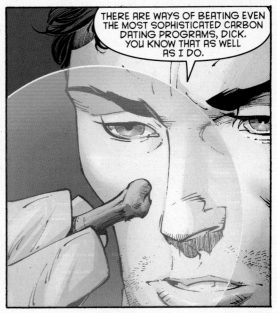

THERE ARE WAYS OF BEATING EVEN THE MOST SOPHISTICATED CARBON DATING PROGRAMS, DICK. YOU KNOW THAT AS WELL AS I DO.

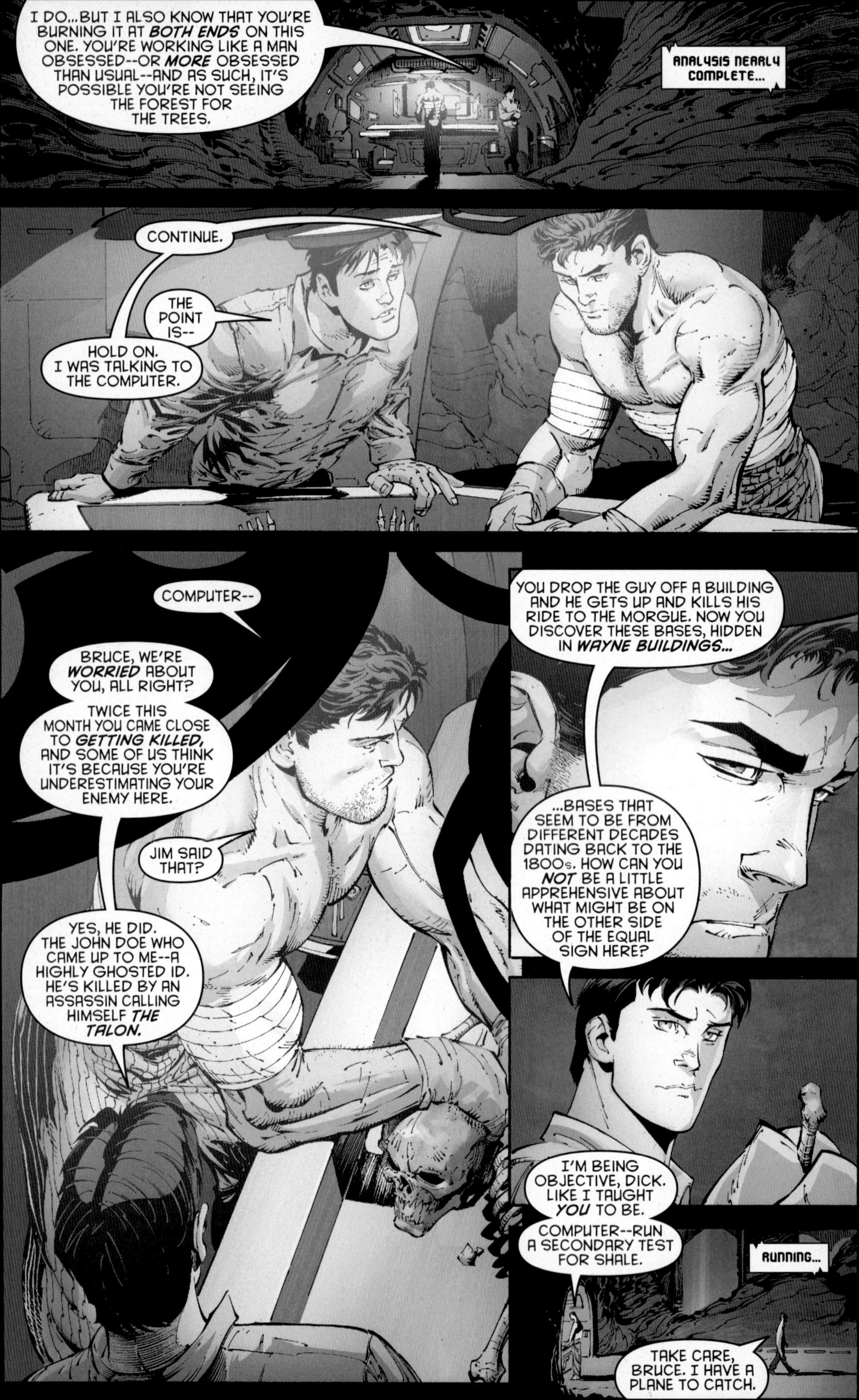
I DO...BUT I ALSO KNOW THAT YOU'RE BURNING IT AT BOTH ENDS ON THIS ONE. YOU'RE WORKING LIKE A MAN OBSESSED--OR MORE OBSESSED THAN USUAL--AND AS SUCH, IT'S POSSIBLE YOU'RE NOT SEEING THE FOREST FOR THE TREES.
ANALYSIS NEARLY COMPLETE...
CONTINUE.
THE POINT IS--
HOLD ON. I WAS TALKING TO THE COMPUTER.
COMPUTER--
BRUCE, WE'RE WORRIED ABOUT YOU, ALL RIGHT?
TWICE THIS MONTH YOU CAME CLOSE TO GETTING KILLED, AND SOME OF US THINK IT'S BECAUSE YOU'RE UNDERESTIMATING YOUR ENEMY HERE.
JIM SAID THAT?
YES, HE DID. THE JOHN DOE WHO CAME UP TO ME--A HIGHLY GHOSTED ID. HE'S KILLED BY AN ASSASSIN CALLING HIMSELF THE TALON.
YOU DROP THE GUY OFF A BUILDING AND HE GETS UP AND KILLS HIS RIDE TO THE MORGUE. NOW YOU DISCOVER THESE BASES, HIDDEN IN WAYNE BUILDINGS...
...BASES THAT SEEM TO BE FROM DIFFERENT DECADES DATING BACK TO THE 1800s. HOW CAN YOU NOT BE A LITTLE APPREHENSIVE ABOUT WHAT MIGHT BE ON THE OTHER SIDE OF THE EQUAL SIGN HERE?
I'M BEING OBJECTIVE, DICK. LIKE I TAUGHT YOU TO BE.
COMPUTER--RUN A SECONDARY TEST FOR SHALE.
RUNNING...
TAKE CARE, BRUCE. I HAVE A PLANE TO CATCH.

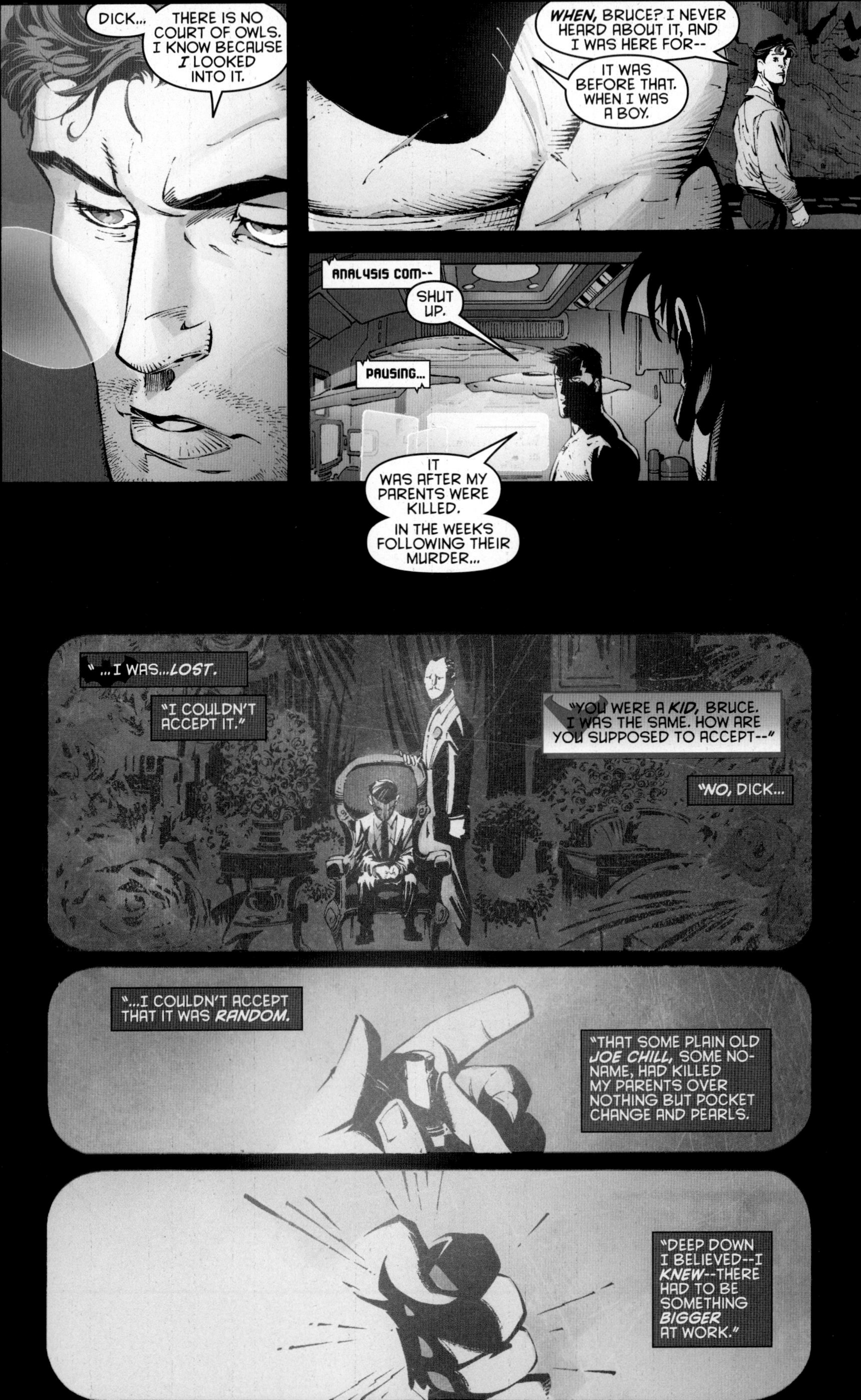
DICK...
THERE IS NO COURT OF OWLS. I KNOW BECAUSE I LOOKED INTO IT.
WHEN, BRUCE? I NEVER HEARD ABOUT IT, AND I WAS HERE FOR--
IT WAS BEFORE THAT. WHEN I WAS A BOY.
ANALYSIS COM--
SHUT UP.
PAUSING...
IT WAS AFTER MY PARENTS WERE KILLED.
IN THE WEEKS FOLLOWING THEIR MURDER...
"...I WAS...LOST.
"I COULDN'T ACCEPT IT."
"YOU WERE A KID, BRUCE. I WAS THE SAME. HOW ARE YOU SUPPOSED TO ACCEPT--"
"NO, DICK...
"...I COULDN'T ACCEPT THAT IT WAS RANDOM.
"THAT SOME PLAIN OLD JOE CHILL, SOME NO-NAME, HAD KILLED MY PARENTS OVER NOTHING BUT POCKET CHANGE AND PEARLS.
"DEEP DOWN I BELIEVED--I KNEW--THERE HAD TO BE SOMETHING BIGGER AT WORK."

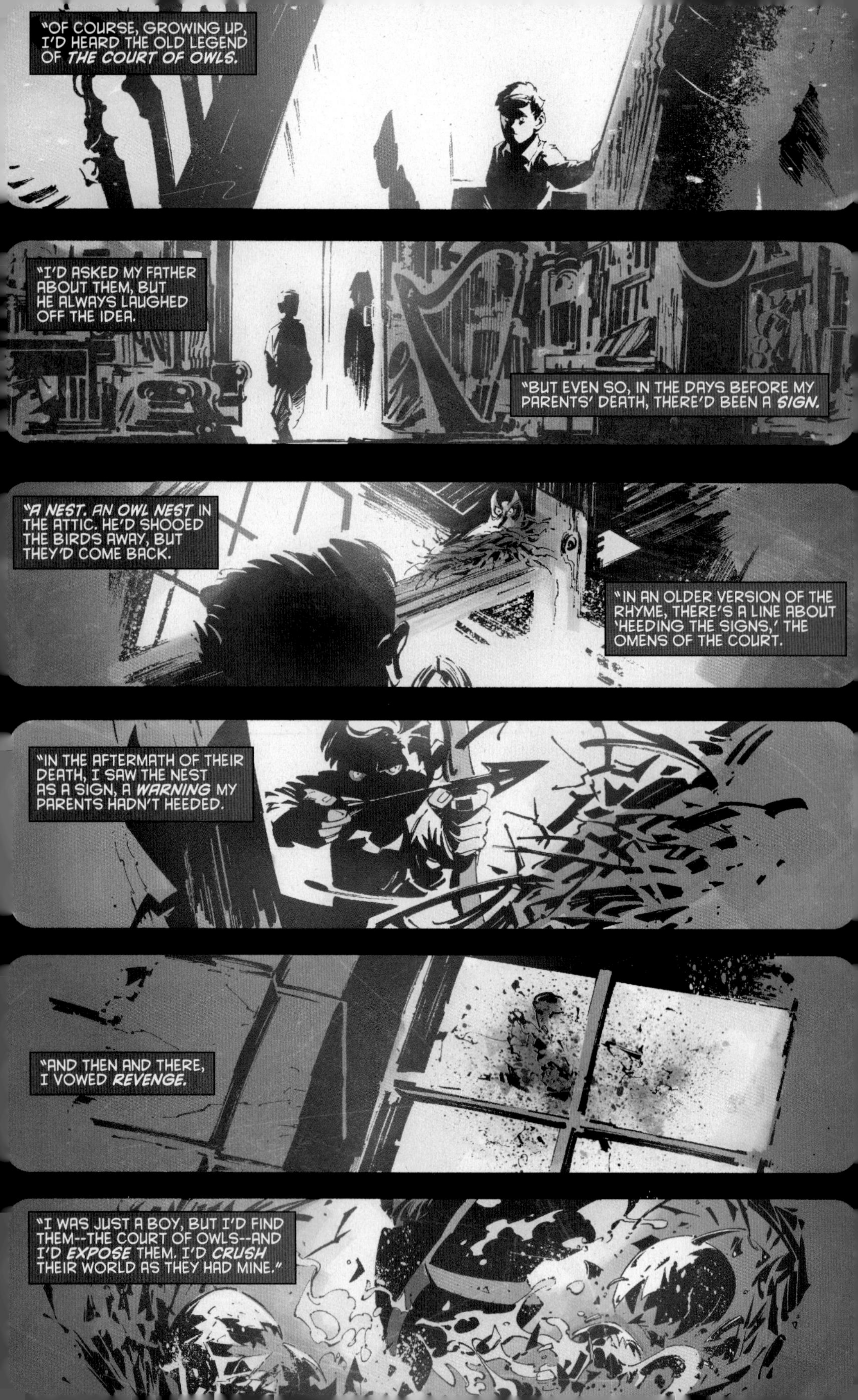
"OF COURSE, GROWING UP, I'D HEARD THE OLD LEGEND OF *THE COURT OF OWLS.*
"I'D ASKED MY FATHER ABOUT THEM, BUT HE ALWAYS LAUGHED OFF THE IDEA.
"BUT EVEN SO, IN THE DAYS BEFORE MY PARENTS' DEATH, THERE'D BEEN A *SIGN.*
"*A NEST. AN OWL NEST* IN THE ATTIC. HE'D SHOOED THE BIRDS AWAY, BUT THEY'D COME BACK.
"IN AN OLDER VERSION OF THE RHYME, THERE'S A LINE ABOUT 'HEEDING THE SIGNS,' THE OMENS OF THE COURT.
"IN THE AFTERMATH OF THEIR DEATH, I SAW THE NEST AS A SIGN, A *WARNING* MY PARENTS HADN'T HEEDED.
"AND THEN AND THERE, I VOWED *REVENGE.*
"I WAS JUST A BOY, BUT I'D FIND THEM--THE COURT OF OWLS--AND I'D *EXPOSE* THEM. I'D *CRUSH* THEIR WORLD AS THEY HAD MINE."

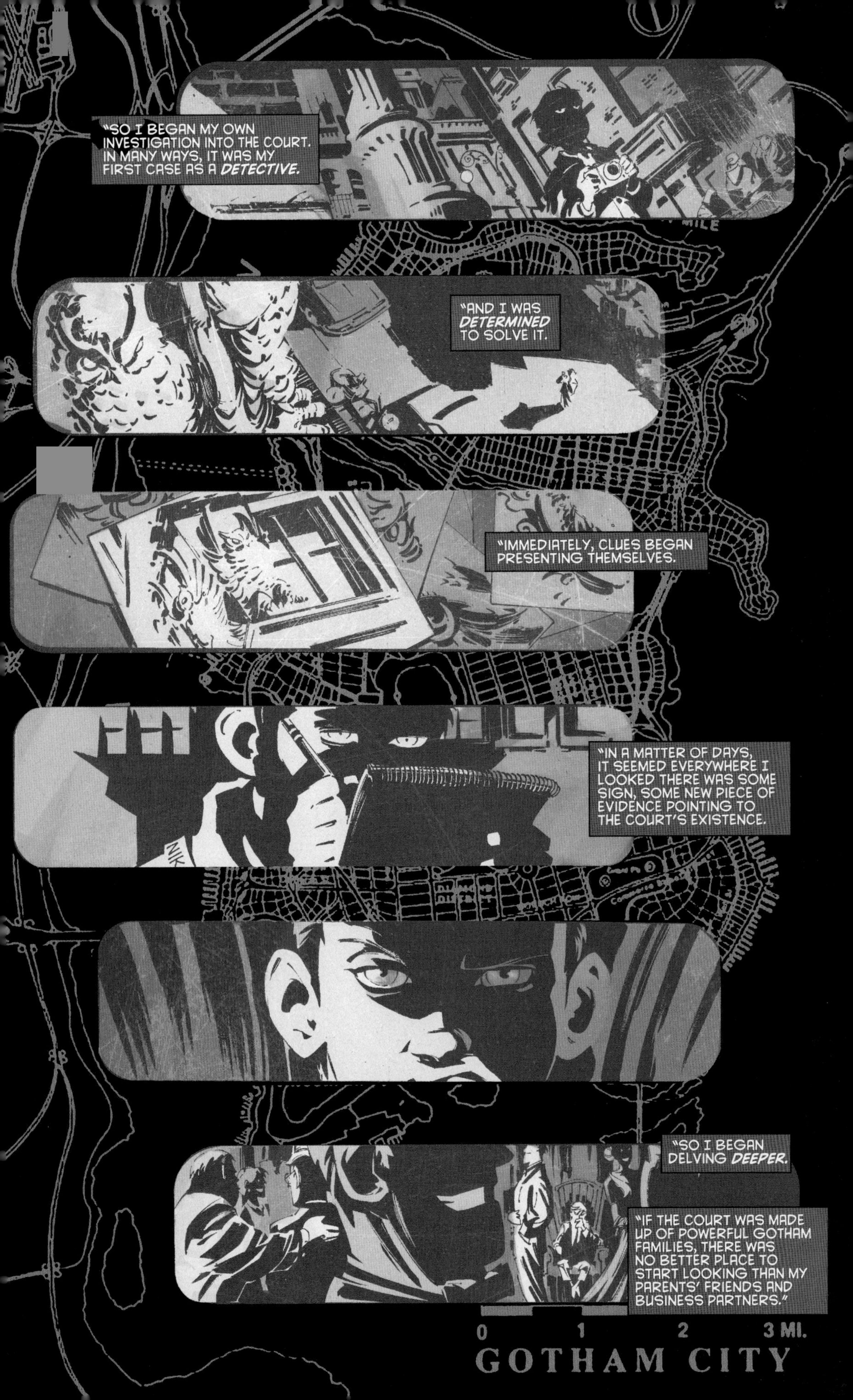
"SO I BEGAN MY OWN INVESTIGATION INTO THE COURT. IN MANY WAYS, IT WAS MY FIRST CASE AS A *DETECTIVE.*
"AND I WAS *DETERMINED* TO SOLVE IT.
"IMMEDIATELY, CLUES BEGAN PRESENTING THEMSELVES.
"IN A MATTER OF DAYS, IT SEEMED EVERYWHERE I LOOKED THERE WAS SOME SIGN, SOME NEW PIECE OF EVIDENCE POINTING TO THE COURT'S EXISTENCE.
"SO I BEGAN DELVING *DEEPER.*
"IF THE COURT WAS MADE UP OF POWERFUL GOTHAM FAMILIES, THERE WAS NO BETTER PLACE TO START LOOKING THAN MY PARENTS' FRIENDS AND BUSINESS PARTNERS."
0 1 2 3 MI.
GOTHAM CITY

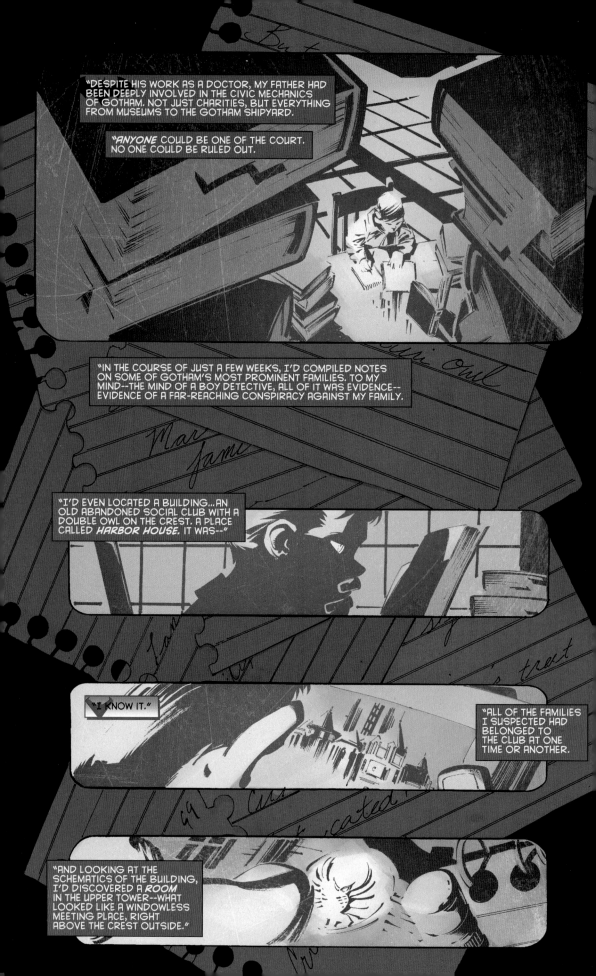

"DESPITE HIS WORK AS A DOCTOR, MY FATHER HAD BEEN DEEPLY INVOLVED IN THE CIVIC MECHANICS OF GOTHAM. NOT JUST CHARITIES, BUT EVERYTHING FROM MUSEUMS TO THE GOTHAM SHIPYARD.

"*ANYONE* COULD BE ONE OF THE COURT. NO ONE COULD BE RULED OUT.

"IN THE COURSE OF JUST A FEW WEEKS, I'D COMPILED NOTES ON SOME OF GOTHAM'S MOST PROMINENT FAMILIES. TO MY MIND--THE MIND OF A BOY DETECTIVE, ALL OF IT WAS EVIDENCE-- EVIDENCE OF A FAR-REACHING CONSPIRACY AGAINST MY FAMILY.

"I'D EVEN LOCATED A BUILDING...AN OLD ABANDONED SOCIAL CLUB WITH A DOUBLE OWL ON THE CREST. A PLACE CALLED *HARBOR HOUSE*. IT WAS--

"I KNOW IT."

"ALL OF THE FAMILIES I SUSPECTED HAD BELONGED TO THE CLUB AT ONE TIME OR ANOTHER.

"AND LOOKING AT THE SCHEMATICS OF THE BUILDING, I'D DISCOVERED A *ROOM* IN THE UPPER TOWER--WHAT LOOKED LIKE A WINDOWLESS MEETING PLACE, RIGHT ABOVE THE CREST OUTSIDE."

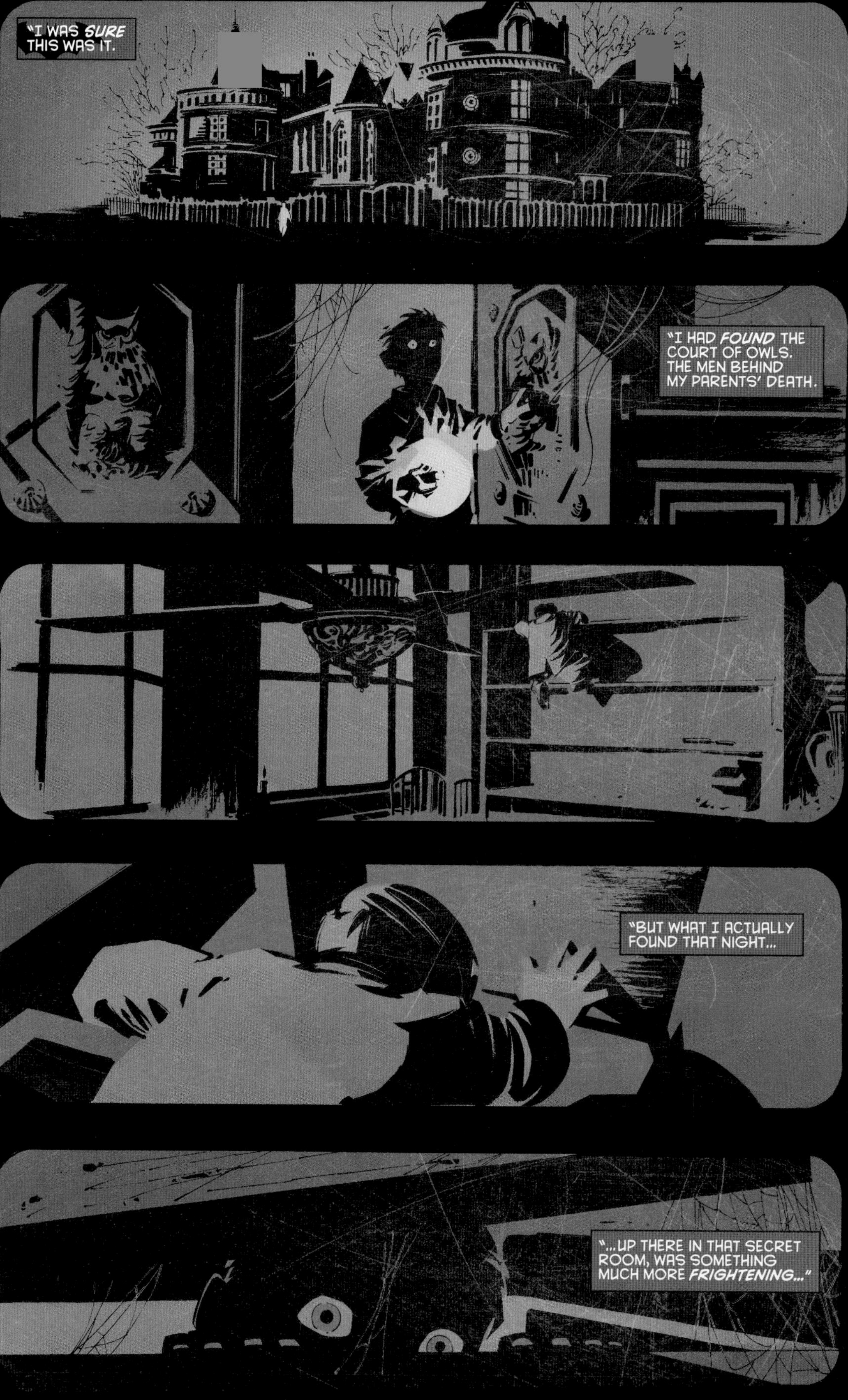
"I WAS SURE THIS WAS IT.
"I HAD FOUND THE COURT OF OWLS. THE MEN BEHIND MY PARENTS' DEATH.
"BUT WHAT I ACTUALLY FOUND THAT NIGHT...
"...UP THERE IN THAT SECRET ROOM, WAS SOMETHING MUCH MORE FRIGHTENING..."

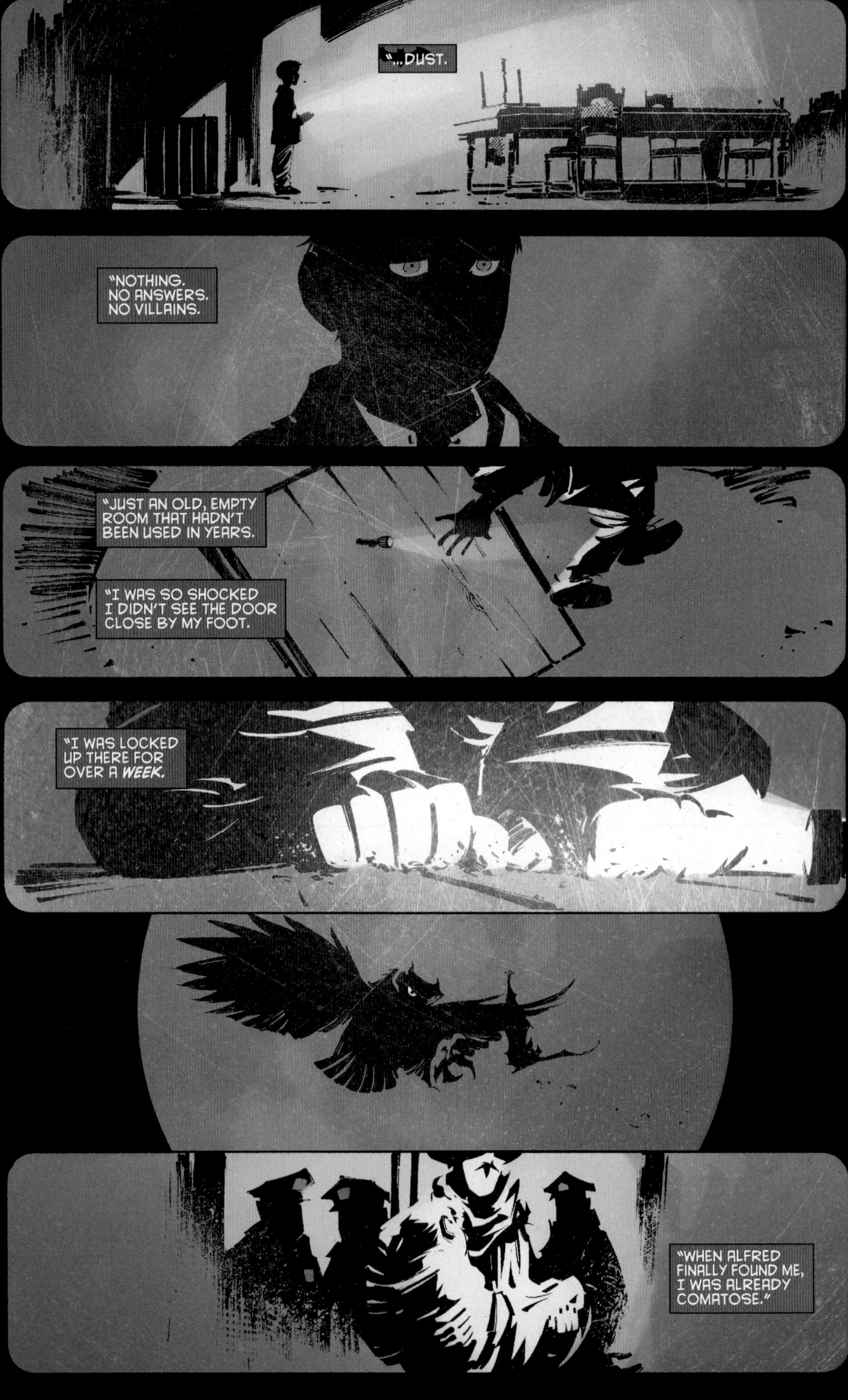
"...DUST.
"NOTHING. NO ANSWERS. NO VILLAINS.
"JUST AN OLD, EMPTY ROOM THAT HADN'T BEEN USED IN YEARS.
"I WAS SO SHOCKED I DIDN'T SEE THE DOOR CLOSE BY MY FOOT.
"I WAS LOCKED UP THERE FOR OVER A *WEEK*.
"WHEN ALFRED FINALLY FOUND ME, I WAS ALREADY COMATOSE."

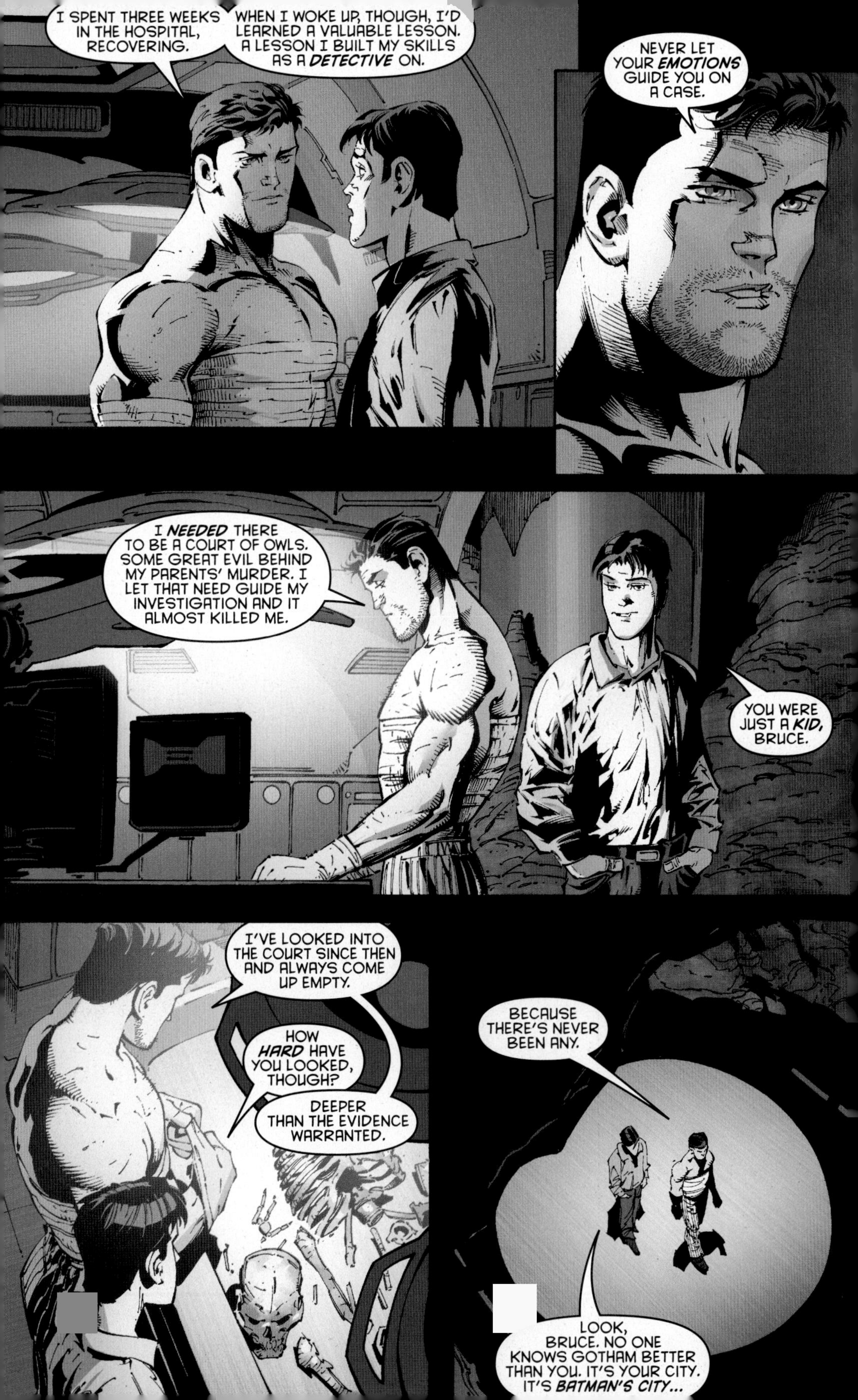
I SPENT THREE WEEKS IN THE HOSPITAL, RECOVERING.
WHEN I WOKE UP, THOUGH, I'D LEARNED A VALUABLE LESSON. A LESSON I BUILT MY SKILLS AS A DETECTIVE ON.
NEVER LET YOUR EMOTIONS GUIDE YOU ON A CASE.
I NEEDED THERE TO BE A COURT OF OWLS. SOME GREAT EVIL BEHIND MY PARENTS' MURDER. I LET THAT NEED GUIDE MY INVESTIGATION AND IT ALMOST KILLED ME.
YOU WERE JUST A KID, BRUCE.
I'VE LOOKED INTO THE COURT SINCE THEN AND ALWAYS COME UP EMPTY.
HOW HARD HAVE YOU LOOKED, THOUGH?
DEEPER THAN THE EVIDENCE WARRANTED.
BECAUSE THERE'S NEVER BEEN ANY.
LOOK, BRUCE. NO ONE KNOWS GOTHAM BETTER THAN YOU. IT'S YOUR CITY. IT'S BATMAN'S CITY...

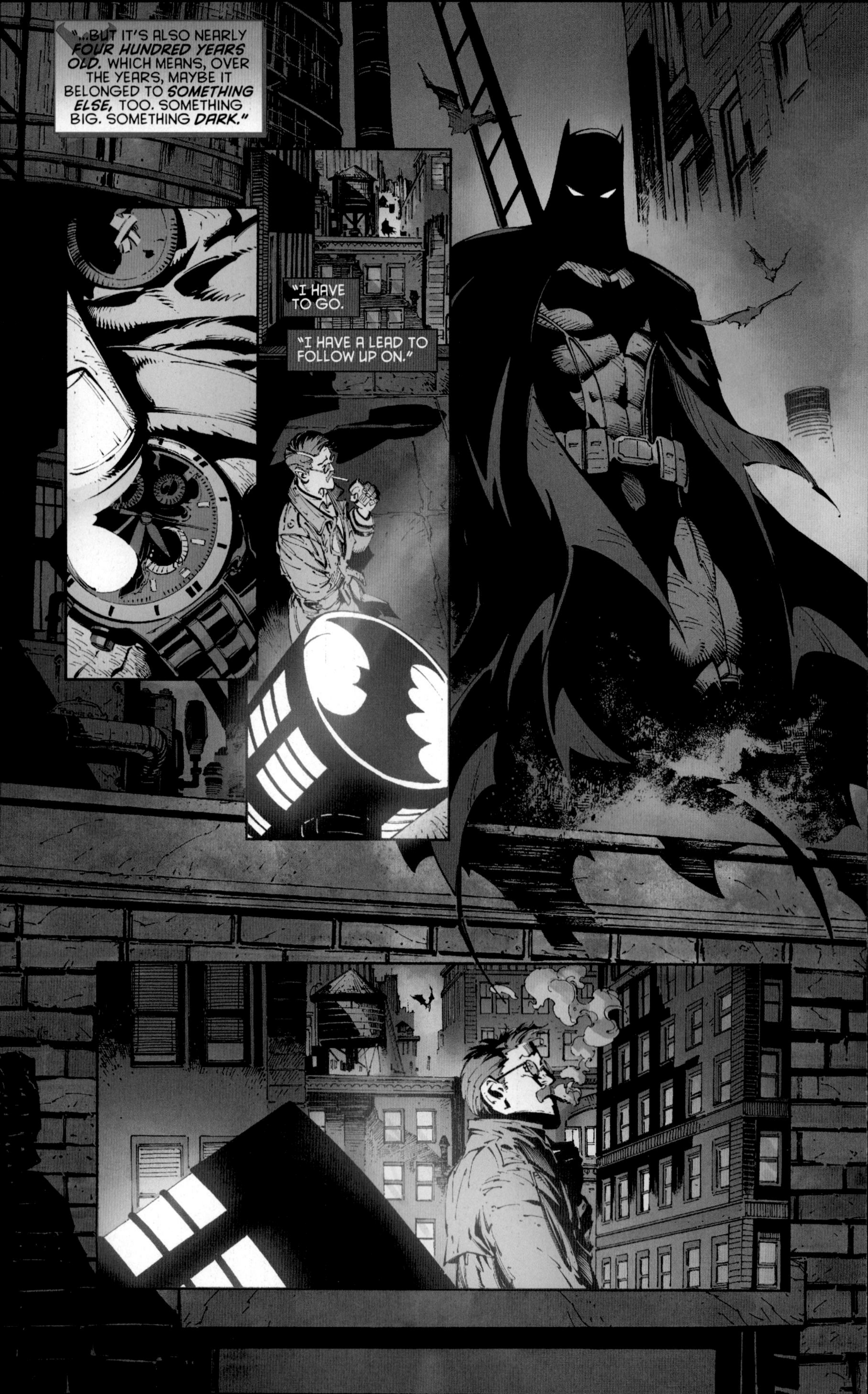
"...BUT IT'S ALSO NEARLY FOUR HUNDRED YEARS OLD. WHICH MEANS, OVER THE YEARS, MAYBE IT BELONGED TO SOMETHING ELSE, TOO. SOMETHING BIG. SOMETHING DARK."
"I HAVE TO GO.
"I HAVE A LEAD TO FOLLOW UP ON."

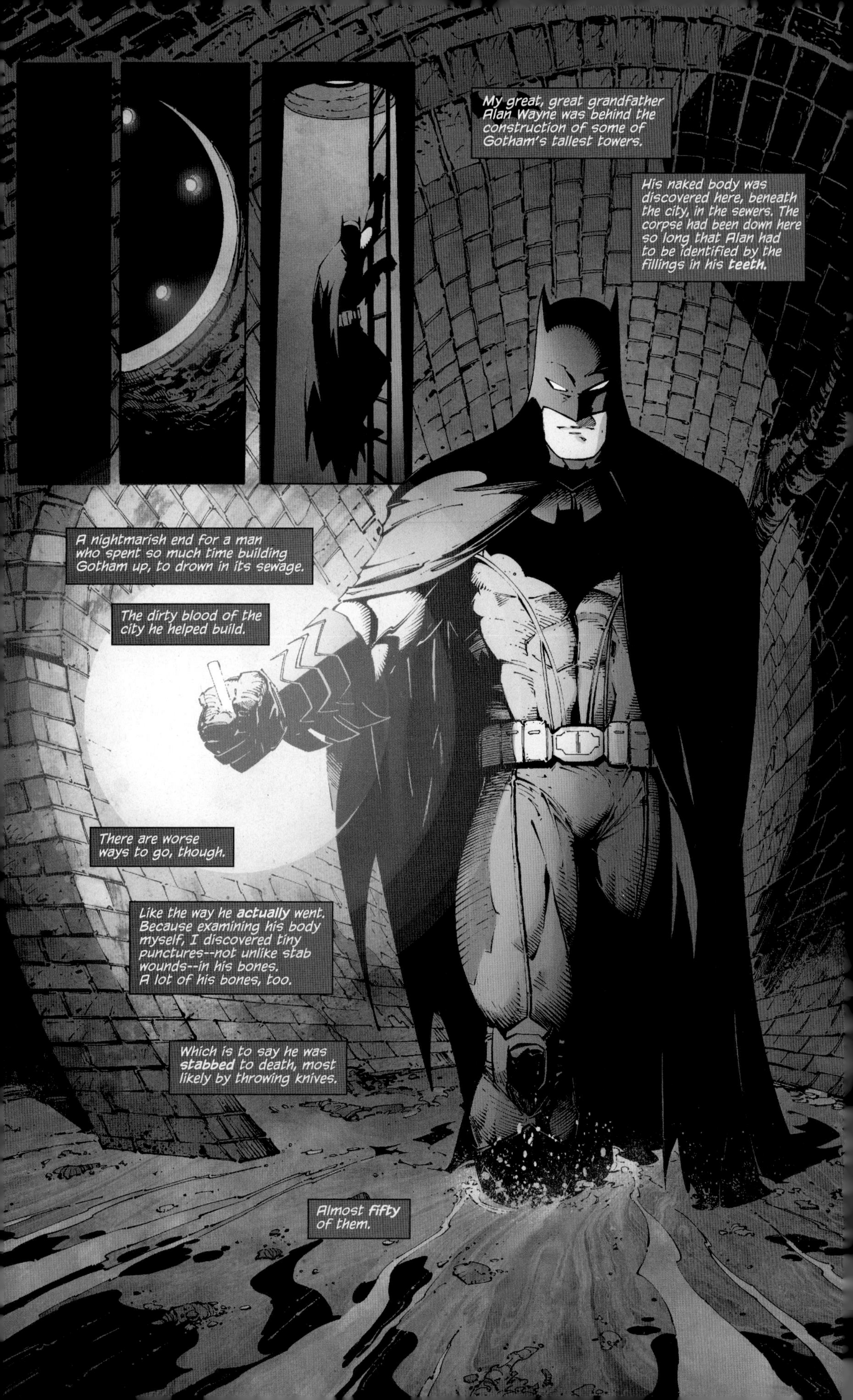

My great, great grandfather Alan Wayne was behind the construction of some of Gotham's tallest towers.
His naked body was discovered here, beneath the city, in the sewers. The corpse had been down here so long that Alan had to be identified by the fillings in his **teeth.**
A nightmarish end for a man who spent so much time building Gotham up, to drown in its sewage.
The dirty blood of the city he helped build.
There are worse ways to go, though.
Like the way he **actually** went. Because examining his body myself, I discovered tiny punctures--not unlike stab wounds--in his bones. A lot of his bones, too.
Which is to say he was **stabbed** to death, most likely by throwing knives.
Almost **fifty** of them.

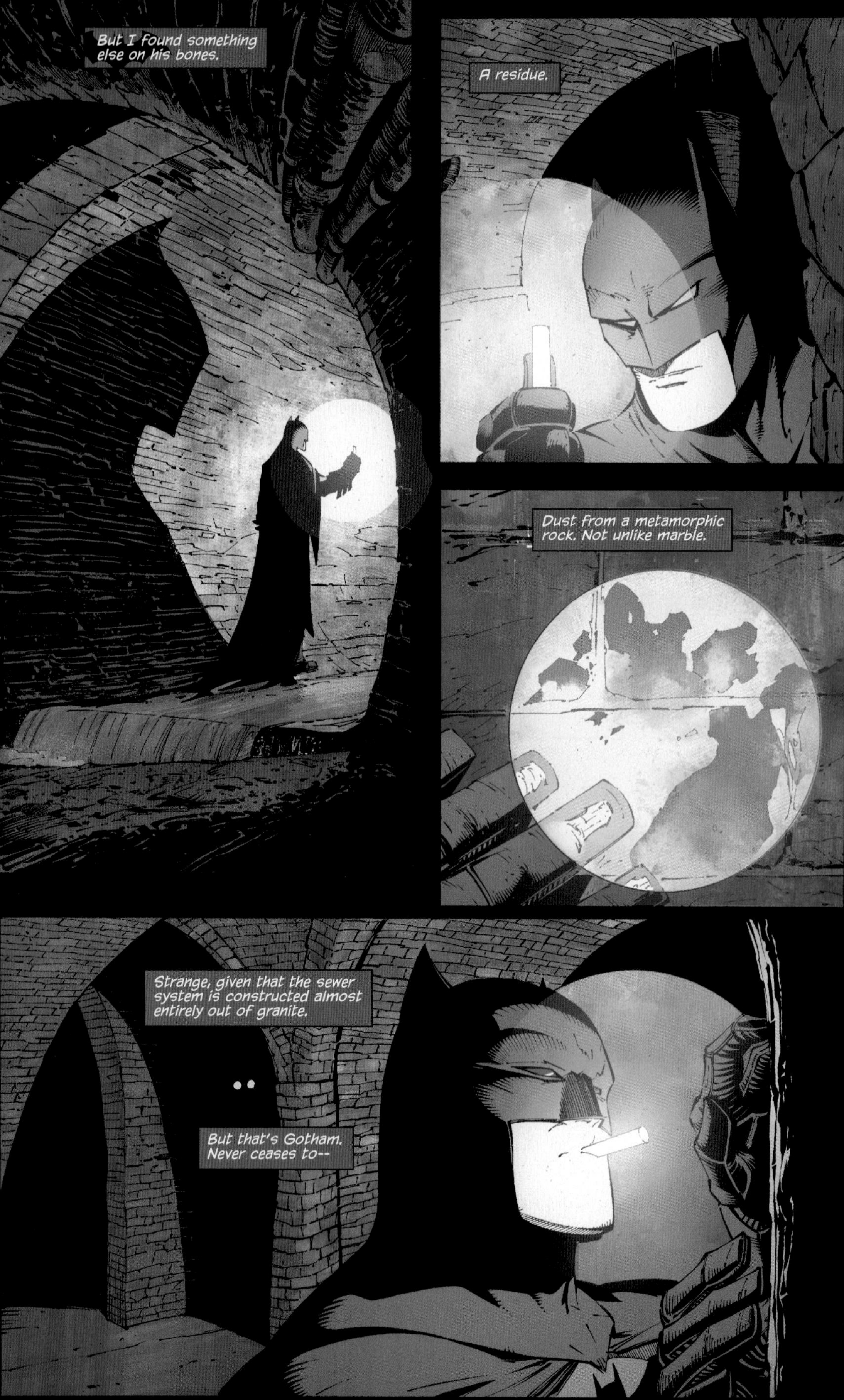
But I found something else on his bones.
A residue.
Dust from a metamorphic rock. Not unlike marble.
Strange, given that the sewer system is constructed almost entirely out of granite.
But that's Gotham. Never ceases to--

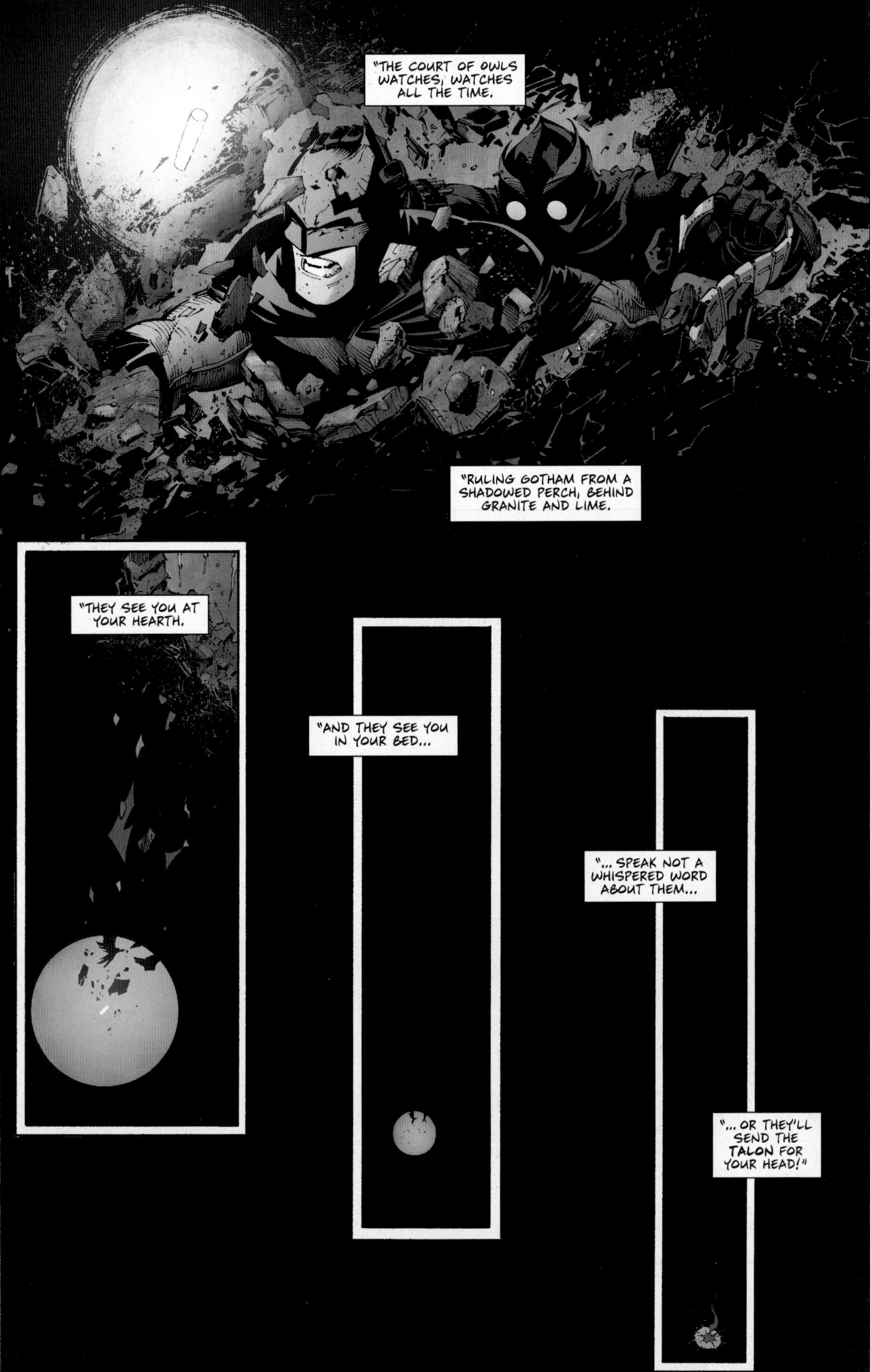
"THE COURT OF OWLS WATCHES, WATCHES ALL THE TIME.
"RULING GOTHAM FROM A SHADOWED PERCH, BEHIND GRANITE AND LIME.
"THEY SEE YOU AT YOUR HEARTH.
"AND THEY SEE YOU IN YOUR BED...
"... SPEAK NOT A WHISPERED WORD ABOUT THEM...
"... OR THEY'LL SEND THE TALON FOR YOUR HEAD!"

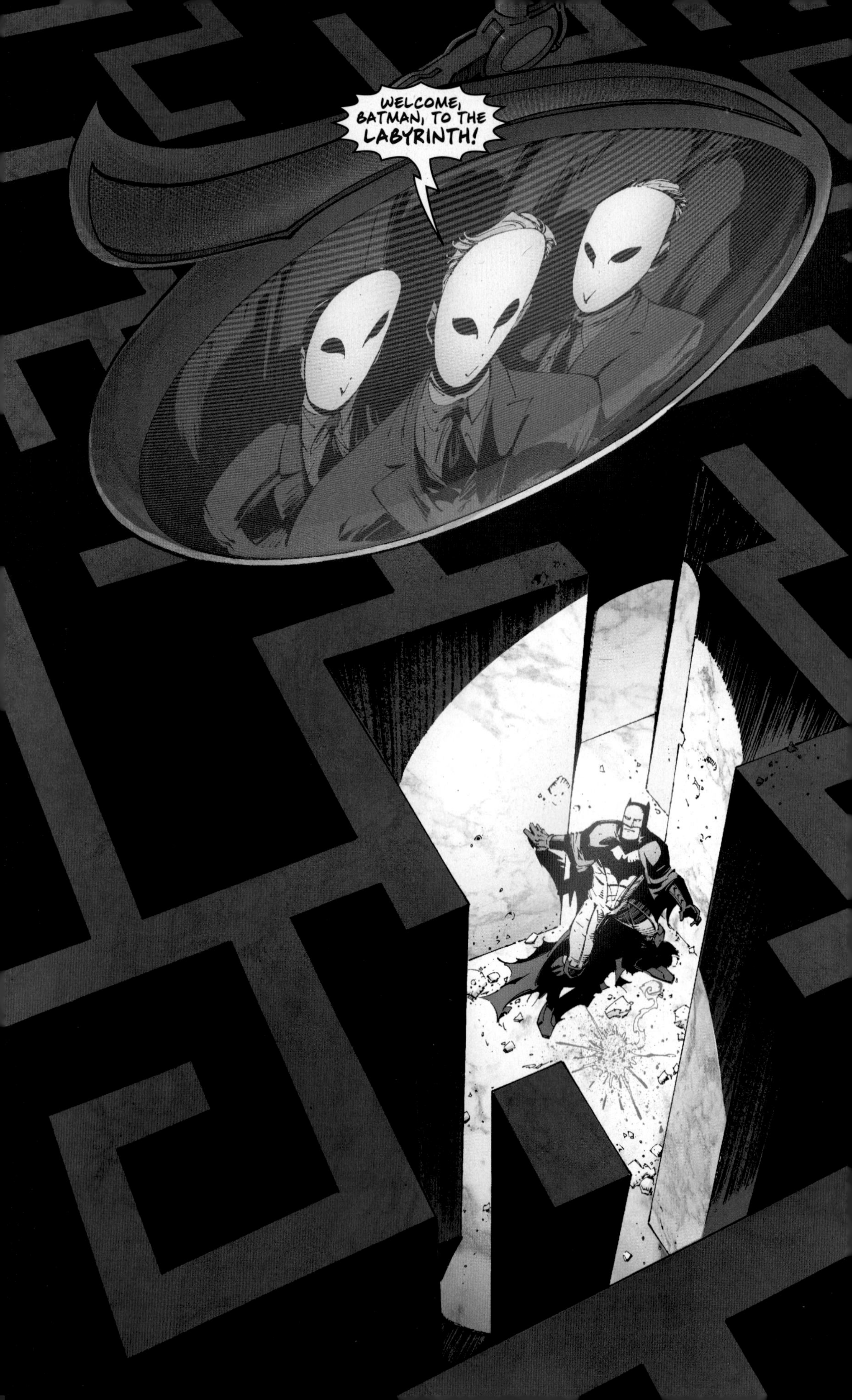
WELCOME, BATMAN, TO THE LABYRINTH!

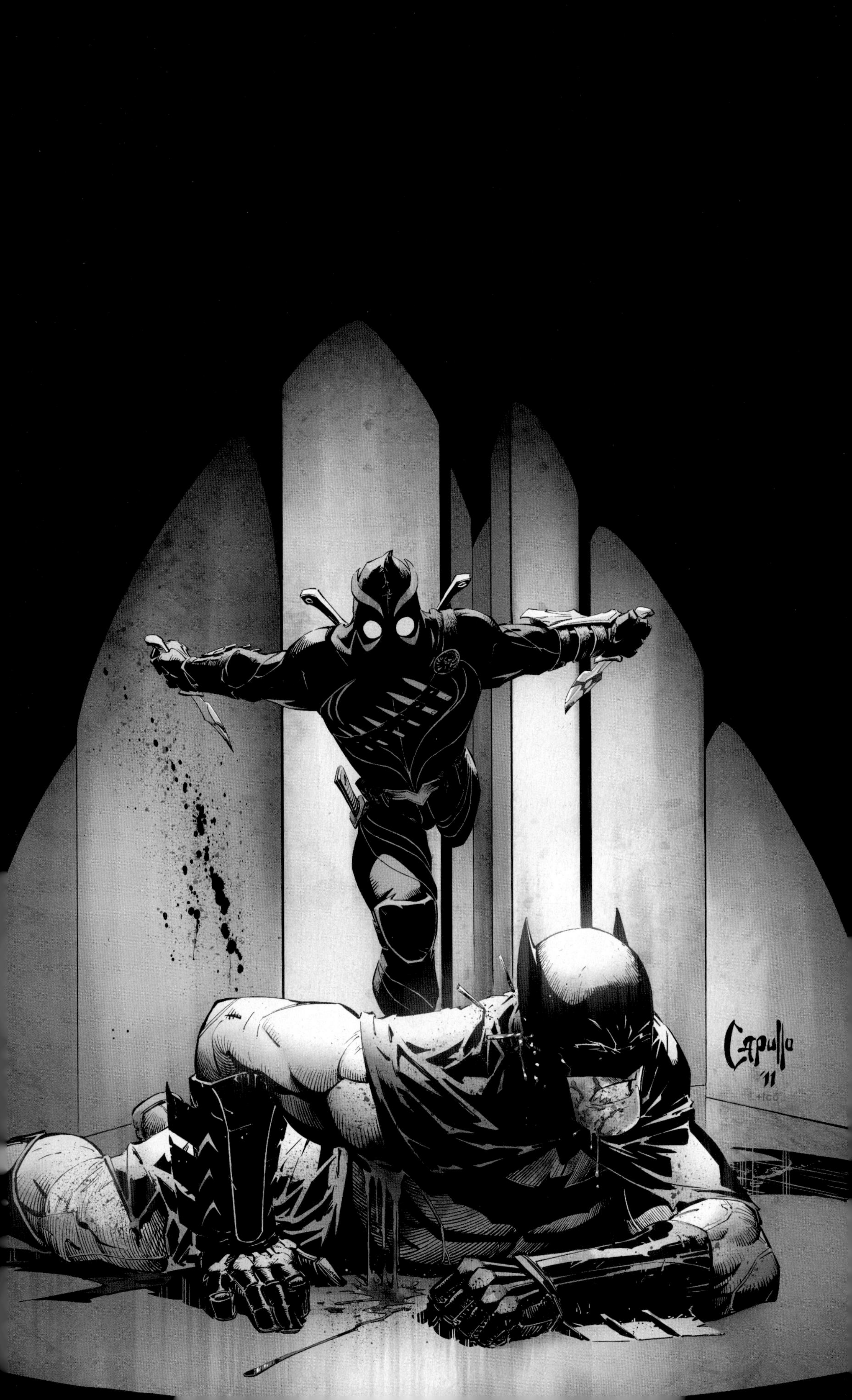

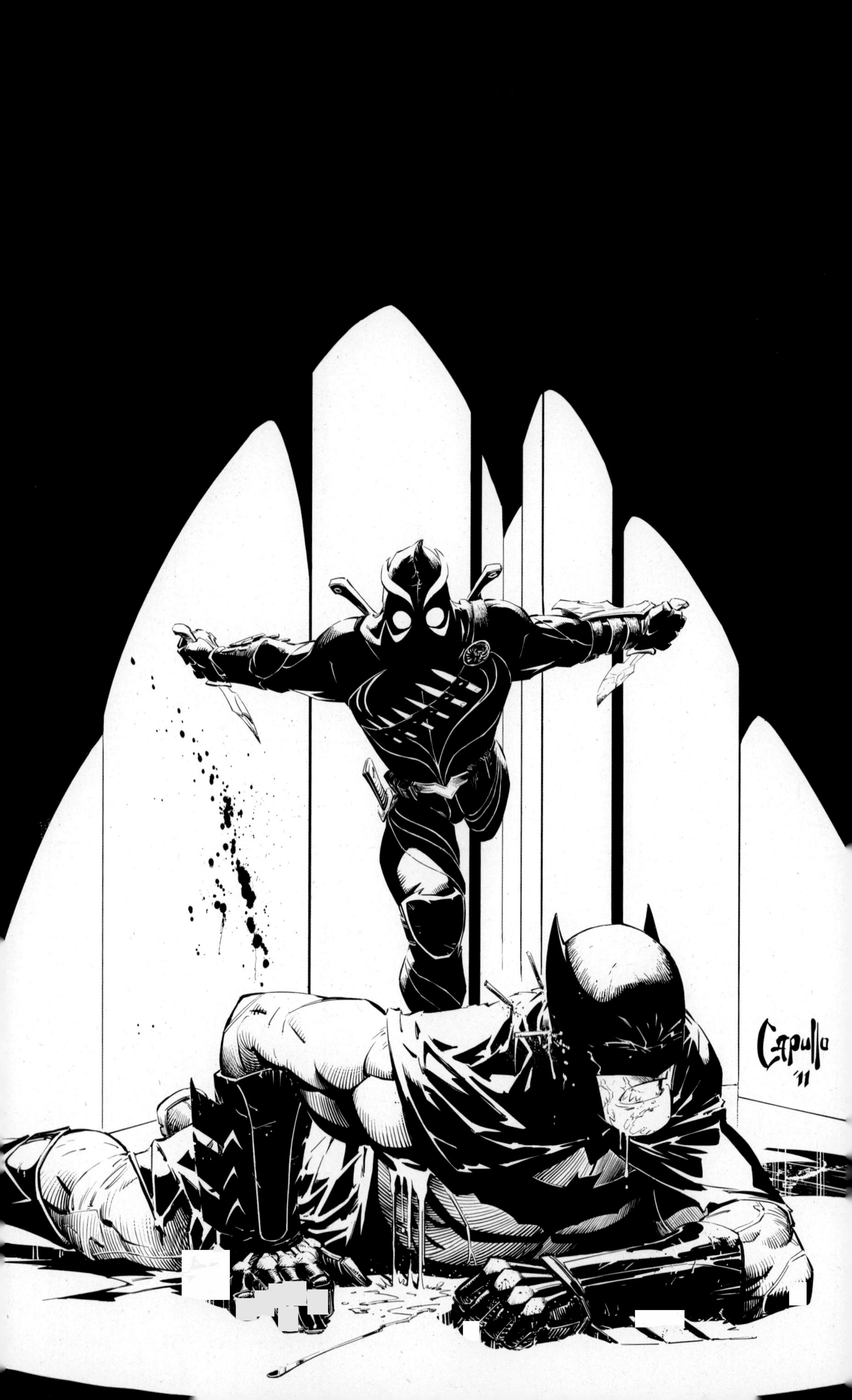
Capullo '11

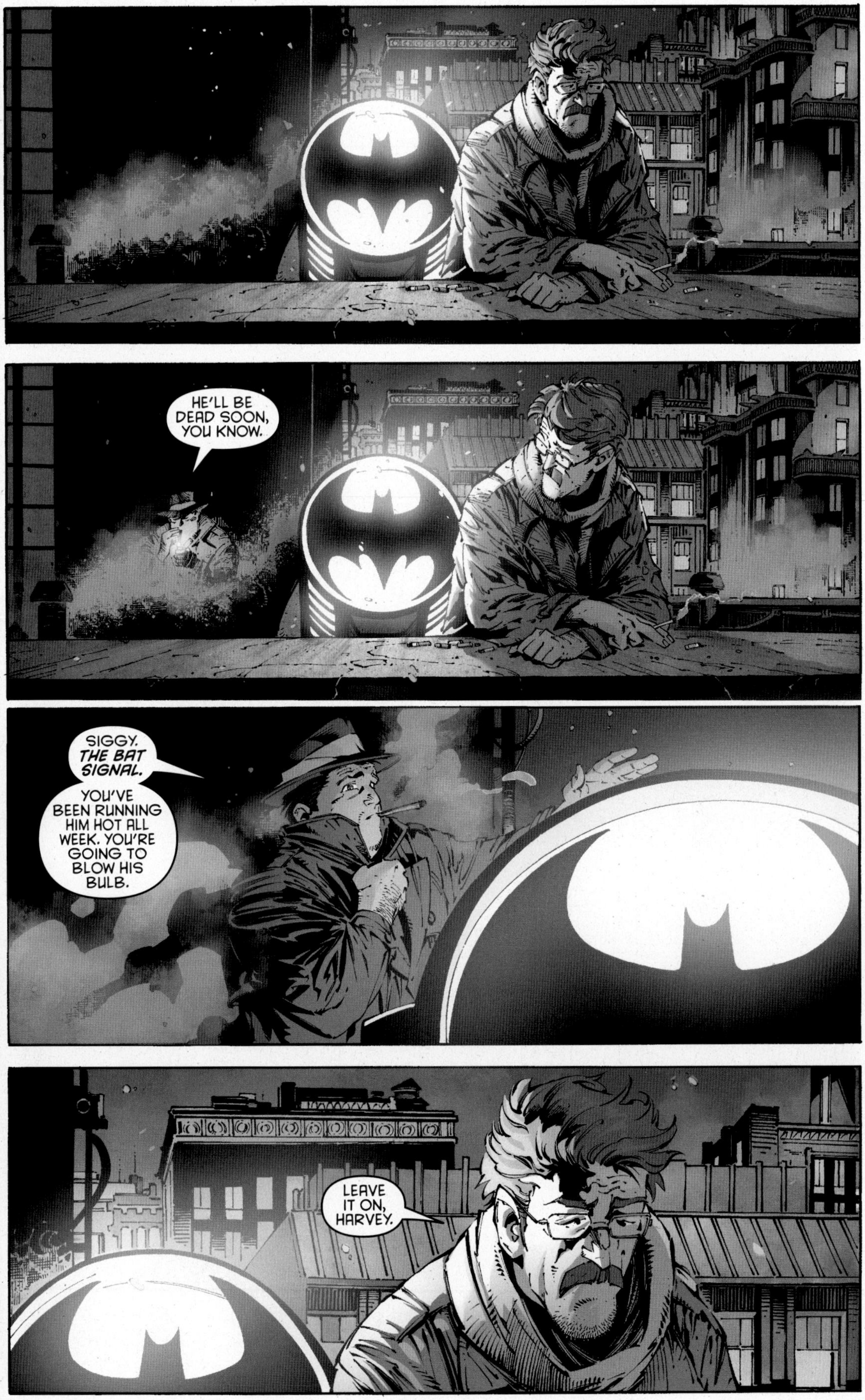
HE'LL BE DEAD SOON, YOU KNOW.
SIGGY. *THE BAT SIGNAL.*
YOU'VE BEEN RUNNING HIM HOT ALL WEEK. YOU'RE GOING TO BLOW HIS BULB.
LEAVE IT ON, HARVEY.

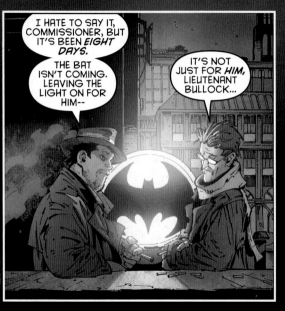

I HATE TO SAY IT, COMMISSIONER, BUT IT'S BEEN *EIGHT DAYS.*

THE BAT ISN'T COMING. LEAVING THE LIGHT ON FOR HIM--

IT'S NOT JUST FOR *HIM,* LIEUTENANT BULLOCK...

"...IT'S FOR THE SCUM WHO THINK GOTHAM'S A DAMN *PLAYGROUND* NOW.

"THE ONES WHO'RE *HURTING.*

NO TRANSMISSION DETECTABLE.

"BECAUSE THEY *KNOW* HIM, THE MAN UNDERNEATH THAT MASK. THE MAN MISSING RIGHT NOW.

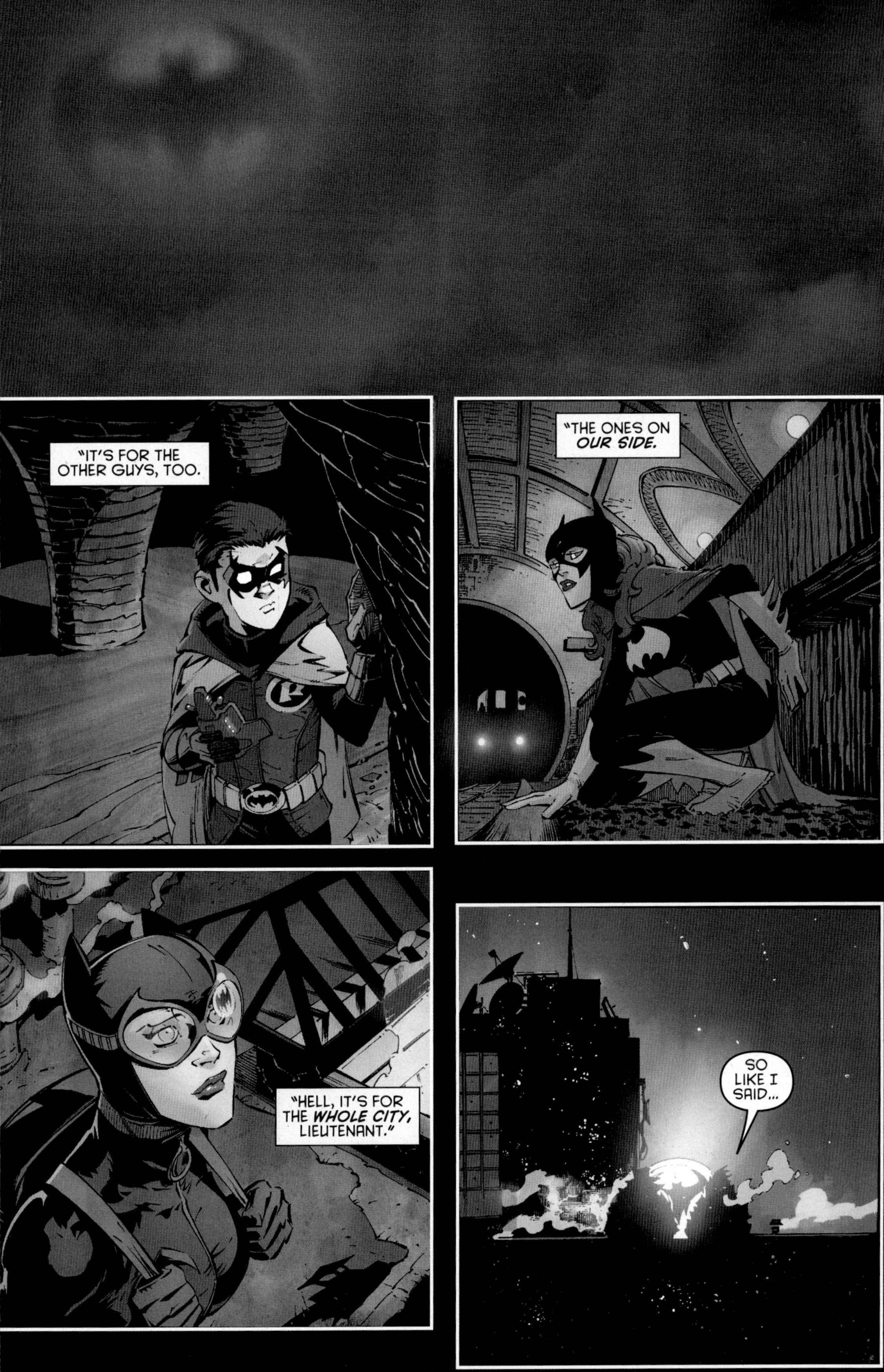
"IT'S FOR THE OTHER GUYS, TOO.
"THE ONES ON OUR SIDE.
"HELL, IT'S FOR THE WHOLE CITY, LIEUTENANT."
SO LIKE I SAID...

They want me to come out of the dark... but I won't.

I won't.

I'll stay here.

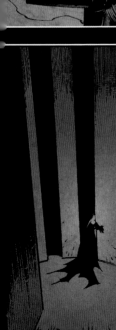

Where it's safe.

Safe from them...

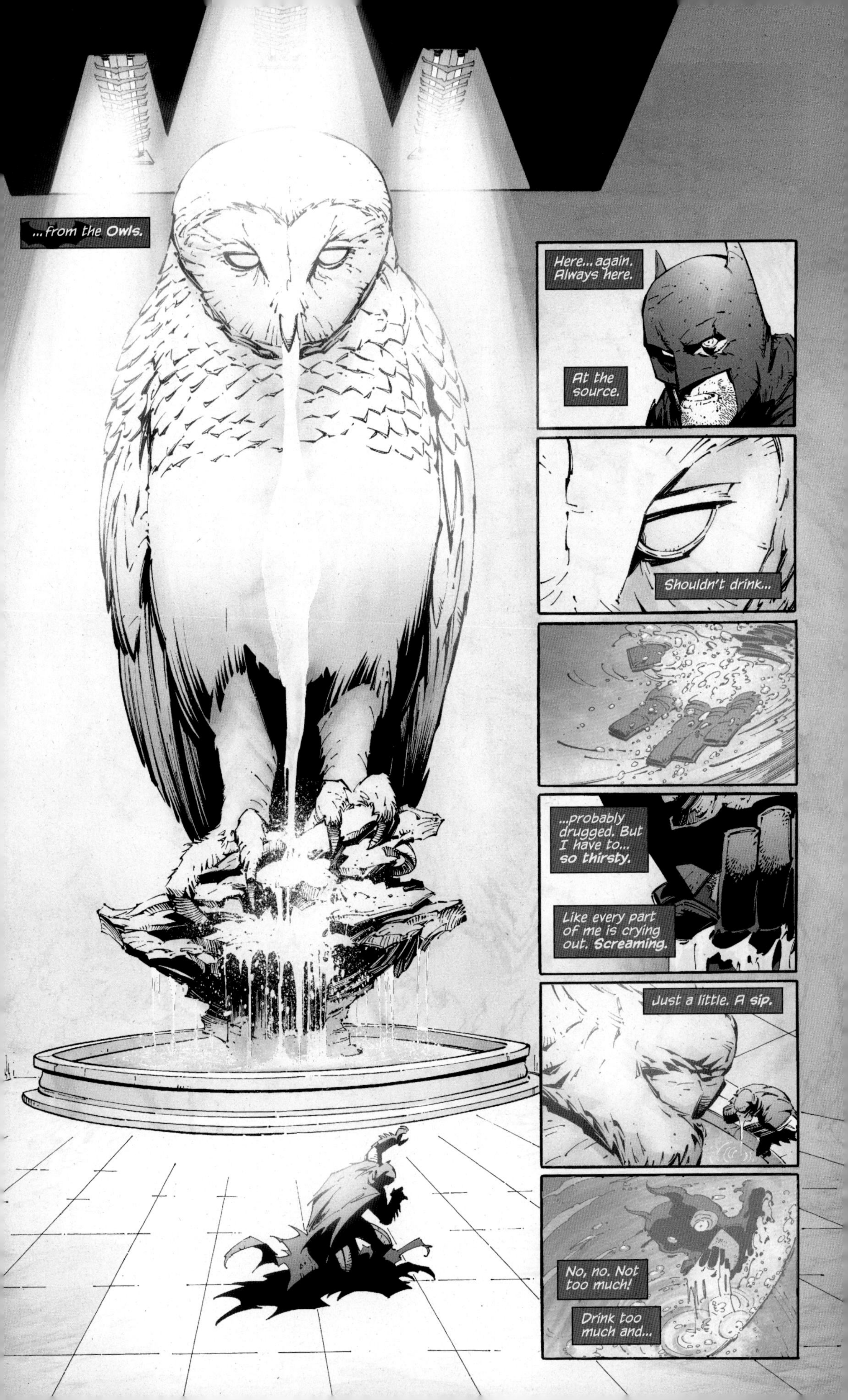
...from the Owls.
Here... again. Always here.
At the source.
Shouldn't drink...
...probably drugged. But I have to... so thirsty.
Like every part of me is crying out. Screaming.
Just a little. A sip.
No, no. Not too much!
Drink too much and...

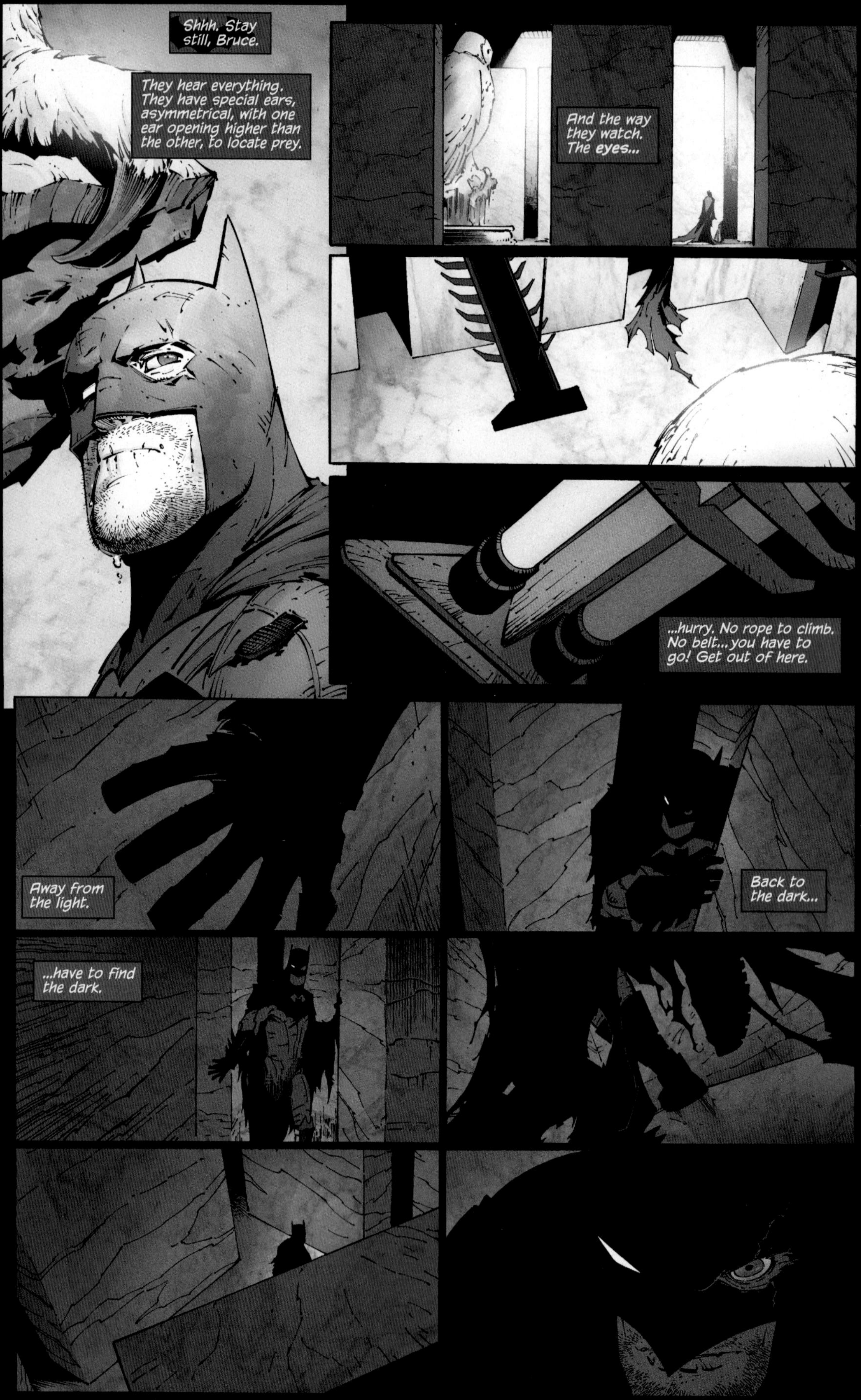
Shhh. Stay still, Bruce.
They hear everything. They have special ears, asymmetrical, with one ear opening higher than the other, to locate prey.
And the way they watch. The eyes...
...hurry. No rope to climb. No belt...you have to go! Get out of here.
Away from the light.
Back to the dark...
...have to find the dark.

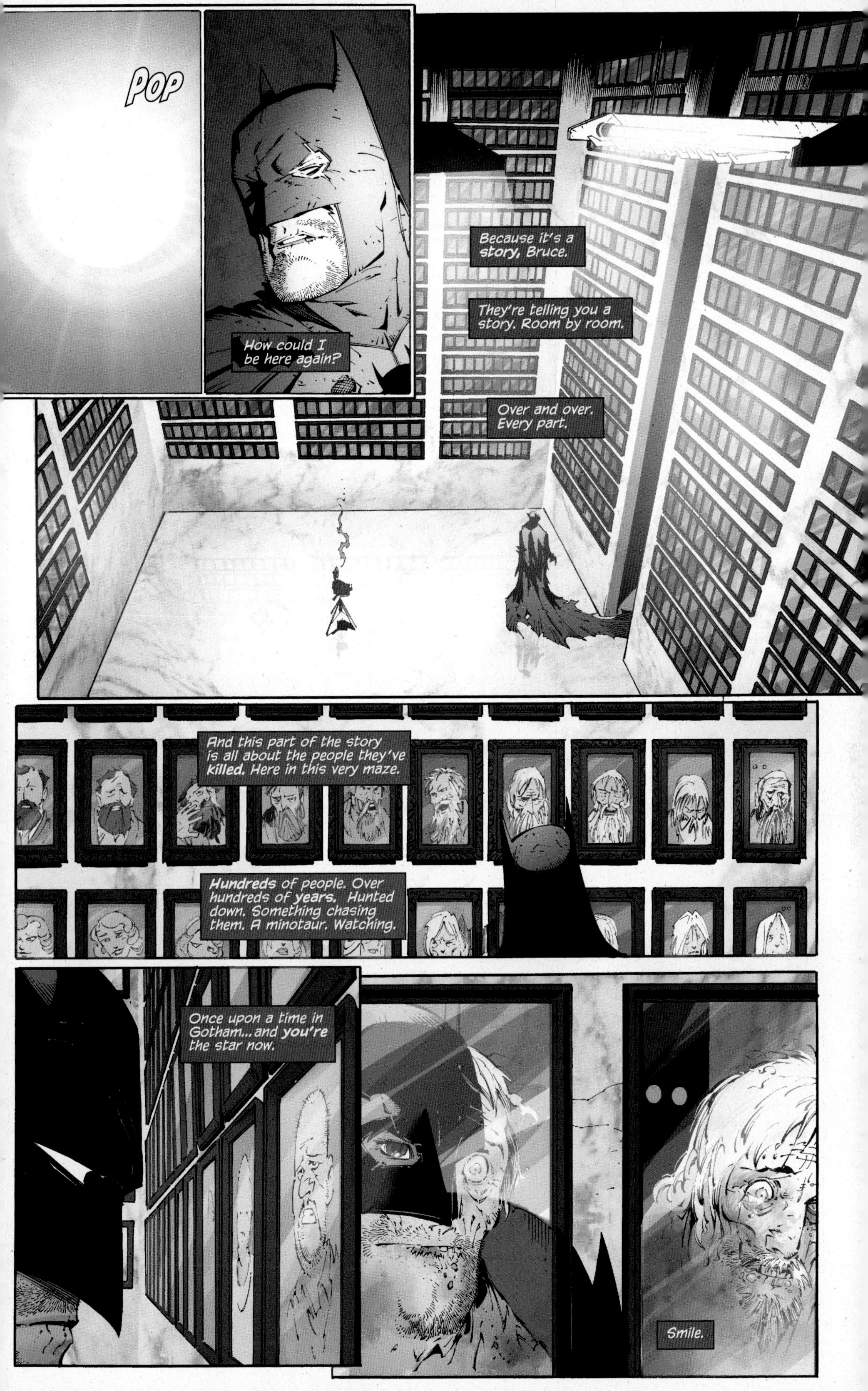
POP
How could I be here again?
Because it's a story, Bruce.
They're telling you a story. Room by room.
Over and over. Every part.
And this part of the story is all about the people they've killed. Here in this very maze.
Hundreds of people. Over hundreds of years. Hunted down. Something chasing them. A minotaur. Watching.
Once upon a time in Gotham...and you're the star now.
Smile.

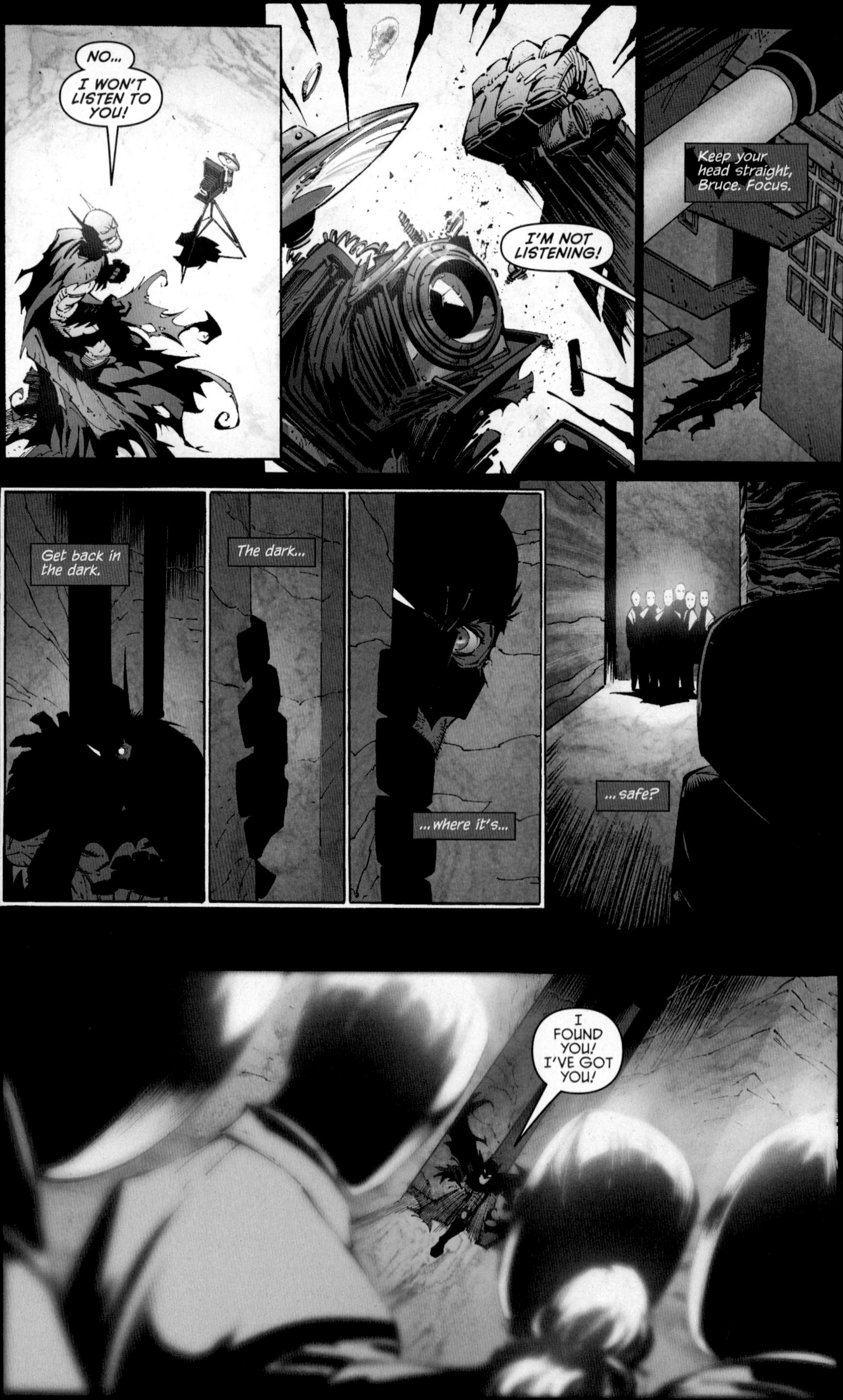
NO... I WON'T LISTEN TO YOU!
I'M NOT LISTENING!
Keep your head straight, Bruce. Focus.
Get back in the dark.
The dark...
...where it's...
...safe?
I FOUND YOU! I'VE GOT YOU!

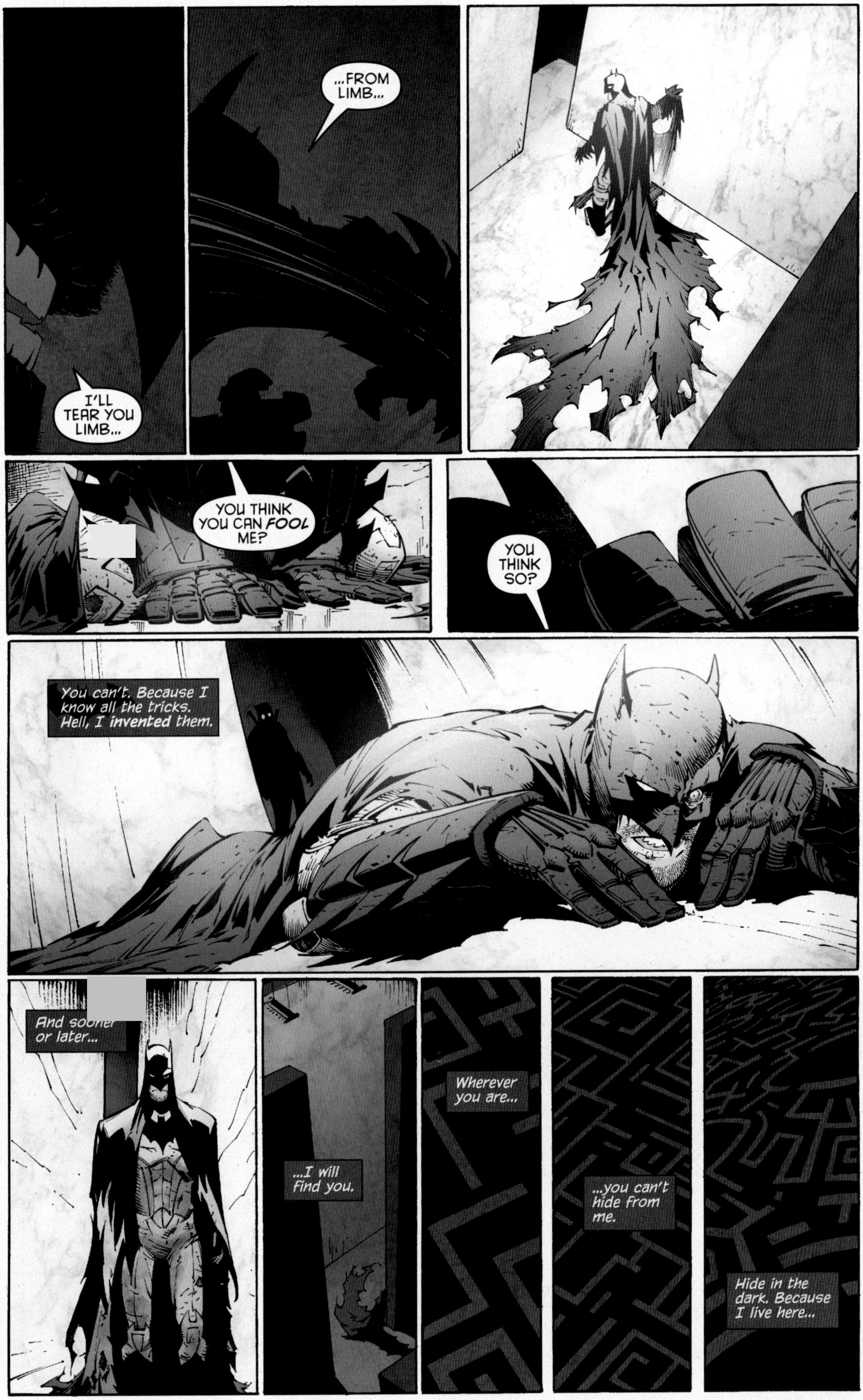
I'LL TEAR YOU LIMB...
...FROM LIMB...
YOU THINK YOU CAN FOOL ME?
YOU THINK SO?
You can't. Because I know all the tricks. Hell, I invented them.
And sooner or later...
...I will find you.
Wherever you are...
...you can't hide from me.
Hide in the dark. Because I live here...

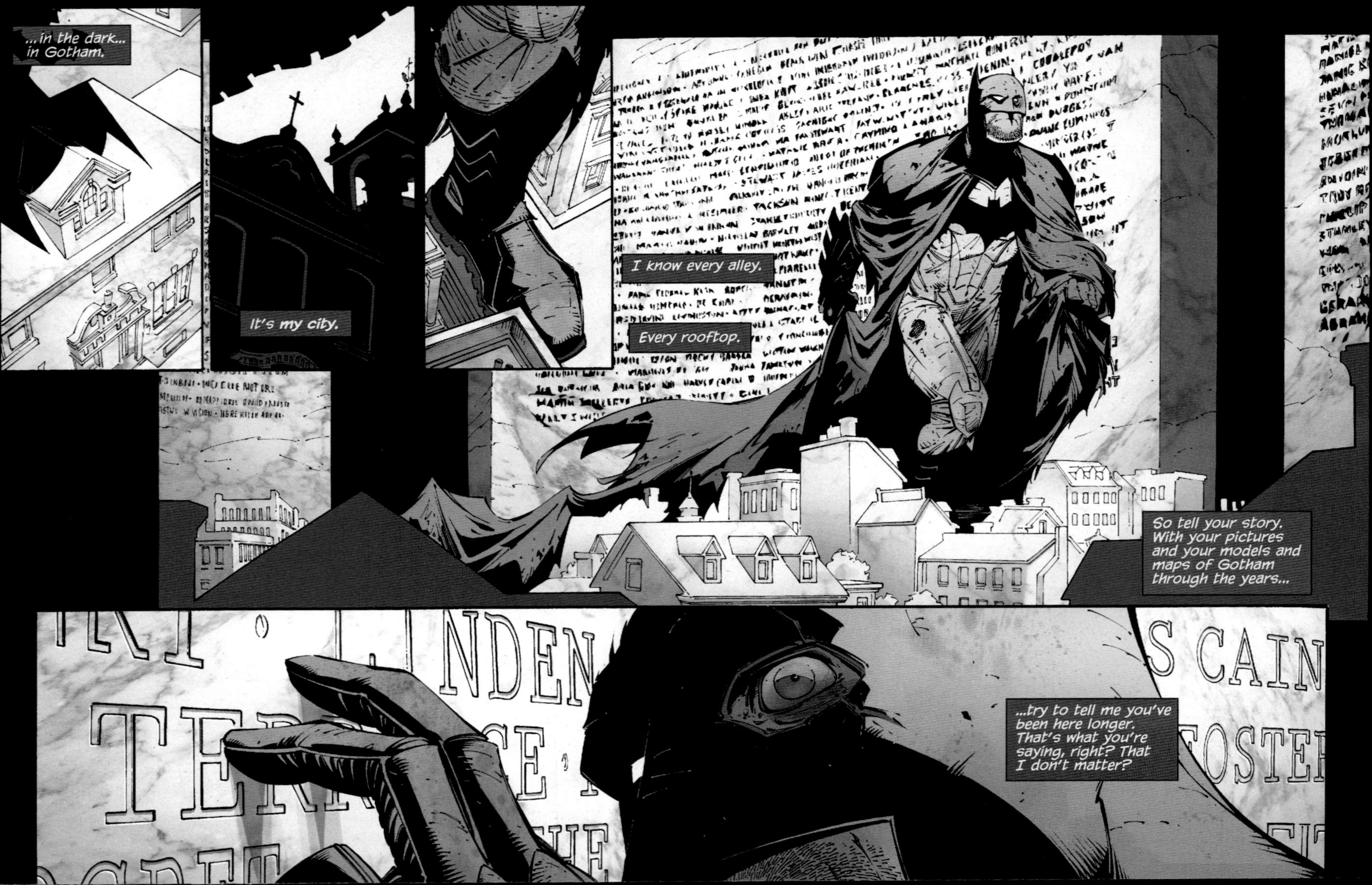
...in the dark... in Gotham.
It's my city.
I know every alley.
Every rooftop.
So tell your story. With your pictures and your models and maps of Gotham through the years...
...try to tell me you've been here longer. That's what you're saying, right? That I don't matter?

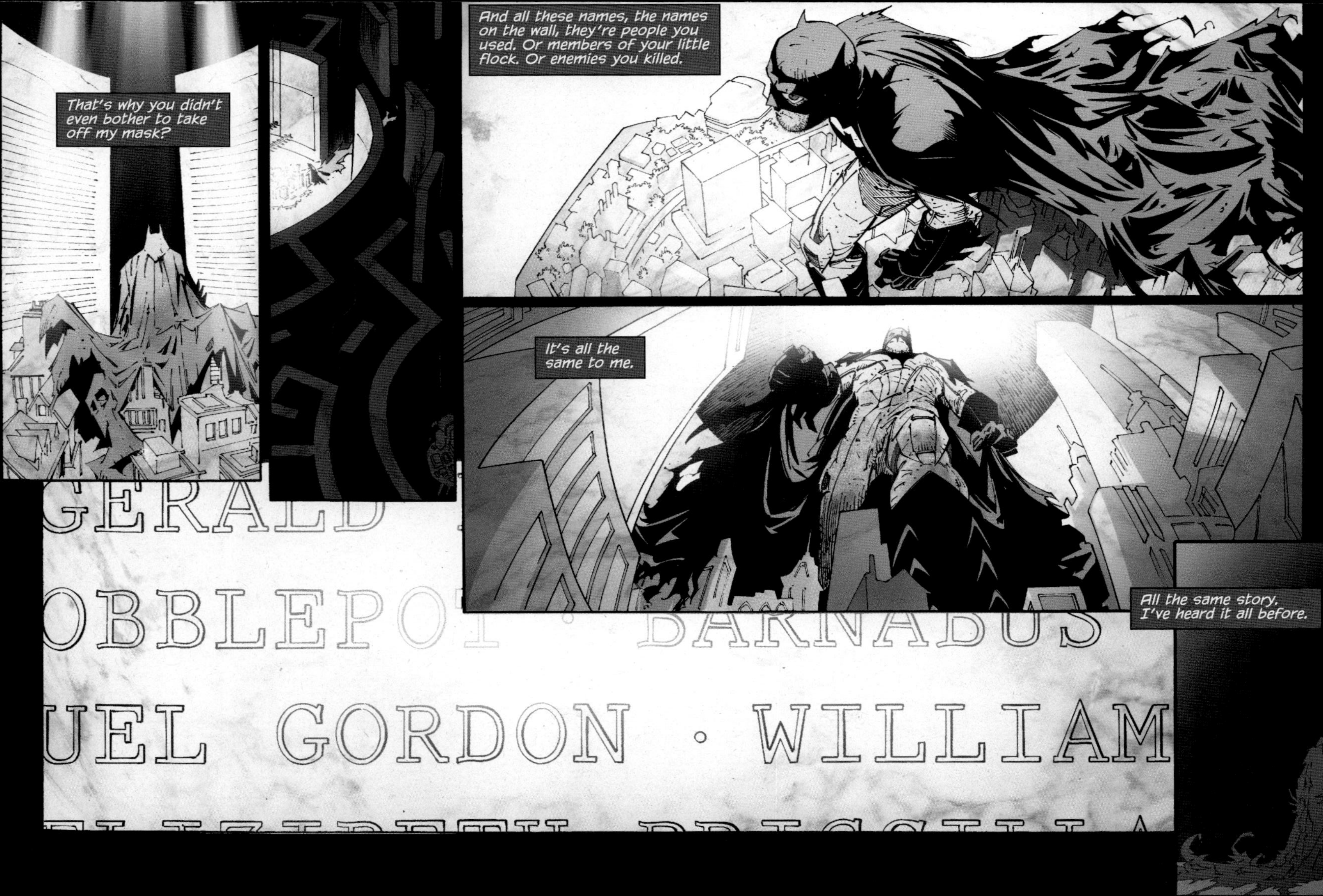
That's why you didn't even bother to take off my mask?
And all these names, the names on the wall, they're people you used. Or members of your little flock. Or enemies you killed.
It's all the same to me.
All the same story. I've heard it all before.
GERALD
OBBLEPOT · BARNABUS
UEL GORDON · WILLIAM

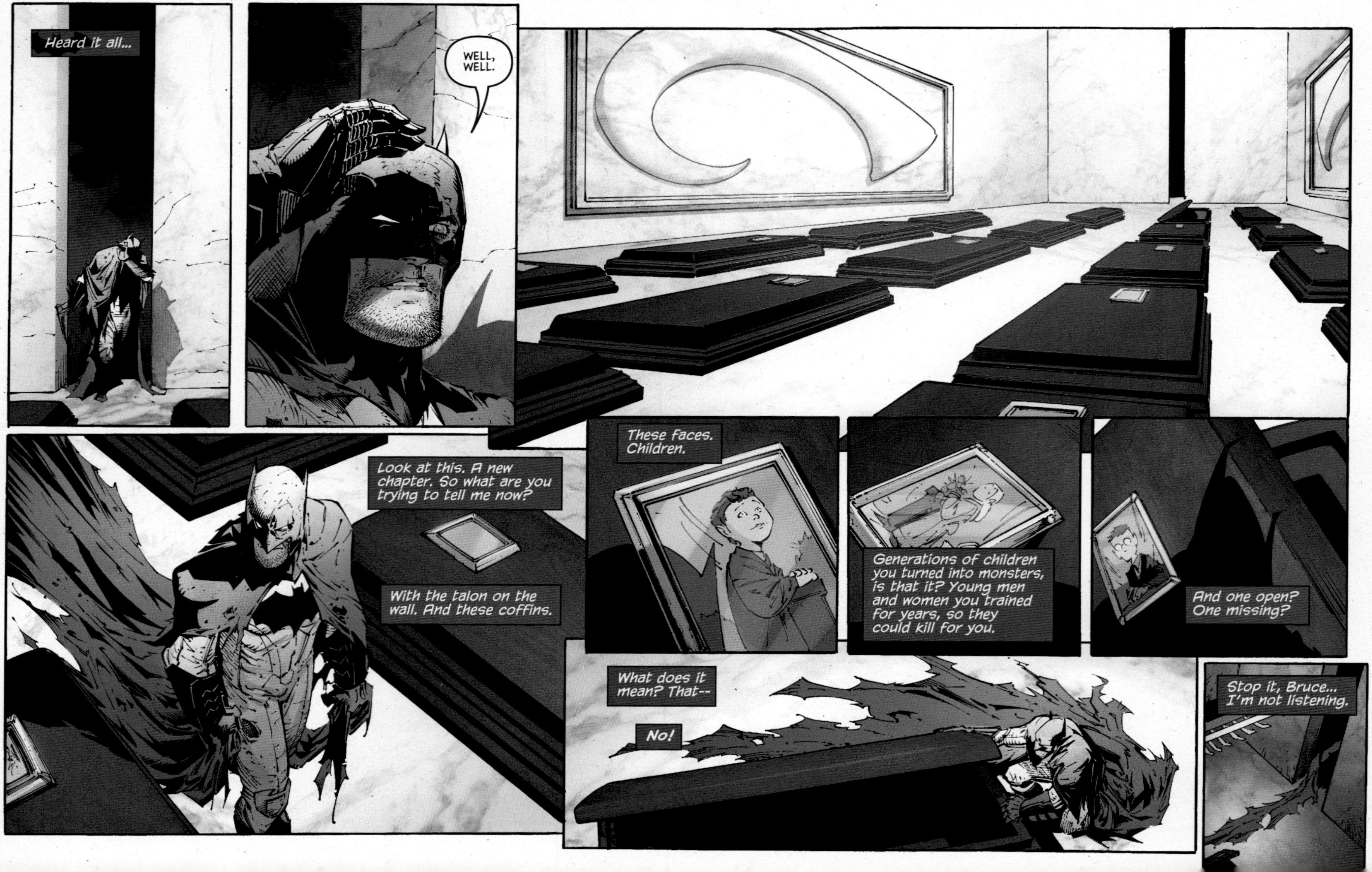
Heard it all...
WELL, WELL.
Look at this. A new chapter. So what are you trying to tell me now?
With the talon on the wall. And these coffins.
These faces. Children.
Generations of children you turned into monsters, is that it? Young men and women you trained for years, so they could kill for you.
And one open? One missing?
What does it mean? That--
No!
Stop it, Bruce... I'm not listening.

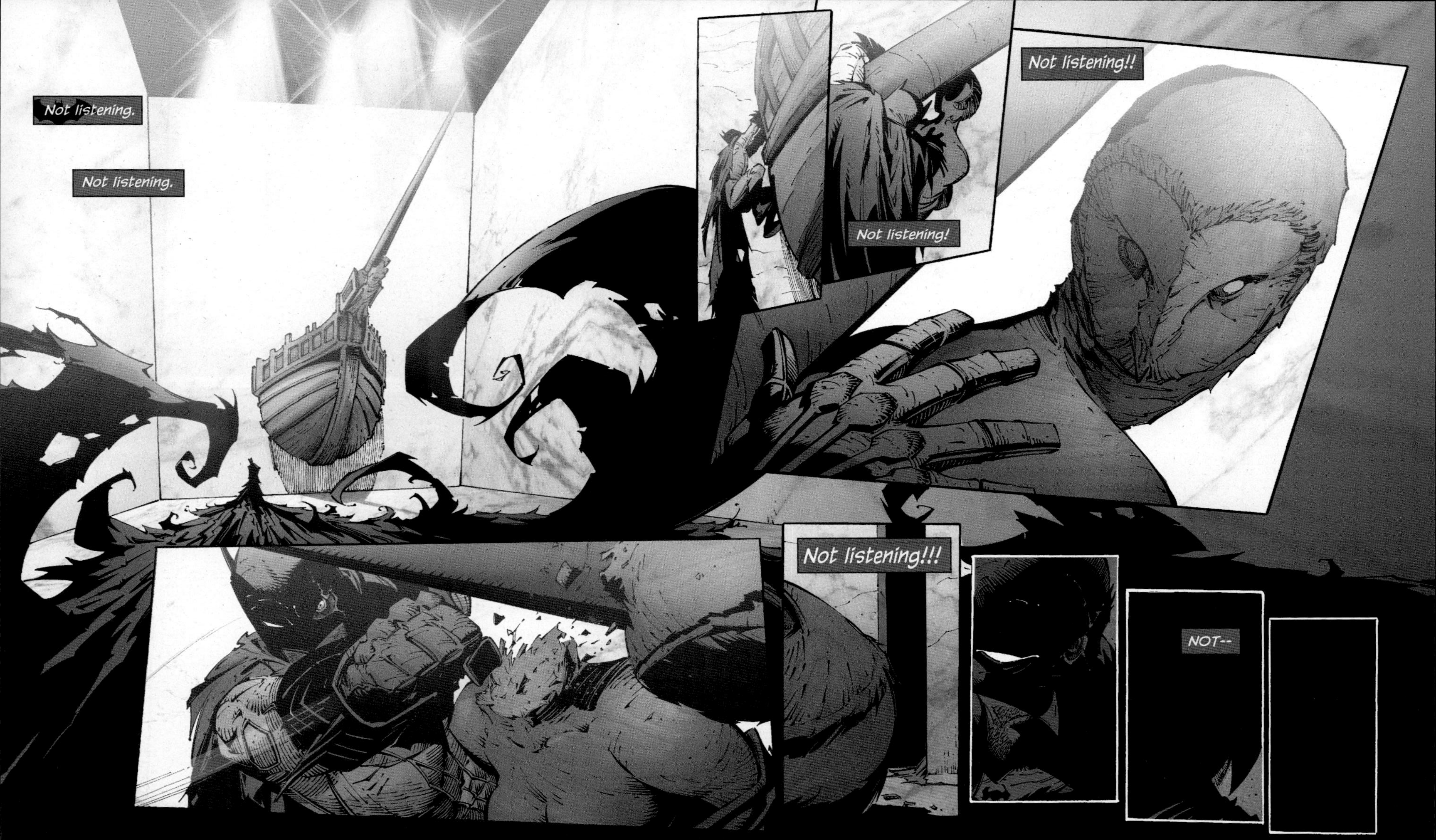
Not listening.
Not listening.
Not listening!
Not listening!!
Not listening!!!
NOT--

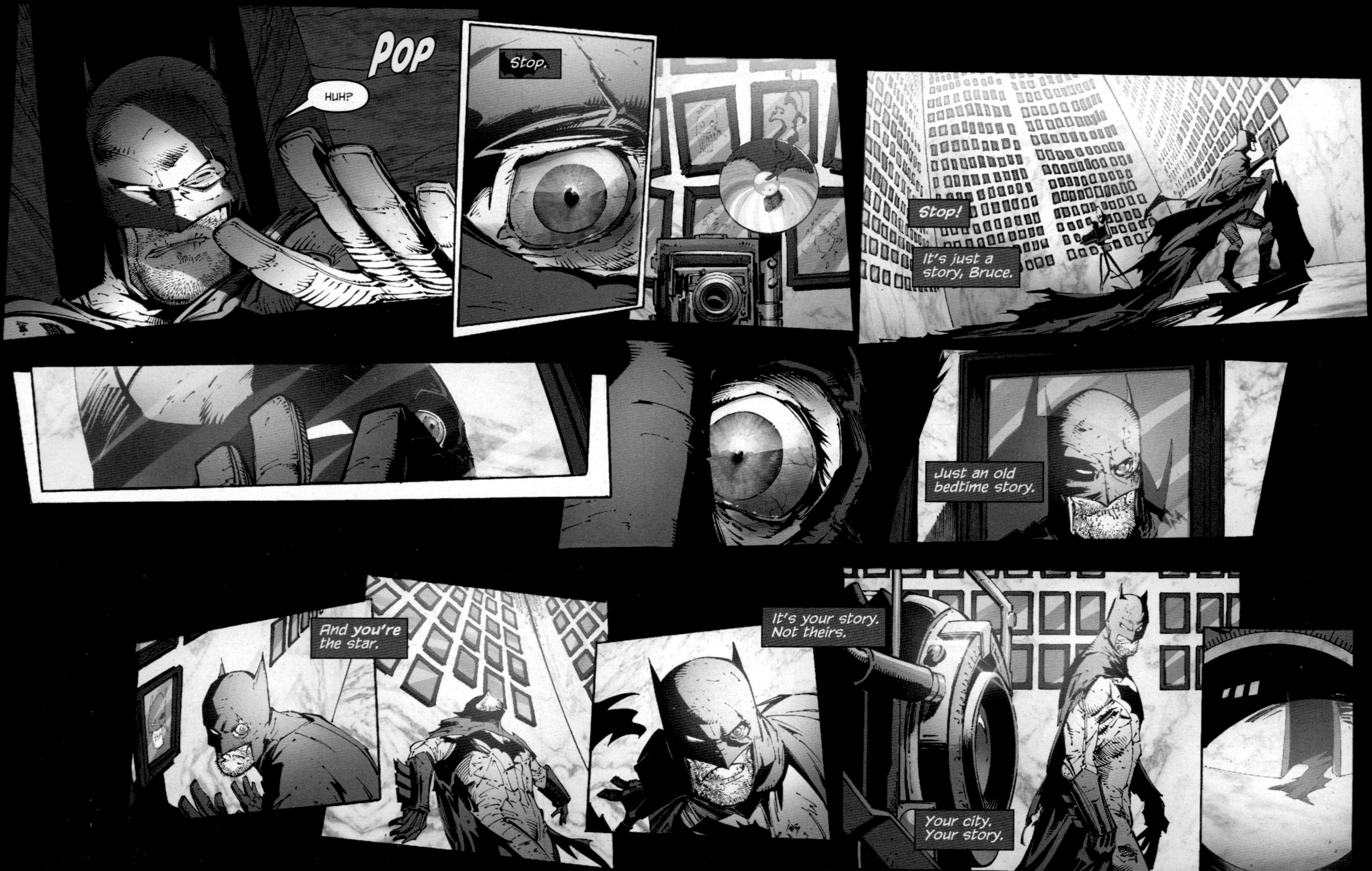

HUH?
POP
Stop.
Stop!
It's just a story, Bruce.
Just an old bedtime story.
And you're the star.
It's your story. Not theirs.
Your city. Your story.

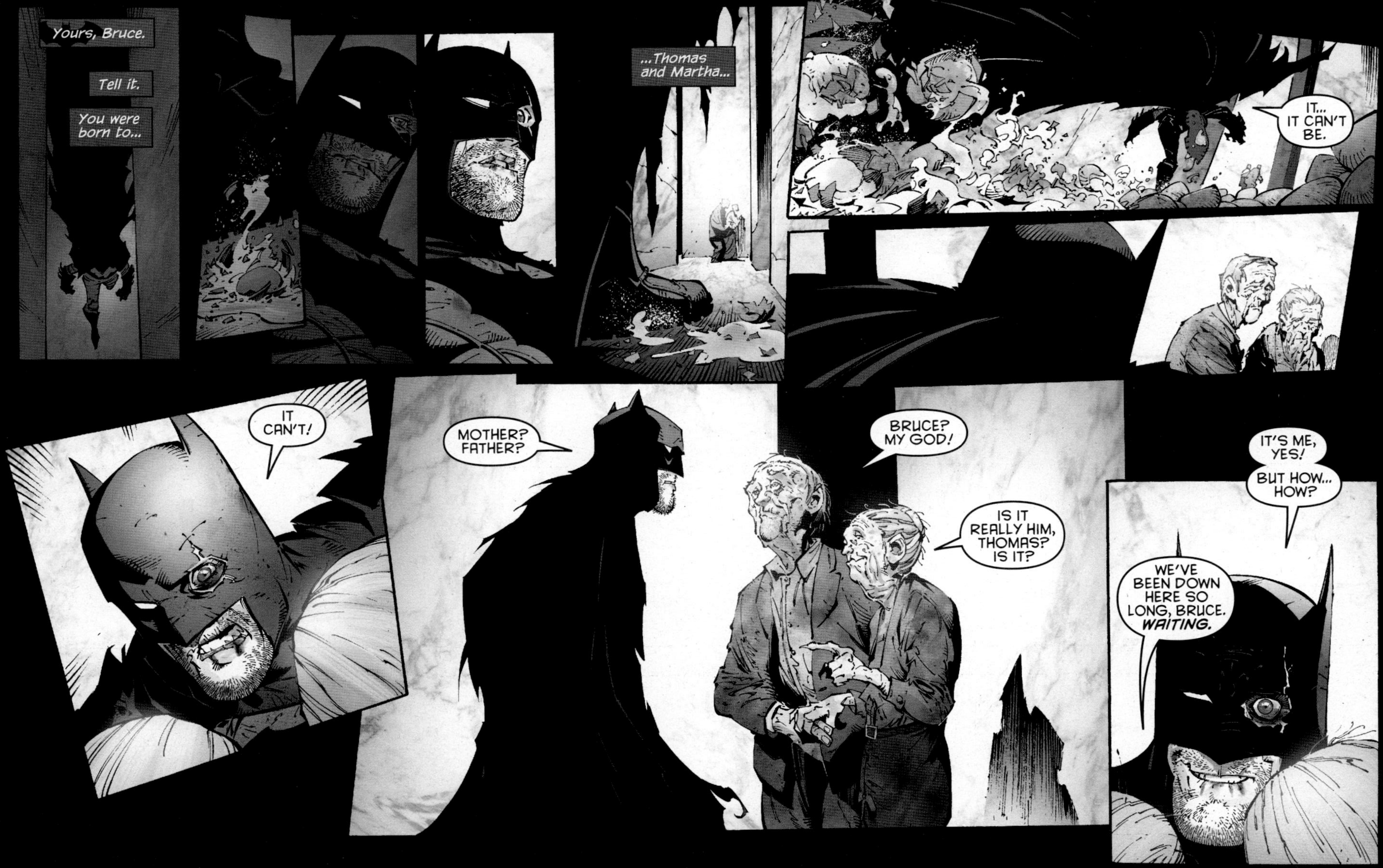
Yours, Bruce.
Tell it.
You were born to...
...Thomas and Martha...
IT... IT CAN'T BE.
IT CAN'T!
MOTHER? FATHER?
BRUCE? MY GOD!
IS IT REALLY HIM, THOMAS? IS IT?
IT'S ME, YES!
BUT HOW... HOW?
WE'VE BEEN DOWN HERE SO LONG, BRUCE. *WAITING.*

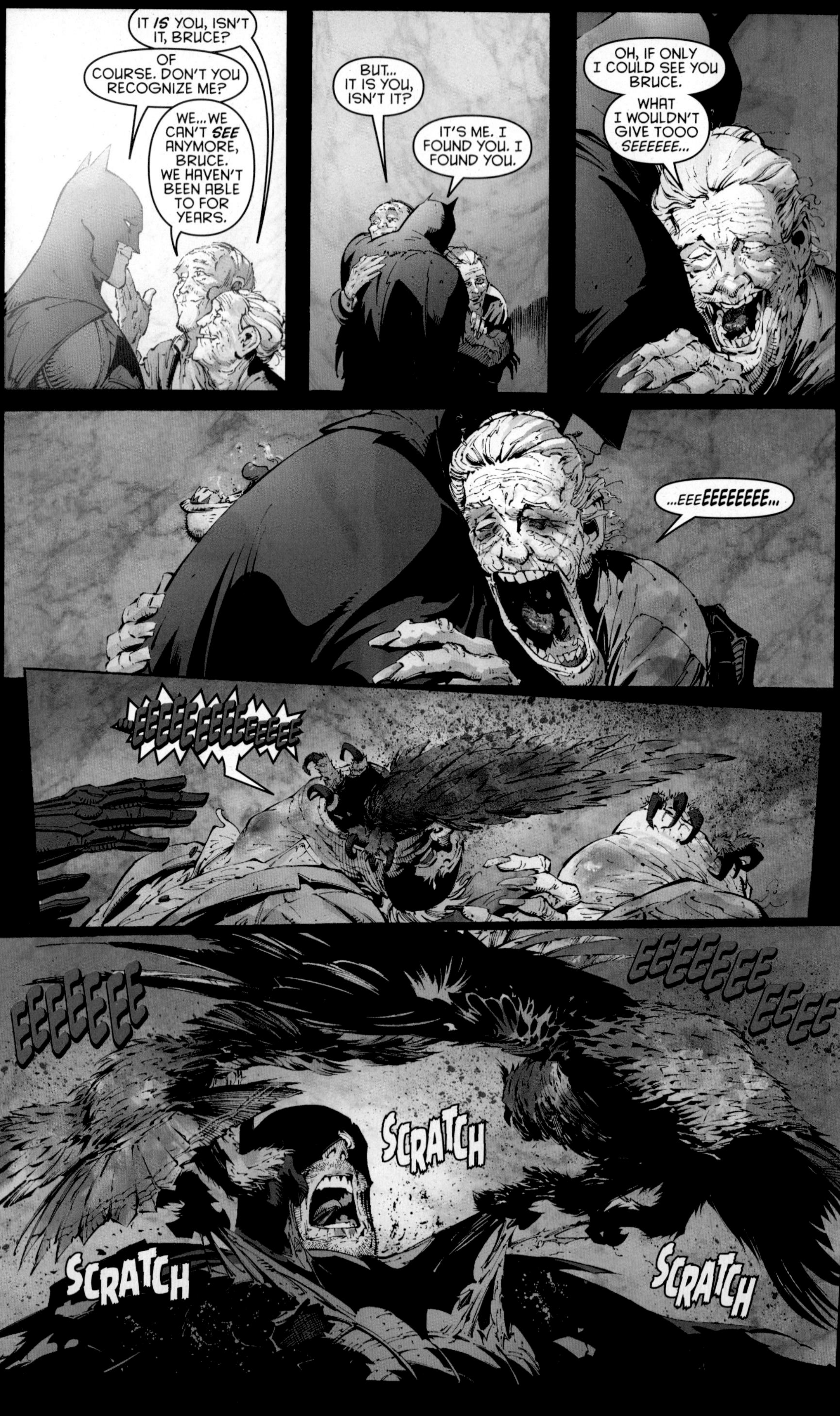
IT *IS* YOU, ISN'T IT, BRUCE?
OF COURSE. DON'T YOU RECOGNIZE ME?
WE... WE CAN'T *SEE* ANYMORE, BRUCE. WE HAVEN'T BEEN ABLE TO FOR YEARS.
BUT... IT IS YOU, ISN'T IT?
IT'S ME. I FOUND YOU. I FOUND YOU.
OH, IF ONLY I COULD SEE YOU BRUCE.
WHAT I WOULDN'T GIVE TOOO *SEEEEEE...*
...EEEEEEEEEEE...
...EEEEEEEEEEEEEEE
EEEEEEE
EEEEEEE EEEE
SCRATCH
SCRATCH
SCRATCH

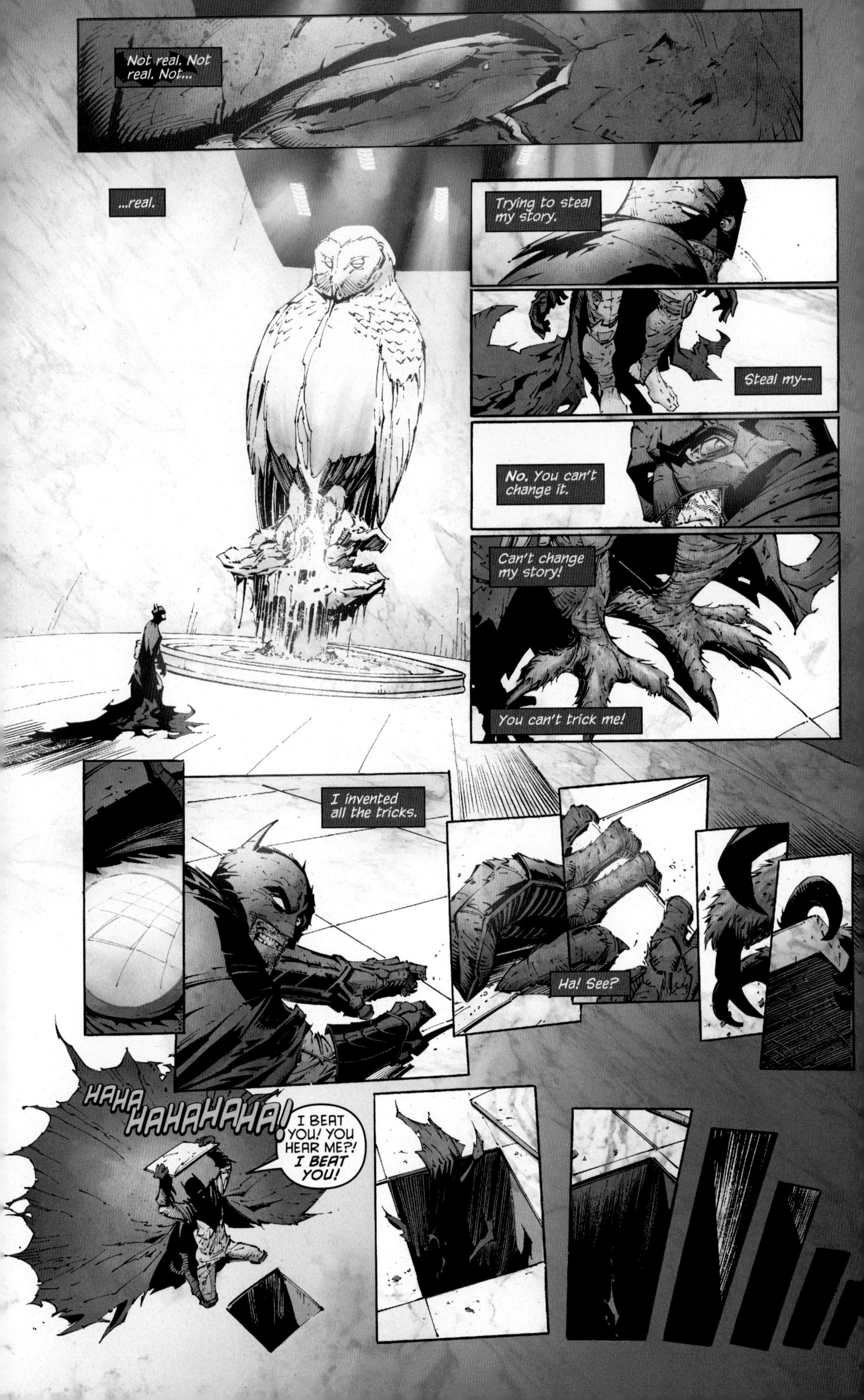
Not real. Not real. Not...
...real.
Trying to steal my story.
Steal my--
No. You can't change it.
Can't change my story!
You can't trick me!
I invented all the tricks.
Ha! See?
HAHA HAHAHAHAHA!
I BEAT YOU! YOU HEAR ME?! I BEAT YOU!

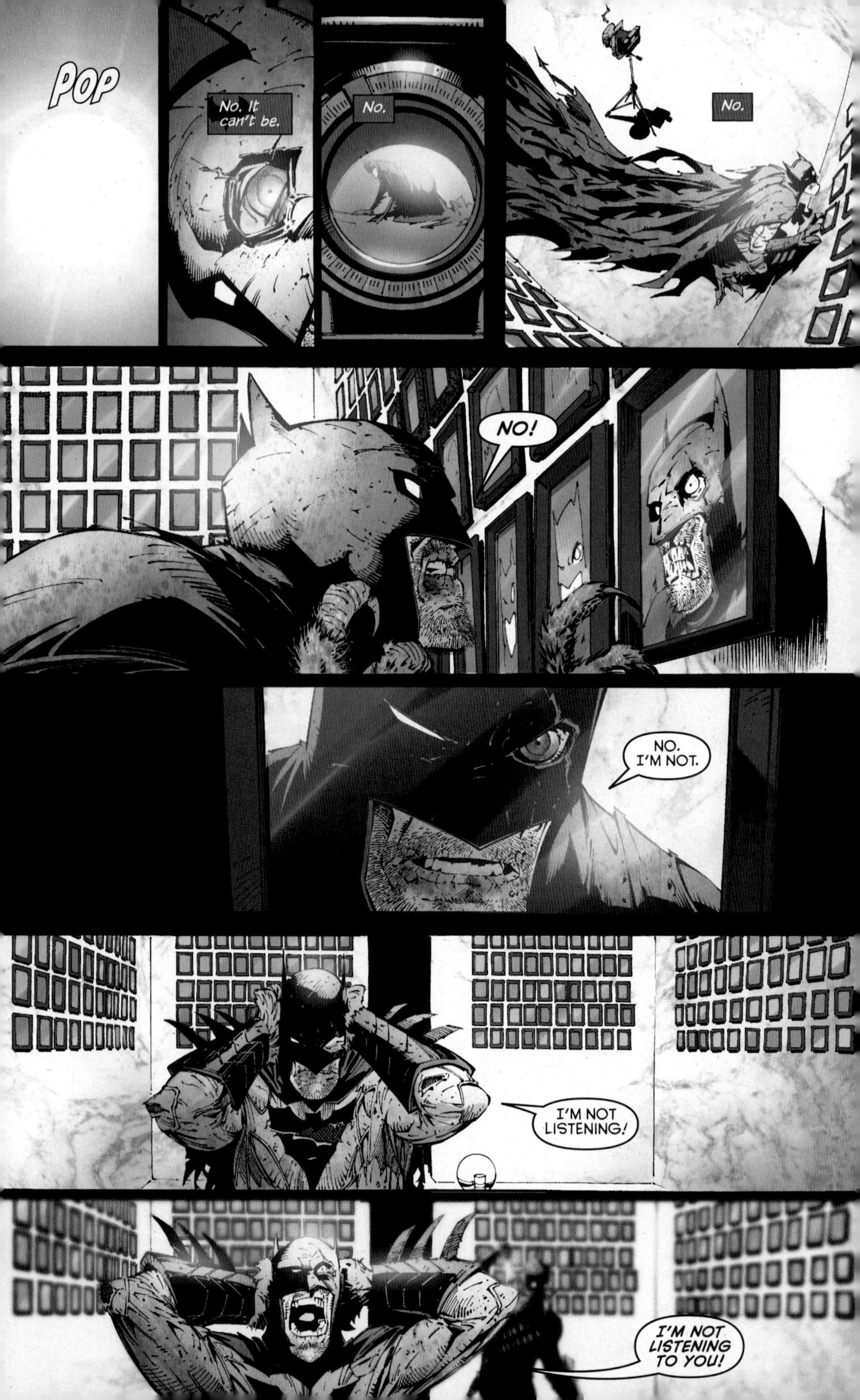
POP
No. It can't be.
No.
No.
NO!
NO. I'M NOT.
I'M NOT LISTENING!
I'M NOT LISTENING TO YOU!

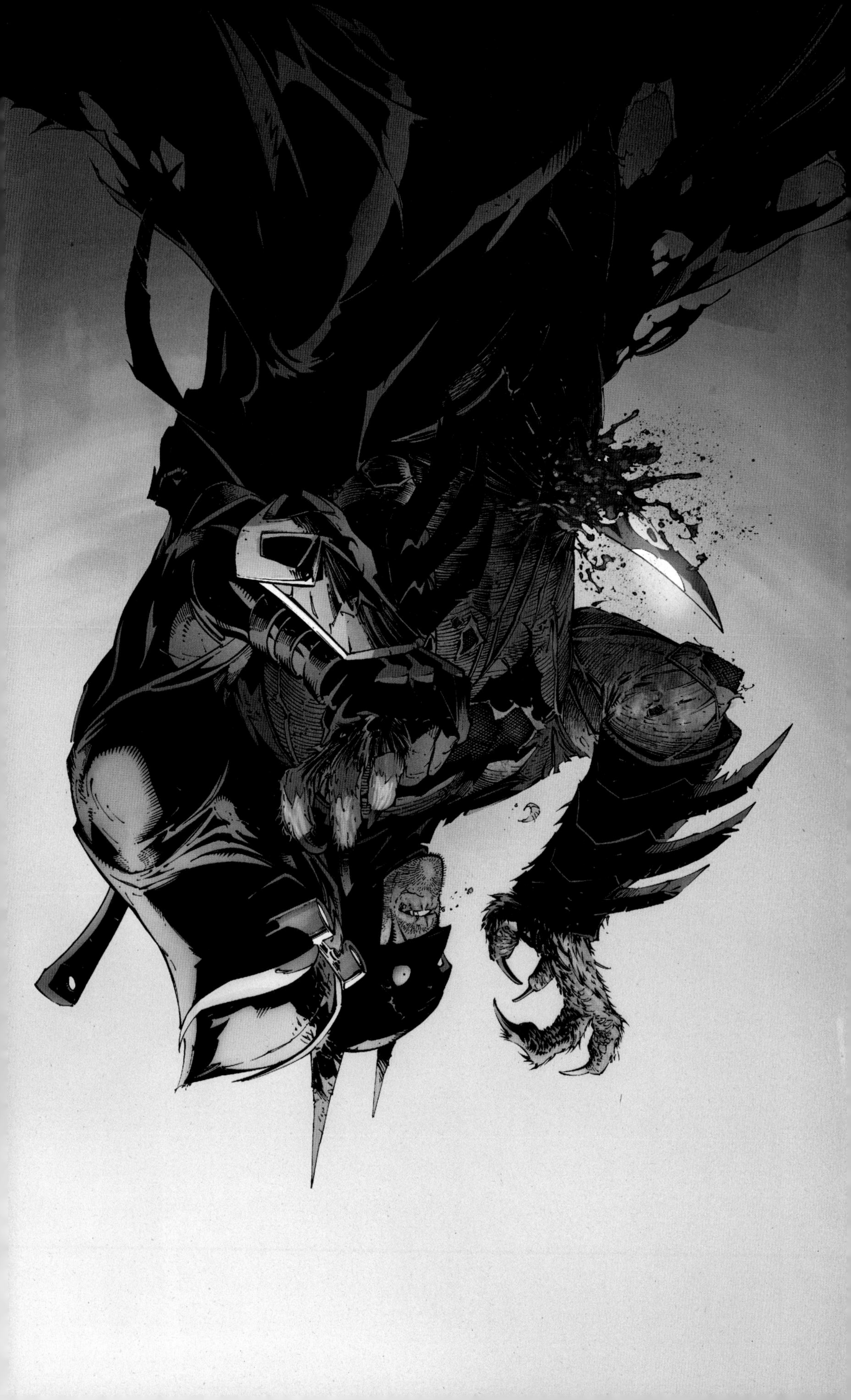

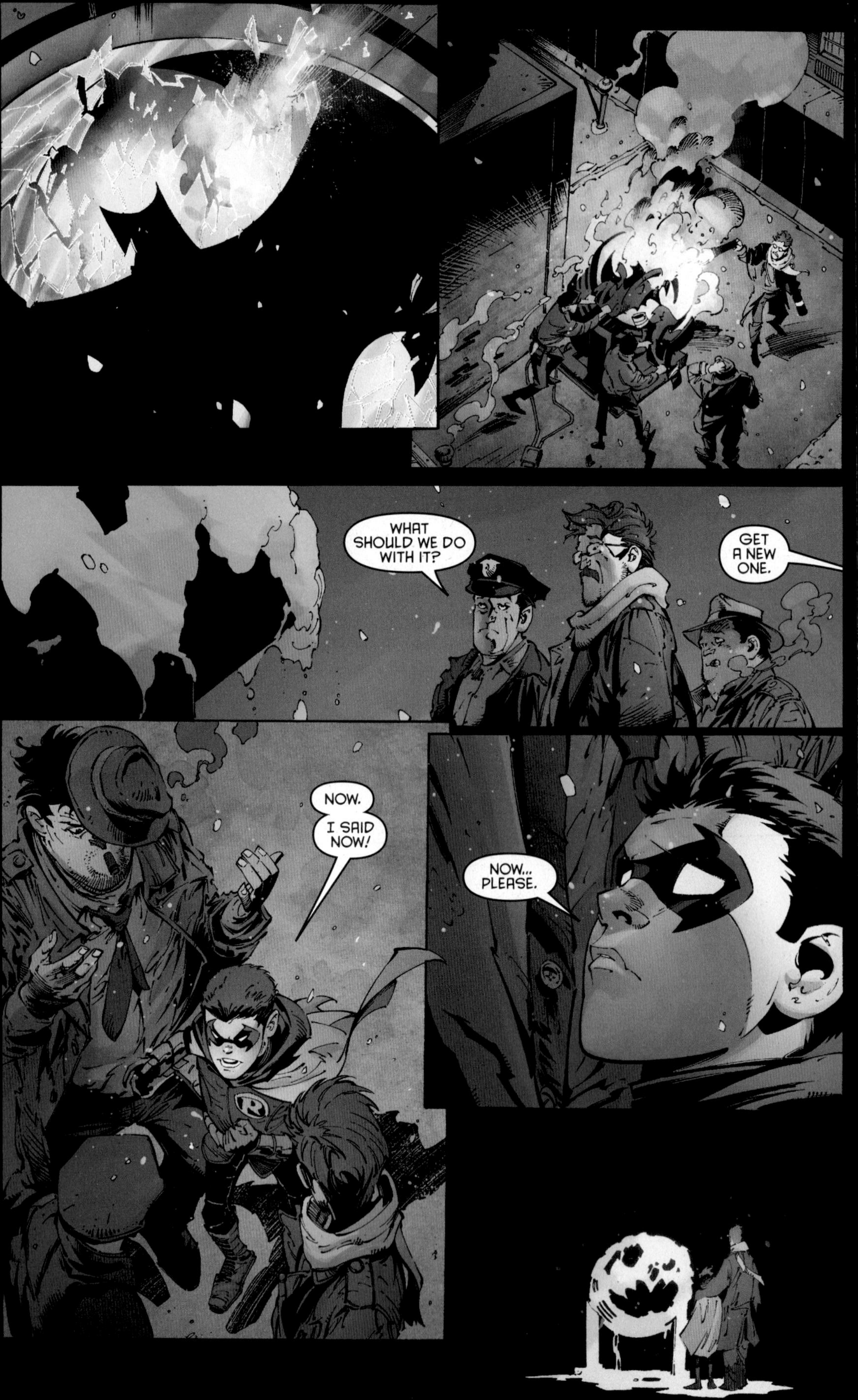
WHAT SHOULD WE DO WITH IT?
GET A NEW ONE.
NOW.
I SAID NOW!
NOW... PLEASE.

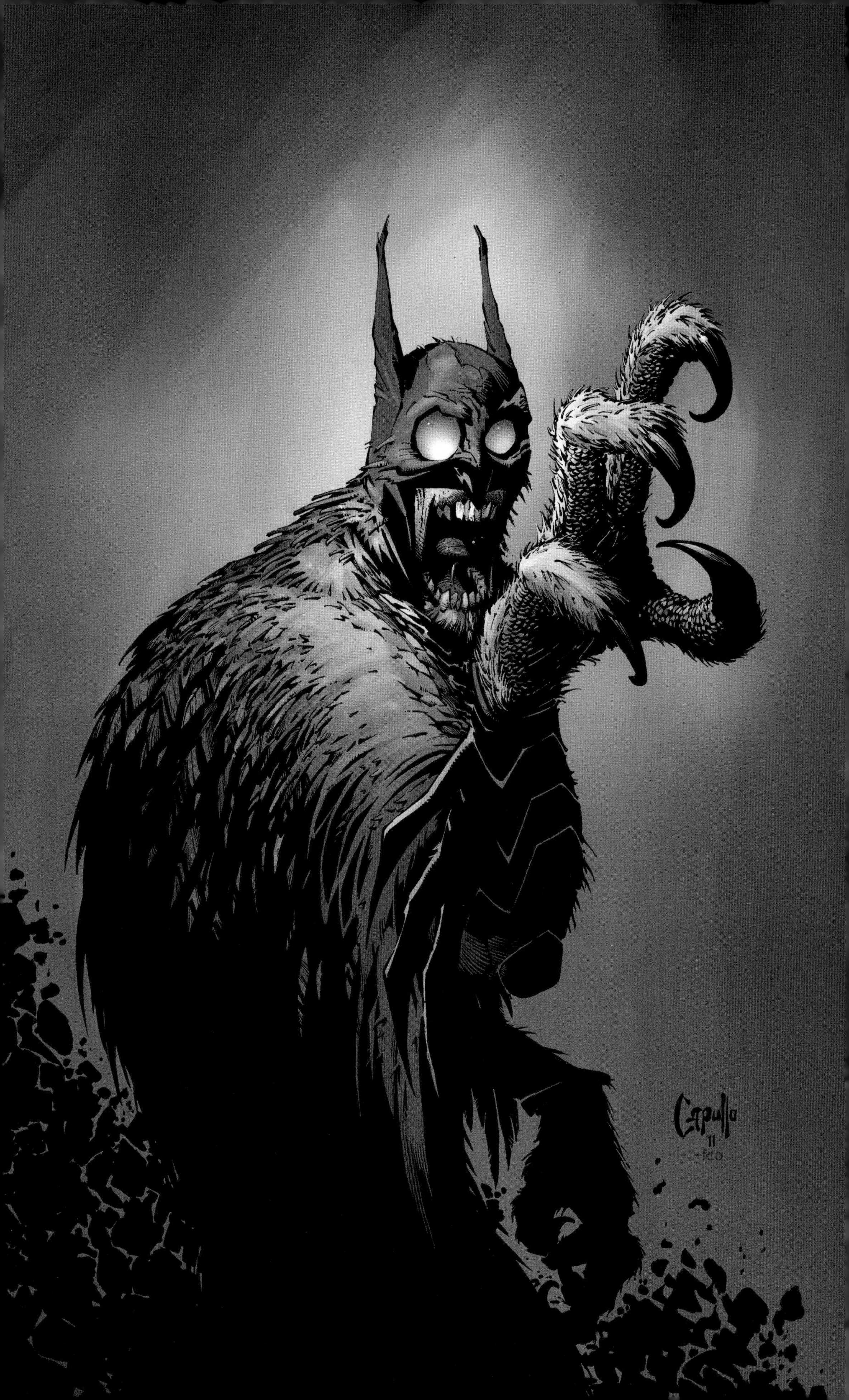
Capullo
'11
+fco

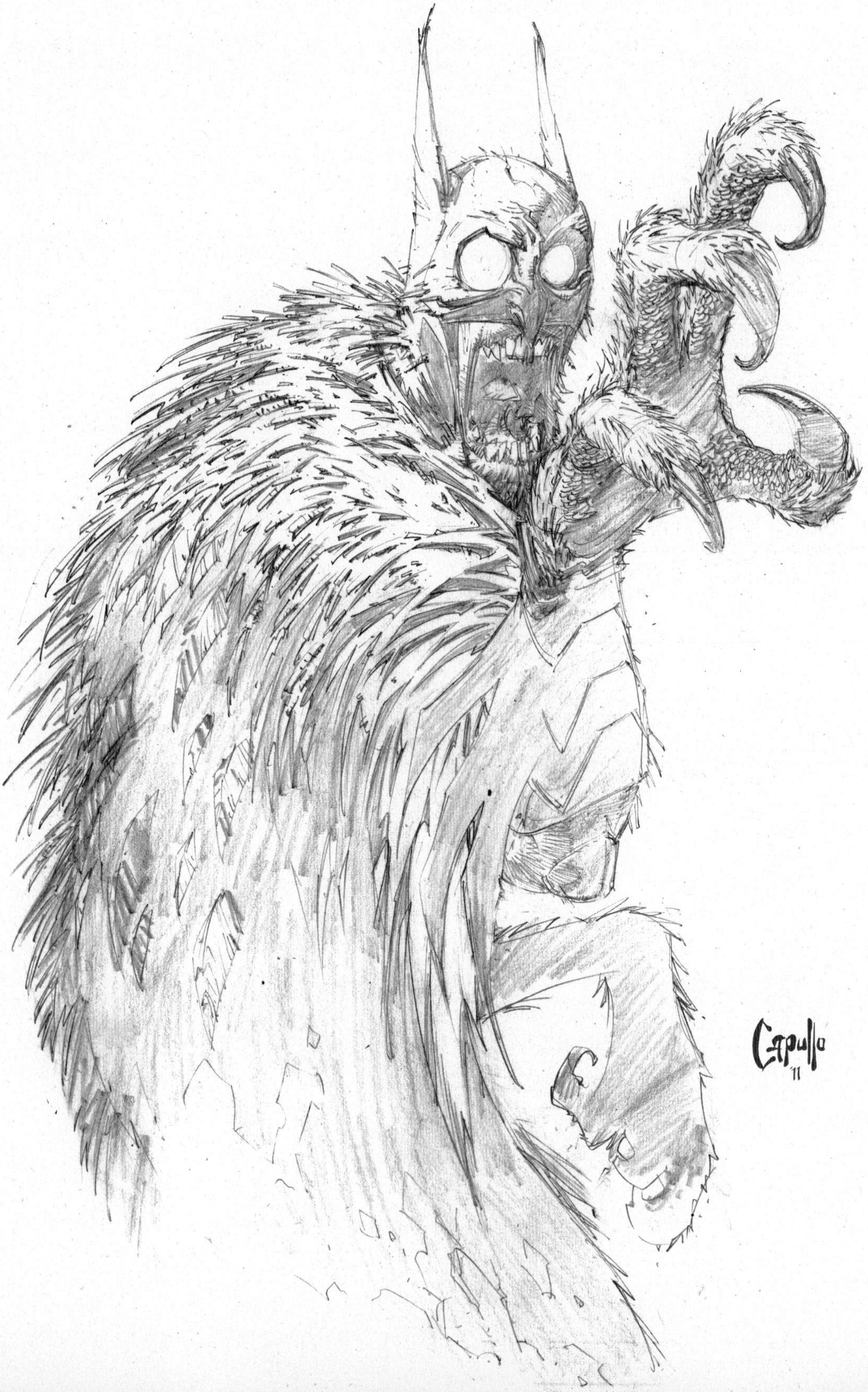

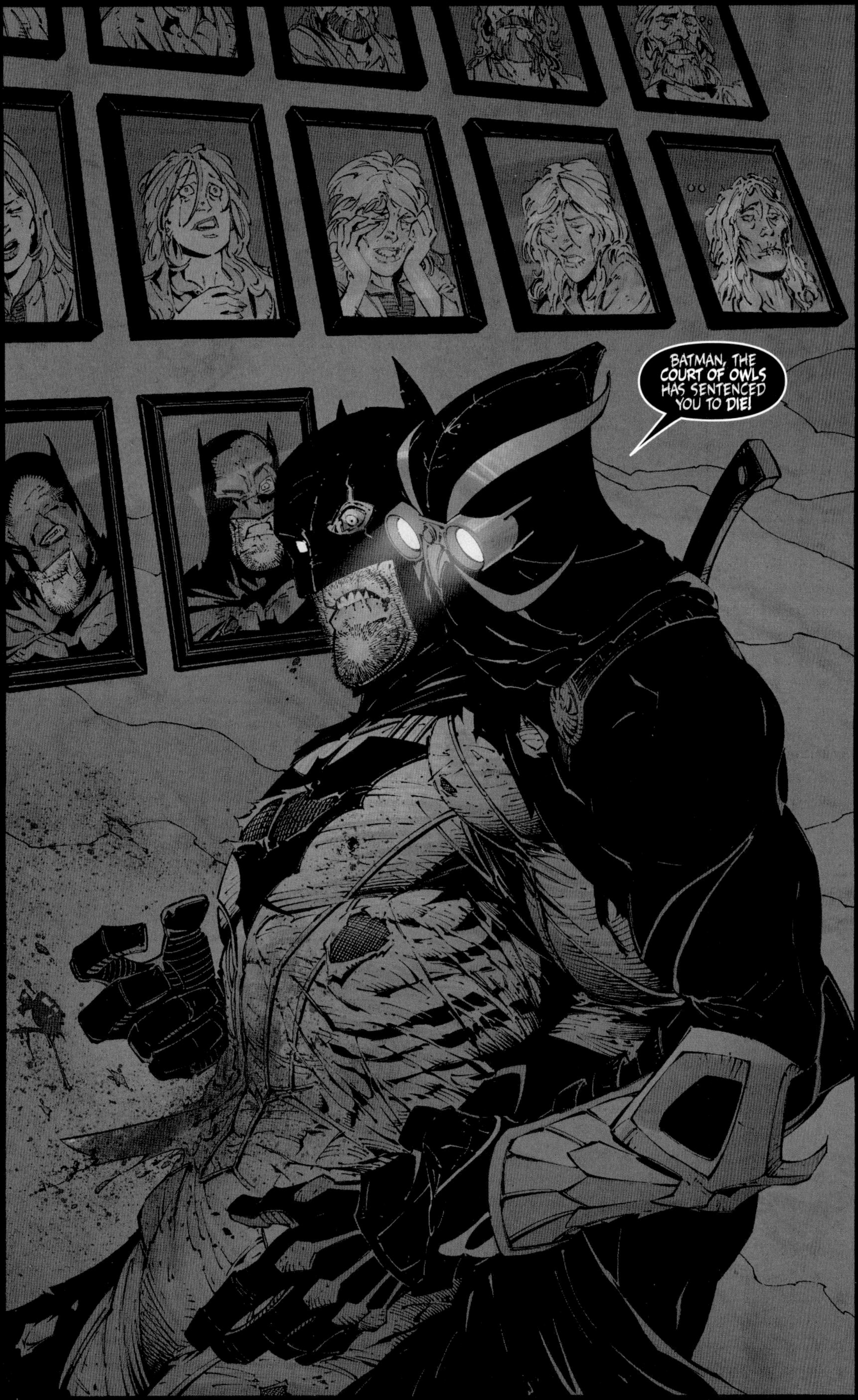
BATMAN, THE COURT OF OWLS HAS SENTENCED YOU TO DIE!

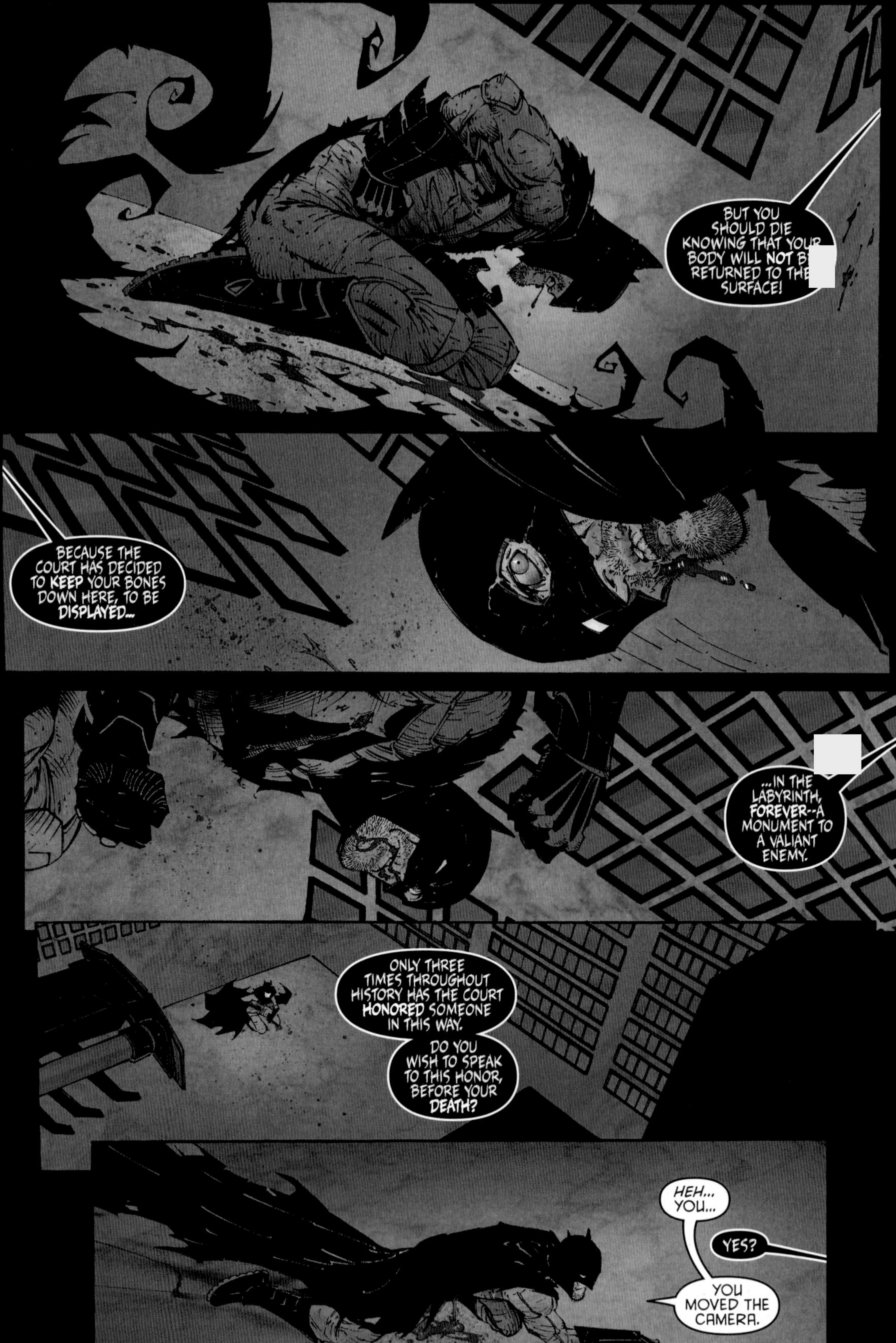
BUT YOU SHOULD DIE KNOWING THAT YOUR BODY WILL NOT B RETURNED TO THE SURFACE!
BECAUSE THE COURT HAS DECIDED TO KEEP YOUR BONES DOWN HERE, TO BE DISPLAYED...
...IN THE LABYRINTH, FOREVER--A MONUMENT TO A VALIANT ENEMY.
ONLY THREE TIMES THROUGHOUT HISTORY HAS THE COURT HONORED SOMEONE IN THIS WAY.
DO YOU WISH TO SPEAK TO THIS HONOR, BEFORE YOUR DEATH?
HEH... YOU...
YES?
YOU MOVED THE CAMERA.

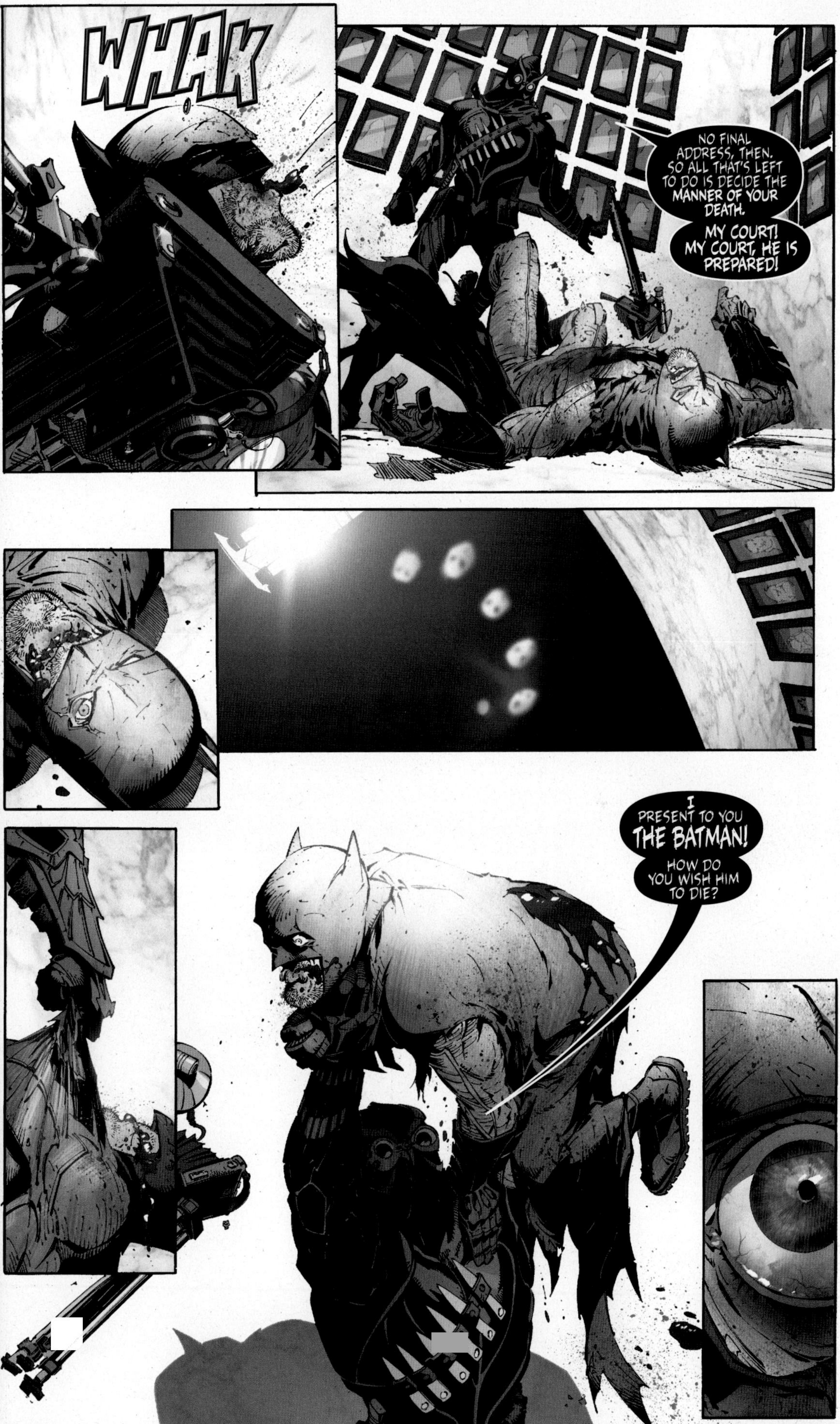
WHAK
NO FINAL ADDRESS, THEN. SO ALL THAT'S LEFT TO DO IS DECIDE THE MANNER OF YOUR DEATH.
MY COURT! MY COURT, HE IS PREPARED!
I PRESENT TO YOU THE BATMAN!
HOW DO YOU WISH HIM TO DIE?

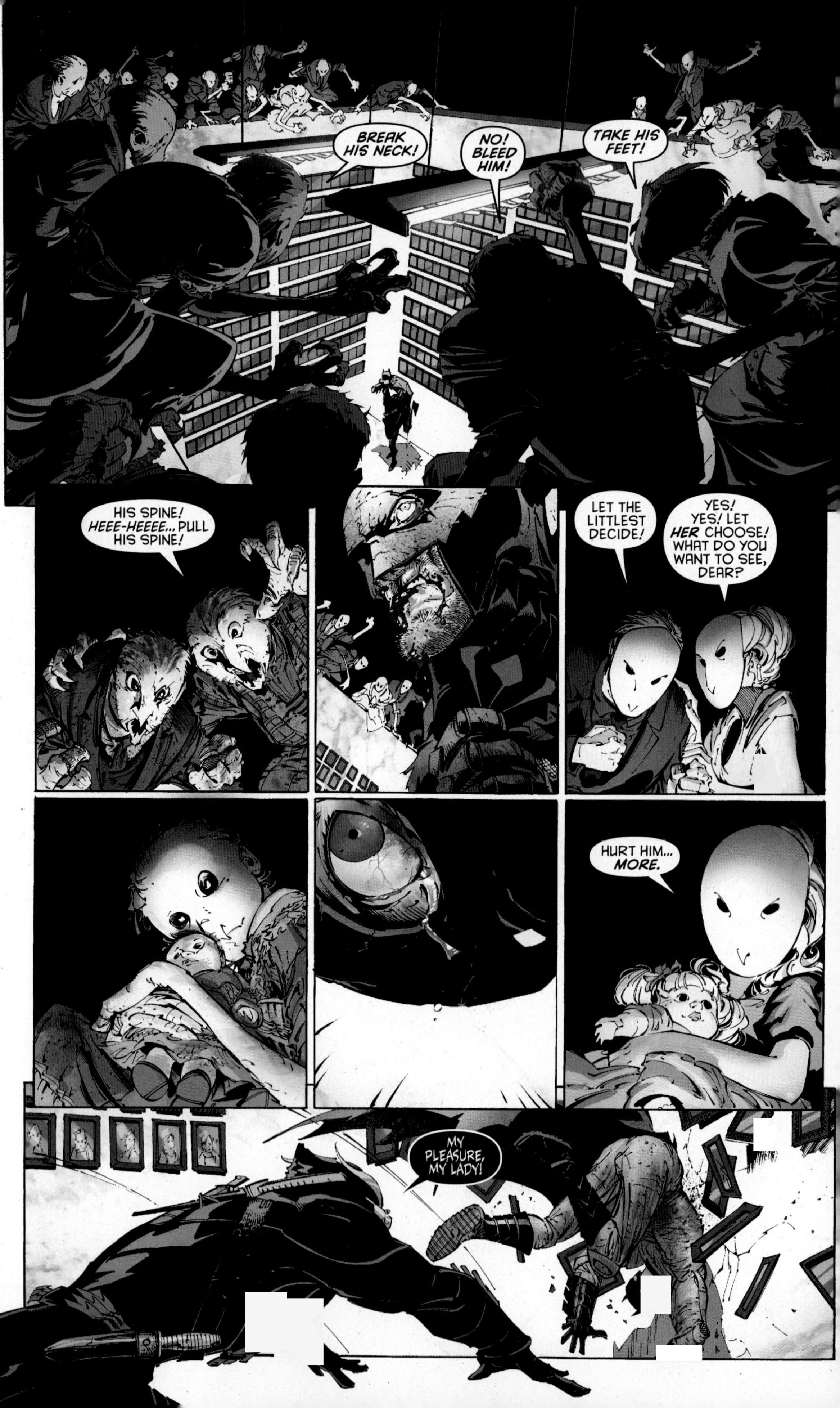
BREAK HIS NECK!
NO! BLEED HIM!
TAKE HIS FEET!
HIS SPINE! HEEE-HEEEE... PULL HIS SPINE!
LET THE LITTLEST DECIDE!
YES! YES! LET HER CHOOSE! WHAT DO YOU WANT TO SEE, DEAR?
HURT HIM... MORE.
MY PLEASURE, MY LADY!

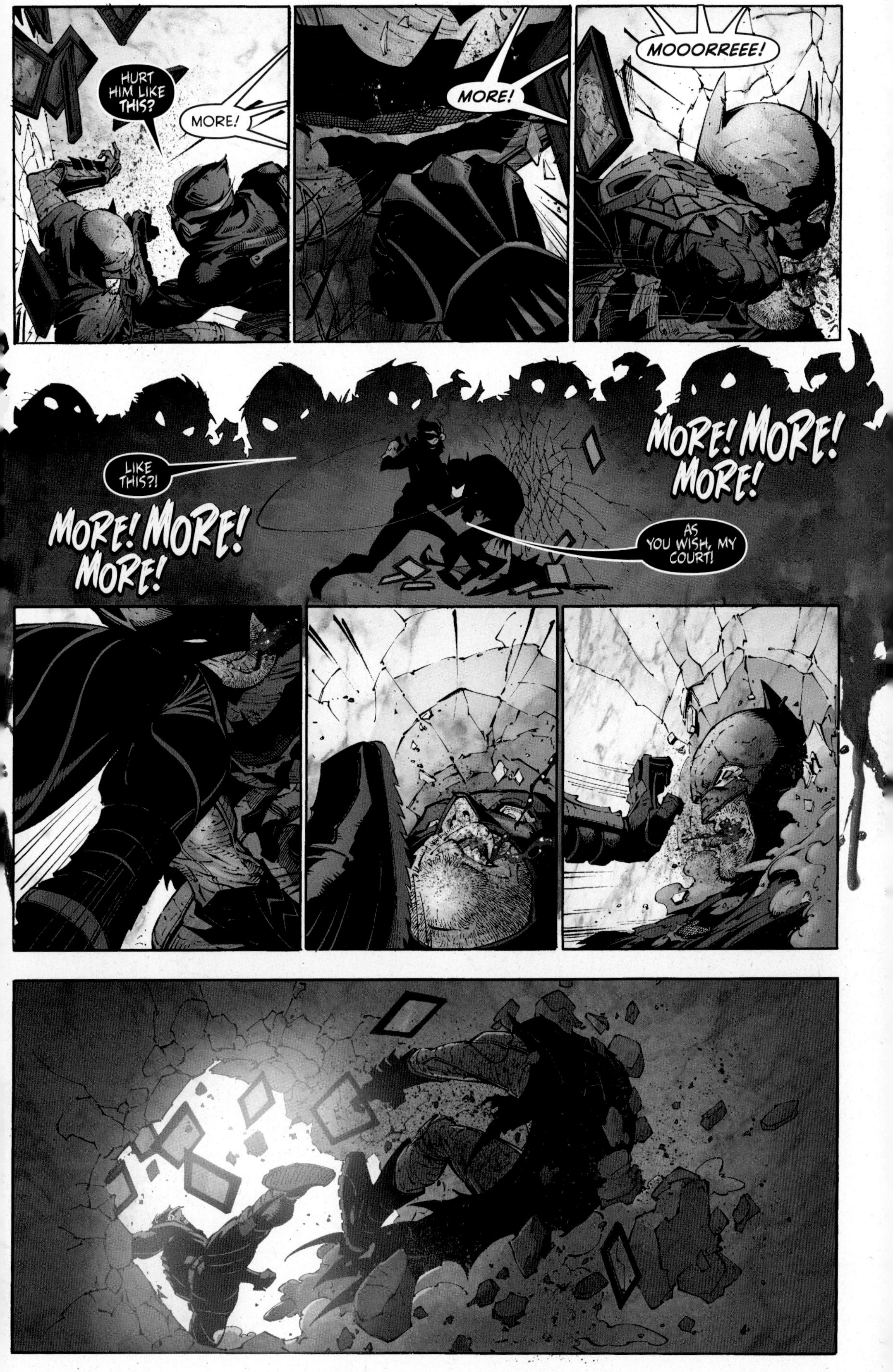

HURT HIM LIKE THIS?
MORE!
MORE!
MOOORREEE!
LIKE THIS?!
MORE! MORE! MORE!
MORE! MORE! MORE!
AS YOU WISH, MY COURT!

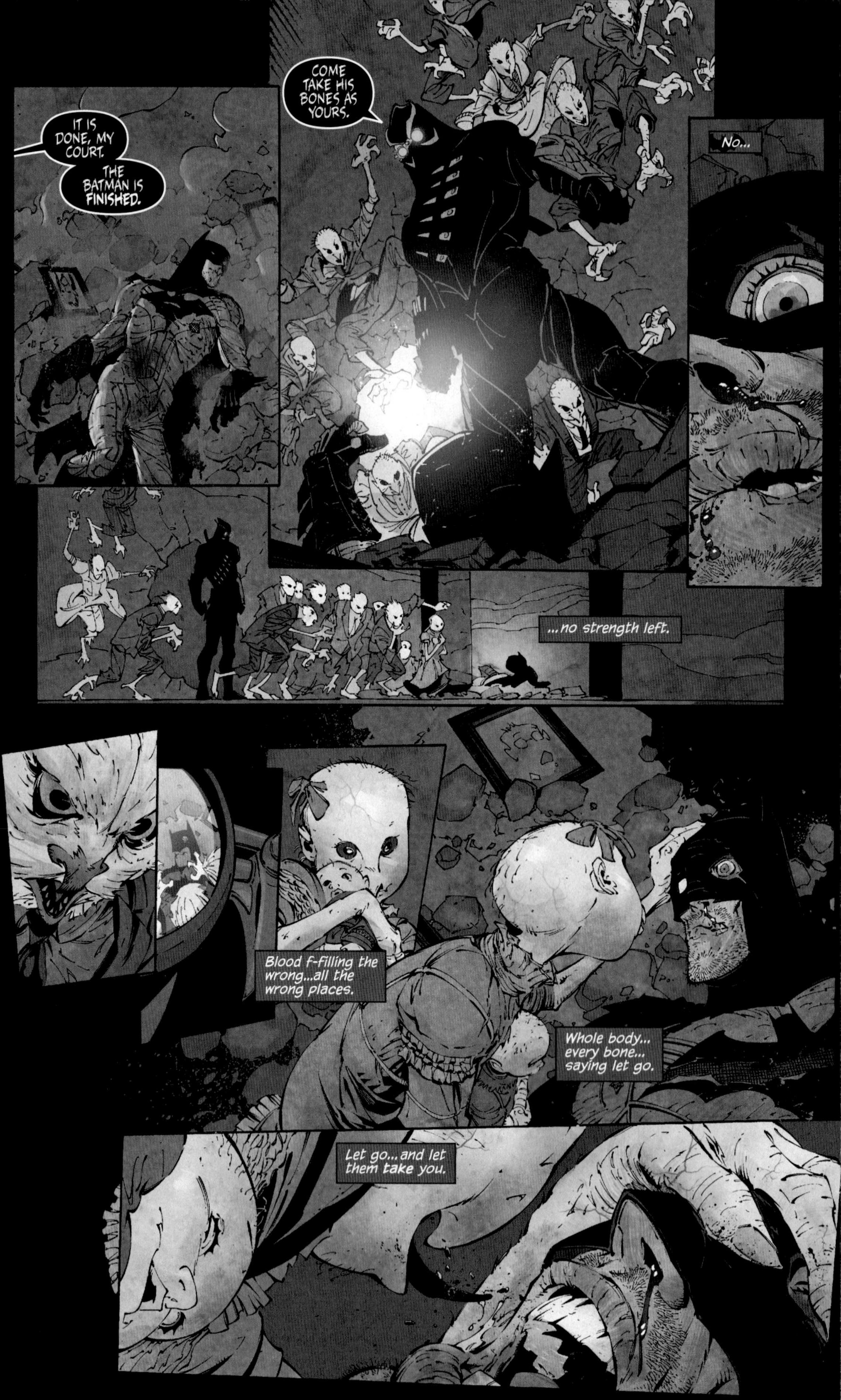

IT IS DONE, MY COURT.
THE BATMAN IS FINISHED.
COME TAKE HIS BONES AS YOURS.
No...
...no strength left.
Blood f-filling the wrong...all the wrong places.
Whole body... every bone... saying let go.
Let go...and let them take you.

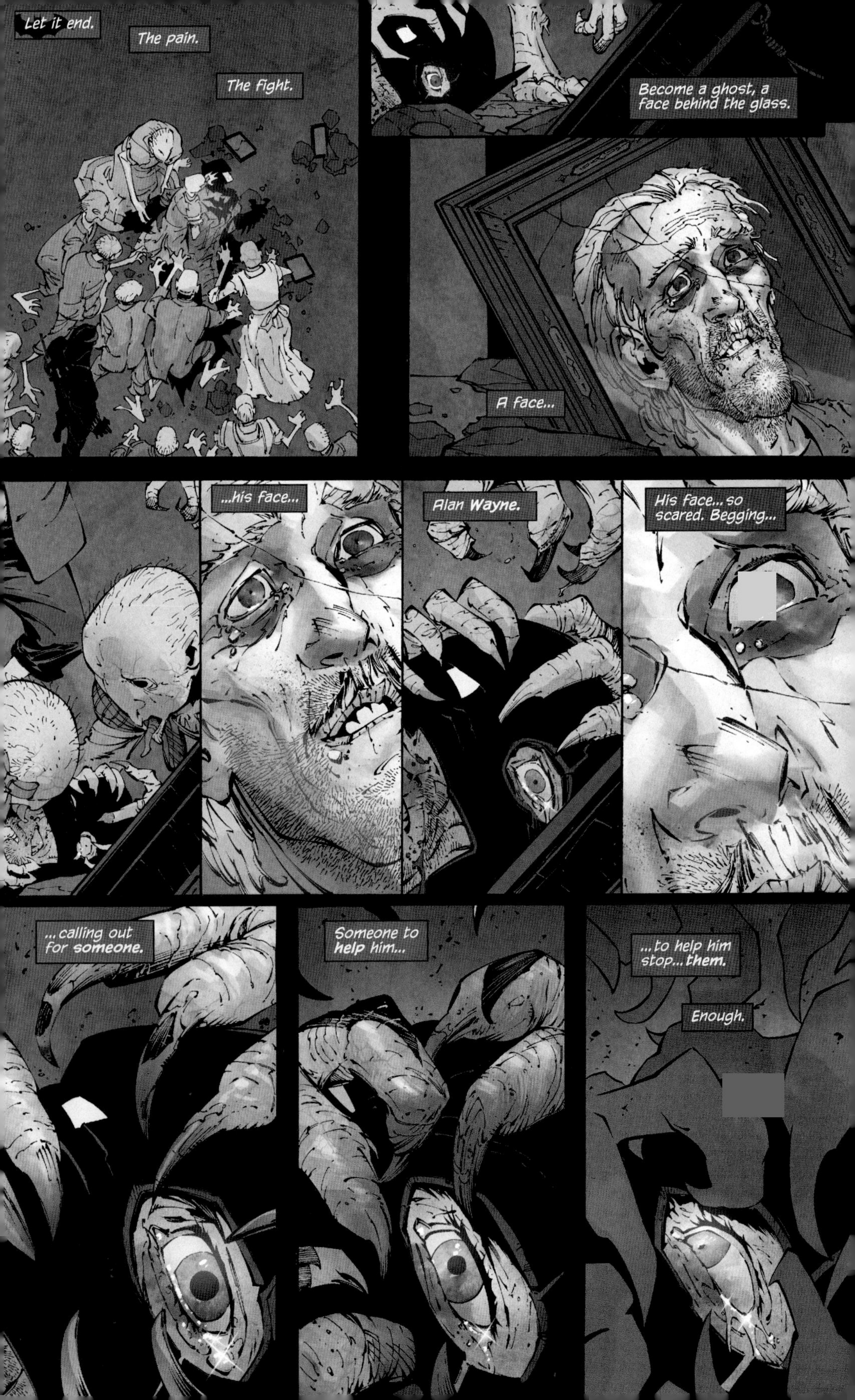
Let it end.
The pain.
The fight.
Become a ghost, a face behind the glass.
A face...
...his face...
Alan Wayne.
His face... so scared. Begging...
...calling out for someone.
Someone to help him...
...to help him stop... them.
Enough.

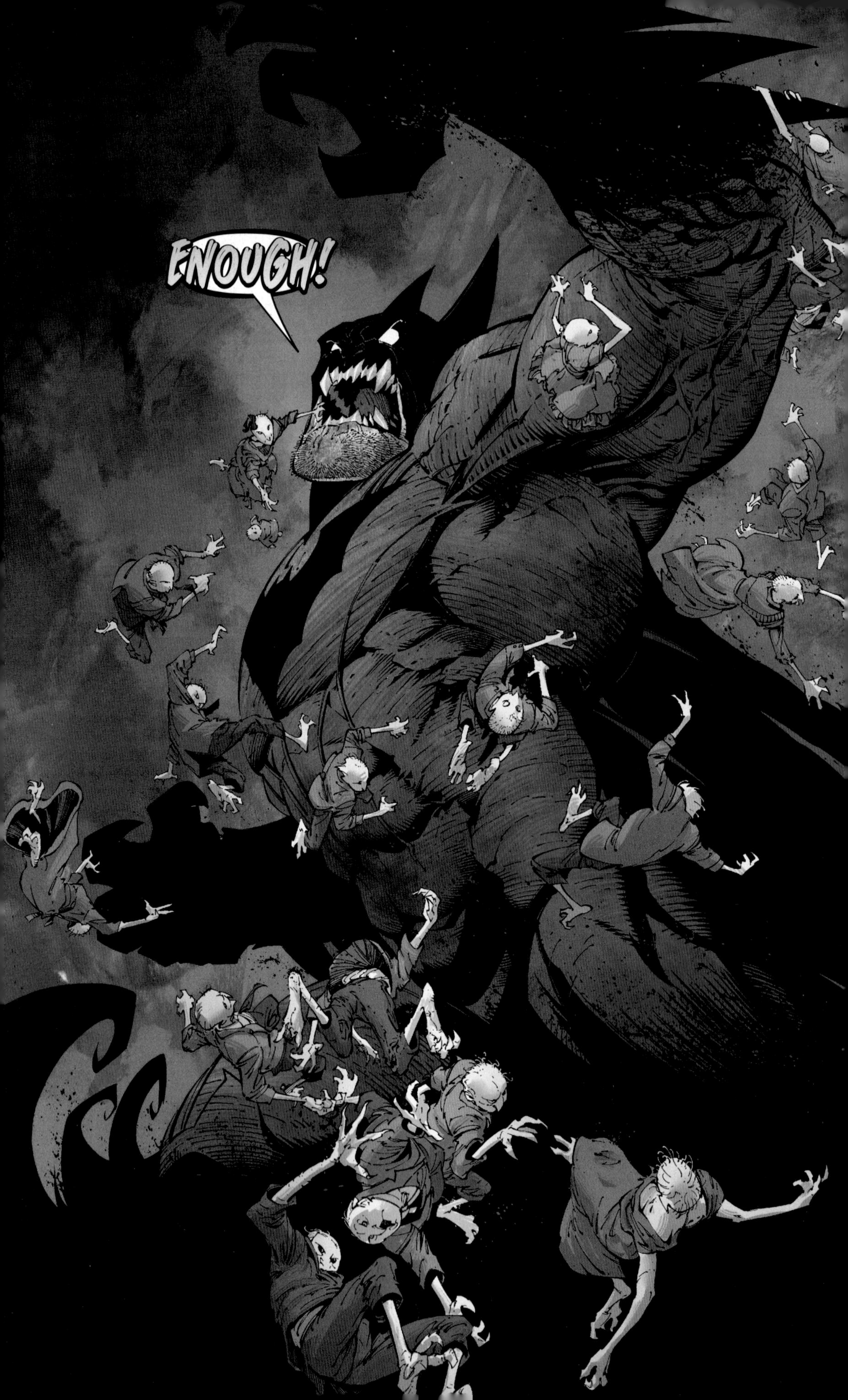
ENOUGH!

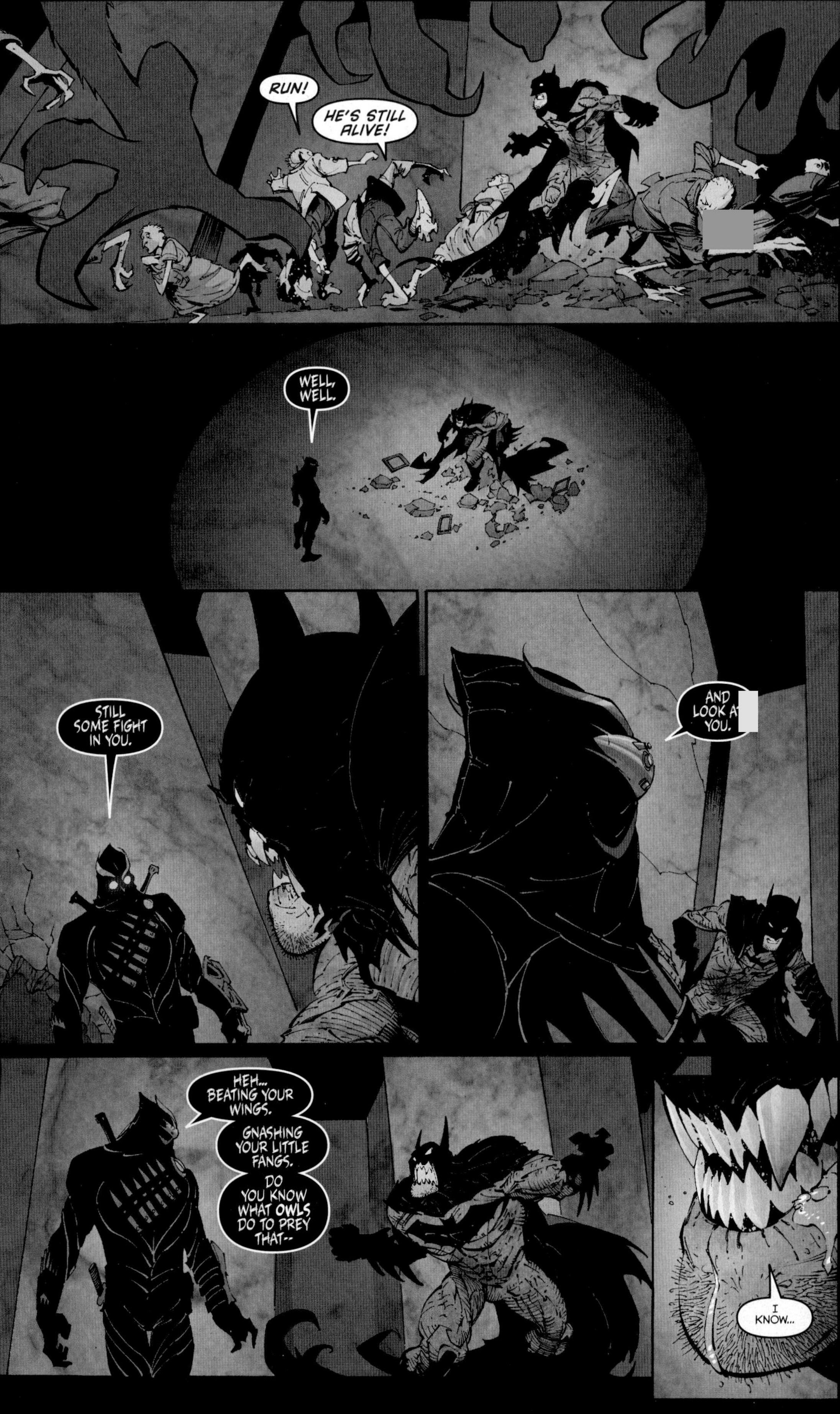

RUN!
HE'S STILL ALIVE!
WELL, WELL.
STILL SOME FIGHT IN YOU.
AND LOOK AT YOU.
HEH... BEATING YOUR WINGS.
GNASHING YOUR LITTLE FANGS.
DO YOU KNOW WHAT OWLS DO TO PREY THAT--
I KNOW...

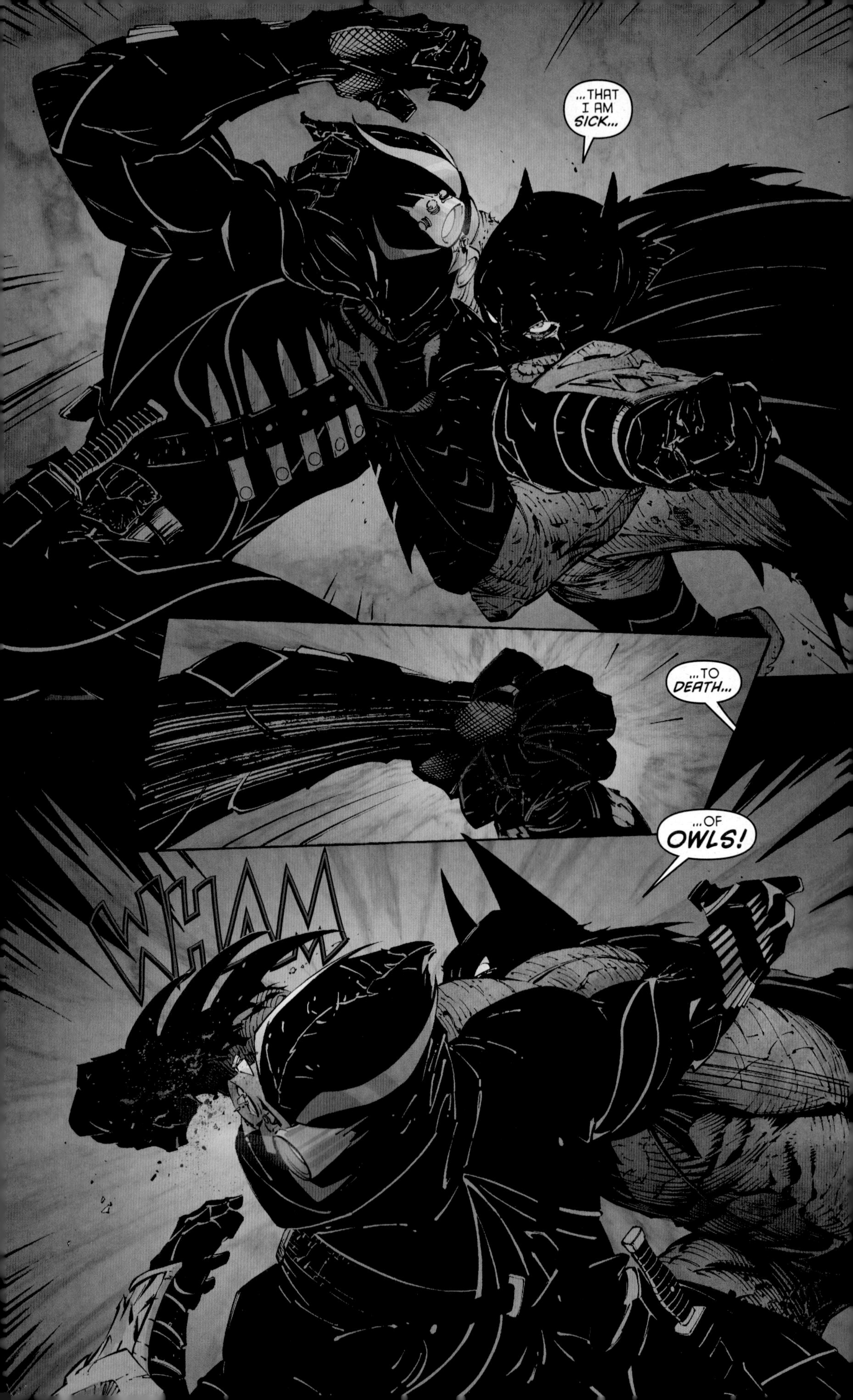
...THAT I AM SICK...
...TO DEATH...
...OF OWLS!
WHAM

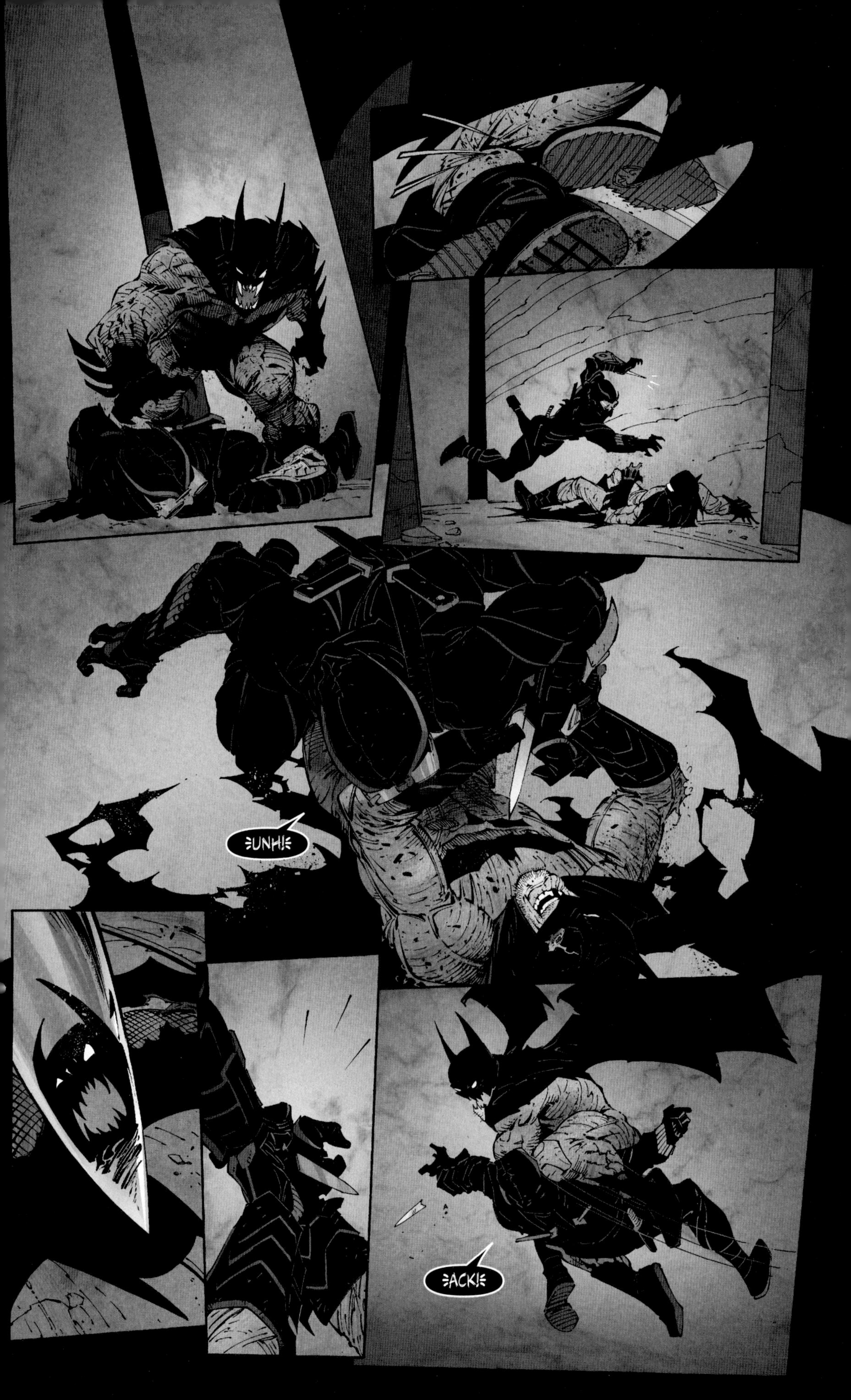UNH!
ACK!

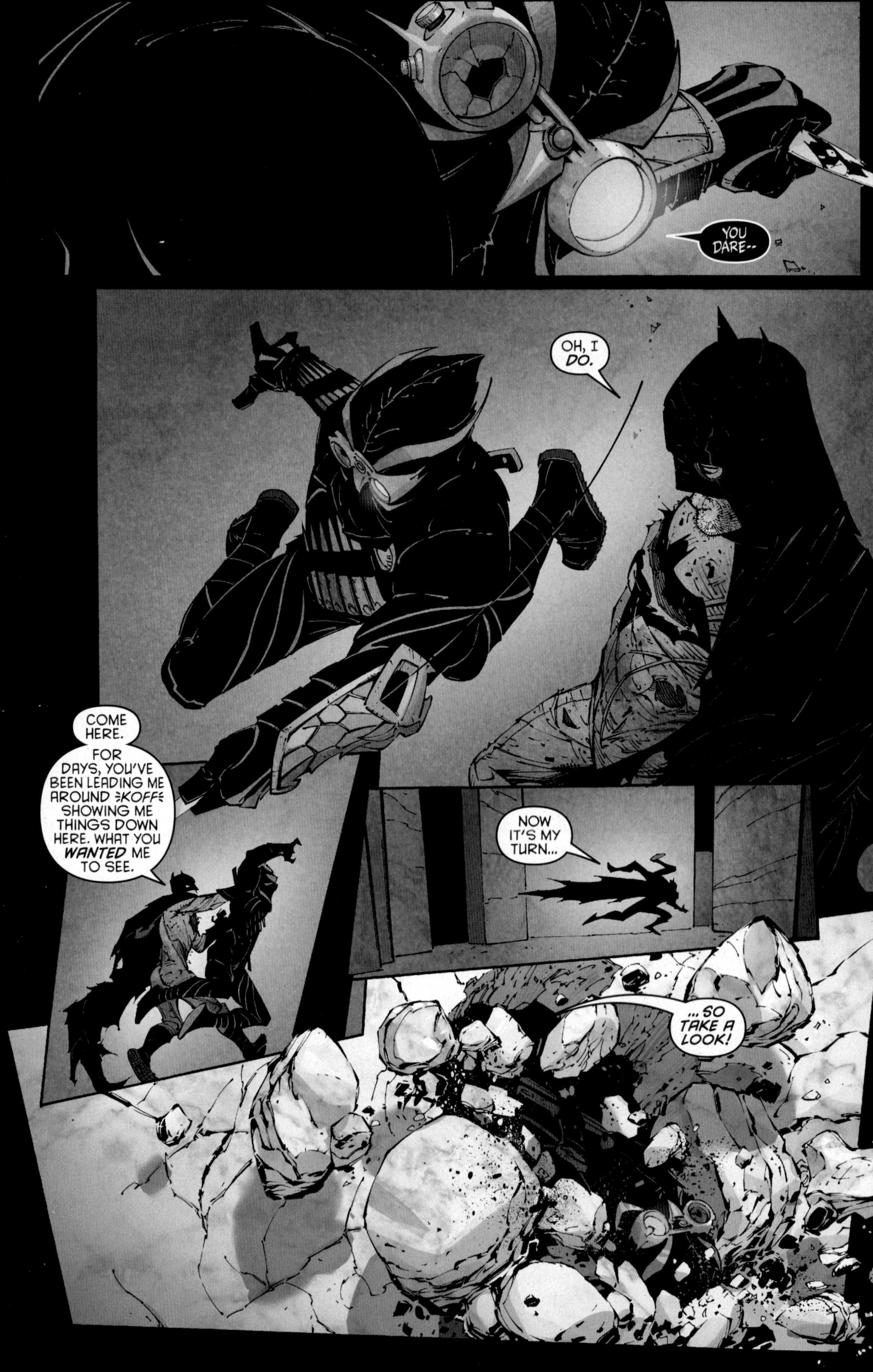
YOU DARE--
OH, I DO.
COME HERE.
FOR DAYS, YOU'VE BEEN LEADING ME AROUND ≠KOFF≠ SHOWING ME THINGS DOWN HERE. WHAT YOU WANTED ME TO SEE.
NOW IT'S MY TURN...
...SO TAKE A LOOK!

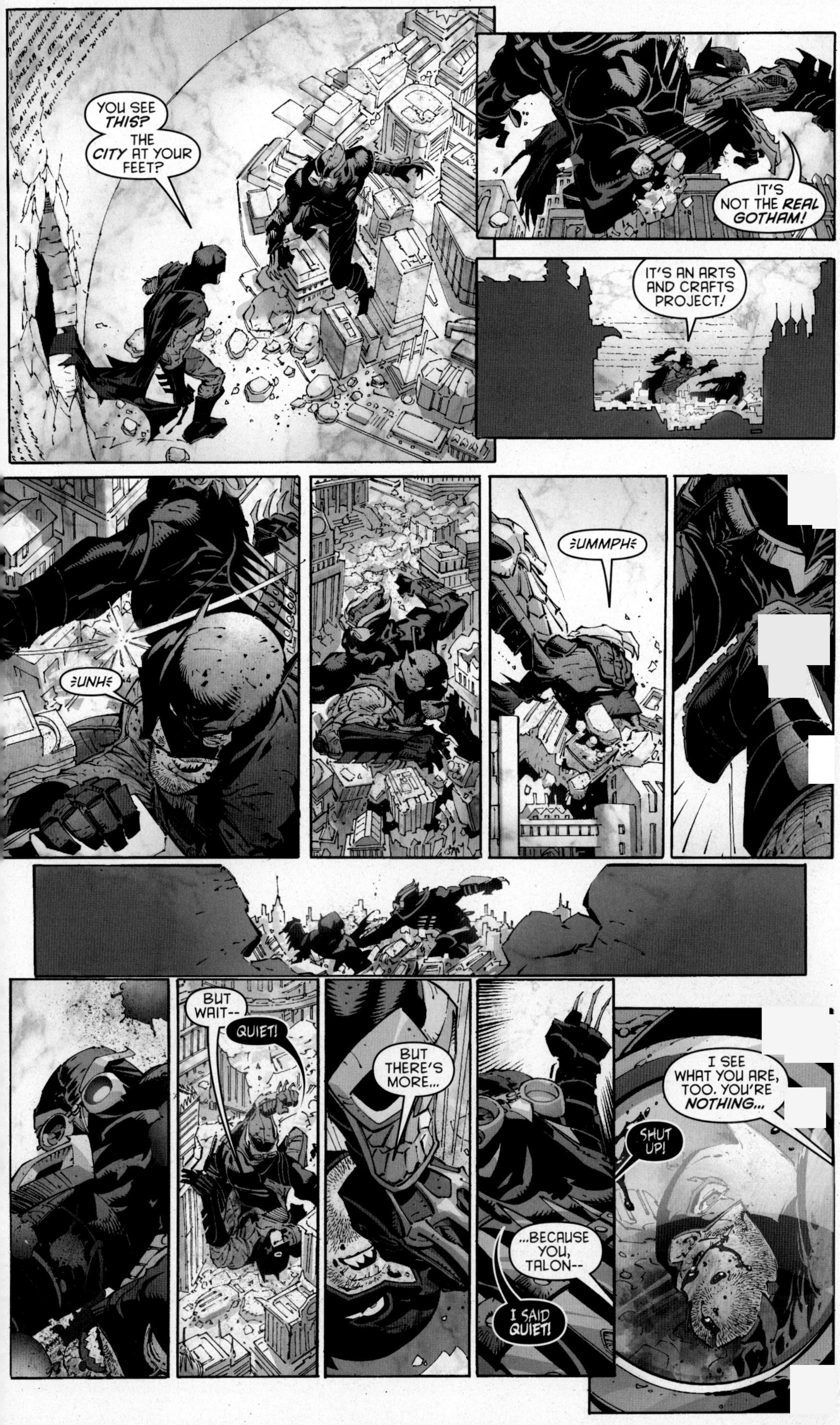

YOU SEE THIS? THE CITY AT YOUR FEET?
IT'S NOT THE REAL GOTHAM!
IT'S AN ARTS AND CRAFTS PROJECT!
UNH
UMMPH
BUT WAIT--
QUIET!
BUT THERE'S MORE...
...BECAUSE YOU, TALON--
I SAID QUIET!
I SEE WHAT YOU ARE, TOO. YOU'RE NOTHING...
SHUT UP!

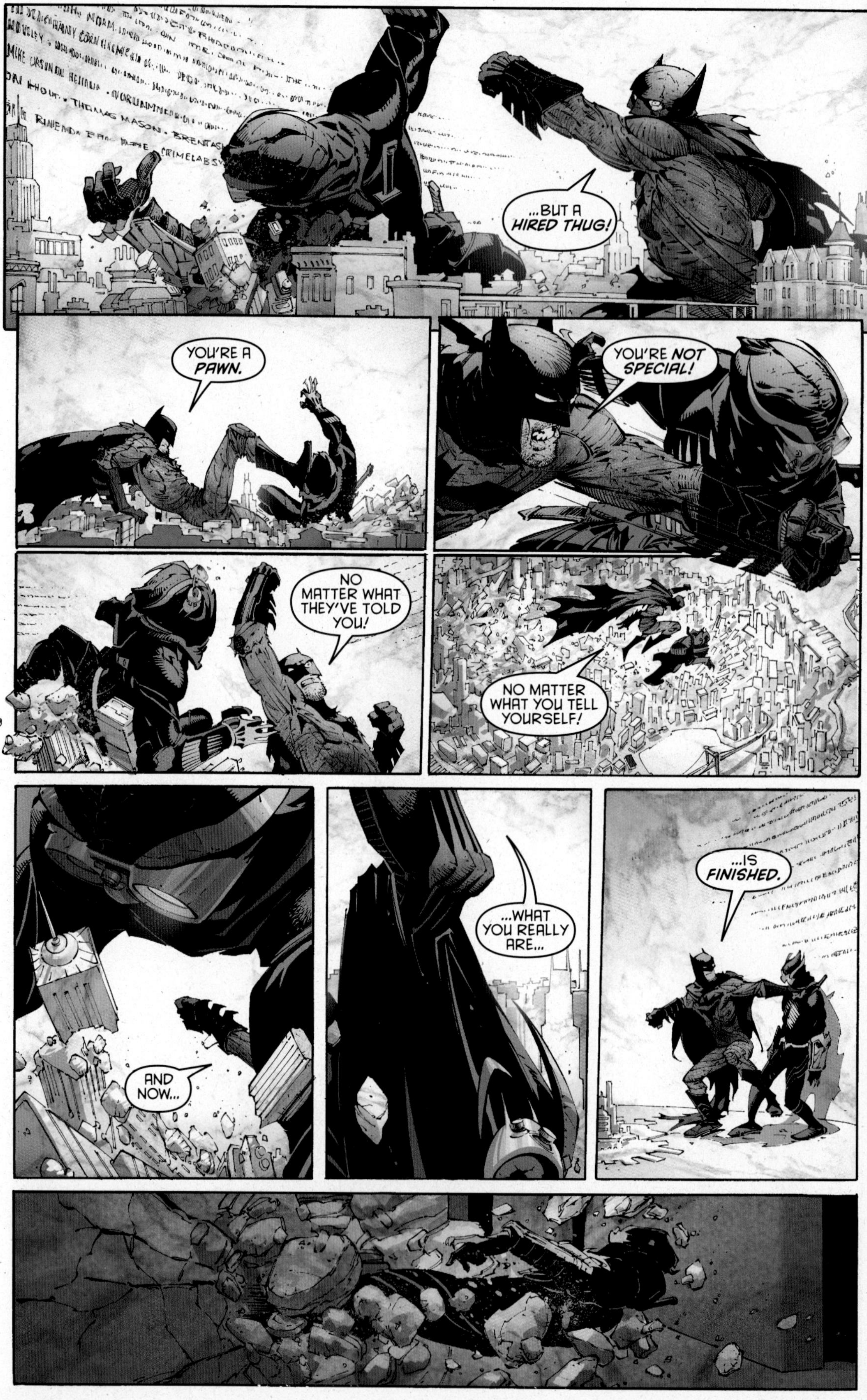
...BUT A HIRED THUG!
YOU'RE A PAWN.
YOU'RE NOT SPECIAL!
NO MATTER WHAT THEY'VE TOLD YOU!
NO MATTER WHAT YOU TELL YOURSELF!
AND NOW...
...WHAT YOU REALLY ARE...
...IS FINISHED.

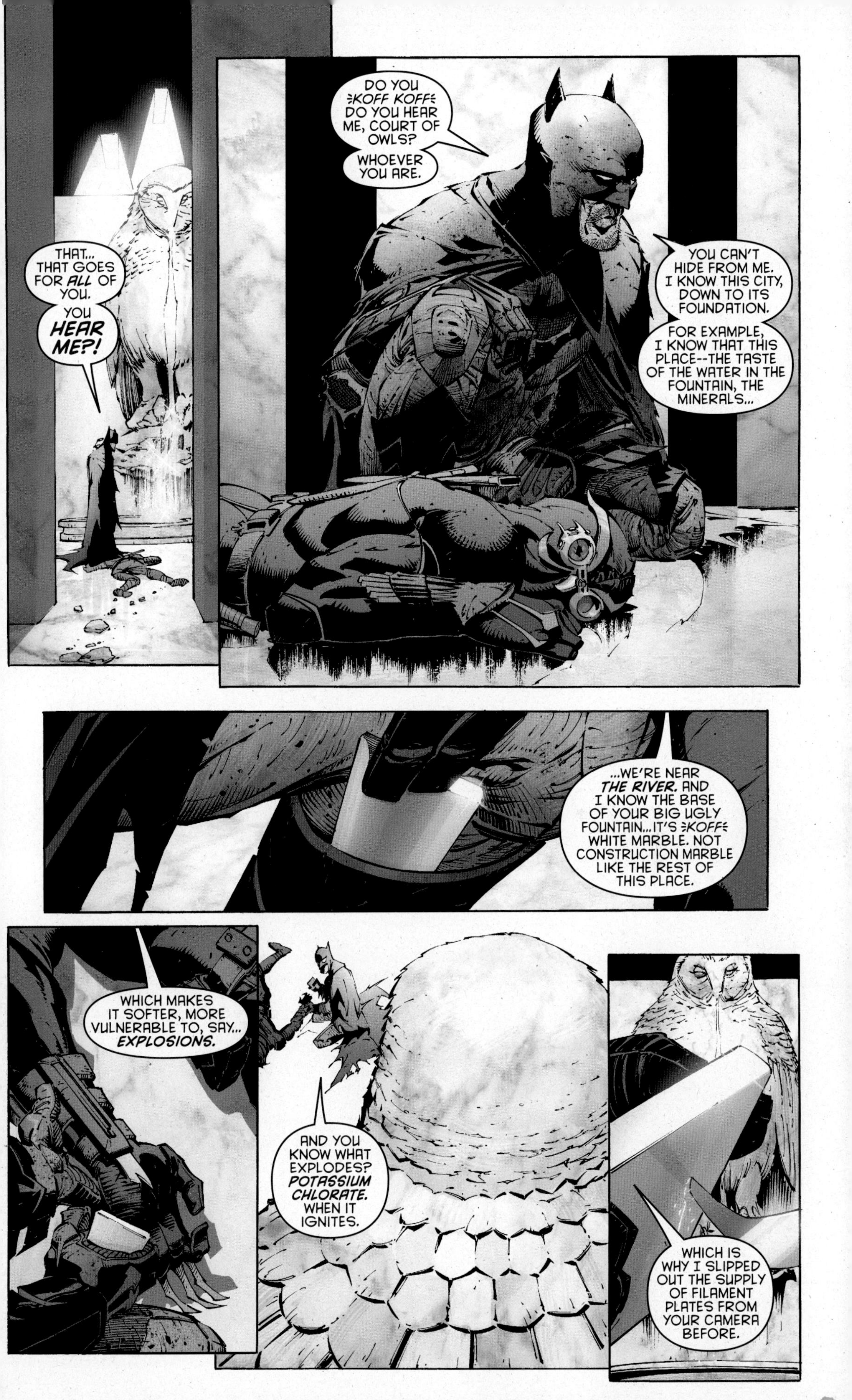
DO YOU
≶KOFF KOFF≶
DO YOU HEAR
ME, COURT OF
OWLS?
WHOEVER
YOU ARE.
THAT... THAT GOES FOR ALL OF YOU.
YOU HEAR ME?!
YOU CAN'T HIDE FROM ME. I KNOW THIS CITY, DOWN TO ITS FOUNDATION.
FOR EXAMPLE, I KNOW THAT THIS PLACE--THE TASTE OF THE WATER IN THE FOUNTAIN, THE MINERALS...
...WE'RE NEAR THE RIVER. AND I KNOW THE BASE OF YOUR BIG UGLY FOUNTAIN...IT'S ≶KOFF≶ WHITE MARBLE. NOT CONSTRUCTION MARBLE LIKE THE REST OF THIS PLACE.
WHICH MAKES IT SOFTER, MORE VULNERABLE TO, SAY... EXPLOSIONS.
AND YOU KNOW WHAT EXPLODES? POTASSIUM CHLORATE. WHEN IT IGNITES.
WHICH IS WHY I SLIPPED OUT THE SUPPLY OF FILAMENT PLATES FROM YOUR CAMERA BEFORE.

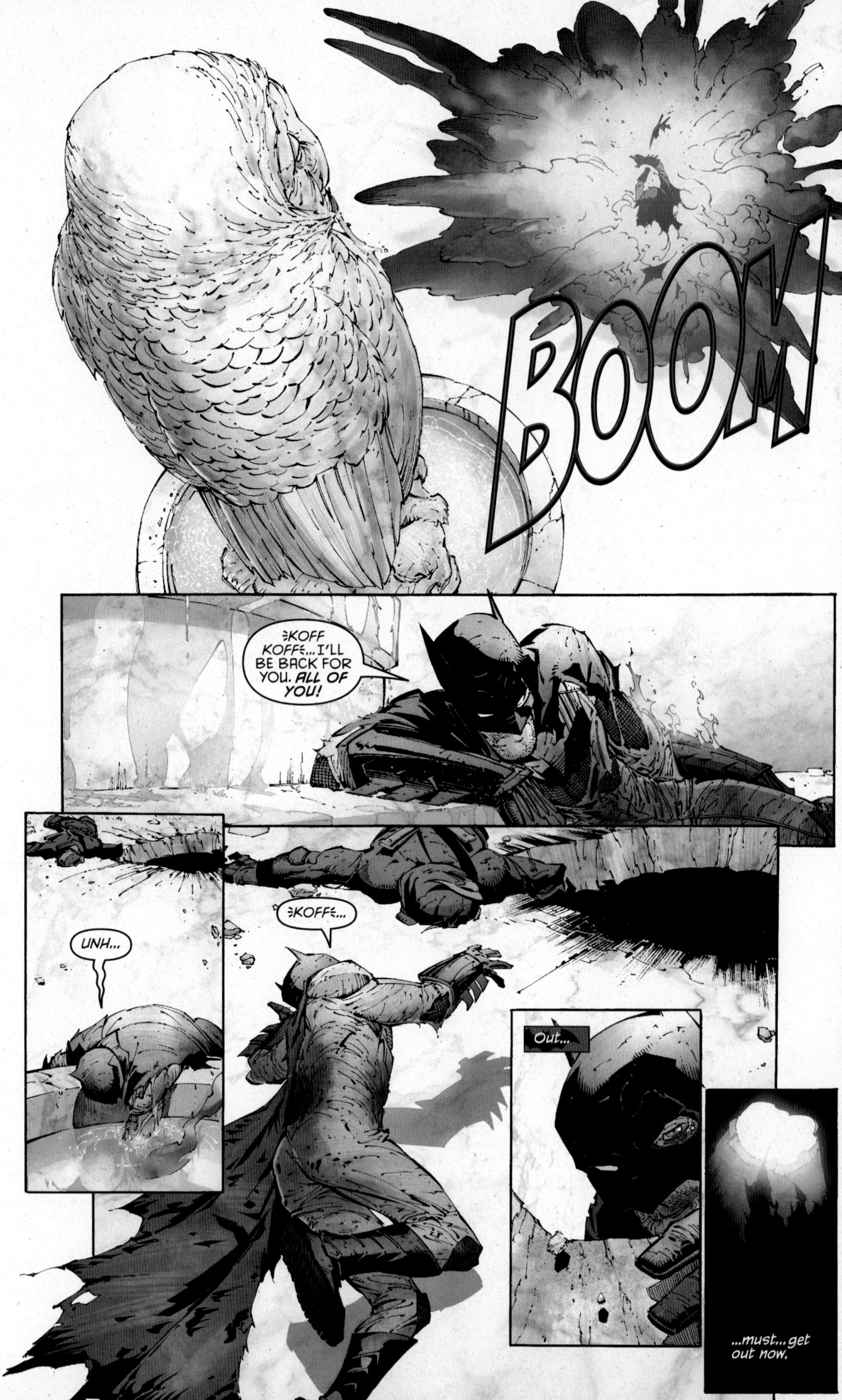
BOOM
ᵏKOFF KOFFᵏ...I'LL BE BACK FOR YOU. ALL OF YOU!
UNH...
ᵏKOFFᵏ...
Out...
...must...get out now.

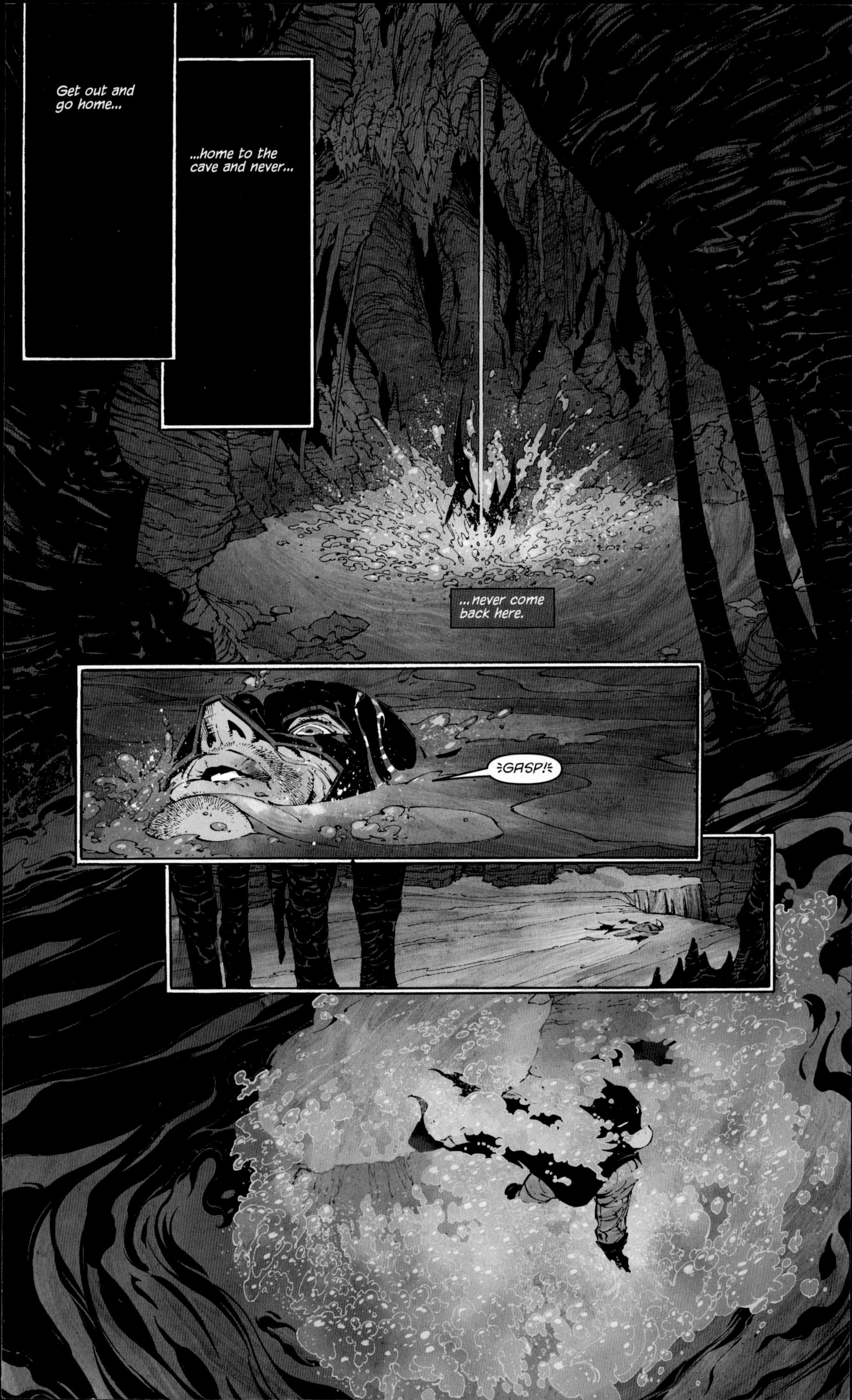
Get out and go home...
...home to the cave and never...
...never come back here.
GASP!

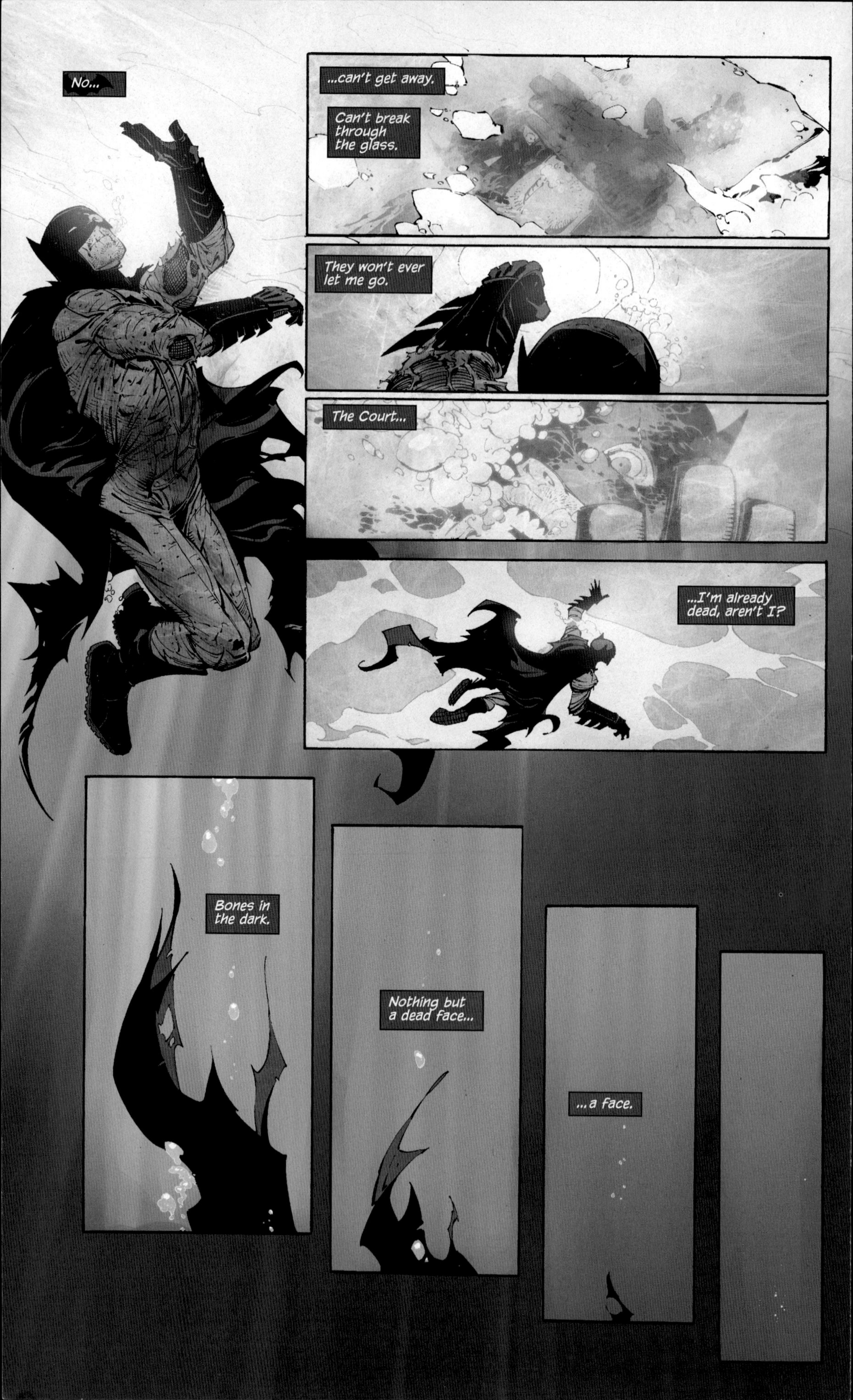
No...
...can't get away.
Can't break through the glass.
They won't ever let me go.
The Court...
...I'm already dead, aren't I?
Bones in the dark.
Nothing but a dead face...
...a face.

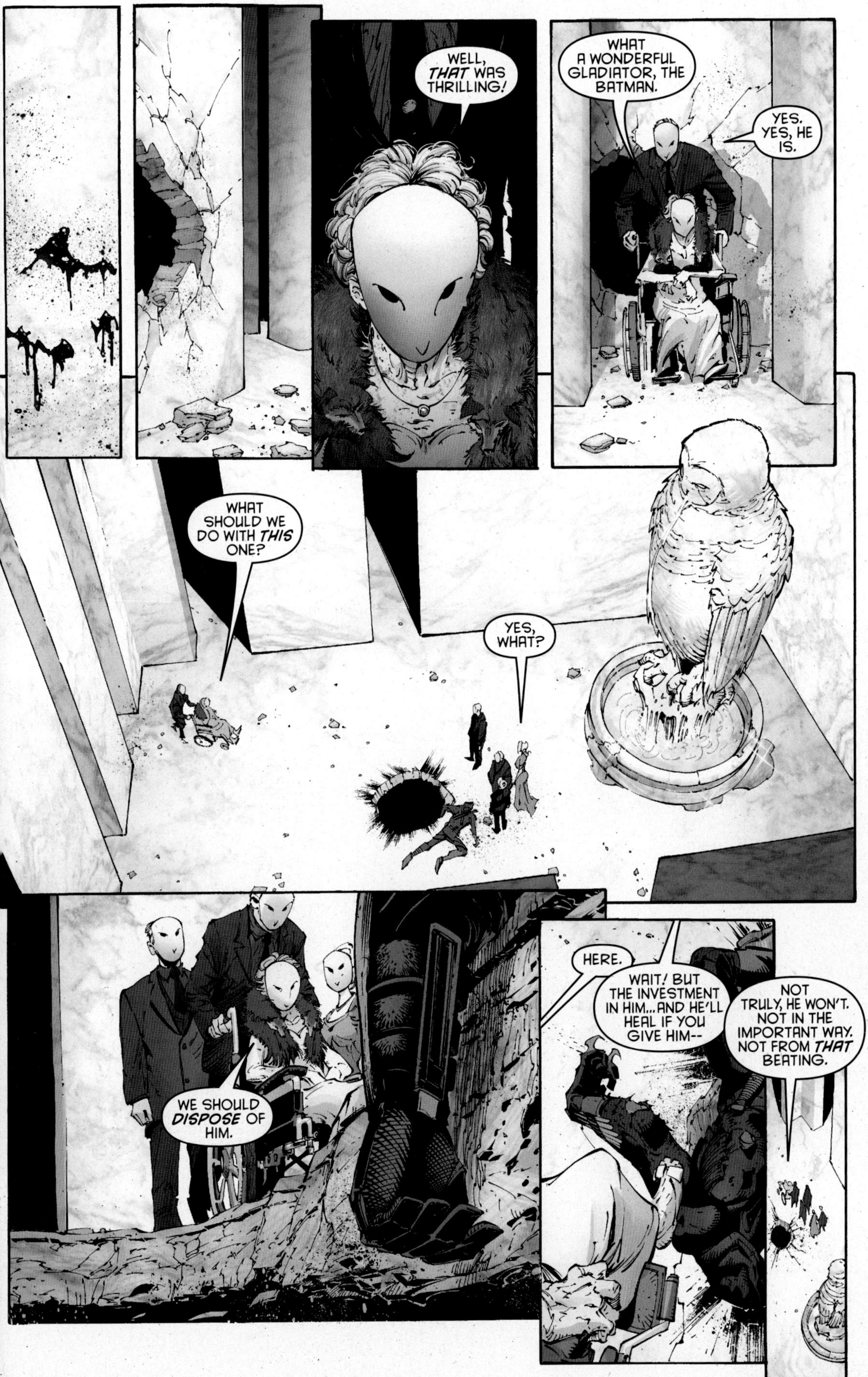
WELL, THAT WAS THRILLING!
WHAT A WONDERFUL GLADIATOR, THE BATMAN.
YES. YES, HE IS.
WHAT SHOULD WE DO WITH THIS ONE?
YES, WHAT?
WE SHOULD DISPOSE OF HIM.
HERE.
WAIT! BUT THE INVESTMENT IN HIM...AND HE'LL HEAL IF YOU GIVE HIM--
NOT TRULY, HE WON'T. NOT IN THE IMPORTANT WAY. NOT FROM THAT BEATING.

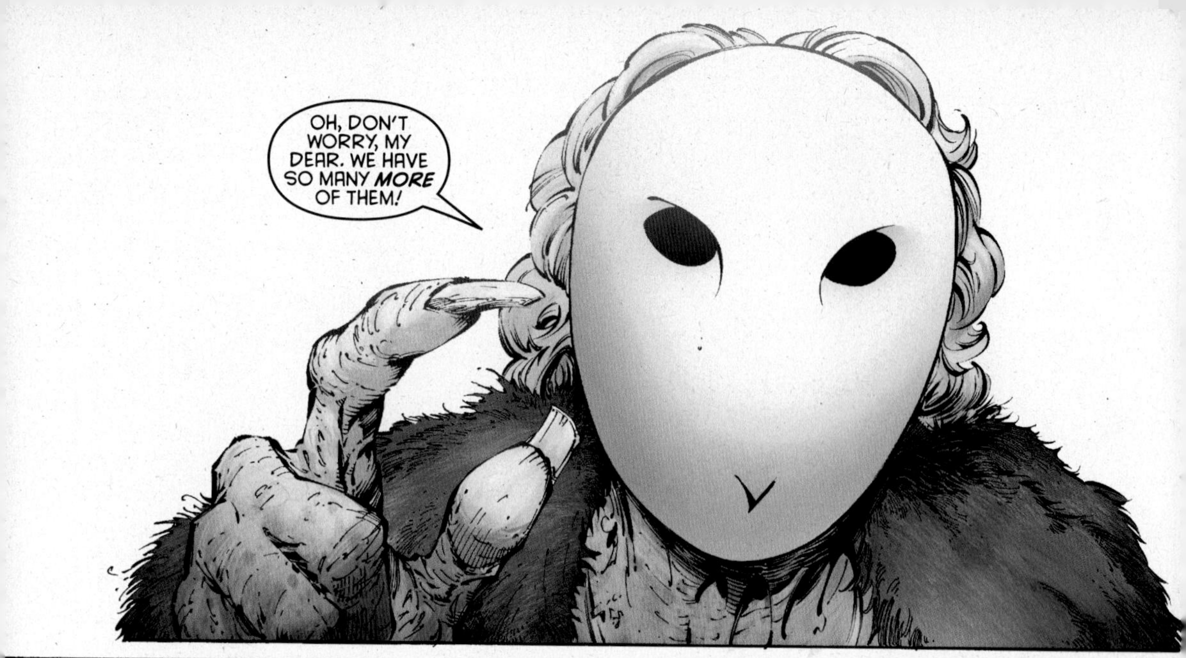
OH, DON'T WORRY, MY DEAR. WE HAVE SO MANY MORE OF THEM!

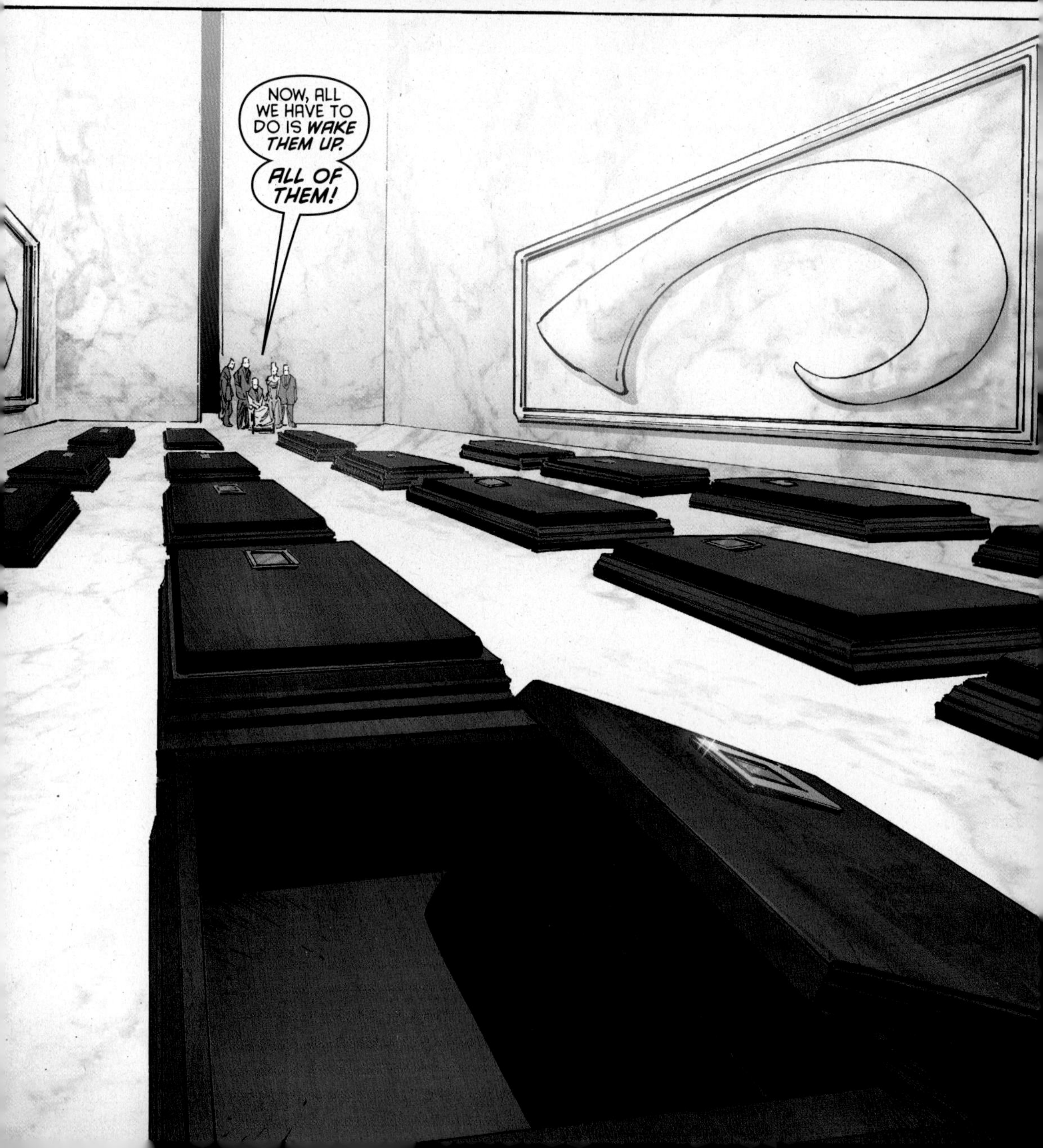
NOW, ALL WE HAVE TO DO IS WAKE THEM UP.
ALL OF THEM!

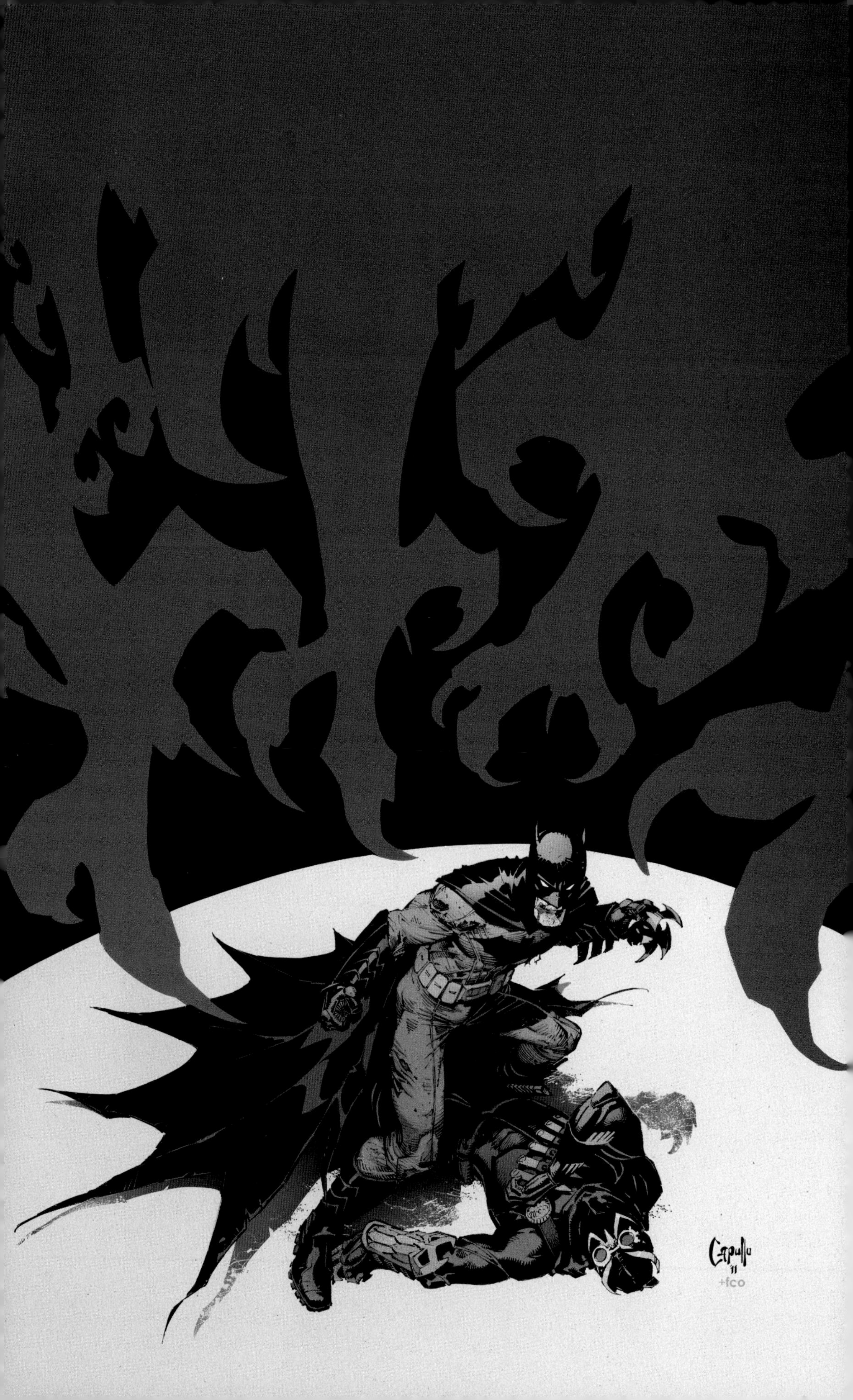

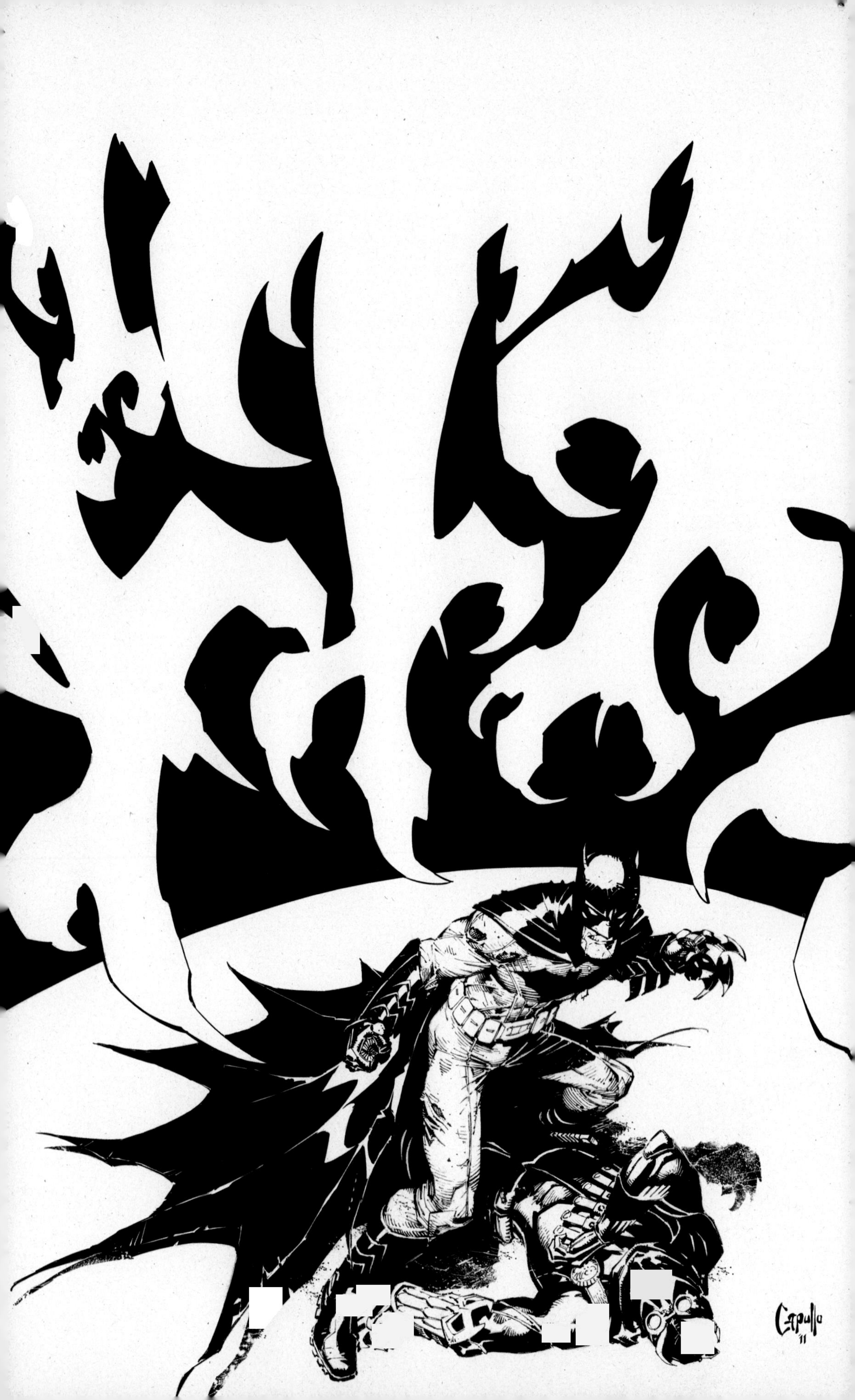

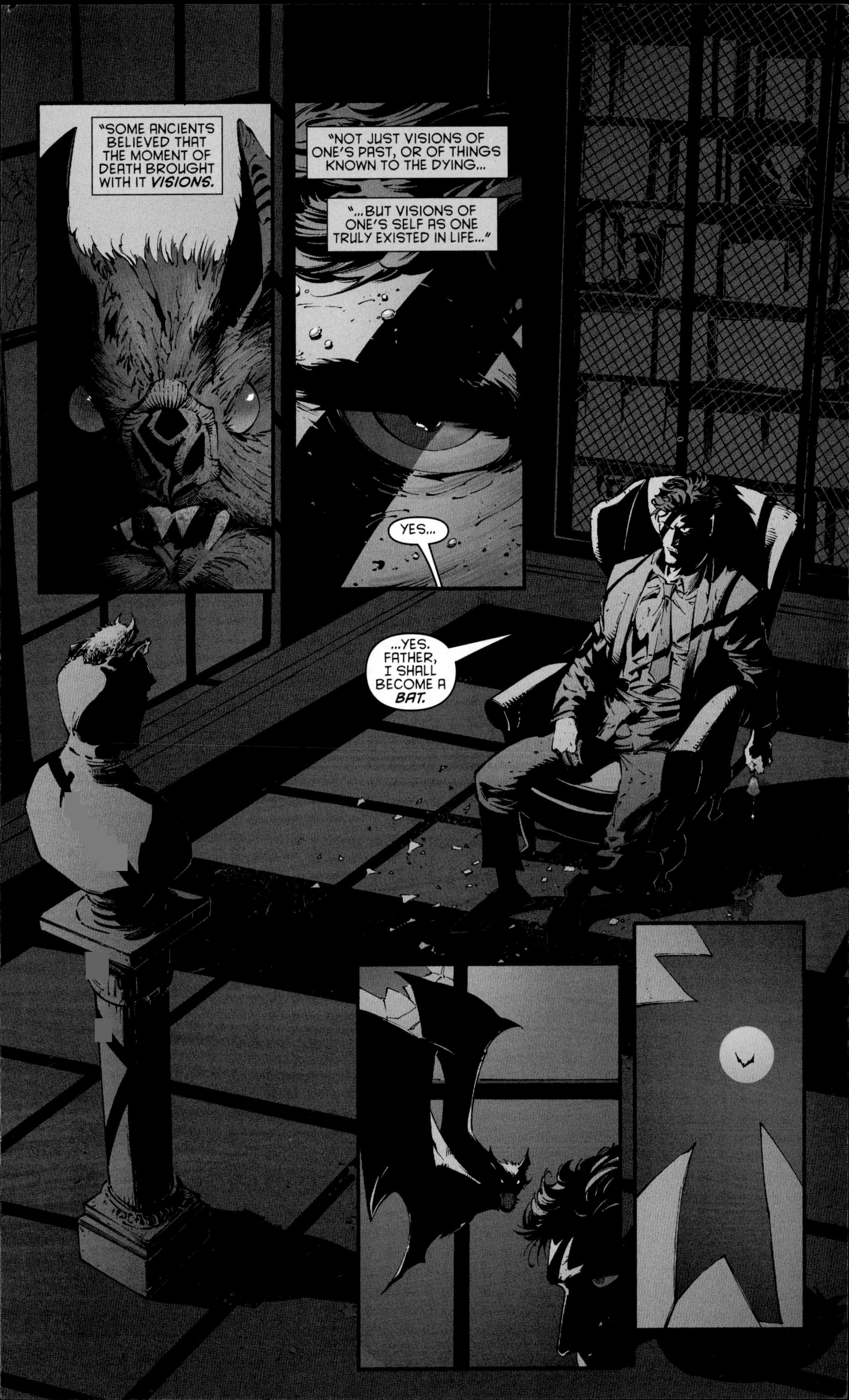
"SOME ANCIENTS BELIEVED THAT THE MOMENT OF DEATH BROUGHT WITH IT *VISIONS.*
"NOT JUST VISIONS OF ONE'S PAST, OR OF THINGS KNOWN TO THE DYING...
"...BUT VISIONS OF ONE'S SELF AS ONE TRULY EXISTED IN LIFE..."
YES...
...YES. FATHER, I SHALL BECOME A *BAT.*

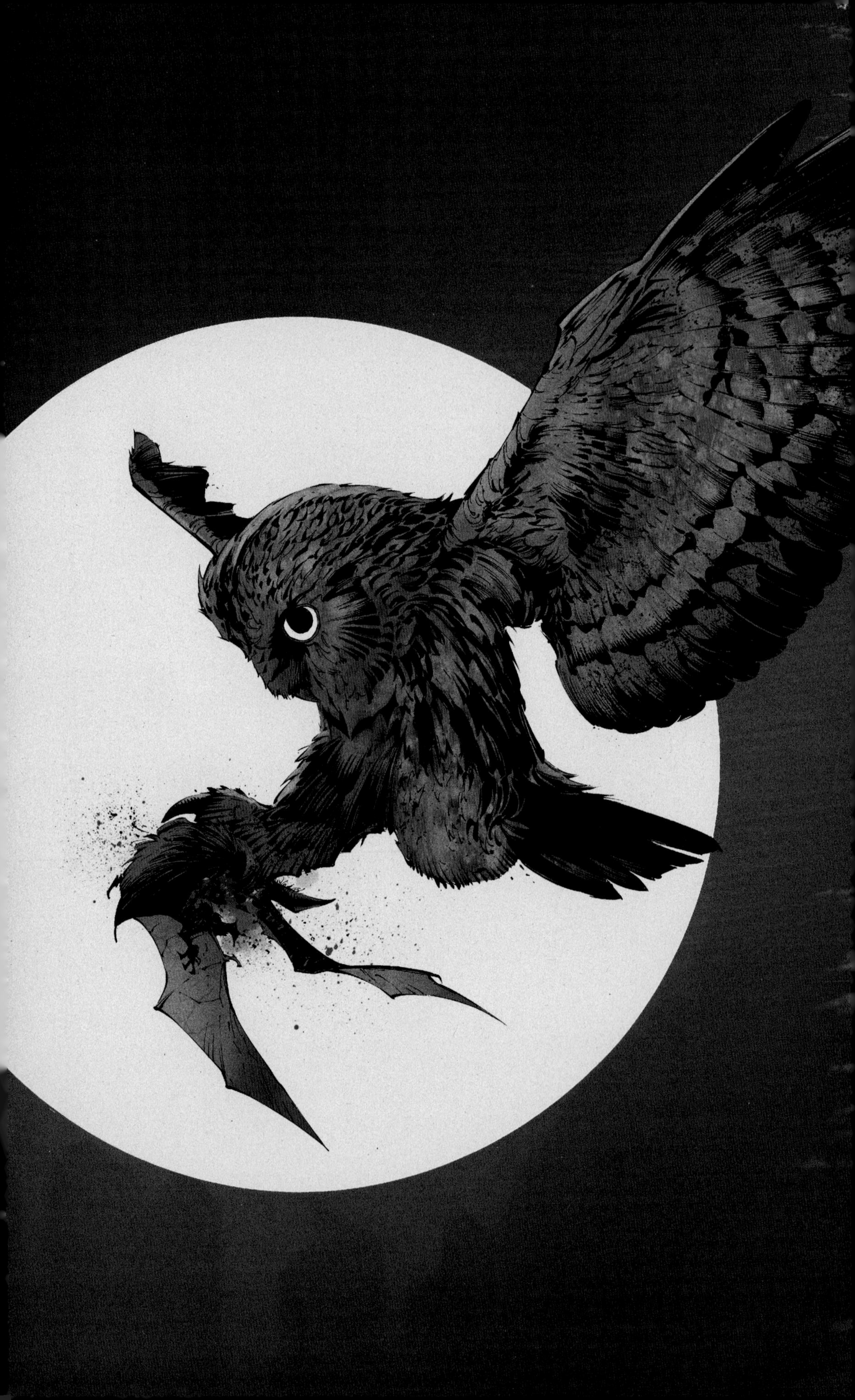

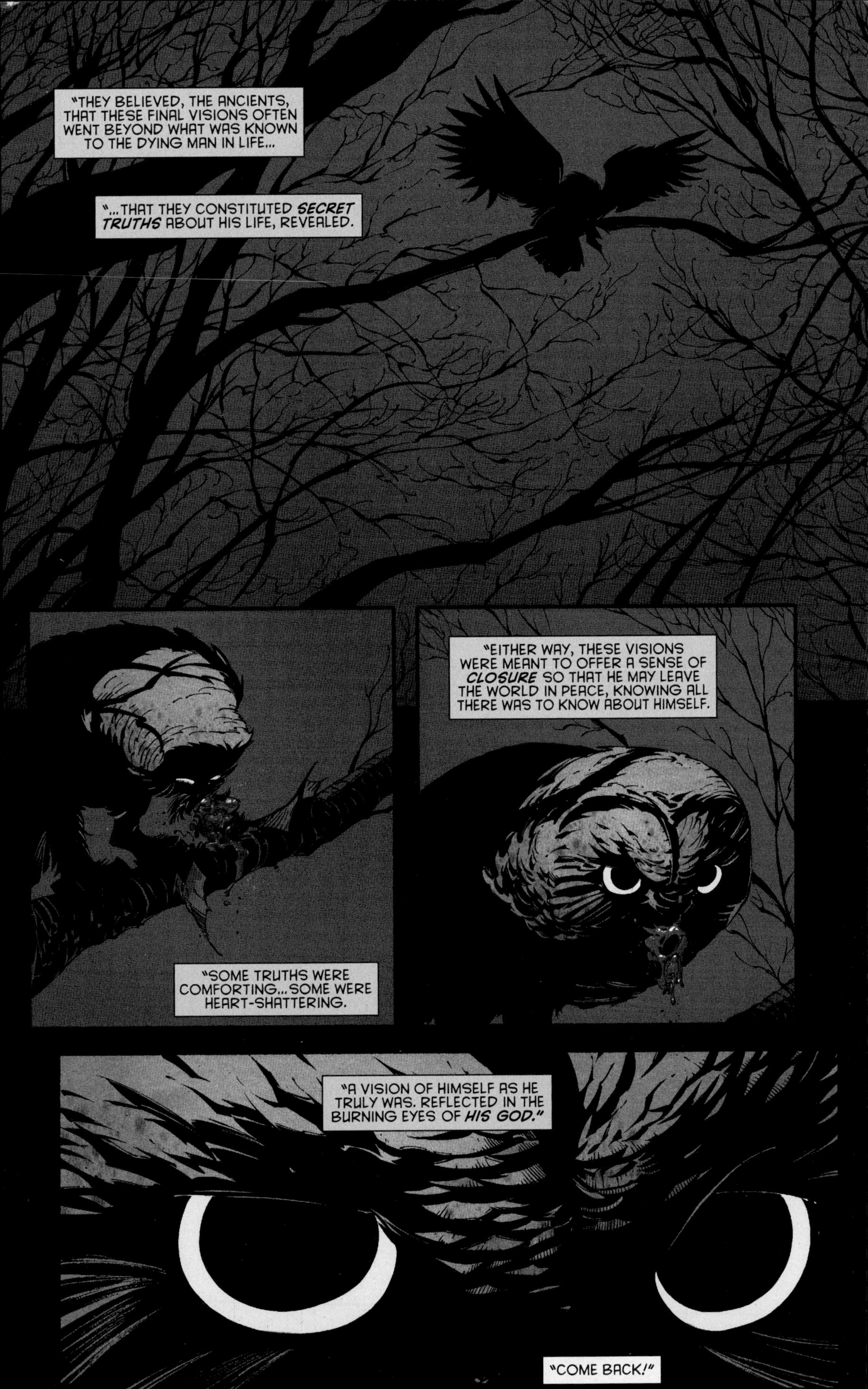
"THEY BELIEVED, THE ANCIENTS, THAT THESE FINAL VISIONS OFTEN WENT BEYOND WHAT WAS KNOWN TO THE DYING MAN IN LIFE...
"...THAT THEY CONSTITUTED SECRET TRUTHS ABOUT HIS LIFE, REVEALED.
"SOME TRUTHS WERE COMFORTING... SOME WERE HEART-SHATTERING.
"EITHER WAY, THESE VISIONS WERE MEANT TO OFFER A SENSE OF CLOSURE SO THAT HE MAY LEAVE THE WORLD IN PEACE, KNOWING ALL THERE WAS TO KNOW ABOUT HIMSELF.
"A VISION OF HIMSELF AS HE TRULY WAS. REFLECTED IN THE BURNING EYES OF HIS GOD."
"COME BACK!"

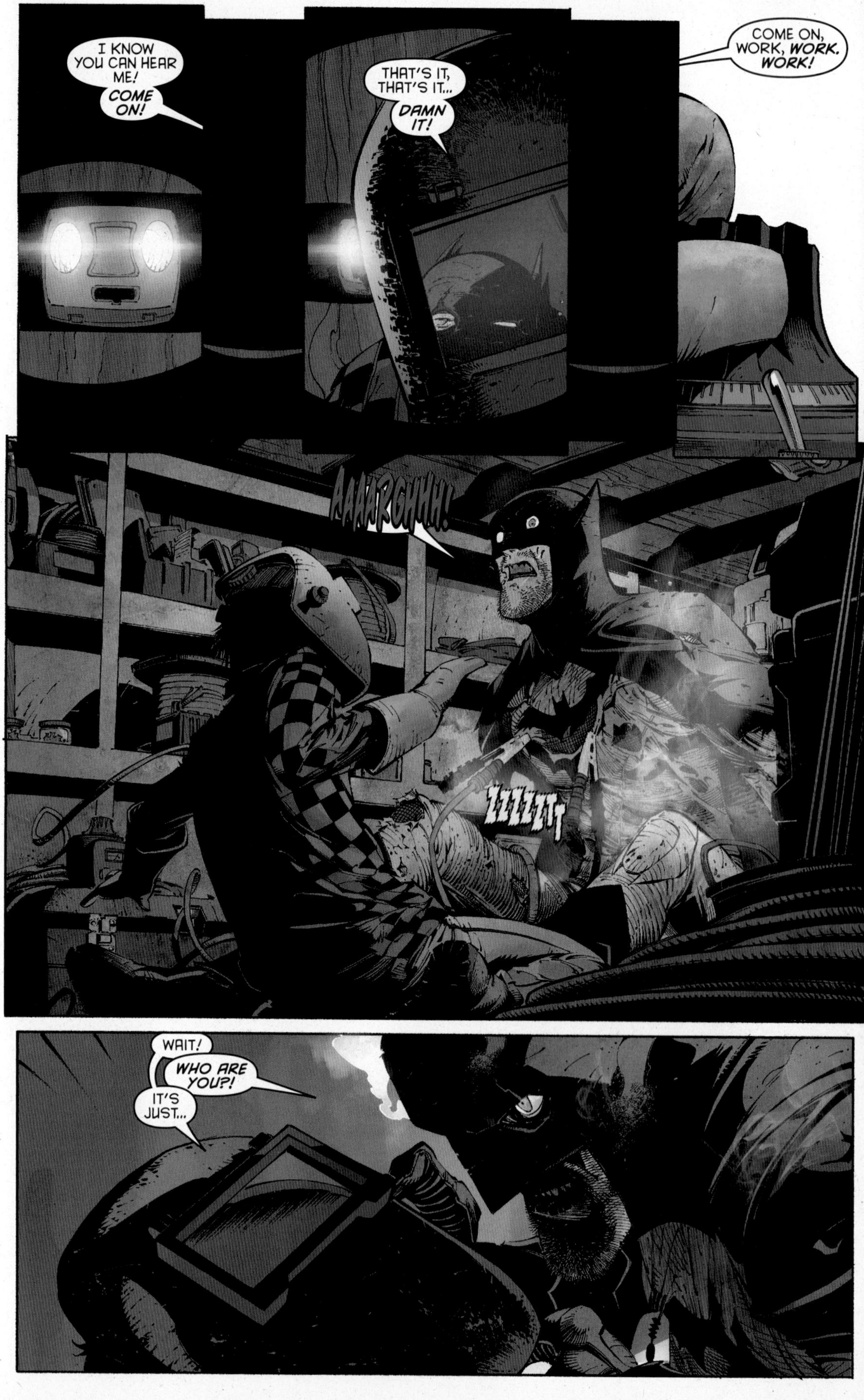
I KNOW YOU CAN HEAR ME! COME ON!
THAT'S IT, THAT'S IT... DAMN IT!
COME ON, WORK, WORK. WORK!
AAAARGHHH!
ZZZZZTT
WAIT! WHO ARE YOU?!
IT'S JUST...

...ME.

YOU.

I'M SORRY...

...THE JUMPERS WERE ALL I HAD. YOU FLAT-LINED AND THIS IS MY BOSS' VAN AND--

I TOLD YOU ONCE ALREADY...

...LEAVE ME ALONE.

I *MEANT* IT.

NICE ONE, HARPER. EPIC BAT-FAIL.

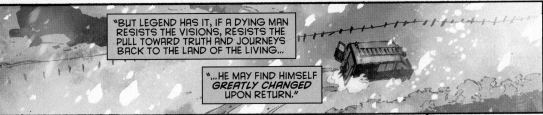

"BUT LEGEND HAS IT, IF A DYING MAN RESISTS THE VISIONS, RESISTS THE PULL TOWARD TRUTH AND JOURNEYS BACK TO THE LAND OF THE LIVING...

"...HE MAY FIND HIMSELF *GREATLY CHANGED* UPON RETURN."

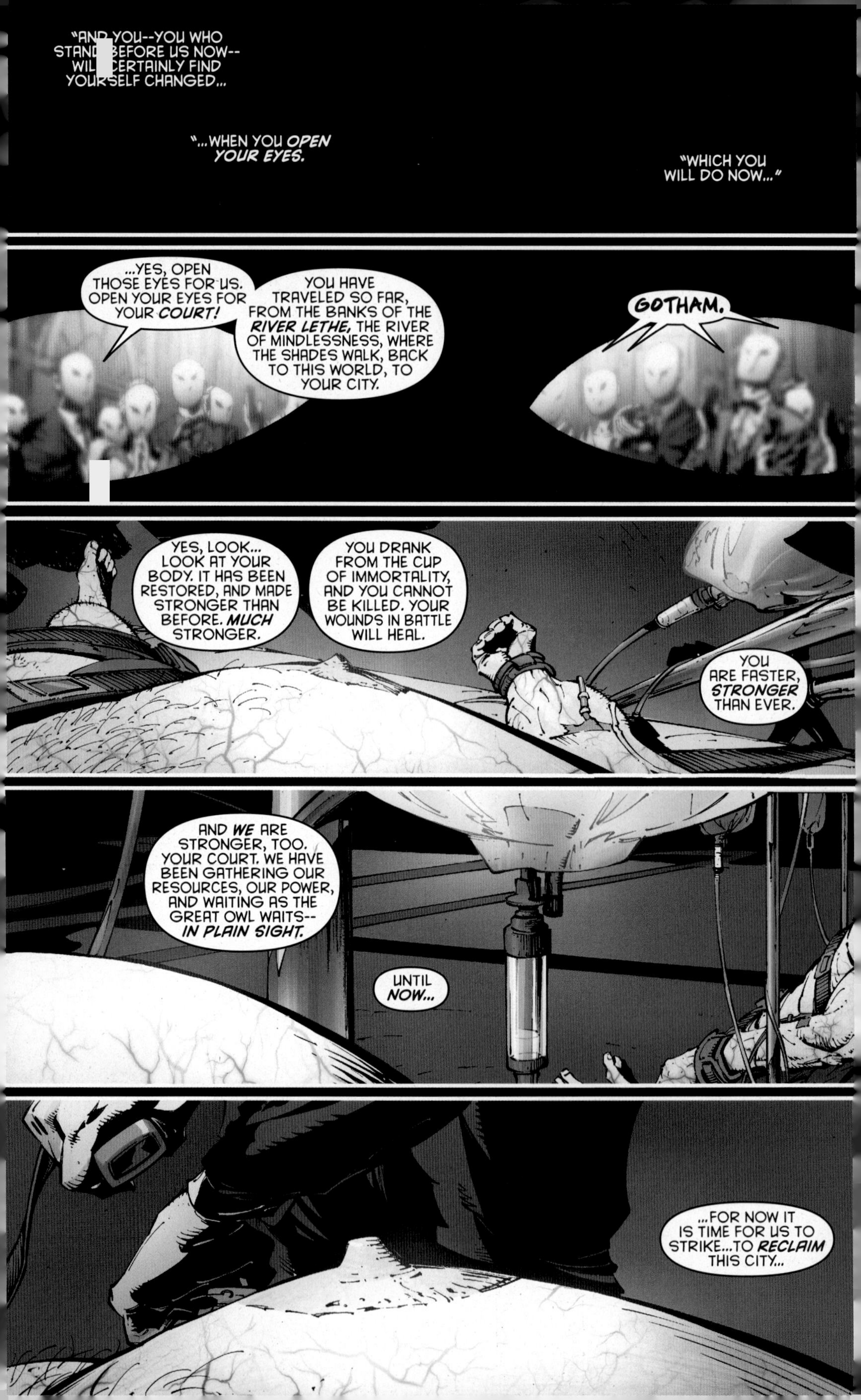
"AND YOU--YOU WHO STAND BEFORE US NOW--WILL CERTAINLY FIND YOURSELF CHANGED...
"...WHEN YOU OPEN YOUR EYES.
"WHICH YOU WILL DO NOW..."
...YES, OPEN THOSE EYES FOR US. OPEN YOUR EYES FOR YOUR COURT!
YOU HAVE TRAVELED SO FAR, FROM THE BANKS OF THE RIVER LETHE, THE RIVER OF MINDLESSNESS, WHERE THE SHADES WALK, BACK TO THIS WORLD, TO YOUR CITY.
GOTHAM.
YES, LOOK... LOOK AT YOUR BODY. IT HAS BEEN RESTORED, AND MADE STRONGER THAN BEFORE. MUCH STRONGER.
YOU DRANK FROM THE CUP OF IMMORTALITY, AND YOU CANNOT BE KILLED. YOUR WOUNDS IN BATTLE WILL HEAL.
YOU ARE FASTER, STRONGER THAN EVER.
AND WE ARE STRONGER, TOO. YOUR COURT. WE HAVE BEEN GATHERING OUR RESOURCES, OUR POWER, AND WAITING AS THE GREAT OWL WAITS-- IN PLAIN SIGHT.
UNTIL NOW...
...FOR NOW IT IS TIME FOR US TO STRIKE...TO RECLAIM THIS CITY...

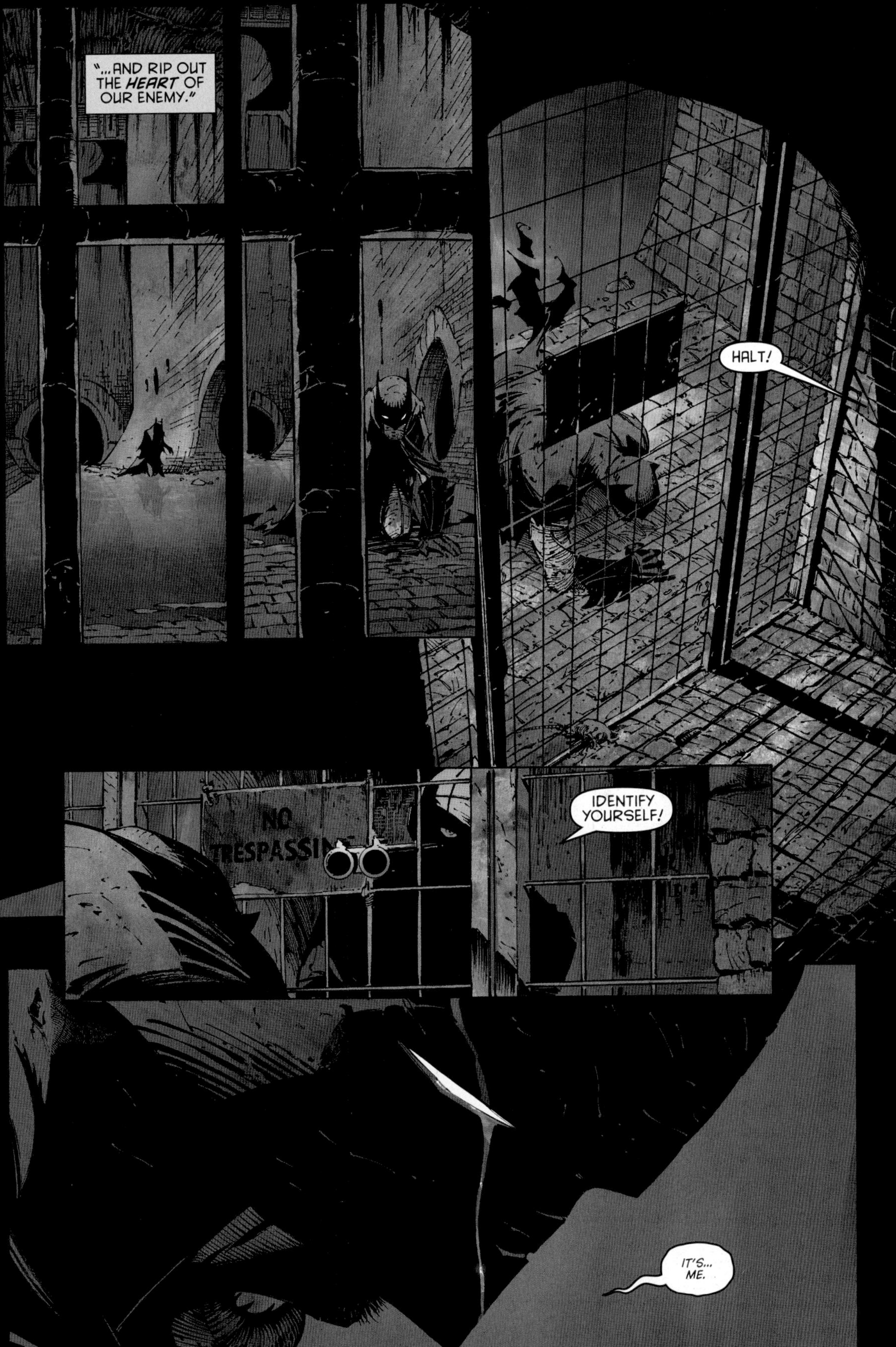
"...AND RIP OUT THE HEART OF OUR ENEMY."
HALT!
NO TRESPASSING
IDENTIFY YOURSELF!
IT'S... ME.

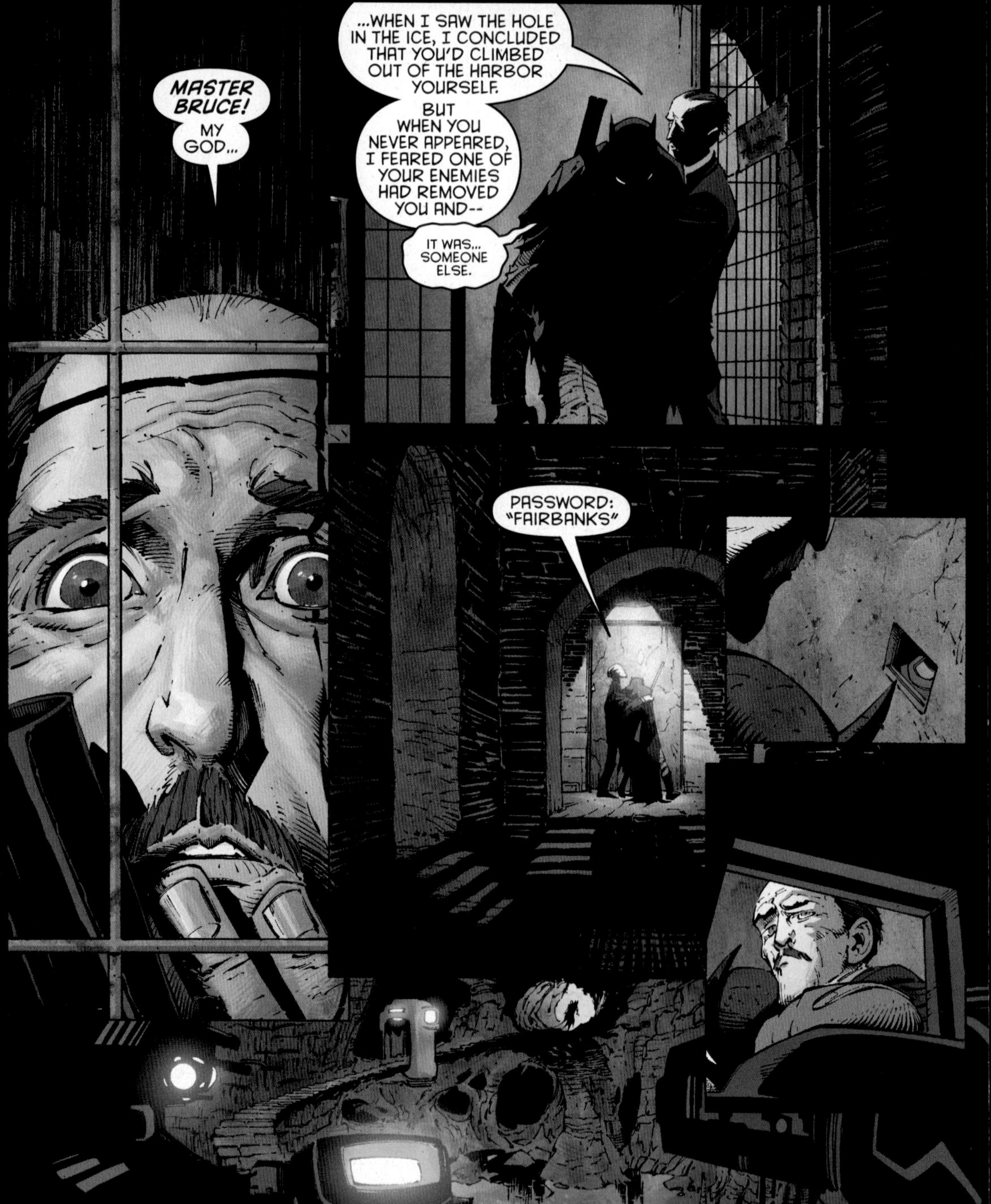
MASTER BRUCE! MY GOD...
...WHEN I SAW THE HOLE IN THE ICE, I CONCLUDED THAT YOU'D CLIMBED OUT OF THE HARBOR YOURSELF.
BUT WHEN YOU NEVER APPEARED, I FEARED ONE OF YOUR ENEMIES HAD REMOVED YOU AND--
IT WAS... SOMEONE ELSE.
PASSWORD: "FAIRBANKS"

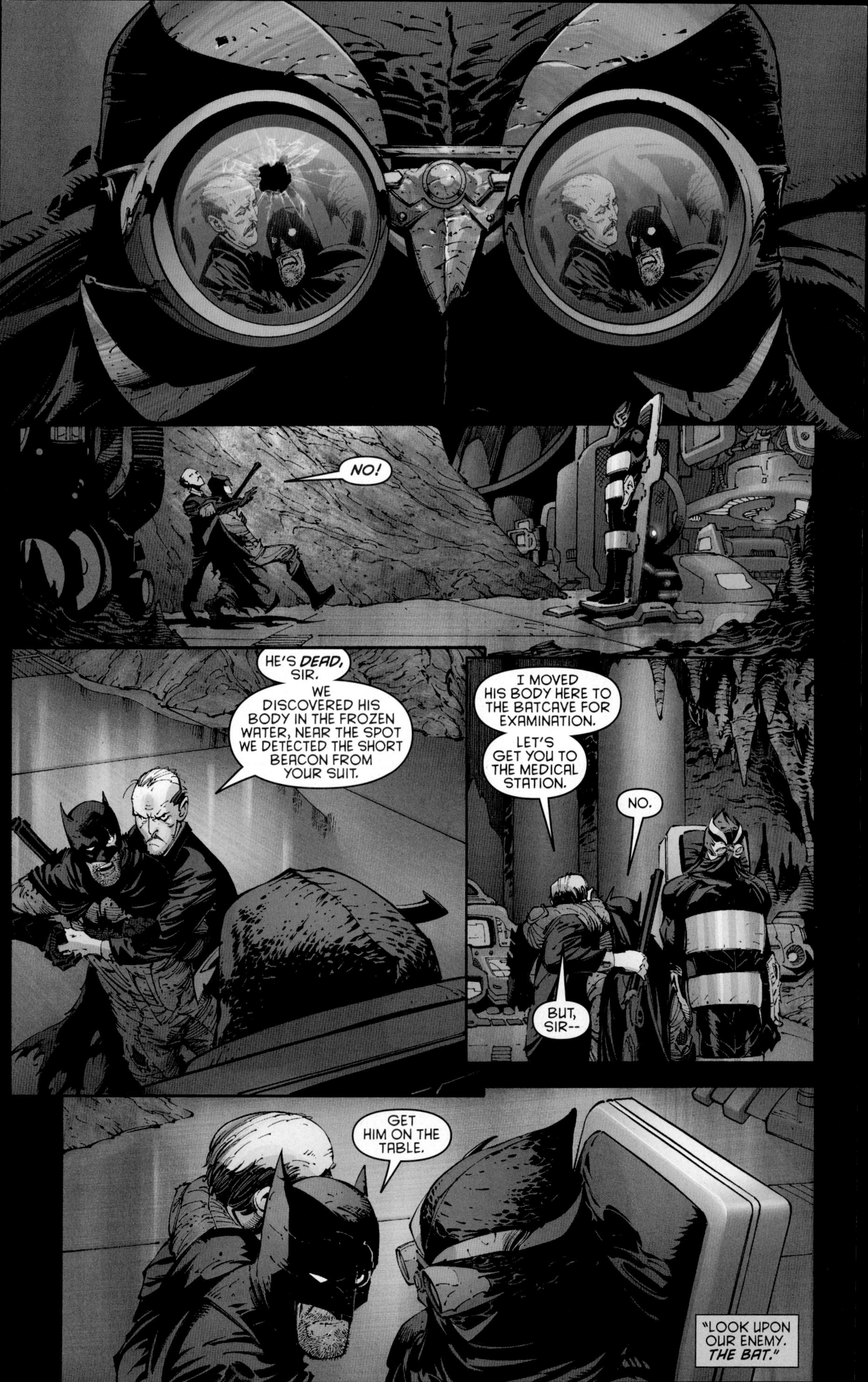
NO!
HE'S *DEAD,* SIR.
WE DISCOVERED HIS BODY IN THE FROZEN WATER, NEAR THE SPOT WE DETECTED THE SHORT BEACON FROM YOUR SUIT.
I MOVED HIS BODY HERE TO THE BATCAVE FOR EXAMINATION.
LET'S GET YOU TO THE MEDICAL STATION.
NO.
BUT, SIR--
GET HIM ON THE TABLE.
"LOOK UPON OUR ENEMY. *THE BAT.*"

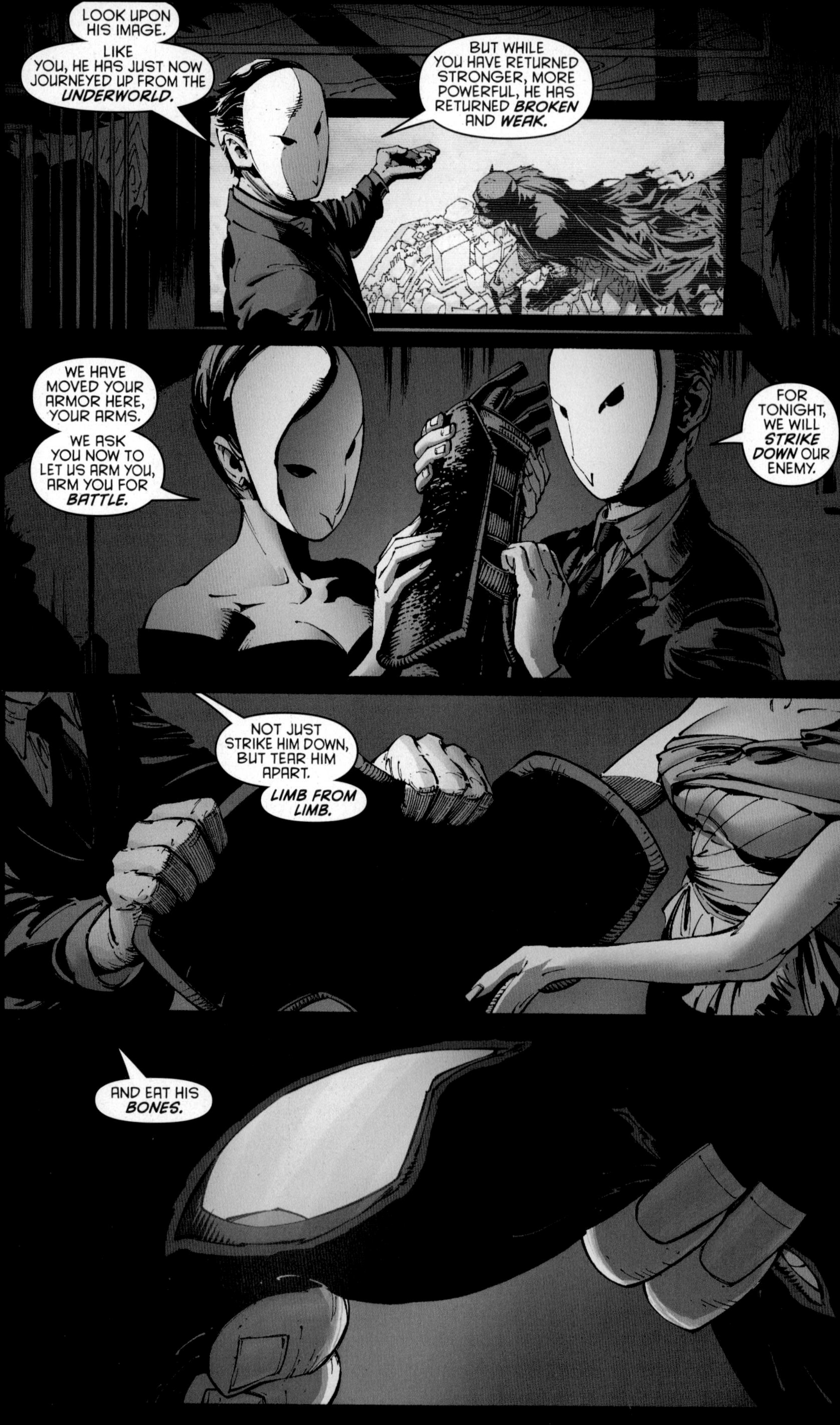
LOOK UPON HIS IMAGE.
LIKE YOU, HE HAS JUST NOW JOURNEYED UP FROM THE UNDERWORLD.
BUT WHILE YOU HAVE RETURNED STRONGER, MORE POWERFUL, HE HAS RETURNED BROKEN AND WEAK.
WE HAVE MOVED YOUR ARMOR HERE, YOUR ARMS.
WE ASK YOU NOW TO LET US ARM YOU, ARM YOU FOR BATTLE.
FOR TONIGHT, WE WILL STRIKE DOWN OUR ENEMY.
NOT JUST STRIKE HIM DOWN, BUT TEAR HIM APART.
LIMB FROM LIMB.
AND EAT HIS BONES.

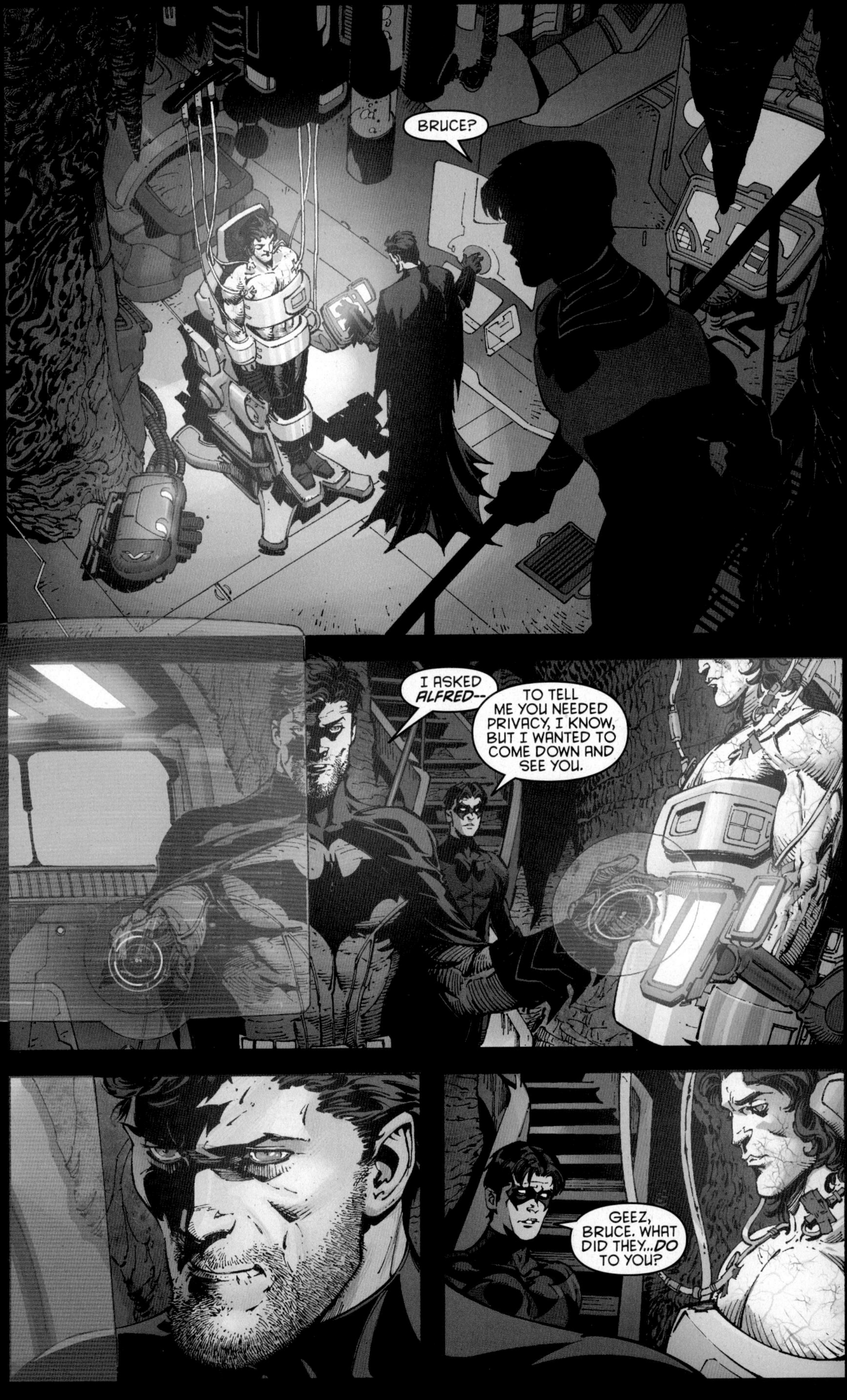
BRUCE?
I ASKED *ALFRED*--
TO TELL ME YOU NEEDED PRIVACY, I KNOW, BUT I WANTED TO COME DOWN AND SEE YOU.
GEEZ, BRUCE. WHAT DID THEY... *DO* TO YOU?

THE MAN ON THE TABLE IS *THE TALON*.

AN ASSASSIN FOR THE COURT OF OWLS.

IS HE... DEAD?

YES...

...AND NO.

THERE'S A COMPOUND I'VE ISOLATED IN HIS CELLS. SOMETHING THE COURT MUST HAVE MANAGED TO SYNTHESIZE. IT'S CAPABLE OF *REANIMATING* DEAD TISSUE.

BRINGING BODIES BACK FROM THE DEAD?

ONLY BODIES SPECIALLY PREPARED.

PREPARED *HOW?*

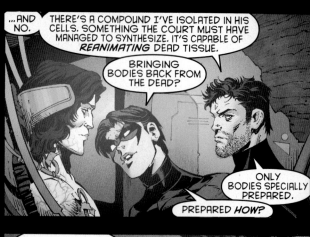

THE COURT HAS AN AFFINITY FOR CLASSICAL ANTIQUITY. IN ANCIENT GREECE, THERE WAS A TRADITION OF PLACING *COINS* BENEATH THE CORPSE'S TONGUE BEFORE BURIAL. SUPPOSEDLY TO PAY FOR PASSAGE INTO HADES.

THE RICH SOMETIMES HAD THEIR COINS MADE FROM A METAL CALLED *ELECTRUM.* A HIGHLY CONDUCTIVE ALLOY OF SILVER AND COPPER.

IN THIS MAN'S BODY, I FOUND A SIGNIFICANT AMOUNT OF ELECTRUM.

NOT JUST IN HIS BLOOD, BUT IN HIS CELLS. THE ALLOY SEEPED DOWN OVER YEARS AND YEARS, FROM A DEPOSIT EMBEDDED IN HIS *TOOTH.* IN THE SHAPE OF A *TINY OWL.*

LIKE THE JOHN DOE HE KILLED--HE CARRIED HIS FERRYMAN'S COIN WITH HIM ALL THE TIME, FOR YEARS.

BY THE TIME HE WAS RETIRED HE WAS A *WALKING CONDUCTOR,* WAITING FOR A SPARK. AND FROM A CHEMIST'S STANDPOINT, THAT'S ALL THIS COMPOUND IS.

A SPARK TO LIGHT UP THE WIRE.

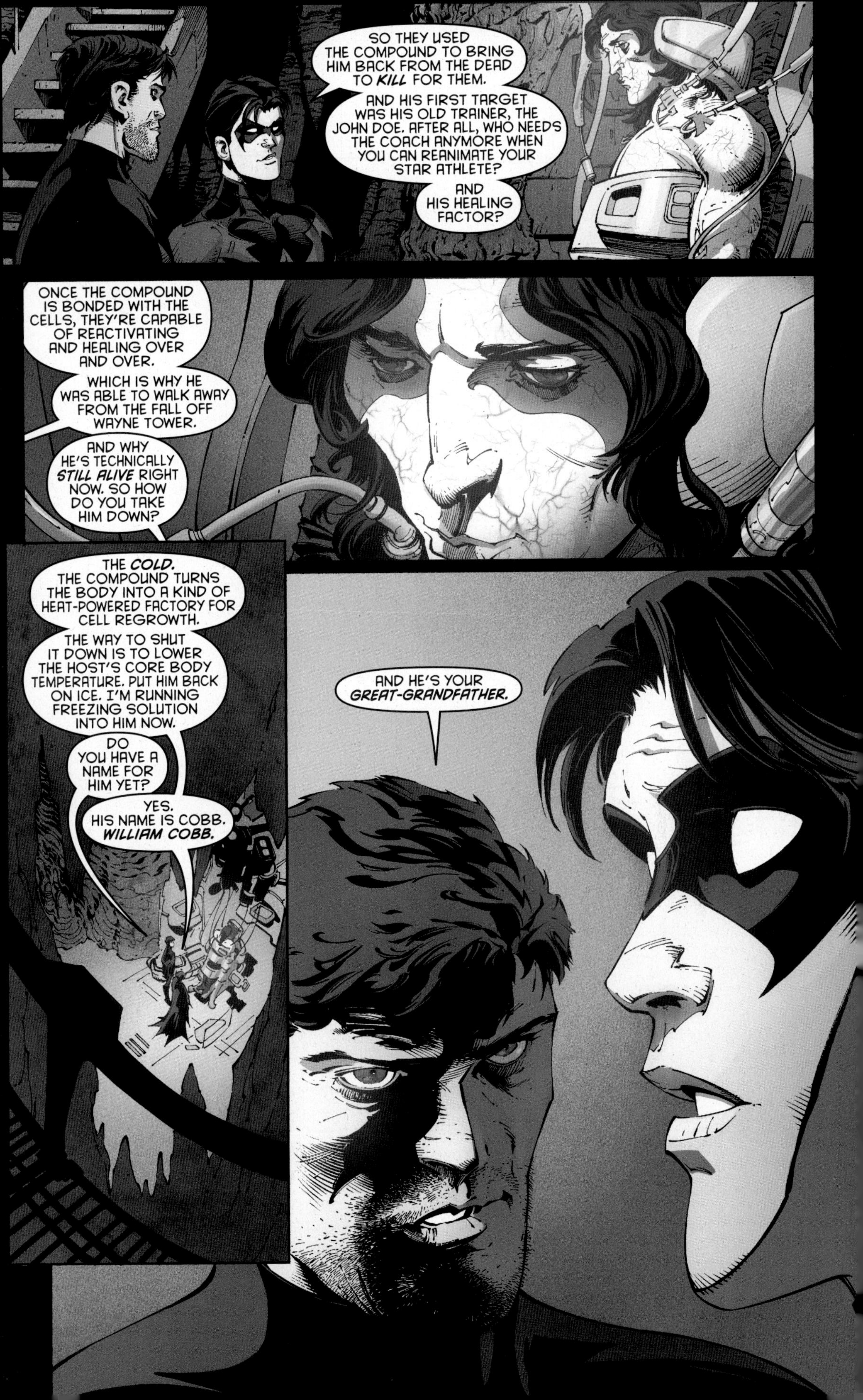
SO THEY USED THE COMPOUND TO BRING HIM BACK FROM THE DEAD TO KILL FOR THEM.
AND HIS FIRST TARGET WAS HIS OLD TRAINER, THE JOHN DOE. AFTER ALL, WHO NEEDS THE COACH ANYMORE WHEN YOU CAN REANIMATE YOUR STAR ATHLETE?
AND HIS HEALING FACTOR?
ONCE THE COMPOUND IS BONDED WITH THE CELLS, THEY'RE CAPABLE OF REACTIVATING AND HEALING OVER AND OVER.
WHICH IS WHY HE WAS ABLE TO WALK AWAY FROM THE FALL OFF WAYNE TOWER.
AND WHY HE'S TECHNICALLY STILL ALIVE RIGHT NOW. SO HOW DO YOU TAKE HIM DOWN?
THE COLD. THE COMPOUND TURNS THE BODY INTO A KIND OF HEAT-POWERED FACTORY FOR CELL REGROWTH.
THE WAY TO SHUT IT DOWN IS TO LOWER THE HOST'S CORE BODY TEMPERATURE. PUT HIM BACK ON ICE. I'M RUNNING FREEZING SOLUTION INTO HIM NOW.
DO YOU HAVE A NAME FOR HIM YET?
YES. HIS NAME IS COBB. WILLIAM COBB.
AND HE'S YOUR GREAT-GRANDFATHER.

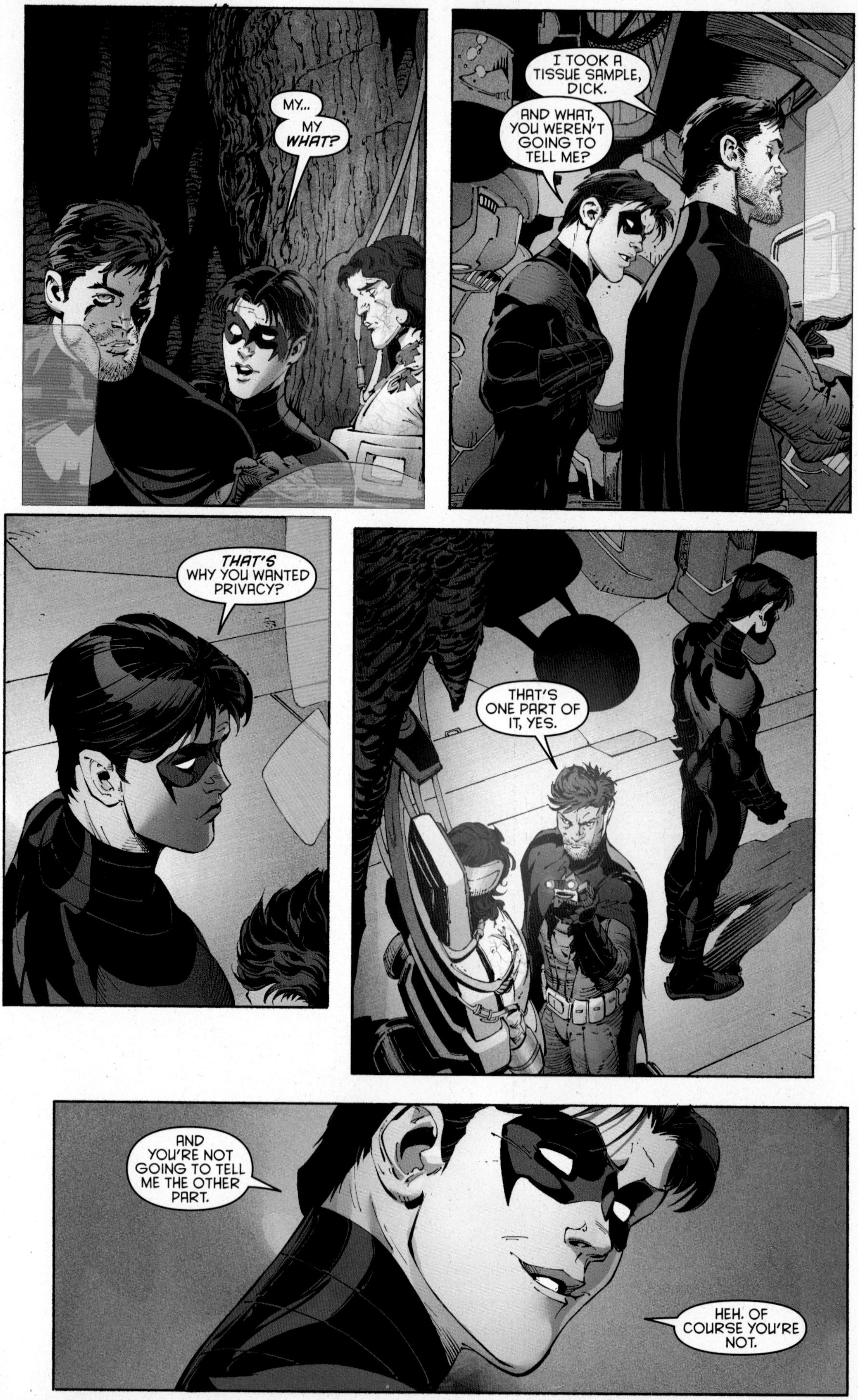
MY...
MY *WHAT?*
I TOOK A TISSUE SAMPLE, DICK.
AND WHAT, YOU WEREN'T GOING TO TELL ME?
THAT'S WHY YOU WANTED PRIVACY?
THAT'S ONE PART OF IT, YES.
AND YOU'RE NOT GOING TO TELL ME THE OTHER PART.
HEH. OF COURSE YOU'RE NOT.

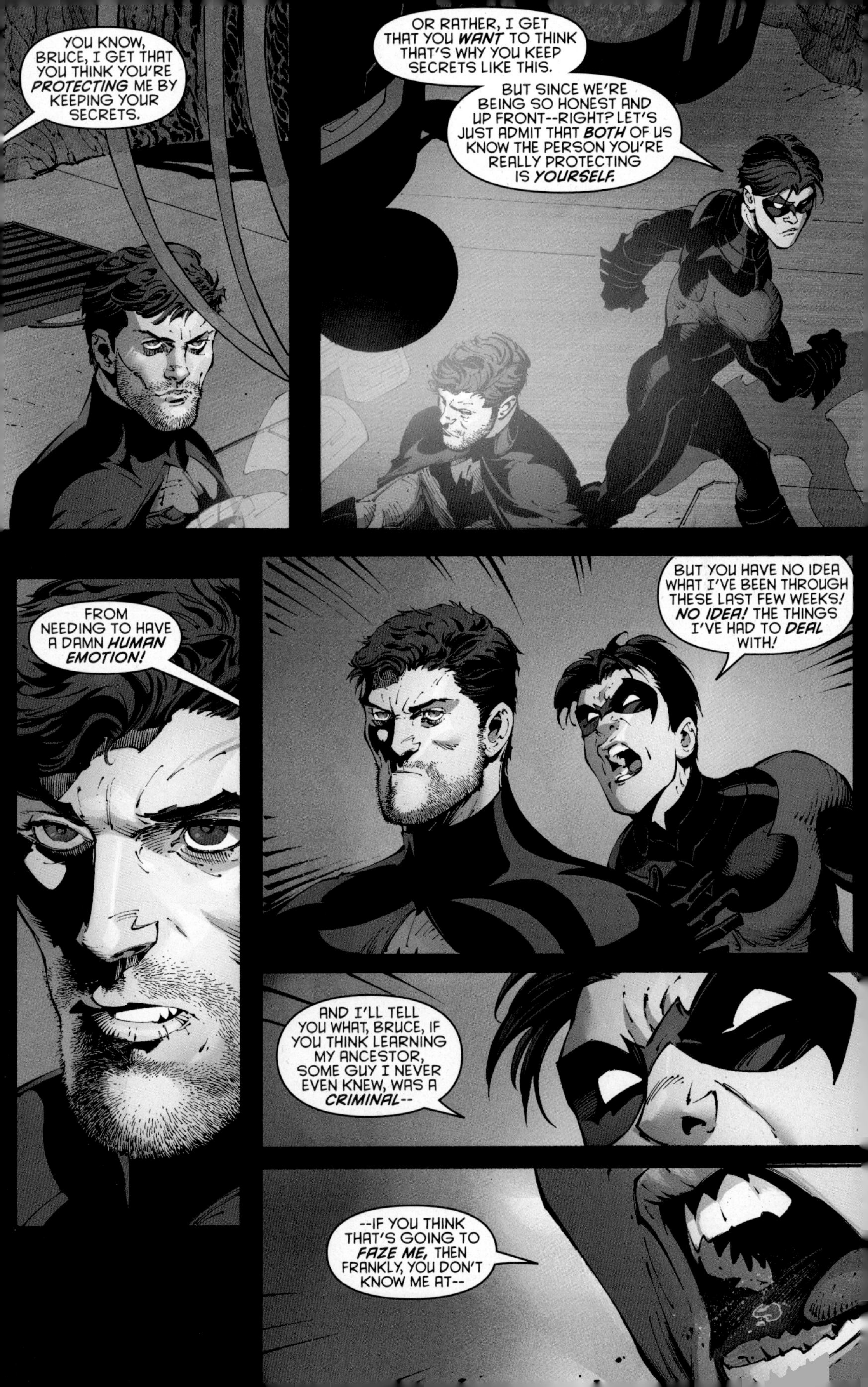
YOU KNOW, BRUCE, I GET THAT YOU THINK YOU'RE PROTECTING ME BY KEEPING YOUR SECRETS.
OR RATHER, I GET THAT YOU WANT TO THINK THAT'S WHY YOU KEEP SECRETS LIKE THIS.
BUT SINCE WE'RE BEING SO HONEST AND UP FRONT--RIGHT? LET'S JUST ADMIT THAT BOTH OF US KNOW THE PERSON YOU'RE REALLY PROTECTING IS YOURSELF.
FROM NEEDING TO HAVE A DAMN HUMAN EMOTION!
BUT YOU HAVE NO IDEA WHAT I'VE BEEN THROUGH THESE LAST FEW WEEKS! NO IDEA! THE THINGS I'VE HAD TO DEAL WITH!
AND I'LL TELL YOU WHAT, BRUCE, IF YOU THINK LEARNING MY ANCESTOR, SOME GUY I NEVER EVEN KNEW, WAS A CRIMINAL--
--IF YOU THINK THAT'S GOING TO FAZE ME, THEN FRANKLY, YOU DON'T KNOW ME AT--

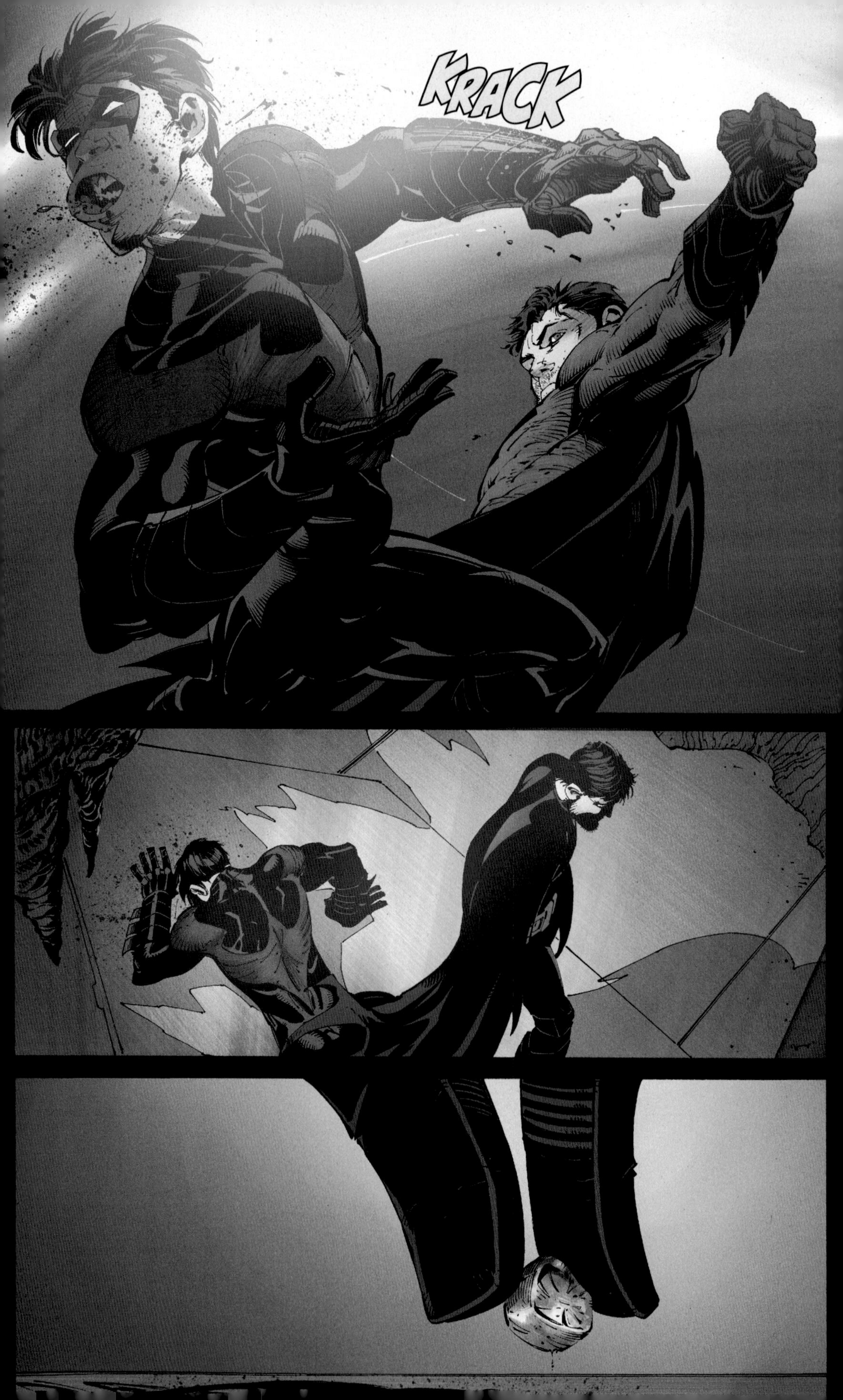
KRACK

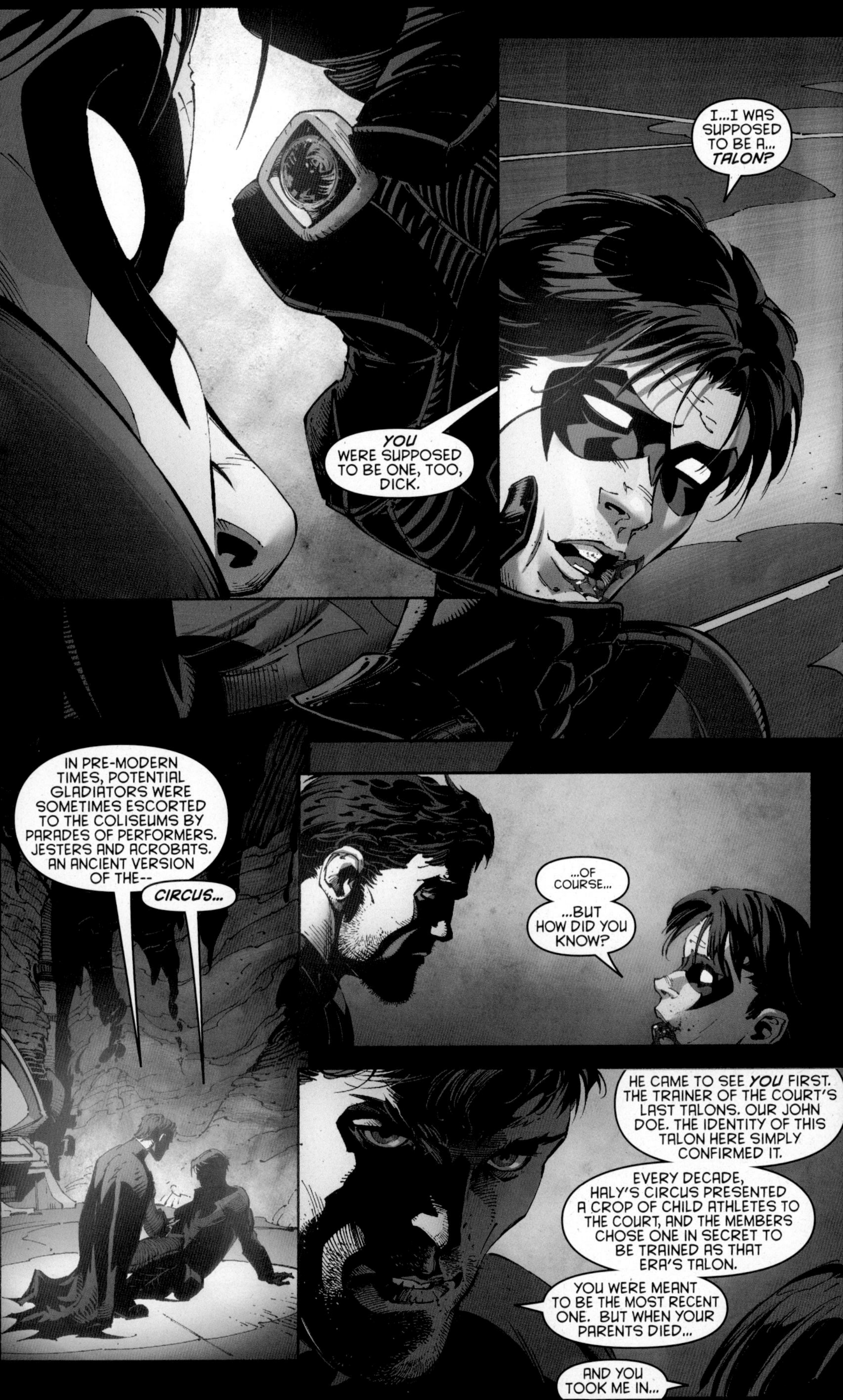
I...I WAS SUPPOSED TO BE A... *TALON?*
YOU WERE SUPPOSED TO BE ONE, TOO, DICK.
IN PRE-MODERN TIMES, POTENTIAL GLADIATORS WERE SOMETIMES ESCORTED TO THE COLISEUMS BY PARADES OF PERFORMERS. JESTERS AND ACROBATS. AN ANCIENT VERSION OF THE--
CIRCUS...
...OF COURSE...
...BUT HOW DID YOU KNOW?
HE CAME TO SEE *YOU* FIRST. THE TRAINER OF THE COURT'S LAST TALONS. OUR JOHN DOE. THE IDENTITY OF THIS TALON HERE SIMPLY CONFIRMED IT.
EVERY DECADE, HALY'S CIRCUS PRESENTED A CROP OF CHILD ATHLETES TO THE COURT, AND THE MEMBERS CHOSE ONE IN SECRET TO BE TRAINED AS THAT ERA'S TALON.
YOU WERE MEANT TO BE THE MOST RECENT ONE. BUT WHEN YOUR PARENTS DIED...
AND YOU TOOK ME IN...

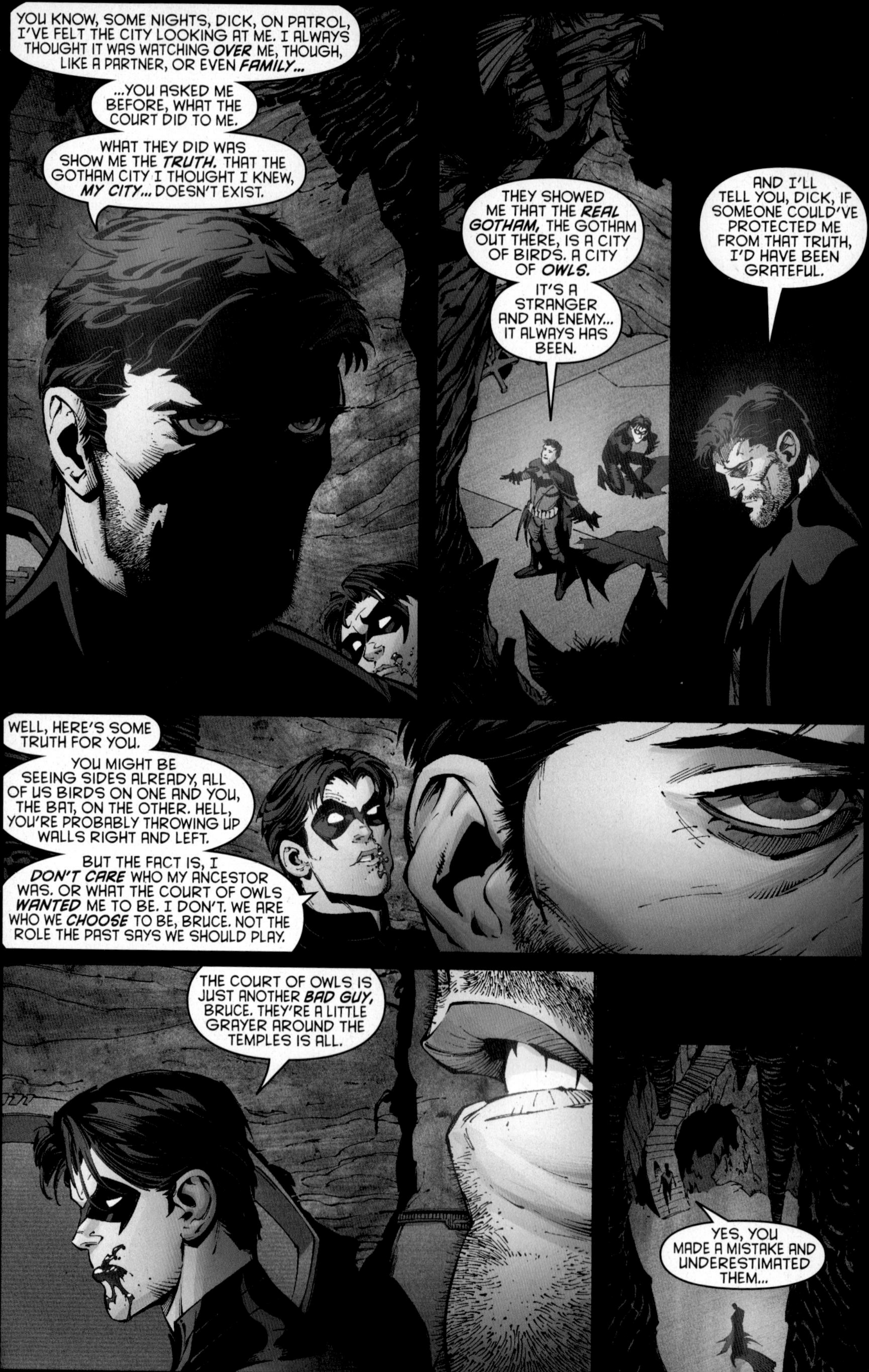
YOU KNOW, SOME NIGHTS, DICK, ON PATROL, I'VE FELT THE CITY LOOKING AT ME. I ALWAYS THOUGHT IT WAS WATCHING OVER ME, THOUGH, LIKE A PARTNER, OR EVEN FAMILY...
...YOU ASKED ME BEFORE, WHAT THE COURT DID TO ME.
WHAT THEY DID WAS SHOW ME THE TRUTH. THAT THE GOTHAM CITY I THOUGHT I KNEW, MY CITY... DOESN'T EXIST.
THEY SHOWED ME THAT THE REAL GOTHAM, THE GOTHAM OUT THERE, IS A CITY OF BIRDS. A CITY OF OWLS.
IT'S A STRANGER AND AN ENEMY... IT ALWAYS HAS BEEN.
AND I'LL TELL YOU, DICK, IF SOMEONE COULD'VE PROTECTED ME FROM THAT TRUTH, I'D HAVE BEEN GRATEFUL.
WELL, HERE'S SOME TRUTH FOR YOU.
YOU MIGHT BE SEEING SIDES ALREADY, ALL OF US BIRDS ON ONE AND YOU, THE BAT, ON THE OTHER. HELL, YOU'RE PROBABLY THROWING UP WALLS RIGHT AND LEFT.
BUT THE FACT IS, I DON'T CARE WHO MY ANCESTOR WAS. OR WHAT THE COURT OF OWLS WANTED ME TO BE. I DON'T. WE ARE WHO WE CHOOSE TO BE, BRUCE. NOT THE ROLE THE PAST SAYS WE SHOULD PLAY.
THE COURT OF OWLS IS JUST ANOTHER BAD GUY, BRUCE. THEY'RE A LITTLE GRAYER AROUND THE TEMPLES IS ALL.
YES, YOU MADE A MISTAKE AND UNDERESTIMATED THEM...

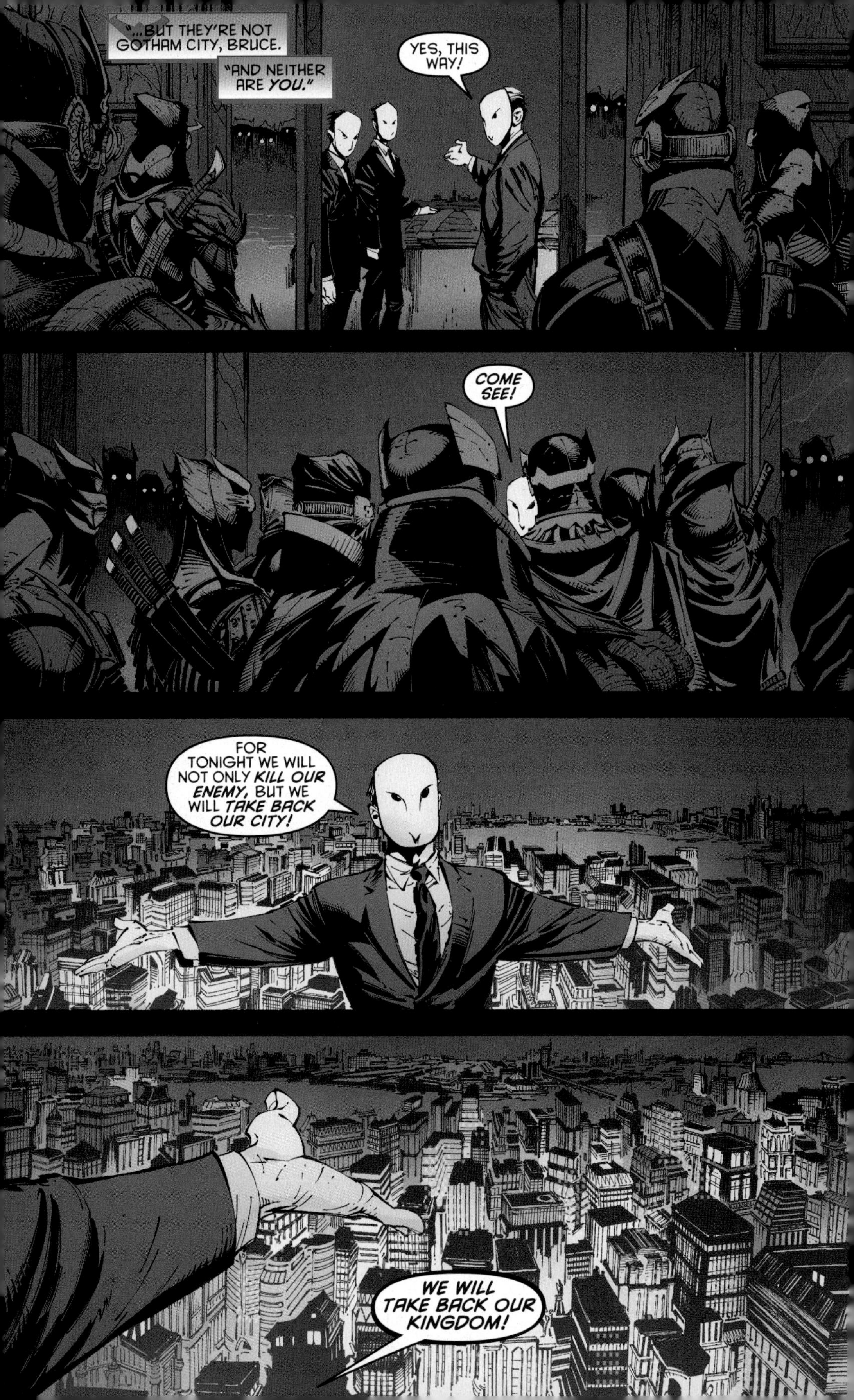
"...BUT THEY'RE NOT GOTHAM CITY, BRUCE.
"AND NEITHER ARE *YOU*."
YES, THIS WAY!
COME SEE!
FOR TONIGHT WE WILL NOT ONLY *KILL OUR ENEMY,* BUT WE WILL *TAKE BACK OUR CITY!*
WE WILL TAKE BACK OUR KINGDOM!

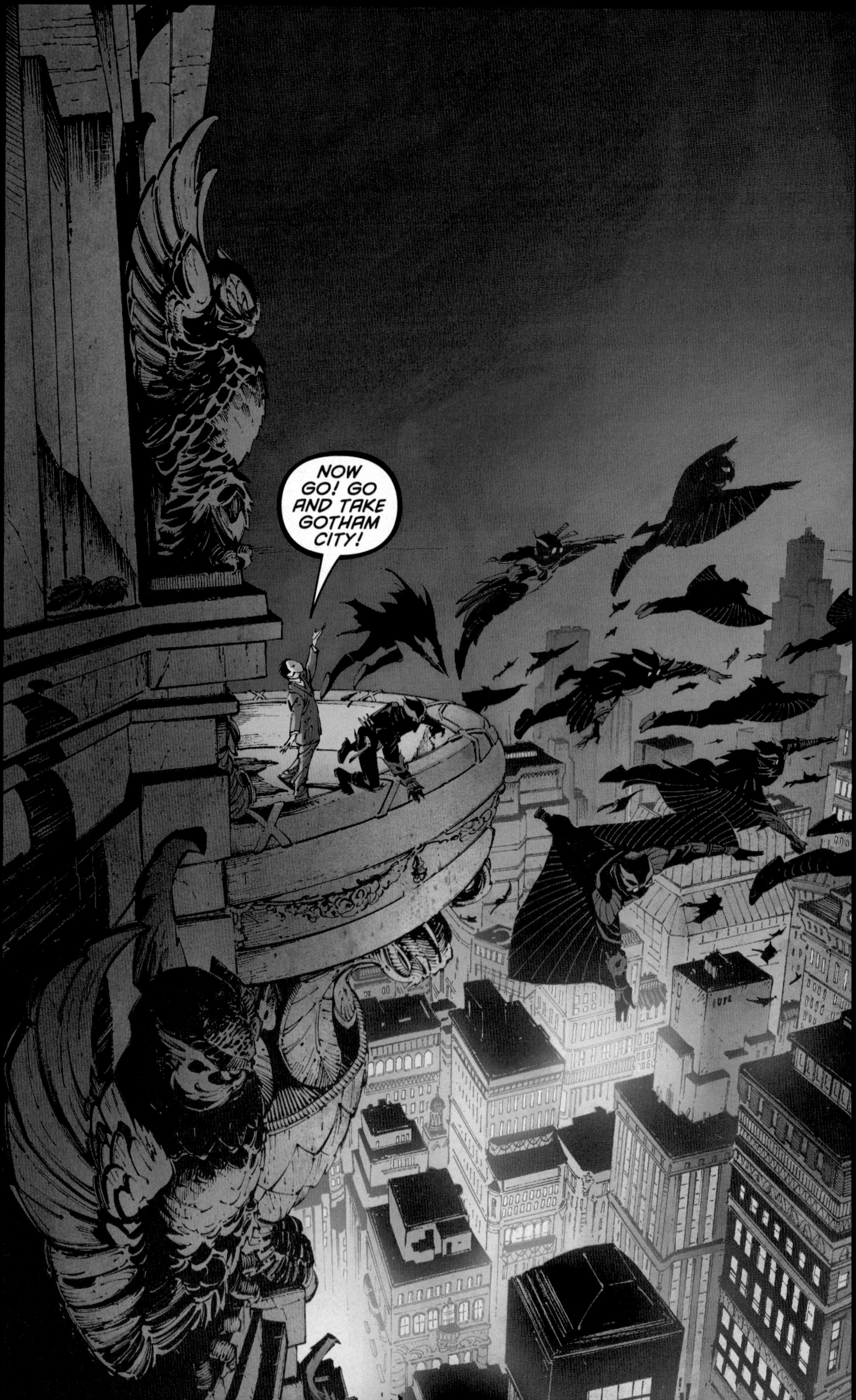
NOW GO! GO AND TAKE GOTHAM CITY!

VARIANT COVER GALLERY

BATMAN 1
by Ethan Van Sciver & Tomeu Morey

BATMAN 2
by Jim Lee, Scott Williams & Alex Sinclair

BATMAN 3
by Ivan Reis, Joe Prado & Rod Reis

BATMAN 4
by Mike Choi

BATMAN 5
by Chris Burnham & Nathan Fairbairn

BATMAN 6
by Gary Frank & FCO

BATMAN 7
by Dustin Nguyen

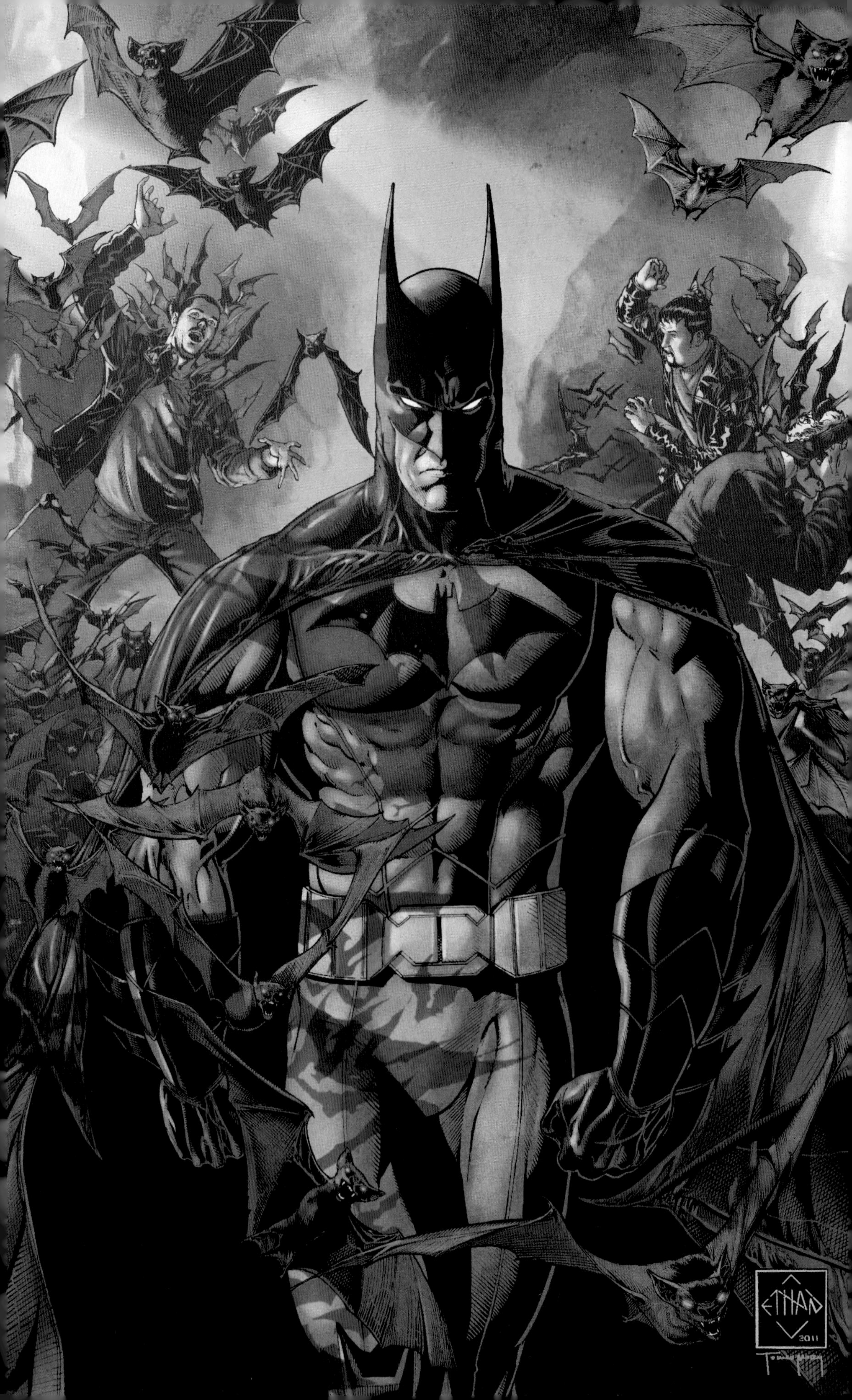
ETHAN
2011

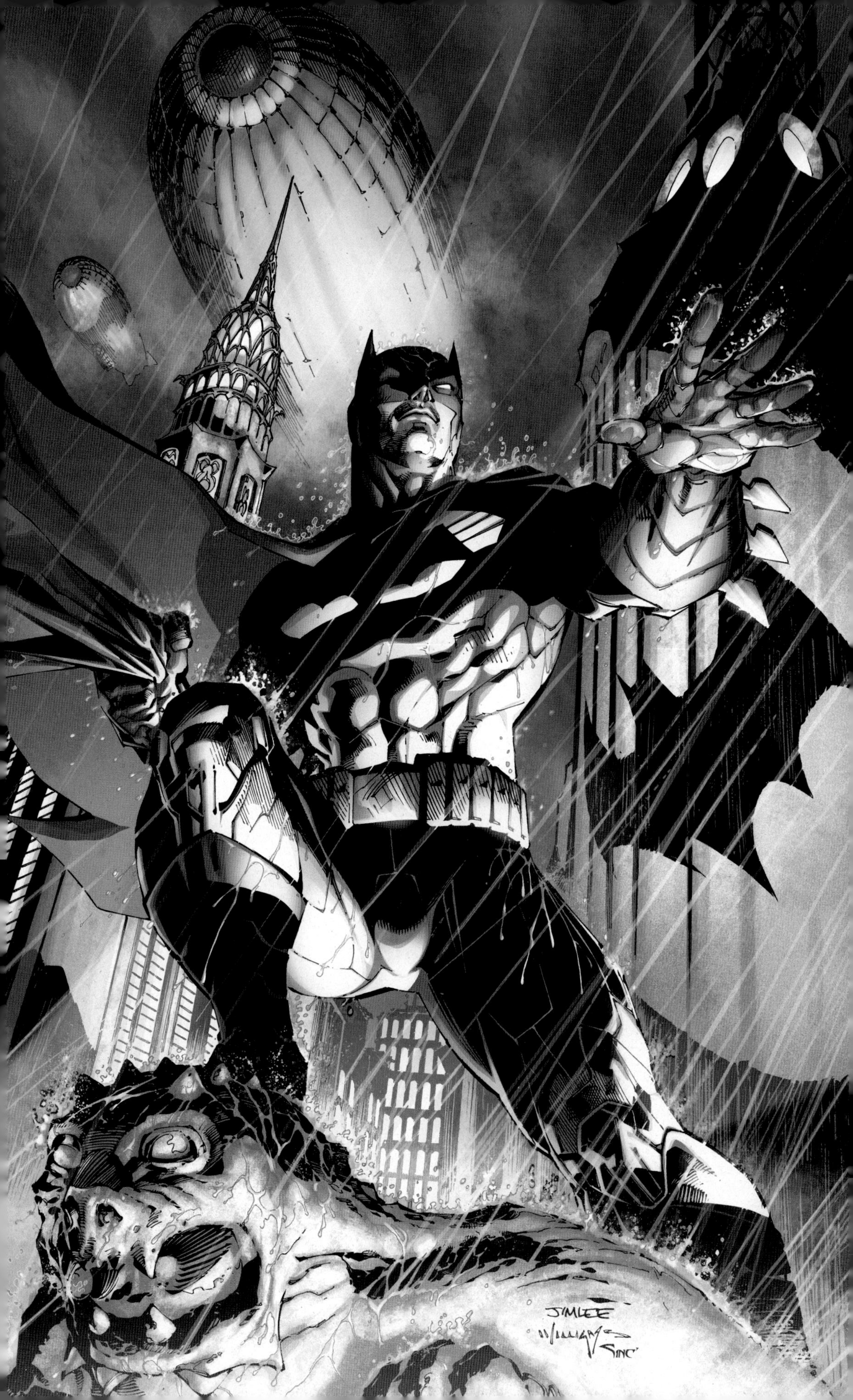
JIMLEE
WILLIAMS
SINC

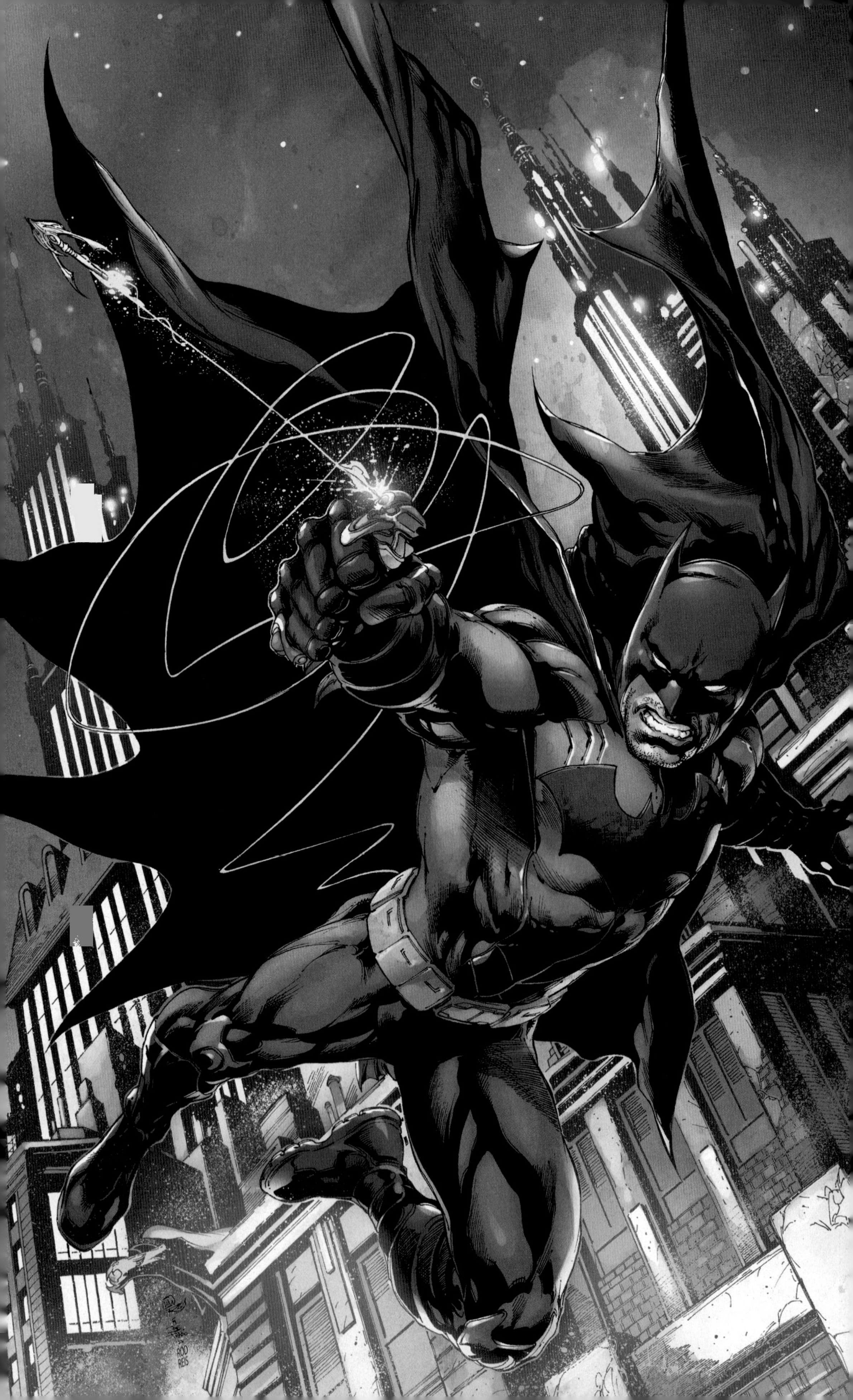
ROD
REIS

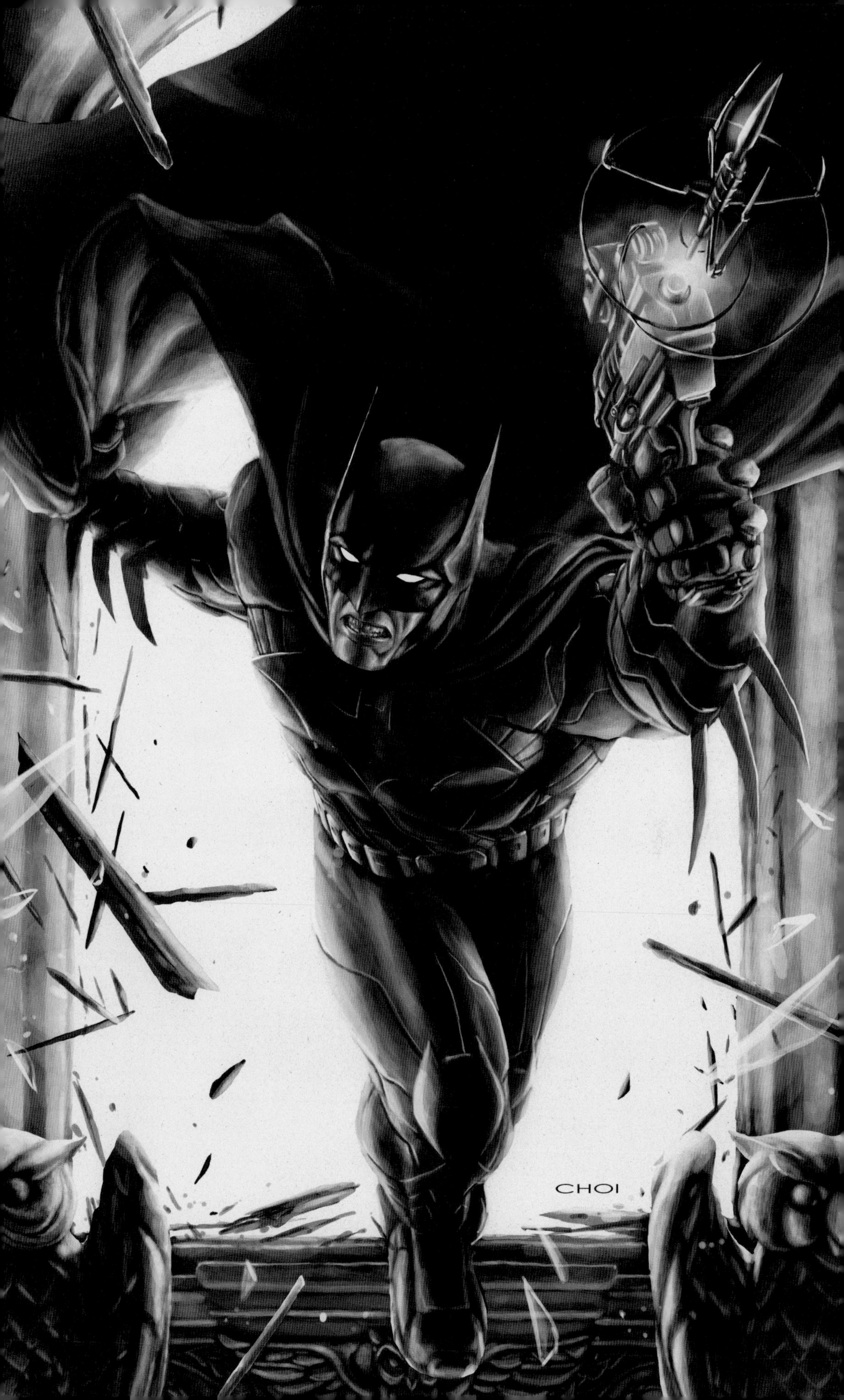
CHOI

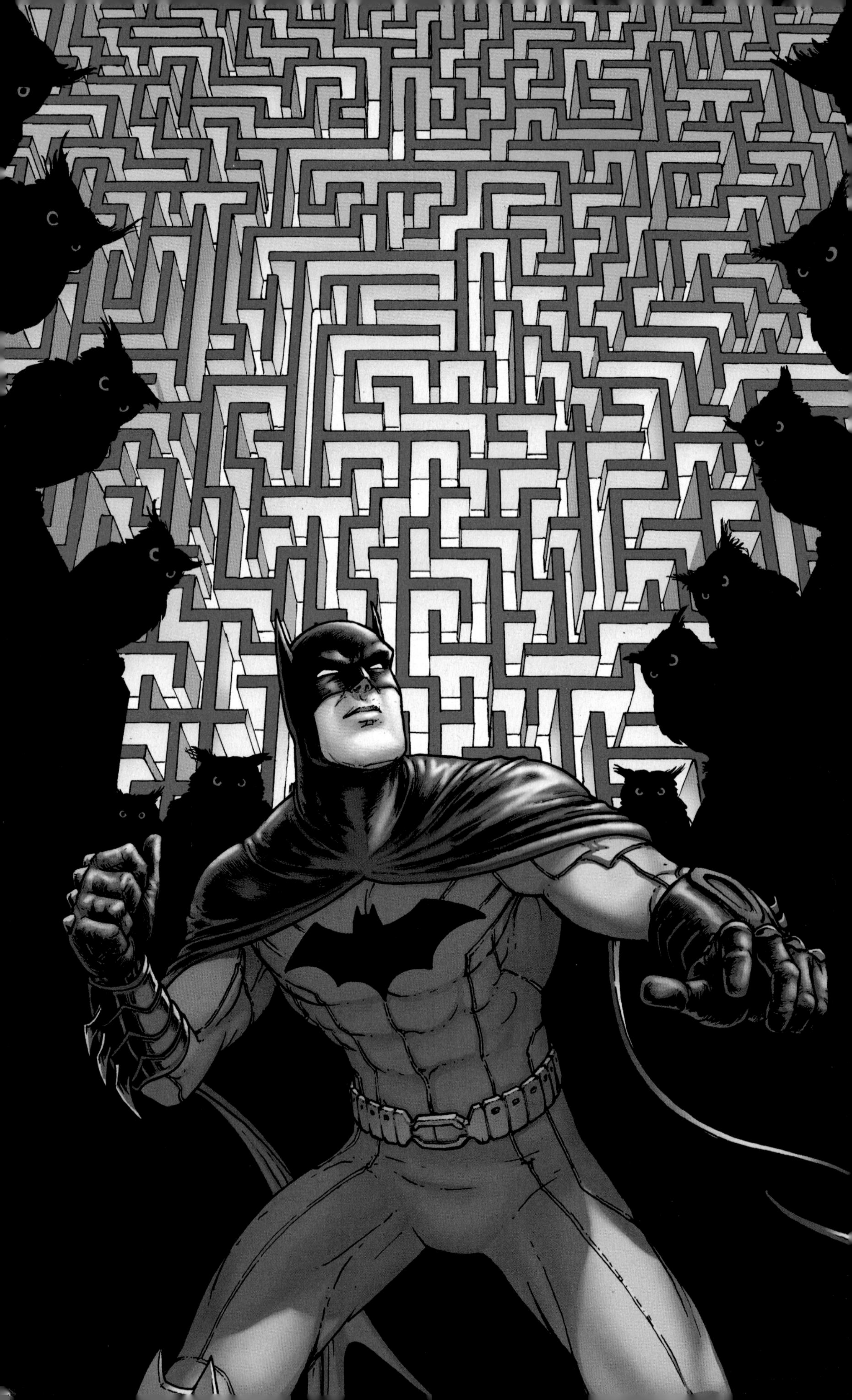

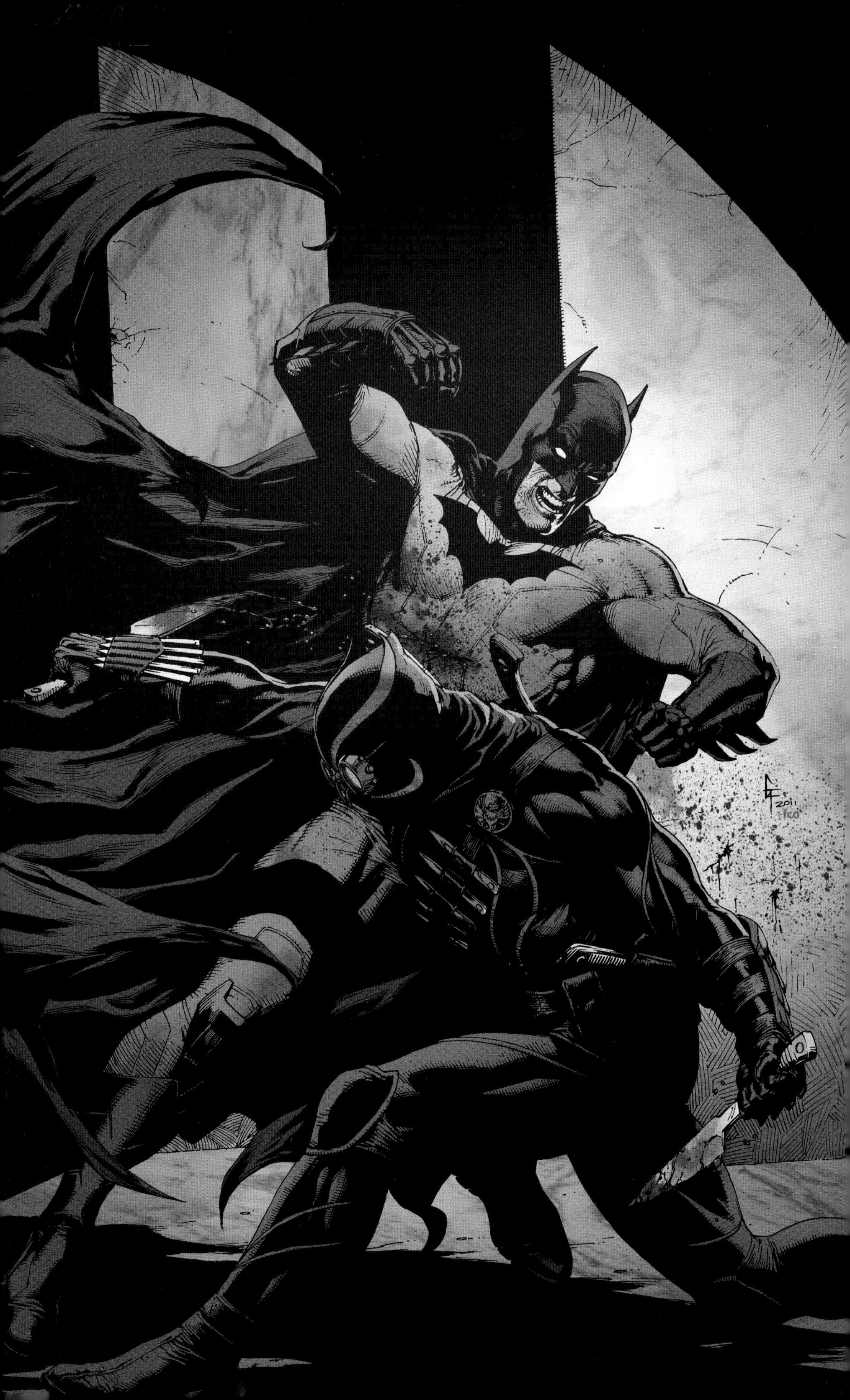

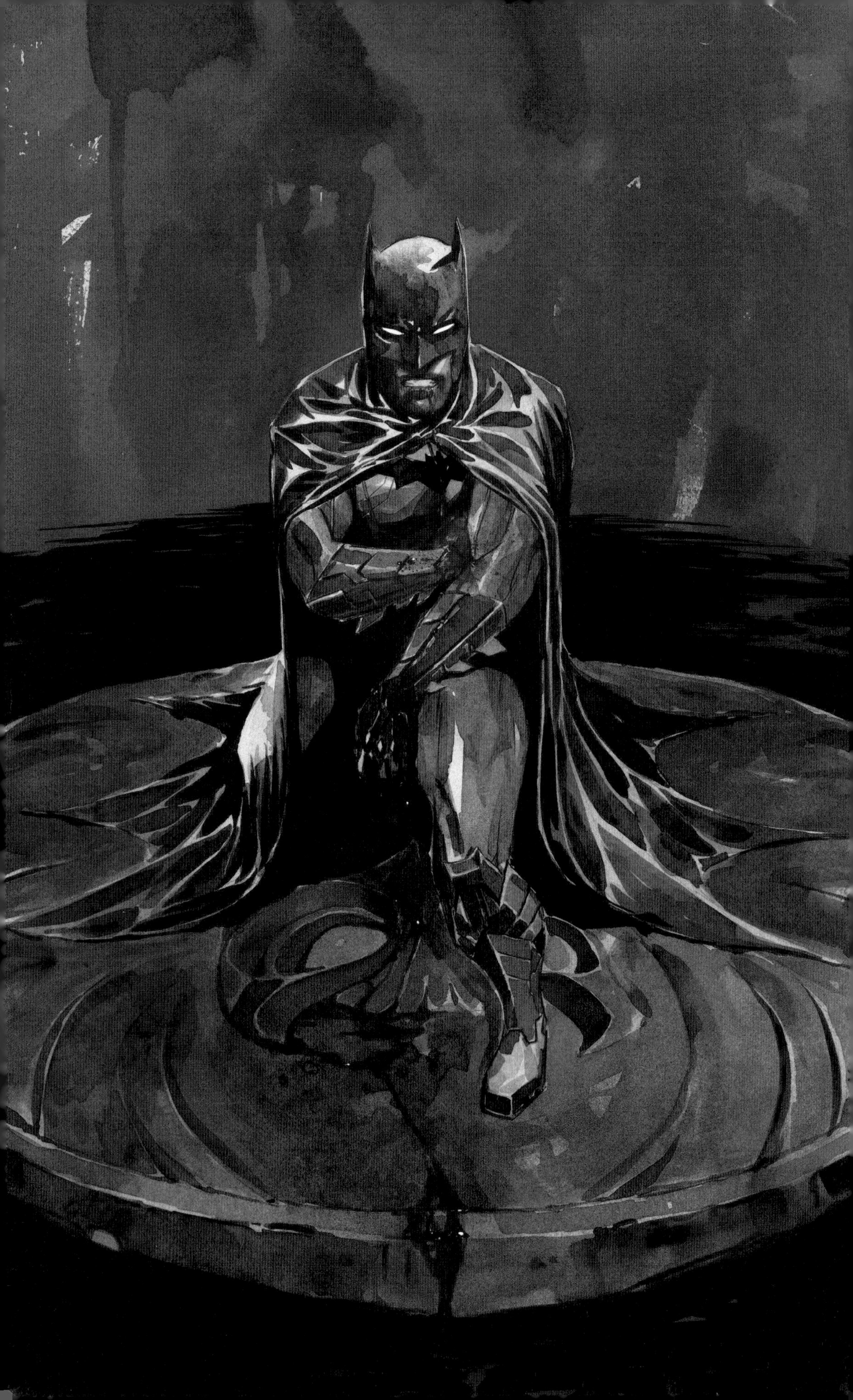

BATMAN #1, PAGES 21-24

SCRIPT BY SCOTT SNYDER   LAYOUTS BY GREG CAPULLO

PAGE 21
21.1
LARGE - the CRIME SCENE - a MAN, pinned to the wall of his loft by DOZENS OF ANTIQUE THROWING KNIVES. The body should be in bad shape - it's been pinned to the wall for almost a week, Greg.

As for the pose, the scene should be reminiscent of one of those circus performances, where someone is strapped to a wheel and spun around while a knife-thrower tosses daggers and always just misses. The thing here, though, is that every knife has hit the victim - all on purpose. So there should be knives in his arms, legs, stomach. One long one - the kill shot - going right into his open mouth, pinning his head to the wooden wall behind.

The MAN himself is a painter in his 50s. He should look a little rakish, maybe a big, broad guy - he was at least, two weeks ago. His loft should be filled with large-scale paintings and canvases.

HARVEY: Collector friend of his found him around six o'clock. Evidence points to a T.O.D. five, maybe six days ago.

HARVEY: So. What do you think?

21.2
BATMAN inspecting the body, HARVEY there, too.

BATMAN: I think whoever did this deliberately missed every major artery.

BATMAN: Meaning, they wanted to hurt Mr. Lockhart very badly, for a very long time.

21.3
And looking at the KNIVES.

BATMAN: The knives are throwing weapons, professional grade. The grooves are filled with mercury for steadier flight.

BATMAN: I'd like to take one.

21.4
HARVEY, as BATMAN examines the VICTIM'S HAND.

HARVEY: Hell, it's not like we're going to run out.

HARVEY: Look like Lockhart got a piece of the killer?

21.5
BATMAN, swabbing beneath the VICTIM'S FINGERNAILS for DNA.

BATMAN (TO ALFRED, THROUGH COWL): Possible DNA analysis. Looks like skin beneath the victims fingernails.

21.6
And placing the flecks of DNA, the skin cells, into a SMALL COMPARTMENT THAT POPS OUT OF HIS GLOVE.

ALFRED (THROUGH COWL): Running AmpFLP now.

ALFRED (THROUGH COWL): Anything else, sir?

21.7
BATMAN, sniffing, smelling something that catches his attention.

ALFRED (THROUGH COWL): Sir?

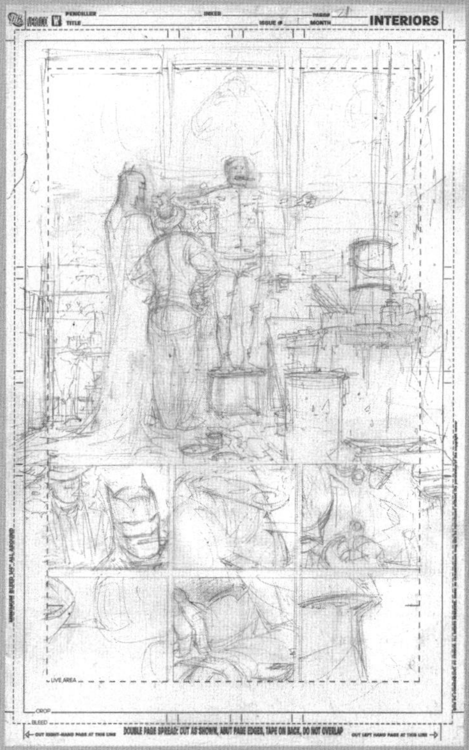
INTERIORS

PAGE 22
22.1
BATMAN – at a wall, looking at a painting. Inspecting. Ever the detective...

22.3
BATMAN, taking the painting down.

HARVEY: What? What is it?

22.4
BATMAN, waiting for HARVEY to hand him his cigar.

BATMAN: Give me your cigar.

HARVEY: My cigar...

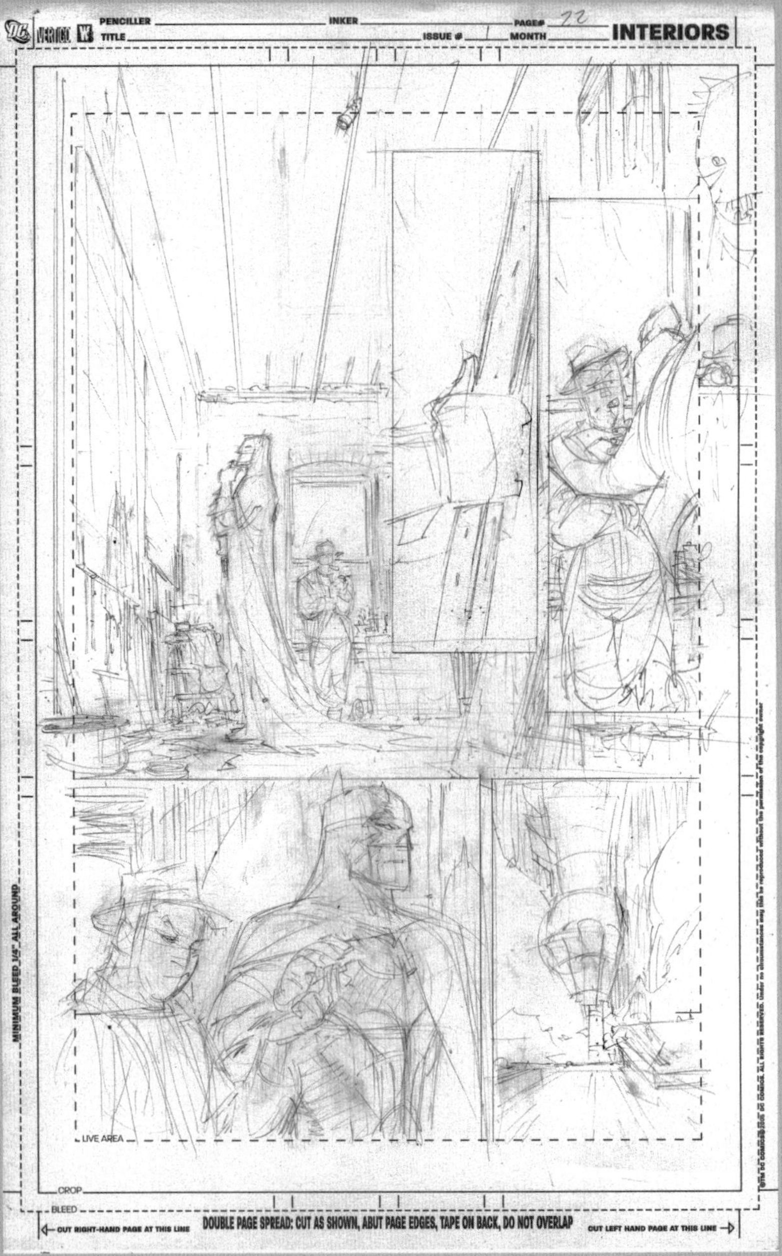
PENCILLER
INKER
PAGE# 22
TITLE
ISSUE # 1
MONTH
INTERIORS
LIVE AREA
CROP
BLEED
MINIMUM BLEED 1/4" ALL AROUND
CUT RIGHT-HAND PAGE AT THIS LINE
DOUBLE PAGE SPREAD: CUT AS SHOWN, ABUT PAGE EDGES, TAPE ON BACK, DO NOT OVERLAP
CUT LEFT HAND PAGE AT THIS LINE

22.5
BATMAN, approaching the wall with the cigar. HARVEY, aggravated in the background.

HARVEY: Fine. Take it. Now. You mind filling me in?

BATMAN: Smell that? It's linseed oil. A common paint thinner. But the intensity is too strong.

HARVEY: So this Lockhart guy spilled a can of paint. So what?

22.6
BATMAN about to touch the wall with the cigar.

BATMAN: Maybe...

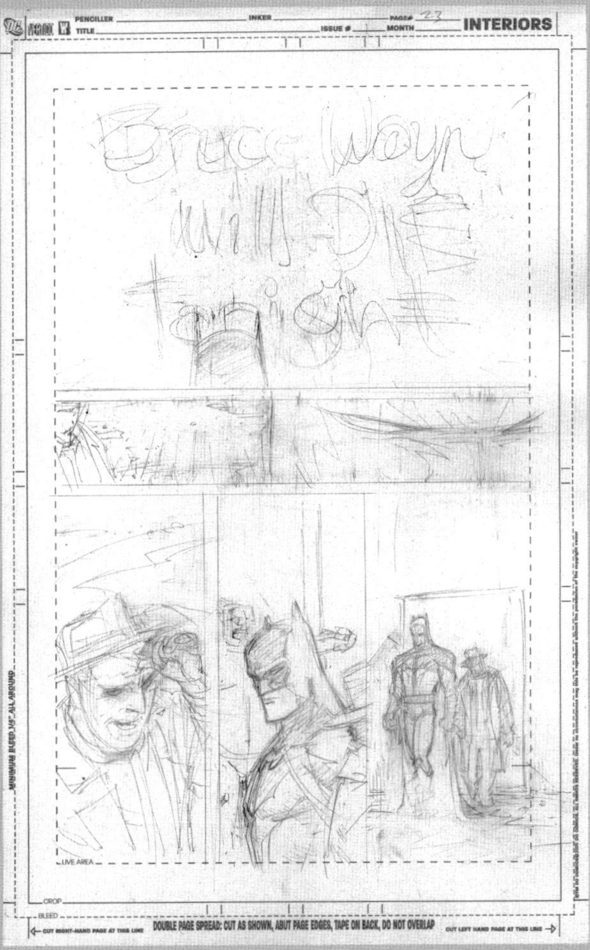
INTERIORS
DOUBLE PAGE SPREAD: CUT AS SHOWN, ABUT PAGE EDGES, TAPE ON BACK, DO NOT OVERLAP

PAGE 23

23.1
Large - A FLAMING MESSAGE ON THE WALL: "BRUCE WAYNE WILL DIE ON SUNDAY"

23.2
BATMAN, looking at the flaming message.

BATMAN: Or maybe he was using it to leave a message, before he was murdered.

HARVEY: Sunday... If Lockhart was killed five days ago, then he's saying Wayne is going to die--

BATMAN: Tomorrow. Whoever did this to Lockhart will try to kill Bruce Wayne tomorrow.

23.3
HARVEY, talking to BATMAN. Flustered by missing the oil clue.

HARVEY: Good luck to him. Wayne's security has security.

HARVEY: Anyone going to take a crack at the guy is going to have to be someone close. Someone in Wayne's circle, would be my guess.

HARVEY: Makes you almost feel bad for the guy.

23.4
BATMAN, looking at HARVEY.

BATMAN: Almost?

23.5
HARVEY, explaining.

HARVEY: Look, I know you're pals and all. But guys like Wayne, they don't get how the city works, the way we do. You and me.

HARVEY: I mean, I listened to his speech tonight on the radio. All about what Gotham is, what it can be. Will be.

HARVEY: I'm just saying. Anyone who thinks they know Gotham, know it now, then or in the frickin' future – he's got a rude awakening coming.

PAGE 24
24.1
SMALL - BATMAN, touching his ear, a message coming in. HARVEY, behind him.

HARVEY: Because you know what I'd answer if I had to do that Gotham Is thing? I'd leave it blank.

HARVEY: Because no one knows Gotham. It's a mystery. If anything, it knows you.

24.2
SMALL - BATMAN, holding a hand up to HARVEY, cutting him off.

HARVEY: You think it's your friend, you try to help it, what does it do? It stabs you in the back. That's what. Stabs you right in the back with a--

BATMAN: Quiet.

BATMAN (TO PHONE): You're sure.

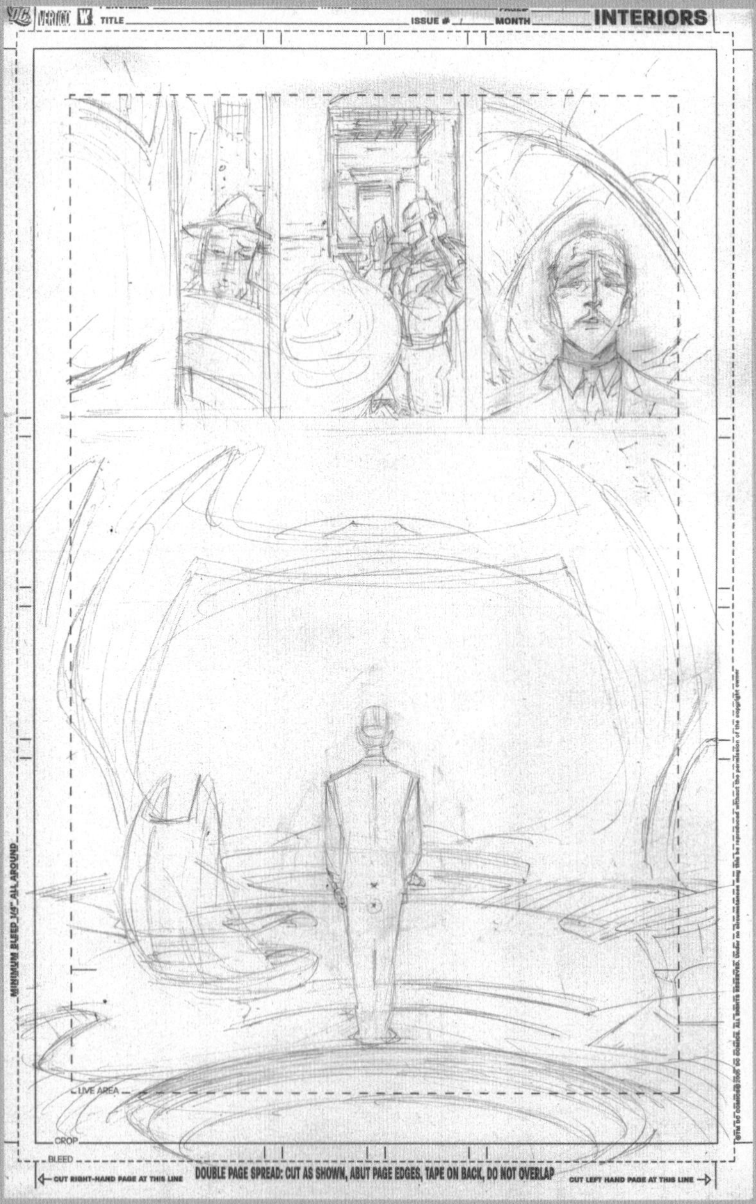

TITLE
ISSUE #
MONTH
INTERIORS
LIVE AREA
CROP
BLEED
CUT RIGHT-HAND PAGE AT THIS LINE
DOUBLE PAGE SPREAD: CUT AS SHOWN, ABUT PAGE EDGES, TAPE ON BACK, DO NOT OVERLAP
CUT LEFT HAND PAGE AT THIS LINE

24.3
SMALL – We're in the CAVE, CLOSE on ALFRED, looking at the BAT-COMPUTER SCREEN (which we cannot see)

ALRED: Quite, sir. The skin cells beneath the victim's fingernails...

24.4
LARGE AS POSSIBLE - We're in the CAVE with ALFRED, who is standing in front of BATCOMPUTER as he talks to BATMAN through the console. And on the screen.

ALFRED: Came back a perfect match.

On the SCREEN is says: "DNA MATCH: DICK GRAYSON"

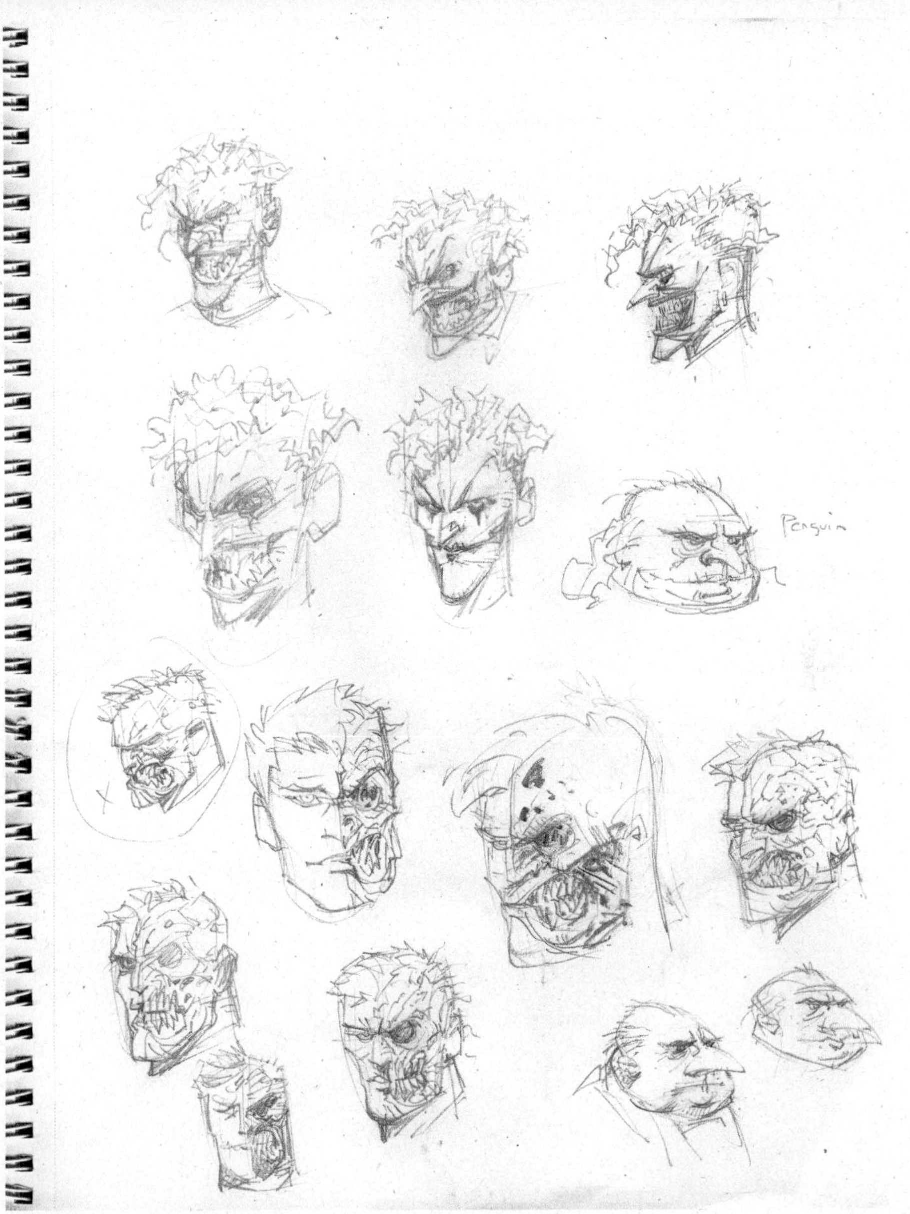
Penguin

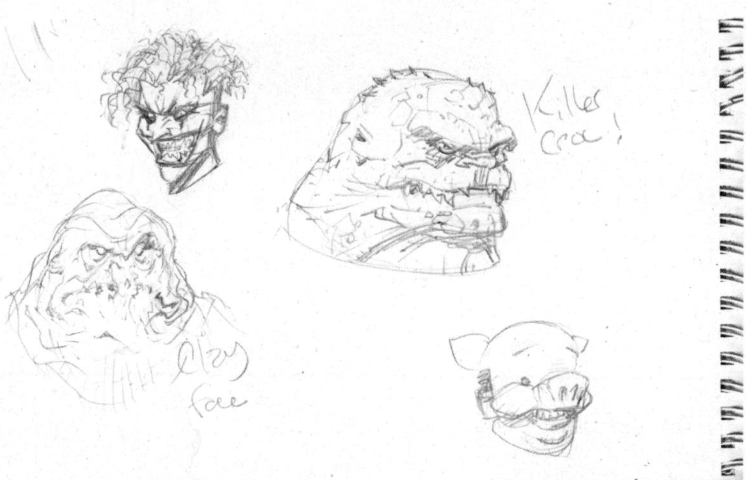
Killer Croc!
Clay face

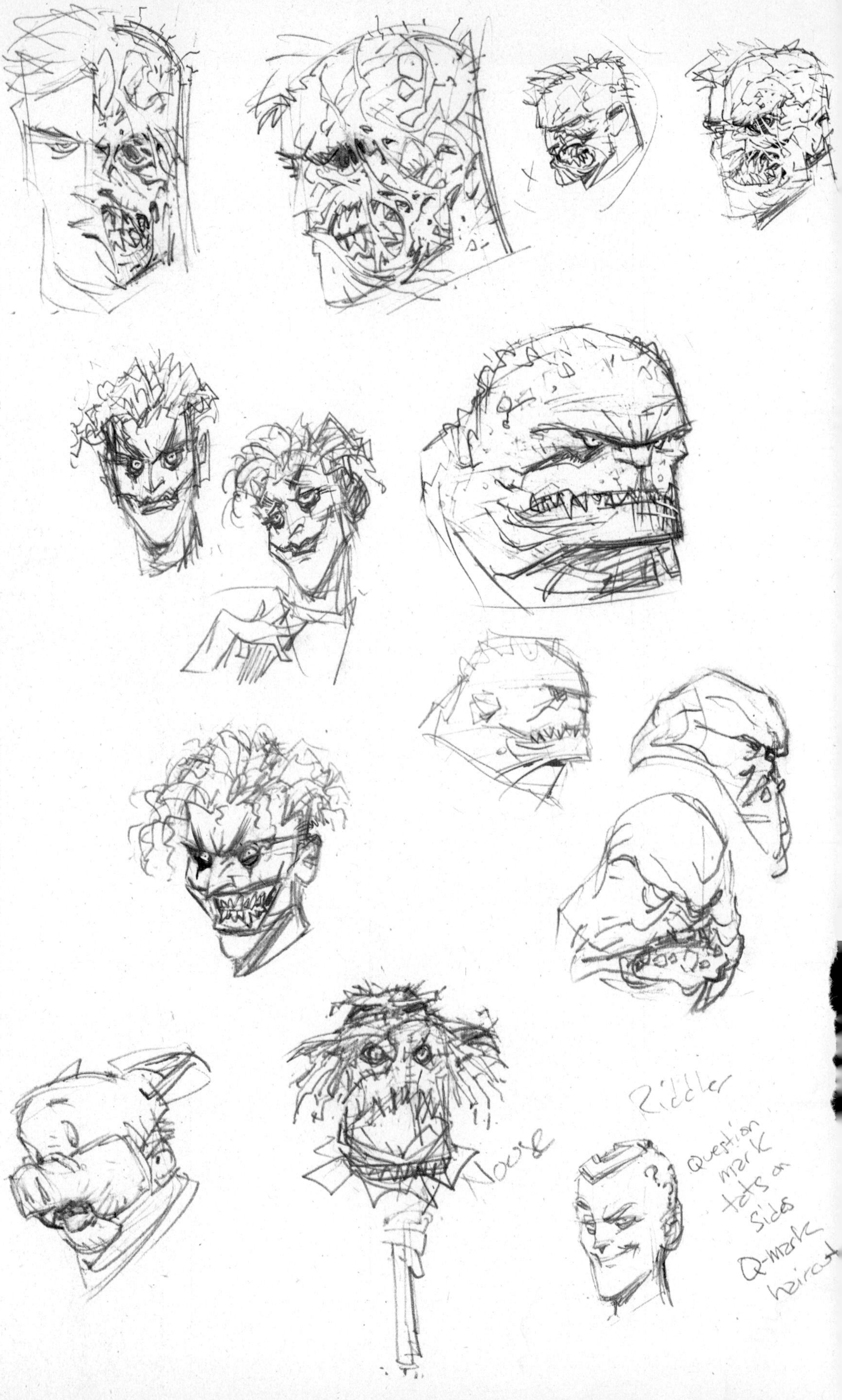
Riddler
Question mark tats on sides
Q-mark haircut